FROM SHORE TO SHORE

The Tour Diaries of
Earl Mountbatten of Burma
1953–1979

FROM SHORE TO SHORE

THE TOUR DIARIES OF
EARL MOUNTBATTEN OF BURMA
1953–1979

Edited by
PHILIP ZIEGLER

COLLINS
8 Grafton Street, London W1
1989

William Collins Sons & Co. Ltd
London · Glasgow · Sydney · Auckland
Toronto · Johannesburg

First published 1989

ISBN 0 00 217606 8

A CIP catalogue record for this book is available from the British Library

Photoset in Linotron Sabon by
Rowland Phototypesetting Ltd,
Bury St Edmunds, Suffolk
Printed and bound in Great Britain by
William Collins Sons & Co. Ltd, Glasgow

CONTENTS

LIST OF ILLUSTRATIONS

CHRISTIAN NAMES AND NICKNAMES
COMMONLY MENTIONED
IN THE TEXT

Alice	Princess of Greece. Mountbatten's sister.
Anne	Princess, Mrs Mark Phillips.
Beppo	King Umberto of Italy.
Bernilo	Prince Bernhardt of the Netherlands.
Bertil	Prince of Sweden. Son of King Gustaf.
Charles	Prince of Wales.
David	David Hicks. Mountbatten's son-in-law.
Dodo	Dowager Lady Brabourne.
Edwina	Countess Mountbatten of Burma.
Freddy	Queen Frederica of Greece.
Gustaf	King of Sweden.
Indu/Indira	Mrs Indira Gandhi.
Jack	John Barratt. Mountbatten's secretary.
Jawaharlal	Jawaharlal Nehru.
John	Lord Brabourne. Mountbatten's son-in-law.
Juanito	King Juan Carlos of Spain.
Lilibet	Queen Elizabeth II.
Louise	Queen of Sweden. Mountbatten's sister.
Marjorie	Countess of Brecknock.
Nan	Mrs Pandit. Nehru's sister.
Norton	Norton Knatchbull, later Lord Romsey. Mountbatten's grandson.
Palo	King Paul of the Hellenes.
Pammy	Lady Pamela Hicks. Mountbatten's daughter.
Patricia	Lady Brabourne, now Countess Mountbatten of Burma. Mountbatten's daughter.
Peg	Princess Margaret of Hesse and the Rhine.
Philip	Duke of Edinburgh.
Ronnie	Vice-Admiral Sir Ronald Brockman.
Solly	Lord Zuckerman.

Nor on this land alone —
But be God's mercies known
    From shore to shore.
Lord, make the nations see
That men should brothers be,
And from one family
    The wide world o'er.

National Anthem

FOREWORD

Every day of his life Mountbatten noted in a small diary the main events of the day, but at first he confined any fuller account of his doings to very special occasions. He kept an unofficial diary of the Prince of Wales's tours to Australia and New Zealand in 1920, and to India and Japan in the winter of 1921/1922, then let the habit drop until he was sent as Supreme Commander to South-East Asia in 1943. His 'Personal Diary' written during this period was copied to members of his family and to the King. He did nothing similar during his time as Viceroy and later Governor-General in India, possibly because time did not permit, possibly because he felt his very full despatches served the purpose equally well. Nor did he resume the habit when he returned to the Royal Navy in 1948. In 1953, however, he recorded a visit which, as Commander-in-Chief in the Mediterranean, he paid to the Emperor Haile Selassie in Ethiopia. Once again the practice was dropped, resumed in 1956 and abandoned the following year. Finally, in 1958, he began to record all the more significant trips abroad in what he described as his 'Tour Diaries'; tours mainly official but, as time wore on, increasingly in the Royal Yacht *Britannia*. Gradually, he began to cover some of the more interesting happenings at home, and in 1976 actually kept a day-to-day diary of all his doings, an experiment which was not repeated.

It is these Tour Diaries, running from 1953 to his death in 1979, which make up this volume. They ran to something approaching 1.5 million words, which I have here reduced to a tenth of that amount. It has therefore been a question of choosing what to put in rather than what to leave out. Often, where people or events of particular interest are concerned, the material chose itself. Otherwise I have tried to keep a balance between the various elements which reflect the nature of Mountbatten's daily life and of his personality.

There has inevitably been falsification as a result. By eliminating the greater part of the trivial and often repetitious detail, I am aware that I have concealed the *density* of Mountbatten's life, the sustained and intense activity that gave his career a touch of the prodigious. For this reason I have occasionally kept the minutiae of a working day intact — those interested to follow blow by blow a hectic, but by no means extraordinary working day might turn, for instance, to 8 March 1962. The heavy cutting that was necessary has sometimes given the text a somewhat scrappy appearance; this is regrettable, but the alternative was to leave in much of minor interest at the expense of material of greater value.

It is always difficult to know how much to supply in the way of notes. Mountbatten used his diaries as an *aide-mémoire* and was therefore usually punctilious in recording the status or occupation of the people whom he encountered. I have tried to identify individuals whom he does not so describe, but have not generally given much additional detail: to take one example, on page 176. Mountbatten identified 'Sam Elworthy' as 'the present Chief of Defence Staff'; from the index it can be established that he was 'Marshal of the Royal Air Force, Baron Elworthy'; it did not seem to me that further detail in a footnote would serve any useful purpose. In general my footnotes are intended to illuminate the occasional arcane reference, to say what happened next in cases where this seems particularly pertinent to Mountbatten's diary entries, and to add detail which I thought might amuse or interest the reader. The editor walks a tightrope between over-officiousness on the one hand, and callous indifference to the reader's needs on the other. I hope I have not fallen too heavily to either side.

1953

In 1953, when Mountbatten began this series of 'Tour Diaries', he was Commander-in-Chief of the Mediterranean Fleet and also CINCAFMED, Commander-in-Chief of the NATO naval forces in the Mediterranean.

An invitation from the Emperor Haile Selassie to visit Ethiopia gave him a chance to perform a worthwhile as well as an enjoyable diplomatic task, and also to indulge his new passion for underwater fishing. He sailed with Edwina from Malta on 20 October 1953 in his despatch vessel, HMS Surprise, *with the cruiser HMS* Glasgow *as escort.*

We had a very pleasant trip and only had one rather rough day which really didn't upset anybody. On the 22nd we passed near Gavdo Island, south of Crete, where the *Kelly* and *Kashmir* were sunk on 23 May 1941; so I stopped the ship and paraded a guard of Marines who fired three volleys and sounded the Last Post and Reveille. On the 23rd the day was so lovely that we stopped in the afternoon and bathed. I tried my new 'Aquaped', which had been given to me by my American Admiral, Jimmy Fife.* This contraption is strapped between the legs so that one can work pedals which drive two contra-rotating propellers, rather like a torpedo. Of course, one has to wear the Aqua-lung air bottles as one is going along beneath the surface, but one can move along quite fast. On the other hand I do not think it is going to be much good for fishing.

At the beginning of the morning watch on Saturday, the 24th, we suddenly ran into a sharp gale as we neared Famagusta [in Cyprus]. The wind was blowing from the south-east straight into the harbour, which

* Admiral Fife was the senior American officer in the international NATO headquarters in Malta, HAFMED.

I

is very small and ill-protected, so the harbour was closed. A pilot boat came out in a very rough sea and with great agility the pilot managed to scramble on board to tell us that nobody could land at Famagusta and recommending us to go to Dhekelia. I need hardly say that Edwina was furious with me, as she wanted to scramble down into the pilot cutter and get ashore, in order to visit the clinic and other places which were expecting a visit from her that morning. However, I was quite firm and said nobody was going ashore in that sea and we went round with the pilot to Dhekelia.

We had a picnic lunch on the beach. Then we drove on to Paphos. Here I was asked to talk to the Company of the Borderers who are busy helping the inhabitants pitch their tents which are still arriving in large numbers for those who are homeless.*

I am quite astonished to see how little damage this earthquake has caused superficially. The trouble, however, is that houses which have not fallen down are so cracked and insecure that it is not safe for the inhabitants to live in them. In many cases the work of pulling them down is almost greater than the work at Argostoli where the earthquake had knocked them all down. I was also shown one of the local designs of prefabricated houses which are going to be put up at the rate of about sixty a day, beginning next week.

We then drove up to Stroumbi, a village in the hills which has been very badly hit indeed. The inhabitants, however, were very cheery, and the local ex-Mayor insisted on giving me some wine and showed me with great pride his pictures of the Queen, and indeed all the Royal Family for the last three generations, which are hanging up in his office.

It is interesting to note that during the Coronation celebrations last June, a detachment of Sappers who were sent down to carry out a ceremonial parade were booed and stoned by the local population in this area because of their desire for *enosis*, or union, with Greece.

These same inhabitants have now of course completely changed their tune and are tremendously friendly and loyal and have given the soldiers a rousing welcome. So perhaps the earthquake has done some good for the Commonwealth!

I was sad to say goodbye to Sir Andrew Wright, for I have got to know him quite well and think very highly of him indeed. He is now two years over the retiring age for Governors, which apparently is fifty-five, and is being thrown away in the prime of his life with an absolutely unique

---

* Parts of Cyprus had been severely affected by an earthquake on 10 September 1953.

knowledge of Cyprus where he has served most of his 32 years in the Colonial service. It seems even more stupid than retiring Sir Knox Helm* at the age of sixty when he has spent 35 years almost entirely in Istanbul and Ankara and knows the Turks backwards. I do feel it is time that we revised the age of retirement of high-grade diplomats and civil servants. We start paying the pension much too early and lose them when they are probably at their most valuable. On the other hand, it might be a good thing for them to have to retire at sixty, unless a medical board found them unusually fit to carry on, as I can think of several Governors who are too old at fifty!

By 31 October Surprise *was in the Red Sea near Aqaba.*

I couldn't possibly describe all the different types of fish I shot on that day and the subsequent days as they were too many and varied. The most interesting was a lion fish which has extremely poisonous spines about four inches long all along its back, but which has fins, if one can call them that, about ten or twelve inches long which are more of the consistency of very wobbly feathers which float about in the water. They are brown and white striped and look quite lovely. One of the sailors in another ship picked one up in his hands, was rushed off to hospital and treated and had to be flown to Fayid for further treatment and then back to Bighi. After three weeks he was returned fit for duty and then started having epileptic fits.

Just before we were going to anchor and start diving, Buster Graham† lost a monster barracuda which we could see spitting the spinner out as it jumped. The others now took the view that we were among a shoal of large barracuda and, as these are much more aggressive than sharks and are known to have bitten cutlets out of bathers in these parts, they endeavoured to dissuade me from going in. When I tried to laugh this off, Captain (Q) said, 'I can't force you to take my advice, sir, but I wish to record in the presence of witnesses my strong opinion that you should on no account take the risk of diving in these waters.' The Commander, himself an enthusiastic diver, who was going with me, defeated me finally by saying, 'I should feel happier, sir, if we didn't try and dive here.' Somewhat weakly I gave in and regretted

---

* The British Ambassador in Turkey.
† Captain (Q) Edward Graham was on the staff of the C.-in-C. in Malta.

not having gone off just by myself with the barge's crew when none of these difficulties would have arisen.

On Thursday, 5 November at 1430 we stopped off Difnein Island, some sixty miles north of Massawa.

On our second dive, as the sun was setting, Ronnie* and Buster set up a fearful commotion, shouting and biffing the water with boat hooks. When we surfaced they screamed, 'Get into the dinghy', which we did and pulled back to the barge.

Not fifty yards away two or three ominous triangular fins were approaching the barge. I came up to the bows and saw a monster pass down the starboard side, rubbing itself against the barge. It was almost as long as the barge, between 25 and 30 feet, mottled grey with hooped stripes. It had a wide head, two triangular dorsal fins and a colossal scimitar tail all out of the water. If my barge's crew had not left my very big harpoon gun in the *Surprise* I could not have failed to harpoon it. Then it joined its mates and kept circling the barge.

On return we consulted the handbook on giant fish and recognized them as a species of giant shark known as 'whale shark'; really quite a thrill.

We reached Massawa at 0800 on Friday, 6 November. It is a very low-lying tropical port. The heat was intense already at that hour. The port buildings were very fine and typical of the Italian colonization.

Although I was not due to land officially for another two hours, a guard of a hundred and a large band were already drawn up on the jetty. We had all been reading Evelyn Waugh's *Black Mischief*† and were delighted to note that the guard had evidently eaten their boots as they were wearing the thinnest of sandals.

The Emperor sent his second son, the Duke of Harar,‡ to meet me. He is thirty-two and was educated at Wellington.

Many other Ethiopian and Eritrean officials also came on board for lunch which was backed up by the party from the *Surprise*.

After the luncheon party had broken up we changed into plain clothes prior to the Duke of Harar and party conducting us to Asmara. We wanted to pick up the Duke so as to save time on the way but His Imperial Highness made a great point that he must come and pick us up. The result was that we were kept hanging about for half an hour when a

---

* Captain (later Vice-Admiral Sir Ronald) Brockman, Mountbatten's most trusted henchman from his time in India onwards.
† A satirical novel set largely in Ethiopia, published in 1932.
‡ Prince Makonnen.

harassed official drove up in a car to say that the Duke's own car had refused to start! I was all for our getting into the Emissary's car and driving over to the Palace to speed things up, but Edwina was very fearful of what the consequences would be for the chauffeur whose car wouldn't start, as flogging is still the most popular punishment in the country! Shortly after this the Duke arrived in a very dashing car to pick up me and his niece, Princess Ruth* (some ten years younger than him), picked Edwina up, and then a large procession of about twelve cars formed and we shot off for Asmara.

Whatever one may say about the way the Italians treated the people in this part of the world, especially when they were fighting, one has to take one's hat off to the way that they set about engineering works, road construction and town planning. The road to Asmara starts off in a dusty, very hot plain alongside the 95 centimetre railway. Both start to climb after about an hour and the road is one of the most sensational *corniches* I have ever driven over. We drove at enormous speed to try and make up the lost time, and as it grew dark we suddenly reached the top of the great escarpment, some 8000 feet above sea level, and found ourselves in the town.

Edwina and I were put up in a six-roomed suite with a big verandah, which was decorated in typical Italian style though rather over-ornate. The bathroom was lined with primrose tiles; the bath, basin, loo and even the bidet were jet black. It all looks very nice, but there was great trouble in getting any hot water and when Princess Ruth was showing Marjorie† how to run her bath she turned one tap to find the water running out of the other!

After an excellent dinner (the food in this country was universally superlative, and we have all put on a lot of weight), Their Imperial Highnesses got up and conducted us out of the room. The moment that they, Edwina and I had got through the door the Duke said to his staff, 'Close the doors.' A couple of ADCs rushed forward, shut the doors and leant against them with their shoulders as the struggling mass inside tried to get out.

We suggested that it might be nice if we were to mingle with the guests and have some conversation before we went to bed, but the Duke was quite firm. He said, 'I am sure you must be very tired after such a long

---

* Princess Hirout, daughter of Princess Tenanya Worq, the Emperor's eldest daughter.
† Marjorie, Countess of Brecknock, Edwina's cousin, who was accompanying the expedition.

day; I am certainly very tired myself, I am sure we ought all go to bed.' I then suggested that at least the Chargé d'Affaires* might be released so that we could discuss next day's programme. The Duke gave some instructions, the door was opened a crack, some enquiries were made and presently the Chargé d'Affaires came out of the door like a champagne cork with the pressure of the indignant guests trying to get out behind him. However, the doors were shut again and the ADCs put their shoulders to them. We then retired to bed, as we had been bidden.

The following day the party continued to the capital, Addis Ababa.

His Imperial Highness startled us by telling us that he had placed his house at our disposal and had himself moved into the old German Legation, which the Emperor uses as an official guest house. Nothing we could say at this late stage, of course, could make the Duke change his mind but it was all very embarrassing.

We drove off with our Chargé d'Affaires in a big Cadillac escorted by nine motor-cycle police.

Fairly large crowds were out in the streets and gave us a surprising sort of welcome. As we drove by, the crowds all bowed low, many of them literally prostrated themselves altogether in the road, their foreheads touching the ground with their bottoms well up in the air. In order to achieve a low bow the men do a sort of curtsey, putting one foot behind, and frequently raising it off the ground to balance their body as they bend forward.

Wherever a group of women had waited in a knot they let out a shrill cry, '*LULLULLULLULLULLULL*'. It is a very high-pitched trilling noise which a European could only reproduce by striking his lips with his fingers in quick succession while letting out a high piercing note.

I could not believe that all this demonstration was in our honour, and the Chargé d'Affaires explained that as the Emperor had given us his own personal Cadillac, and as he had never allowed anybody else before to have an escort of motor-cycle outriders, not even the Crown Prince or Prime Minister, and certainly not General de Gaulle, the last VIP to visit him last week, that it was more than likely that the people mistook us for the Emperor!

A day or two after my visit had been announced the Emperor ordered

---

* Caryl Ramsden. The Ambassador was on leave.

Addis Ababa to be 'cleaned up'. All the streets through which we were to pass were to be widened to 36 metres (117 feet), and ramshackle houses were to be pulled down and new fronts built and old houses painted up. Although not even the Chargé d'Affaires thought that this was entirely in honour of our visit, he thought it probable that the Emperor linked it up so as to make all the people get a move on. At all events, during the six or seven weeks since the order was given all the main streets in Addis Ababa have now been widened to 117 feet. Even the walls of the Imperial Palace grounds have been pulled down and moved back about 20 feet and rebuilt with new iron railings. In some places a whole street will consist of brick fronts, with doors and windows not yet filled in and with nothing whatever behind the frontage. In other places new fronts have been built and one can see behind them partly demolished houses which are to be rebuilt in a more modern manner.

I was riveted to see the Embassy so frequently referred to in such a brilliantly amusing and sarcastic way in Evelyn Waugh's book. The Consul, old Colonel Curle, DSO, told me that *Black Mischief* was not much of an exaggeration as far as the British Embassy was concerned, and that our then Minister, Sir Sydney Barton, did indeed open the Embassy bags on the dining room floor to distribute the gramophone records, silk stockings, etc. which came out with the official papers. The daughter, Esmé Barton, was in fact the heroine of Evelyn Waugh's book who was finally eaten by the cannibals. The reason why the book was written was that Lady Barton refused to receive Evelyn Waugh at the Embassy, since she considered that he was living in open sin with Irene Ravensdale at the local hotel! Evelyn Waugh's revenge is certainly very amusing, though the book can only be mentioned to a very few high-grade Ethiopians who have a strongly developed sense of humour; the bare mention of *Black Mischief* to any other Ethiopian is regarded as an insult. Curle told me that Evelyn Waugh has written an even better book on Ethiopia called *Remote People*,* which I must get hold of.

The usual *Daily Express* correspondent arrived in Addis Ababa to cover our visit. We have yet to visit any important country without this delicate attention from Max Beaverbrook.† The correspondent was seen by my Staff Officer, and all he had really been briefed to do was to

---

* Published in 1931, a highly entertaining and by no means wholly unreliable travel book.
† Lord Beaverbrook, proprietor of the *Daily* and *Sunday Express*, had had a vendetta against Mountbatten since the latter had taken a leading role in dismantling the Empire in India and Burma.

enquire about the *Surprise* and the *Glasgow*. How much time had I spent in the *Surprise* and how much in the *Glasgow*? Did Lady Mountbatten ever go to sea in the *Glasgow*? What other friends or relations were on board? My Staff Officer, who knew the form, thinks he managed successfully to put him off with harmless answers, but I suppose something fairly odd will come out in the *Daily Express*.

November 8th being Remembrance Sunday, we had to start off the proceedings by my laying a wreath at the Liberation Monument in the town, and then we all went on to the British cemetery at Gulale. Here we found most of the British community and the Ambassadors and Ministers of the Allied countries. The band of the Imperial bodyguard had been promised for 0830 but when we arrived at 0928 they were not yet there. The Chargé d'Affaires suggested we should start without them, but as I noticed that in the order of service we had to sing hymns I suggested we should wait until the band came. They arrived at 0931 at the double. To my surprise when the service started the band took no part and we had to sing the hymns without musical accompaniment. The explanation apparently was that the band could only play tunes that they already knew and they didn't know any of these hymns. After the service was over they played lustily those tunes and hymns which they did know.

Everybody placed wreaths on the War Memorial and then a rather nice ceremony occurred when the representatives of the Jewish, Hindu and Moslem communities laid wreaths on the graves of their co-religionists in the various cemetery plots. I was quite astonished to find the number of British soldiers of all creeds who lost their lives in the liberation of Addis Ababa; no wonder the British are beloved there.

> *The party drove that afternoon to Ambo, a sulphur spring resort seventy miles to the west of Addis Ababa.*

Driving the Emperor's car is rather a risky business because every few miles pedestrians are found lying in the road, stretched fully across the middle, so that one cannot pass them and has to pull up with a screeching of brakes. General Mered* used to explain to the pedestrians that I was not the Emperor, and they were to wait until His Imperial Majesty came next time to deliver their petitions.

* Mountbatten's Ethiopian ADC, General Mered Mangesma.

Another charming habit of Ethiopians who believe themselves to be pursued by evil spirits is to dash across the road in front of a car, timing matters in such a way that they will just not be run over whilst the evil spirit is, of course, cut off by the car.

The rest of the inhabitants prostrated themselves in an even more active form in the country than they had done in the city. It is rather disturbing at first, but after a while one grows used to passing rows of posteriors humped in the air while their owners' heads are in the dust! Whenever we pass any car on the road, it pulls into the side of the road and all the occupants tumble out as fast as they can and stand bowing as the Emperor's car goes by. If they ever discover that they have got out for the wrong chap I should think they must all be very annoyed.

We had asked to be called at 0600 on Monday, the 9th as we had a long programme ahead of us at Addis Ababa. At 0630 Edwina came in to find me still asleep and said she had not been called either. Luckily, everybody else woke up without being called and so we were all ready to leave the house at 0700. The mystery was solved by the fact that the servants came round and knocked so gently that we none of us heard them. I don't know what happens when the Emperor wants to be called early, but perhaps he is a lighter sleeper than we are.

After a visit to the General Wingate Secondary School:

I had to go back to the Harar Palace to get into No. 3s for the official call on the Emperor.* Edwina and Marjorie had to dress in full-length dresses, with sleeves and gloves, and appeared to have had quite a time in getting themselves dressed up and both thought it vastly amusing; though to a mere man their dresses looked no odder than what they wear at any other time.

When the moment came to be shown into the Throne Room, the Emperor's ADC manoeuvred us about with both hands, rather like an aircraft handler manoeuvres aircraft on the flight deck of a carrier. He is a regular Hercules, eighteen stone of sheer muscle. He plays regular polo on a mount like a cart horse and is responsible for the personal safety of the Emperor. He is never without a loaded revolver when with His Imperial Majesty and has been known to use it. High-level floggings

---

* The gradations of naval uniform appropriate for each occasion preoccupied Mountbatten greatly. No. 3s were about as formal as you could get.

are also administered by him, which must be most unpleasant for the culprits on account of his very great strength.

The double doors of the Throne Room were thrown open as we appeared. Edwina and I advanced together and in accordance with the protocol bowed and curtseyed low in the doorway. We then manoeuvred across to a position opposite the throne and started to advance, ready to carry out our second bow and curtsey half way down as instructed, prior to the third bow and curtsey at the steps of the throne. However, the Emperor advanced smilingly towards us with both hands out and intercepted us with a very warm welcome before we could do our second bow and curtsey. He led us up by the hand to the throne where the Empress was and introduced us personally.

Although the Emperor speaks extremely good English, he decided that he would talk French to me, and so, of course, I had to follow suit. On the other hand, I am told that when he first met Monsieur Auriole, the Director of the Addis Ababa—Djibouti railway, he decided to speak English to him, and although M. Auriole can hardly speak any English, he of course had to answer in the same language. Ever since, the Emperor always speaks to him in English, and for the rest of the time we were in Addis Ababa the Emperor spoke to me in French!

It is impossible to exaggerate the warmth of the welcome which we received. He kept repeating how deeply touched and delighted he felt that we should deign to visit his humble country. He said that the people who meant most to him in this world were the British. We had given him asylum in the days of his exile and we had striven to stop the Italian aggression.

When the moment came to depart we got into some difficulties with our manoeuvring. Edwina and I had to walk out backwards, which is the protocol here, stopping to bow and curtsey about every ten or fifteen yards, during which time the rest of our party advanced outside us, closed into the throne and then followed us backwards. By the time we got to the end of the Throne Room, our last bow and curtsey was to the posteriors of the seven people who had come with us, who were all in the process of bowing and curtseying ahead of us. We had to manoeuvre sideways through the door, which is unfortunately not in the centre of the Throne Room but we all got out without any collisions.

> *The following day the Emperor gave an official banquet for his visitors.*

The servants were all in their full dress livery of green velvet coats and red velvet waistcoats and knee breeches. Everything was done in the most sumptuous manner and the food was unbelievably good.

I understand that His Imperial Majesty is distressed at the absence of gold plate and has ordered a dinner service of solid gold plate for 100 people at the cost of £75,000 from Asprey. Asprey's were apparently very good to him during his exile and refused to send in any bills. Now that he is restored to the throne he has had the Directors of Asprey out as his guests for three weeks, bringing a large selection of their goods, and everybody in Addis Ababa has ordered great quantities of things from Asprey. Rather a nice story.

After dinner the Emperor kept me by his side for the whole of the rest of the evening gossiping hard. He asked me what I thought of Chiang Kai-shek, Stalin, Roosevelt, Churchill, Marshall, etc. . . . . He expressed the greatest apprehension of what the Americans were doing, kind-hearted as they undoubtedly were.

He told me that he always stayed at Brown's hotel in Dover Street because it was such a nice English family hotel, and above all they employed no Italians!

The Emperor has shown the most inordinate personal interest in our welfare. He personally rang up his representative in Eritrea on the day we arrived to get an account of how the visit was progressing and whether we were comfortable. He sent round some Ethiopian porridge to us each morning for breakfast. When Edwina rather light-heartedly remarked to General Mered that she had always wanted to have one of the Ethiopian monkeys with black faces and white whiskers, the General reported this conversation to the Emperor who immediately had monkeys of this breed sent to the Palace where he personally selected the tamest one and presented it to Edwina! It is now on board the *Surprise* together with a baby gazelle and two chameleons.*

I forgot to mention that in the cathedral the dome has three mural paintings. The centre one depicts the crucifixion; the one to the right depicts Haile Selassie addressing the League of Nations after the Italian invasion; the left-hand one depicts Haile Selassie rehoisting the

---

* Mountbatten appears to have had an insatiable appetite for chameleons, see e.g., 14 October 1964 and 13 May 1965.

Ethiopian flag after the defeat of the Italians by the British. All are by the same artist and all are treated with equal reverence.

All the Imperial children are looked after by Scottish or English nurses, of whom there are four. They all learn to speak English at the same time as their native Amharic. All are the most ardent admirers of everything British, and I am sure that this admiration, and indeed devotion, is deeply sincere.

That evening there was a dinner party at the British Embassy for the Emperor, the Empress, the Imperial Family and the Prime Minister and Ministers.

At the end of the evening the Emperor spoke to me alone and said that it had been the greatest grief to him to hear that the Foreign Office would not permit him to make a present to me which he had set his heart on.

It appears that the moment my visit was announced the Emperor sent for the court jeweller and instructed him personally to prepare the star of the Grand Cross of his highest order set in diamonds. The diamonds were telegraphed for to Europe and sent out by air mail and the jewellers worked overtime to get this elaborate diamond-mounted star ready. Meanwhile the Foreign Office had written to the Chargé d'Affaires asking him to find out whether the Emperor was contemplating conferring a decoration on me so that he could be warned that this could not be accepted.

Part of the trouble lies in the fact that when Monty* came here three or four years after the war, he accepted the same decoration, although the Eighth Army boundaries were no nearer to Ethiopia than the South-East Asia boundaries!† Furthermore, the Ethiopian court live by Debrett, from which they could see that I had Spanish, Rumanian, Swedish and Portuguese orders, which clearly had not been given for war service. With restricted permission there would be no question of ever wearing any of these orders, except on the very rare occasions of being in Ethiopia or in the presence of the Emperor, and I really wonder whether the amount of ill-feeling the Foreign Office have caused in Morocco, Jordan and Ethiopia can possibly be justified by strict adherence to the regulations. However, this incident passed off reasonably well and we were given the Emperor's portrait in a large silver

---

* Field Marshal Viscount Montgomery.
† A curious interpretation of zonal boundaries. Most people would conclude the SEA zone was at least twice as far away.

frame. Edwina received a beautiful gold filigree bracelet and I received a gold filigree cigarette case. In return the Emperor said that he would accept small gifts from us for himself and his two sons. It is an expensive game as we would not have had to give back anything in return for a decoration!*

We flew back in two aircraft, and made a detour to pass over Lake T'ana. The name is sometimes spelt Tsana, but the Ethiopians pronounce the 't' with an explosive effect by blowing out hard against the teeth when the 't' is pronounced. I practised this under General Mered's instruction at Ambo with such success that poor Marjorie who was sitting opposite me had to wipe her face.

Of many visits I have paid to strange parts of the world, such as Nepal, Siam, Borneo and the various states of India, Ethiopia has proved by far the most interesting and enjoyable.

---

* Mountbatten collected decorations as others collect stamps. This story had a happy ending on 23 July 1965.

1956

Mountbatten did not resume keeping a journal of his travels until March 1956, by which time he had been First Sea Lord for some eighteen months. On 12 March he set off with Edwina on a visit to India, Burma, New Zealand and Australia.

WEDNESDAY, 14 MARCH   At 0330 Delhi time I was woken by the Captain of the aircraft with a signal from the Air Control Traffic Centre at Karachi which read as follows: 'You are not, repetition, not permitted to fly over Pakistan territory or territorial waters. Acknowledge.' As we were half way on the trip before we got the message, it meant a diversion of over one hundred miles to avoid Pakistan, and, with an aircraft whose maximum speed is less than 190 knots, the Pakistan authorities had every reason to suppose that they would cause us to arrive at least half an hour late at Delhi, which presumably was the object of this extraordinary signal forbidding a British aircraft to fly even over Pakistan territorial waters.

As luck would have it we had a following wind and had allowed enough time in hand to arrive on the dot at Palam. Here I was received, not as First Sea Lord, but as former constitutional Governor-General of India with the highest honours. The Vice-President, the entire Cabinet, headed by the Prime Minister and down to and including all the junior Ministers and the Secretaries of Government Departments, were drawn up on the tarmac. All the senior officers of the three Services, Ambassadors, High Commissioners and leading citizens of Delhi were there too. The Indian Navy provided a Guard of Honour and the Indian Air Force a band.

The route from Palam to New Delhi is a long one, about five miles, yet there were almost continuous crowds on both sides of the roads; sometimes two or three deep. It is difficult to estimate but the numbers must have run into tens of thousands.

1956

The Mountbattens stayed at the President's House.

Edwina and I walked in the gardens where the various head gardeners came up to greet us and old friends came up at every turn.

We have been put in the VIP suite, which was originally intended for the Viceroy and which we occupied during the first days of my Viceroyalty. We wandered round the house, which has been beautifully kept up, and at every turn emotional memories surged up.

I and my staff met the High Commissioner (Malcolm MacDonald) before lunch. Jawaharlal and his daughter Indira* lunched with us on the balcony of our suite. At 1630 we called on the President† in my old study and I was much touched to note that he still had all the badges of my South-East Asia Formations hung round the walls.

THURSDAY, 15 MARCH. DELHI   We got into our finery for the State Banquet. The President very politely came and fetched us from our rooms in person. A further courtesy, which I do not remember extending to any of our guests, was that the route from our rooms, the full length of the house to the ballroom, was lined by the Body Guard.

The dinner was as beautifully done as ever, with 100 guests at the one long table. The only change is that instead of dear old head Abdar controlling the service by means of raising his arms, there are coloured traffic lights rigged up all round the room by which the service is controlled. The President proposed the Queen's health and it was nice to hear 'God Save The Queen' being played in the traditional way in the Banqueting Hall. I proposed the President's health and then Jawaharlal made one of his most charming speeches, proposing Edwina's and my health, to which I replied.

It was all so beautifully done, with such care to ceremonial and dignity, but what struck me most was that the members of the President's staff were not bidden to sit down at the table. To see the Maharoa Raja of Bundi (an ADC) and the Maharaj Kumar of Jaipur (Adjutant of the Body Guard) stand throughout dinner behind old Dr Rajendra Prasad's chair appeared to me to epitomize the complete passing of the old order in India.

---

* Jawaharlal Nehru, Prime Minister of India, and his daughter, Mrs Indira Gandhi.
† Dr Rajendra Prasad.

FRIDAY, 16 MARCH   I forgot to mention that the Queen of Afghanistan, with a large suite, has been occupying the floor above us, but as she is. in purdah none of us have seen her and she left this morning to continue her interrupted flight.

What a commentary on this gigantic house, that a Queen and her retinue can be fellow guests without one discovering this until the day of her departure.

SUNDAY, 18 MARCH   Jawaharlal and Indu came and collected us at 0730 and drove with us to Palam airfield.

We were amused to see that Ghazanfar Ali Khan was among the High Commissioners who came to see us off. This must have required considerable courage since the Karachi newspaper *Dawn* published a letter attacking him for being present at Palam 'To receive Serpent Lord Mountbatten'. It continued, 'A man like Mountbatten whose hand is stained with the blood of thousands of innocent Muslims, is nothing but the enemy of Pakistan. He is the declared enemy of Islam, the Musulmans and Pakistan. The ghastly crimes committed by the Lord on the eve of Partition, are still fresh in public memory and time cannot obliterate them.'

We arrived at Vera Cruz Airport, Bombay, punctually at 1100.

This was the last occasion on which we were to see Mr René McColl,* Max Beaverbrook's special agent sent out to write up our visit to India, for he confessed to the Indian Public Relations Officer that he had been unable to obtain transport either to get him to Wellington or to Cochin.

He has been carrying round a copy of Ray Murphy's book,† saying that this man started as an admirer but as he got to know me he realized what a rotter I was and that this comes out clearly in the book! As he has not lent the book for more than half an hour to anybody, they have not been able to verify his statement.

As Mr McColl was preceded by Mr Harper of the *Daily Express* to prepare his coming, this little bit of publicity must have cost Max something in the region of four figures.

---

* Author and Chief Foreign Correspondent of the *Daily Express*.
† *The Last Viceroy*, published in 1948; by no means hagiographical but not justifying Mr McColl's description of it.

WEDNESDAY, 21 MARCH. RANGOON   We arrived at Mingaladon Airport, Rangoon, just as the sun had set at 1830. The Prime Minister* had brought with him the most important members of his Cabinet to meet us. There was also an extremely smart naval guard and band and 24 of the most lovely little Burmese girls from the National Institute and Rangoon University, each of whom gave us a bouquet.

That hideous Government House which, by some oversight, the RAF failed to destroy, really looked rather nice in the gloaming, for the entire house was illuminated and so were the trees and the roads in the grounds, so it almost looked like fairyland.

THURSDAY, 22 MARCH   At 1630 the Investiture was held in the Throne Room, immediately in front of the throne of King Theebaw which I presented to Burma on behalf of the Government of India in 1948.

Incidentally, the Prime Minister said he would like to move it to the museum they intend to build, but as it has to be stripped into 5000 parts he has been advised that it would be too difficult to move it again, so he laughingly suggested that they had better have a new Palace built for the President† and put the museum here.

[The order Mountbatten was about to receive] confers the title *Agga Maha Thiri Thudhamma*. I am told by the President that the expression *Agga Maha Thiri Thudhamma* is a Pali expression:

Agga	means Highest
Maha	means Great
Thiri	means Glorious
Thu	means True
Dhamma	means Law

Put it literally, it means The Highest and the Great Glorious Commander of the Most Exalted Order of True Law; but put it liberally, it means The Highest and the Most Glorious Commander of the Most Exalted Order of Truth. It is based on an old Burmese decoration which is stated to have been instituted a thousand years ago.

The whole order is of solid gold and platinum. There is an embossed plate, angled to go over the left shoulder, from which 12 gold chains

* U Nu.
† Ba U.

suspend holding a modern-looking star in front and an ancient embossed plaque at the back. It continues rather like the Sash of the Grand Cross to the side where it joins three embossed gold plates joined together.

The President unfortunately picked up the order the wrong way round and got hopelessly mixed up in trying to put it on. Luckily, while the President was holding it over my head to put my arm through I could read instructions in English gummed on the inside of the plates, saying in capitals 'LEFT SHOULDER, FRONT, RIGHT HIP and BACK' respectively. I was thus able to persuade His Excellency to try again, and with much difficulty we eventually got it on the right way round.

The President pronounced a very charming citation:

> I confer this title of *Agga Maha Thiri Thudhamma* on you in recognition of signal services rendered by you, firstly, in liberating my country from the Japanese occupation; secondly, in treating my countrymen kindly, humanely, and sympathetically after liberation and, thirdly, in paving the way for the quick restoration of our birthright. The title is the highest in the gift of the people of the Union of Burma.

I must admit it is rather unique that the President of Burma should have endorsed in a manner of speaking the King's original grant of the 'of Burma'* title in this way, and I feel duly proud.

*   *   *

The President had invited me along to tea to have a heart to heart. He informed me that in June 1945 just before I came to Rangoon there had been a meeting of the leaders of political parties, at which they decided on their future policy. In view of the fact that it was already clear that the British were coming back as friends and to give the Burmese Dominion status, it was agreed that their goal should be to accept Dominion status and not to leave the Commonwealth. The President sadly added, 'It was only the events after you gave up the Military Government which forced us out of the Commonwealth.'†

---

* Mountbatten took the territorial appellation 'of Burma' when created an Earl in 1947.
† Ba U was being too kind. Best opinion is that Burma would have left the Commonwealth in any case.

SATURDAY, 24 MARCH   Looking through the vast amount of luggage
we seem to have brought with us on this trip, which was all stacked up in
an adjoining dressing room, I came across two years' supply of loo-loo
paper which staggered me. On enquiry I found that this was paper
which had been delivered at Wilton Crescent the evening before we left
and Pullen was under the impression that it was a special supply we got
in for the trip!

*On 27 March the Mountbattens arrived in Welling-
ton. The following morning:*

I attended a meeting of the New Zealand Chiefs of Staff and then went
on to call on Mr Macdonald, Minister of External Affairs and Defence,
who took me on to call on Mr Holland, the Prime Minister.

The Prime Minister took me in to attend a full meeting of the New
Zealand Cabinet, which I addressed for some forty minutes and
answered questions for the remaining twenty minutes, before the State
Luncheon in Parliament House.

Mr Holland and the Leader of the Opposition, Mr Nash, made very
flattering speeches. Mr Nash, who had been the Prime Minister in 1946,
was quite absurdly lyrical in his praise. As I had been told that this
speech would not be broadcast I was horrified to find microphones on
the table. The Prime Minister also thought it was not going to be
broadcast and we only discovered at the last moment that it was a live
broadcast being followed by a national broadcast that evening, which
meant I would have to prepare completely separate speeches for other
occasions in New Zealand.

*On 29 March the Mountbattens continued to
Auckland.*

A huge Civic Reception was arranged in the most formal way at which
3000 people were present. The speeches were once more broadcast,
which is reducing the material I can use more and more. I have found
one useful dodge is to quote extracts from my diary of what we did in
each place in 1920, and to read Pammy's diary and find any interesting
pleasant pieces of the Royal Tour to refer to.*

* Lady Pamela, Mountbatten's younger daughter, attended the Queen on the Royal
Tour during the winter of 1953–4.

After a short break for some fishing, on 3 April:

We flew in Lilibet's Dakota to Paraparaumu. Originally we were going to fly straight through to Dunedin, but the Prime Minister had telephoned and said he specially wanted to see us for a moment.

He met us at the airfield, took us to his little weekend bungalow nearby and presented us each with a New Zealand rug. He said he had been so anxious to see us again and have a last talk that he had even cancelled a Cabinet Meeting to come up!

We flew on to Dunedin in the South Island. A high-level press conference of editors was awaiting us and then we went off to the State Reception in the Royale Ballroom at which 1500 people were present.

Having imagined the people would be sitting and I would have a lectern from which to make a speech, I had prepared a lot of notes which proved quite useless as I had to stand surrounded by a vast crowd at a microphone and speak extemporarily.

There was no special organization after this so we suggested we should shake hands with the assembled crowd, which we did at the rate of 40 a minute.

Ex-Leading Seaman Solomon, the Coxswain of the *Kipling*'s motor boat, was there with his wife and was brought over by one of the officials who, in the presence of a large crowd, said, 'This is the man who saved your life', so I said, 'I am very delighted to see him, but not because he saved my life but because I risked his life by leaving him behind in the wrecked motor boat without realizing it and I congratulate him on finding his way back from Crete.' Luckily Pammy's diary had warned us of this line, but it made no difference as far as the papers are concerned as Solomon is definitely one of the many people who saved my life in the war!

By 7 April they were in Melbourne.

I was taken to what I thought was going to be an excessively boring event; namely the one-mile race in the Victoria Amateur Athletic Championships at the Olympic Park. The stadium and track is almost finished and looked quite magnificent, but I was informed that this was only one of the training tracks!

Landy, the great Australian miler, was running and there were colossal crowds in all the stands. I felt very embarrassed at being introduced by loud speaker and having to wave to them, for all of us had only come to see Landy.

Rangoon, 22 March 1956. Mountbatten thanks the President of Burma after being invested with the order of Agga Maha Thiri Thudhamma.

Paris, 11 April 1957. A meeting at SHAPE, between Generals Norstad (left) and Ely.

Washington, 16 October 1958. Mountbatten at the White House sits between President Eisenhower and General Twining. Admiral Denny makes up the front row.

New London, 20 October 1958. Aboard the USS *Skipjack* with Admiral Rickover alongside.

I would not have believed that such an ordinary athletic race could be so exciting, as we all thought that there was a chance that Landy might break the world record and indeed it took a long time to work out the result.

The whole of the last lap the crowd went wild with excitement and cheered themselves hoarse. He sprinted faster and faster and clearly passed the post in under 4 minutes, in fact 3 minutes 58.6 seconds; equal to the Australian record but 0.6 of a second longer than the world record which in fact Landy himself holds. I have a feeling he will beat the world record in the Olympic Games.* I met him afterwards and found him quite charming.

On 10 April they arrived in Canberra. Next day:

The Prime Minister† conducted me into the House of Representatives and the Speaker announced my presence and asked if it was the pleasure of the House that I should be given a seat on the floor of the House (presumably as a member of the British Upper House). The House made polite noises and I was then conducted by the Sergeant at Arms to shake hands with the Speaker and sit on a specially placed chair next to him.

Question time followed. In Australia they have a pernicious habit that verbal questions are asked without notice and Ministers have to reply without briefing. The written questions, on the other hand, are only answered in writing and once a written question has been submitted no other questions on the same subject are allowed. It is the simplest thing in the world for a Minister to get a friend to submit a written question on a topic he wants to evade in the House and it cannot be raised.

The House was extraordinarily noisy and boisterous and I can well understand Winston describing Australian politics as having an eighteenth-century robustness.

What made it more difficult for me to follow was that front benchers from both sides came up in turn to talk to me and of course had to whisper in my ear.

I went at 1530 to call on the Leader of the Opposition, Dr Evatt. He has a reputation for being one of the rudest men in Australian public life but he was very charming to me.

---

* An Australian duly beat the world record in 1958, but it was J. H. Elliot, not Landy.
† Sir Robert Menzies, Prime Minister 1939–41 and 1949–66.

At 1600 I attended a meeting of the Australian Cabinet and addressed them for about an hour and answered questions for another half an hour.

[The Governor-General, Field Marshal Viscount Slim, that evening gave] a dinner for about 46. After walkie-talkies were over, Bill was very anxious for another talk with me so we stayed gossiping until 1 a.m.

He told me an absolutely fascinating thing. While he was CIGS it became known that he was writing the story of the Burma Campaign. He was approached by two representatives of the *Daily Express* who offered him an unusually large sum for the serial rights, provided he could finish the book quickly.

He asked what the hurry was and they said that they were anxious that the true story of the Burma Campaign should be told while it was fresh in people's minds, and they wished to afford him the opportunity of stating his side of the quarrels and disagreements which they understood he had had with me.

When Bill replied that we had never had the smallest disagreement they were not interested in his story. Since that he has been included in the vendetta and they have written nothing but foul things about him.

> *On their return journey the Mountbattens called in on Ceylon, arriving there on 18 April.*

We drove to Temple Trees, the official residence of the Prime Minister, which has been put at our disposal with the staff. The new Prime Minister, Mr Bandaranaike, is not living here; but neither did the late Prime Minister, Sir John Kotelawala. It is very pleasant having the house to ourselves.

We just had time to unpack our mess dress and evening clothes and then we had to depart to call on the Governor-General, Sir Oliver Goonetilleke.

Goonetilleke told us what a shock it had been to him and all the members of his Party to find that they were so heavily defeated at the polls. He gave me some very helpful advice for my meeting with the Prime Minister, and kept us in all for one and a quarter hours.

We then went on to a dinner given by the Syers* at the lovely dashing new modern house just completed by the Ministry of Works. After

---

* Sir Cecil Syer, UK High Commissioner.

the muggy heat of Colombo a modern air-conditioned house was delightful.

It was quite a big dinner party and to everybody's delight and surprise the Prime Minister and Mrs Bandaranaike accepted to come. This is the first engagement of this nature he has accepted since his election, and he turned out to be an extraordinarily intelligent, pleasant and well-intentioned man, who clearly worships Jawaharlal and all he stands for.

THURSDAY, 19 APRIL. COLOMBO   I was joined by the High Commissioner and the C.-in-C.* and we all went in for my formal call on the Prime Minister. Instead of lasting 20 minutes, he kept us for close on an hour, and I had the unusual gratification of being told separately and individually by de Zoyza† and Charles Norris and Syer that they thought it had been a most opportune and invaluable interview for putting the right ideas into the Prime Minister's head in a manner which was evidently acceptable to him. As there has been talk of leaving the Commonwealth and severing all connections with the British forces, anything we can gain on this position will be to the good.

Before concluding their visit to Ceylon the Mountbattens went briefly to Kandy, arriving on 20 April.

The emotions which the King's Pavilion‡ has awakened in me are even stronger and in a way more upsetting than others on this trip. I have now returned as a guest to three houses which I occupied; the Viceroy's House, the President's House, Rangoon, and King's Pavilion, and have visited two other houses I occupied; Government House and Flagstaff House, Singapore. Although staying in Viceroy's House was an extraordinary experience it was too big ever to have been 'home'.

On the other hand, the little King's Pavilion in which I never had more than my personal staff and two guests, really was my complete home for 20 months. Almost every corner of the house and grounds evokes a memory of some incident and it is an unusually peculiar feeling sleeping once more in my bedroom.

---

* The Commander-in-Chief, East Indies, Vice-Admiral Sir Charles Norris.
† Permanent Secretary of the Ministry of External Affairs.
‡ Mountbatten's headquarters for much of the time that he was Supreme Allied Commander in South-East Asia.

1958

*Another gap of a year followed, and then in 1958
Mountbatten began to record all his more significant trips abroad. That year he visited Canada and
the United States.*
On Monday, 6 October he was in Ottawa.

After lunch I met the Canadian Naval Board for over an hour's valuable
discussion. The Minister of Defence* then took me over to call on the
Prime Minister.† This was supposed to be a quarter of an hour's
courtesy call, but he kept me an hour talking about India and matters
affecting our two Navies. We discussed at great length the opening of
the St Lawrence sea-way, when he said how disappointed the Canadians were about it not being possible to arrange the time of the
Canadian National Exhibition in Toronto so that the Queen would be
able to open it.

He told me that the Canadian Government hoped I would do it, and
he then produced the President of the Exhibition to convey the formal
invitation in the Prime Minister's office.

I pointed out that we had done it ten years ago and I thought they
never had the same man to open it a second time. He realized that this
was true in principle, but he wanted me to bring a squadron of frigates
up the St Lawrence sea-way and anchor them off the Exhibition
grounds. I thought there was a catch in it!

I said I would have to consult HMG before I could give an answer,
though of course I was very flattered.

Karsh, the famous photographer, had asked if he could come and
take a photograph and as he is an old friend I agreed. In any case, I
haven't got a good one with the right number of stripes yet!

I forgot he really likes to take an hour over his photographing and this

* Hon. George R. Pearkes, VC, DSO, MC – 'a really fine old veteran,' wrote Mountbatten, 'very alert and progressive.'
† John Diefenbaker.

24

made me rather late for a meeting of the representatives of the Ontario Branch of the Royal Life Saving Society.

On 10 October Mountbatten arrived in San Diego, California, and the following morning:

At 0930 I left for the US Marine Corps Recruit Training Centre. I went round all their various activities in great detail and just don't believe that our recruits would stand the extraordinarily rough treatment to which these men are submitted, but then it must be remembered that the US Marine Corps is the *Corps d'Elite* of the whole nation. They turn down all but the highest class recruits, for they are heavily over-subscribed with volunteers. They pass 25,000 recruits a year through this centre and the same number at Paris Island on the East Coast. Last year they threw out 2500 who had not matched up to the high standards they expect after 90 days.

Any man who is overweight on arrival is put in a special squad to bring his weight down to normal, or if underweight he is put in another squad to bring his weight up. If the rough treatment damps their ardour they are put in a special motivation squad to make them feel good about the Marines, and backward men are given a final chance in a separate squad before they are flung out.

Even at the recruit stage they have obviously a great pride in their Corps and take the merciless bullying of their drill instructors in good part.

At one of the Commando obstacle courses a Marine trying to climb an 8-foot vertical wall unaided got stuck. The drill instructor shouted, 'You are not in the Army, you are a Marine', which had an electrical effect on him, for he reached the top of the wall in one more stupendous effort.

We flew in Arleigh Burke's* magnificent aircraft to Los Angeles Municipal Airfield. Mr Frank Freeman, the head of Paramount Studios, was there to receive me with a large Cadillac. He suggested we should visit the MGM lot which was on the way. When we got to the gate one of the studio policemen held us up and my host said, 'I am Mr Freeman, the head of Paramount. This is Lord Mountbatten.' I was in uniform,

---

* Admiral Arleigh Burke, American Chief of Naval Operations and a close ally of Mountbatten's.

but the guard replied emphatically, 'Mr Freeman, nobody gets in here without a permit.'

After some futile argument we drove round to another gate where the guard again refused to let us in. By this time Mr Freeman was getting quite angry. He demanded the right to use the gate telephone and rang up one of the head people and finally we got permission to drive in.

Mr Freeman apologized and explained, 'So many people try different dodges to break into the studios, hire Cadillacs and drive up in uniforms just to get in, that the guards have to be very careful.' He did not explain how the gate crashers made themselves up to look like the head of Paramount!

We drove on to the Beverly Hilton, by far the most expensive hotel in the world. Here a party of some sixty Hollywood notables were collected.

Spyros Skouras* had flown especially from the East Coast to spend a few hours in Hollywood for this luncheon. He spoke with deep emotion about the British Navy, and said that if it had not been for our ships penetrating to all parts of the world, bringing the English language with them, and teaching the benighted foreigner how to understand English, they would never have been able to have such a wide sale for American films.

As a token of their gratitude he called upon the American film industry to give copies of their future films to the British Navy, gratis. This caused quite a sensation. He called upon the representative of MGM across the table, 'Don't you agree?' and received the reply, 'This must be dealt with in New York.' He called on Frank Freeman, 'Don't you agree?' and Freeman said, 'I will have to think it over.' He then called on all those who did agree with him to show it by their applause, and I must say the whole of the rest of the table clapped enthusiastically.

This created an embarrassing situation, since the last thing I wanted to do was to get the American film people to pay for the prints, which they already let us have without rent, at cost price. So, when my turn came to speak, I accepted the spirit of the offer, but asked that the present arrangements should continue, and this was met by even more applause, so that I hope the position of the Royal Naval Film Corporation will be all the more secure in the future with the US film industry.

We were then taken on to some of the stages and had the luck to see Orson Welles as the Lawyer Clarence Darrow making his famous

---

* President, Twentieth Century-Fox.

address to the judge in a crowded courtroom, asking for a life sentence for Loeb and Leopold, instead of the electric chair. This film will probably be called *Compulsion* and is the story of those horrible young lust murderers of 1925.*

Orson Welles went through a rehearsal so brilliantly that the large audience of film extras in the courtroom scene broke into spontaneous applause at the end of his rehearsal.

> *On 14 October Mountbatten arrived at the naval base at Norfolk, Virginia. A press conference was held.*

The press were quite friendly when I resolutely refused to answer questions about Quemoy,† and I steered them off the $64,000 question, 'Are you satisfied with Britain's NATO contribution?' by pointing out that if I answered 'Yes' I could hardly stay on as a guest of Admiral Wright,‡ and if I answered 'No' I was unlikely to retain my job when I got home.

In the afternoon they gave me the same presentations which they had given Duncan Sandys.§ Sandys told me the questions he had asked and the answers they had given, which I am sure will be extremely useful to me when I see Duncan again.

> *On 15 October Mountbatten continued to Washington.*

I arrived for my stay at the White House at 1645 and was told that the President¶ was out practising golf but would be in by 1700 to give me tea.

From 1700 to 1900 we gossiped ceaselessly, fighting the war over again and finally discussing the current situation. The President discussed how the Quemoy situation might be handled, and as I am never one for holding back what I think, I told him my views. He said, 'Will

---

* The film did appear under that title in 1959, but whatever the merits of the rehearsal, it was not generally felt to be one of Welles's happier efforts.
† Quemoy and Matsu were islands off the shore of China which were occupied by Chiang Kai-shek's forces and under bombardment from the mainland. Some people were advocating American intervention.
‡ Admiral Jerrauld Wright was Supreme Allied Commander in the Atlantic.
§ Later Lord Duncan-Sandys. Minister of Defence at the time.
¶ Dwight D. Eisenhower.

you go and tell Foster that', and immediately rang through to the Secretary of State* to say that he was to see me the following morning.

FRIDAY, 17 OCTOBER. WASHINGTON   I was bidden to breakfast in the dining room with the President at 0745. He had a huge rare steak and held forth more garrulously than ever. He told me he had to be in his office at 0815 but in fact continued talking until 0845. Finally at 0905 I saw Ike and Mamie off on their electioneering trip to Iowa.

I thought they were both in cracking good form and good health. Mamie kept saying, 'You have done Ike so much good by letting him gossip with you, that is what he really enjoys.'

I was taken over to the old Main Navy Building where the British Joint Staff are housed, to meet the forty or fifty members of the British Naval Staff and to address them.

Rear Admiral Al Mumma, the Head of the Bureau of Ships, called and after a good gossip took me down to the Atomic Top Secret Room in which they kept their models and sketches of nuclear propulsion, where that brilliant, cantankerous genius, Admiral Rickover,† gave me a presentation. He loves being rude to people and enjoys it even more being answered back.

He started, 'Admiral, I think your British set-up is lousy because you haven't got a tough enough man at the top. What you want to run a show like this is a real son of a bitch!' He was delighted with my reply, 'That is where you Americans have the edge on us, you have the only real son of a bitch in the business!' He was furious to hear that on Monday, instead of having the whole day for nuclear propulsion, I was going to waste my time for one and three quarter hours eating lunch with unimportant Admirals and Mayors, and going round conventional submarine schools at New London. He insisted on having the pro-gramme re-cast, to which I agreed subject to Arleigh Burke giving the necessary ruling and not cutting out the official luncheon to which all the guests had been invited. He kept saying to me as he showed me new and fantastic models of nuclear propulsion for all sorts of ships, 'You are the first Britisher to be allowed to see this!'

---

* Foster Dulles.
† Hyman Rickover was the architect of and chief force behind the American nuclear propulsion programme.

After this I was taken over to the State Department, where I met Harold Caccia,* who took me in to see the famous Foster Dulles.

I repeated the views I had expressed to the President and then I told him that I had had to deal continuously with the Generalissimo† during the war, and that when he had sacked the American General Stilwell on the day of my first arrival in Chunking, I had forced him to take Joe Stilwell back by saying I would not allow any of the five Chinese divisions in my theatre to take part in the campaign except under his command, and that contrary to the belief of all the 'experts', the Generalissimo had believed I would carry out my threat and had given way and reinstated Stilwell.‡

Mr Dulles said that this example was most encouraging to him as he would be seeing the Generalissimo in Formosa on Tuesday, but I shall be very surprised if my talk has any effect on this curious native of Cape Cod, who has been christened by his own countrymen 'The piece of Cod which passes all understanding'.

MONDAY, 20 OCTOBER We took off at 0625, had breakfast on board, and landed at 0810 at Schenectady County Airport and were driven at once to West Milton, where the Atomic Energy Commission have erected the famous steel sphere in which the sodium-cooled reactor had first been tested for the submarine *Sea Wolf*.

They were now in the midst of constructing a complete section of their new nuclear-powered destroyer, bigger even than our guided missile destroyers, in which they are going to try out the destroyer reactor.

We then moved over to a large building which housed the *Triton* prototype reactor. The *Triton* is an enormous submarine, about the same tonnage and length as our *Euryalus* Class cruisers. The entire section of the reactor room, engine room etc., has been constructed in this building to full scale and of the same materials.

The reactor was working at full power driving a huge water-brake propeller. I was invited to work the extremely simple controls and took the reactor down to half power and very quickly up to full power with startling ease.

---

* The British Ambassador, later Lord Caccia.
† Chiang Kai-shek.
‡ A somewhat over-dramatic statement of Mountbatten's role in the reinstatement of General 'Vinegar Joe' Stilwell.

At the submarine base at New London:

I was taken straight on board USS *Skipjack*, whose reactor had gone critical three days before. The whole shape of the submarine is a fantastic peep into the future (or perhaps a throwback to the past – for her hull resembles that of the first Holland boat).

I spent one and a half hours crawling all over the *Skipjack* from stem to stern along each of her four decks. She makes the *Nautilus* look very old-fashioned and clumsy. I was allowed in the reactor compartment for they had closed down the reactor again, but what astonished me most was the really beautiful lay-out of all this complicated machinery, piping and valves. Unlike any other submarine, British, American or any other nationality I have ever seen, the *Skipjack*, with her immensely more complicated machinery, has been so carefully laid out that everything is straightforward and access to every part is easy. I was to discover the reason for this later.

Next we went on board the monster *Triton*, by far the biggest submarine the world has ever seen, with a Post Captain in command. Rickover told me that the Navy Department, with typical lack of imagination, had christened this monarch of the deep by the ridiculous name of *Halibut*, but he arrived in time to discover this and managed to get the name painted out, and the fine name *Triton* substituted, before she was launched.

Next we went to see the mock-up shops, where every class of nuclear submarine has had its reactor machinery compartments built to full scale, but in wood. I saw some five different classes, from the biggest to the smallest, but what fascinated me most was going over the *Skipjack* mock-up.

Rickover and his staff had spent months in re-siting every component, pump, valve and pipe, until they had a really clean run with easy access to every part. The cost of the mock-up itself is fabulous but must pay for itself over and over again. After the wooden mock-up they then build a full scale model with the proper materials at even more fabulous cost, but the result when they put to sea is perfection first time.

Rickover certainly is an absolute genius, and honest people in the know admit that the USN would not even now have nuclear propulsion but for his own valiant efforts.

Rickover, who is habitually rude and quarrelsome with everybody, was in an amazing mood, cooing like a turtle dove.

As we left by air he took me aside, pressed my hand hard, put his left hand round me and said, 'I can never thank you enough for today's visit. You have shown all my team that there is an Admiral who really does understand nuclear propulsion, can ask intelligent and stimulating questions and is capable of inspiring us on. Couldn't we fuse the USN and the RN into one Service with you as the International Chief?'

I thanked him and gently pointed out how impracticable this suggestion was, but told him I would always be glad of his candid advice and help for British Naval nuclear propulsion.

> *Mountbatten returned to Britain in the* Queen Elizabeth, *sailing on 22 October.*

I asked those passengers whom I knew on board (about a dozen) to help me finish the US Navy magnums of champagne in my cabin.

Among them was Trevor Howard, whom I knew slightly. He told me that he had been engaged by Darryl Zanuck* to act in his new film, *The Roots of Heaven*, of which an essential ingredient was a herd of wild elephants. They had not, however, felt it worthwhile sending out a reconnaissance party, and so the entire cast, camera units, etc., had to go to four different countries in Central Africa before they came across the requisite number of elephants!

---

* President of Darryl F. Zanuck Productions for Twentieth Century-Fox release.

1959

In August 1959 the Mountbattens visited Canada,
in particular for the Canadian National Exhibition.
Mountbatten had by this time ceased to be First Sea
Lord and had become Chief of the Defence Staff.

MONDAY, 24 AUGUST. ST LAWRENCE SEA-WAY We drove down
to the St Lawrence sea-way where HMS *Scarborough* was secured
alongside.

Edwina and I went on board and I must say I felt quite a thrill to see
my Admiral of the Fleet's flag broken out at the main and the Trinity
House flag at the fore.

TUESDAY, 25 AUGUST We went through the two American locks,
Snell and Eisenhower, this morning. They are incomparably better laid
out and organized than the Canadian locks and everybody could not
help remarking on it. The Canadians really will have to do something to
their locks if they want to keep the traffic flowing.

SATURDAY, 29 AUGUST. TORONTO At 1015 Edwina and I drove
to the Stadium of the Canadian National Exhibition. The Grandstand
was full to overflowing with over 20,000 people in it to watch the
famous Warriors' Day Parade.

The Parade was led by the band of the Royal Marines and 1000
sailors from the NATO Fleet, who marched past in 19 companies,
one from each ship. They were followed by the various Ex-Service
Organizations. There were only about a dozen left who had fought in
the South African War, but they put up a brave show as they hobbled
past.

Quite a number of men who had lost an arm or an eye were in the
Parade, including one who was totally blind, led by means of a stick.

Between 30 and 40 different bands took part and as the last band could always be heard by the approaching procession at the same time as their own band, this caused great confusion. The really smart bands were the Militia bands, the Canadian Grenadier Guards and the Rifle Brigade – all in uniforms scarcely distinguishable from their British opposite numbers.

But there were a lot of ludicrous bands dressed in the most extraordinary costumes. A favourite form of band here consists of drums and trumpets and German glockenspiels.

After the Parade had passed, a band of about 100 massed pipes and drums marched the colours and standards in for The Last Post and Reveille ceremonies.

I had written to Aunt Olga* to ask if I could come and call and had assumed that everybody would know where she lived in Cooksville. In fact no one knew her address and we had a desperate time trying to find out where she lived, as of course she does not use the title 'Grand Duchess'. We eventually found the address and arrived as arranged at 1515. She, her elder son and his fiancée were there. They could not have been sweeter.

What courage for the daughter and sister of the richest men in the world, Alexander III and Nicholas II respectively, to live in a tiny bungalow so small that her daughter-in-law has to sleep on a sofa in the minute sitting room.

They have, of course, no servants and live in the simplest possible way, but she enjoys life painting rather beautiful pictures.

By 31 August Mountbatten was in Washington.

Admiral Rickover came to see me. The account of his visit with Vice-President Nixon to Russia was fascinating, not only on the Atomic Propulsion side, but particularly on Soviet education and standard of living. His conclusions were that the people were happy and contented and would never revolt; a point which has been obvious to the British all along but apparently is news to the Americans.

He also considered that unless the Americans change their educational system the Soviets will have them licked in the next ten years in this field alone.

---

* The Grand Duchess Olga, sister of the Tsar Nicholas II who married Mountbatten's Aunt Alix of Hesse.

He had his usual bellyache about the way the British were behaving in connection with Atomic help over the *Dreadnought*, etc., but I told him this no longer had anything to do with me and turned him on to our Naval Chief of Staff.

Mountbatten was back in the United States by 5 October 1959, visiting the Strategic Air Command at Omaha, Nebraska.

We were shown the fantastic organization by which a very high proportion of the nuclear bombers are at less than fifteen minutes' readiness, and some are even constantly in the air.

General Power* can never be more than ten seconds away from a telephone without turning over to one of his Deputies to be available in his place ready to give the order 'go'.

The Strategic Air Command can be sent off instantly under positive control, which means that if within about one and a half hours they do not obtain a further message to go ahead and drop their bombs, they have to come back. This is known as the 'fail safe' procedure, since if a message fails to get through the situation remains safe as they come back.

Next day he was at the Vandenberg Air Force Base in California.

The Air Force Base here is the first operational inter-continental ballistic missile base to be activated. It stretches along 24 miles of the Pacific Coast with a depth of up to 7 or 8 miles.

There are three types of missiles deployed here. The intermediate ballistic missile THOR, of which we have a large number now in England, and the inter-continental ballistic missiles ATLAS and TITAN.

We spent the morning mainly with THORs. This beast is 65 feet long and 8 feet in diameter, and I was amused to see the RAF roundels painted on the one that was due to be fired, since it belonged to the RAF and was entirely operated by an RAF crew who had received their instruction from the Americans.

---

* Commander-in-Chief of Strategic Air Command.

The trouble is that they cannot fire the THOR missiles in England, so the RAF crews have to come to Vandenberg to be trained and to carry out actual firings.

Having inspected the missile in a horizontal position, under cover of quite a big hangar, we went to the Command Position for the actual firing. Anybody who has seen a space travel film can very easily visualize the scene during the 'count down'. Television cameras showed the hangar being withdrawn, the missile coming to the vertical, and one could even see the liquid oxygen blowing off as the tanks were filled.

When there was only 30 seconds left to go we all went outside and watched. No film of a firing gives an adequate idea of this awe-inspiring event. The missile rises surprisingly slowly into the air and the flames are so bright as to be almost blinding. The roar of the rocket motor far exceeds anything produced by a jet engine, and can only be likened to an unbroken rumbling of thunder.

As the rocket gathered speed and flashed into the layer at which contrails develop, these appeared suddenly with a white burst at 32,000 feet, but a few seconds later the missile had passed above the level at which contrails stop. Seven minutes later it was reported that the THOR had reached a height of 350 miles, and 17 minutes after firing it landed in the Pacific Ocean, 1500 miles away. The exact accuracy will be measured and reported later on, but the flight seemed to go very well and I went and congratulated the RAF crew and was photographed with them.

After lunch we went first to inspect the ATLAS Squadron. This is a fully operational squadron with a range of about 6000 miles, and is set to fire over the North Pole at certain rather obvious targets in Russia. It will normally be at 15 minutes' notice, though a check routine was being carried out today.

I must confess I had no idea that the Americans already had the operational capability of hitting Russia with nuclear ICBMs.

We then went on and saw further ATLAS sites being developed, which will in future be horizontal and then raised to the vertical like the THOR, whereas the first three are permanently vertical under big movable gantries. These gantries are made specially big to allow for the bigger space rockets which are being developed out of ATLAS. What these will look like I cannot imagine, for the present ATLAS weighs 120 tons and looks as big as the Nelson Column.

We next went on to see the TITAN sites being prepared. They are excavating nine with underground headquarters and associated testing rooms, etc. The cost of this TITAN Squadron when installed will be over 120 million dollars, but this is only a drop in the ocean compared to the cost of the US Air Force Ballistic Missile programme, for which four and a half billion dollars have been appropriated. This does not include the enormous appropriations for the US Army missile JUPITER, or the US Navy missile POLARIS, but it does include the new solid fuel US Air Force missile MINUTEMAN.

Nothing I had been told prepared me for the staggering shock of seeing a TITAN hole. This is 40 feet in diameter and 165 feet deep, big enough to house a 20-storey skyscraper.

The various sites are all inter-connected by tunnels. To get from the open air past the underground headquarters to the first TITAN hole I counted 397 steps in the tunnel, which must therefore be about 1000 feet long.

The TITAN comes up on a gigantic lift after the heavy doors at the top of the hole have been opened. The whole complex has been designed to stand up to a pressure of 100 lbs per square inch, and they say that nothing but an absolute direct hit from a nuclear weapon can knock it out.

The whole thing has a gruesome and horrific effect, which makes one really fear for the sanity of mankind.

WEDNESDAY, 7 OCTOBER. VANDENBERG   At 1000 we flew on by helicopter to NORAD* Headquarters.

Air Marshal Slemon† gave a first-class presentation without notes, and then, without warning, invited me to comment on their set-up and offer any criticism I liked.

He cannot have known me very well for I need hardly admit that I took advantage of the invitation and pointed out that once the Russians had gone over to using Inter-Continental Ballistic Missiles instead of manned bombers, I thought the whole fabulously expensive set-up would prove a waste of time and money. I gave my reasons in some detail. Slemon was kind enough to say afterwards that, though my remarks had caused a great stir, they were in line with some of their own thinking.

---

* North American Air Defense (an integrated United States–Canada Command).
† Charles Slemon was a Canadian Air Marshal, currently Deputy C.-in-C. of the North American Air Defense Command.

We then went over to Combat Operations Centre where a magnificent presentation was laid on. At my suggestion they got through to SHAPE in one minute, and through to Alaska to their northernmost radar station of the distant early warning line in 30 seconds.

I was staggered to hear they keep track of over 200,000 daily air movements in the North American continent. Each time an aircraft takes off and lands again is counted as one movement. If they have more than about six that they cannot account for at any one time, they get worried. They have a staggering number of fighters and missiles at five minutes' notice, round the clock, 365 days a year.

The constant and fantastic degree of readiness to deal with Soviet aggression is a cardinal feature of SAC, NORAD and indeed most of the forces in North America. This is a very sobering thought.

THURSDAY, 8 OCTOBER. WASHINGTON   We arrived at the White House at 1930 for dinner. Besides the President and Mrs Eisenhower, the only other people were Al and Grace Gruenther* making six in all. The President had just flown back from California and had brought back some specially succulent steaks which he insisted on cooking himself for dinner and which were indeed very delicious.

The President was in absolutely wonderful spirits the whole evening. After dinner there was a film, *It Started With A Kiss*. The President gave us all the choice of whether we went to the film or stayed and gossiped. The ladies went to the film and the men stayed and gossiped.

This was election day in the UK and every half hour the President was on the telephone getting the latest news. He was considerably more excited than I was as the results came in, and could not conceal his pleasure when Gaitskell conceded the election. He said that though he would personally have no difficulty in working with Gaitskell, he could not see Herter working happily with Bevan.† But what pleased him most was being able to work once more with his old friend Harold Macmillan, and that he thought that his re-election would be a notable contribution to summit negotiations and world peace.

---

* General Gruenther had been Supreme Commander of Allied Forces in Europe from 1953 to 1956.
† Christian Herter, Eisenhower's new Secretary of State, might indeed have found it difficult to work with Aneurin Bevan, though it was by no means certain that Gaitskell would have appointed Bevan Foreign Secretary.

Ike, Al and I gossiped over old times and I heard an account of the President's visit to Europe and of Khrushchev's visit to the US.

The President told us that he considered Khrushchev the brightest man he had ever met, with the greatest detailed knowledge of any subject, and that the displays of temper were all carefully calculated to produce effect.

The President was proud of his achievement in getting 'the ultimatum' lifted over Berlin, but could not get Mr Khrushchev to agree to put it in the Communiqué. He promised, however, that if Ike made the statement unilaterally on Mr K's departure he would confirm it after his first meeting in Moscow. Ike's advisers were doubtful whether they could trust Mr K to do this, but the President was sure that he must, and indeed could, be trusted.

We were together for more than four hours and discussed a number of fascinating subjects, including India. I have never seen him so bright and alert for a long time.

On 12 October Mountbatten visited the Hunter Air Force Base at Savannah.

I was taken to all the activities in the base and was fully briefed on all that they do. Sixty operational B47 bombers and forty-three KC 97 refuellers are always ready within twenty-four hours. Of these, fifteen bombers and a corresponding number of refuellers are at instant readiness throughout the year. Of these six do a week in Europe at a time and nine are on specially prepared hard standings with their crews permanently on the alert.

We visited them and then the alert klaxons were sounded, the nine crews dashed out at a terrific speed and jumped into nine motor-cars with flashing red police lights and sirens. We joined up at the end of the mad procession screaming through the Air Force Base to the aircraft, which were immediately started up and taxied off ready for take-off.

We were then shown the new buildings actually at the end of the runway in which the alert crews will live. This will cut four minutes off the time taken to get into the air since they will never be more than fifty yards from their aircraft.

We were shown their missions, their fantastically detailed briefs on how to get to their target and what to do.

Perhaps the most terrifying aspect is that when these aircraft take off they actually carry one or two H Bombs apiece. The conviction that the whole of Strategic Air Command have that at a moment's notice they could blot out Russia, is really quite frightening, whereas the Americans, of course, only feel safe because of it.

1960

*On 21 February 1960 Edwina Mountbatten died
while visiting Jesselton in North Borneo. Her health
had been poor for some time but no one had antici-
pated her sudden death. A month later her husband
took a trip to the Middle East. On Thursday, 24th
he was in Libya.*

At 1020 I drove with the Oriental Secretary of our Embassy to Tobruk,
where King Idris was in residence. Knowing it was Ramadan and that
the King did not receive guests while fasting, I had light-heartedly
offered to call on him. The reply was that His Majesty never received
guests during Ramadan, but would be delighted to see me. He was very
friendly and paid touching tributes to Edwina. He told me that he kept
the photograph of her and me, which we had given him after our last
visit, always on his writing desk, and that he would never forget
her.

*On 26 March Mountbatten continued to Teheran
for a meeting of the Military Committee of the
Central Treaty Organization (CENTO).*

Our Ambassador, Sir Geoffrey Harrison, collected me and drove me to
the Embassy along the magnificent wide and straight avenues through
this vast city of two million inhabitants.

The Embassy was built by the Indian Army about ninety years ago
and stands in its own large compound. The ground was bought for
£8000 and is now worth £1,000,000! We had a very small dinner with
Sir Geoffrey and Lady Harrison and after dinner worked on the latest
Foreign Office briefs for the CENTO meeting.

I could not help feeling pretty depressed tonight because this was the
night when Edwina was to rejoin me from Delhi.

MONDAY, 28 MARCH. TEHERAN   We drove to the marble palace to sign our names in the Shah's book. This palace was built about thirty years ago entirely out of the rather beautiful translucent yellowy green marble.

We were taken round the rooms, which were quite fantastic and out-do any Indian Maharaja's palace. The audience room is made of thousands upon thousands of pieces of cut mirror set in different patterns at different angles. These catch the sunlight in such a way as almost to blind one, and you almost feel as though you were inside a huge diamond.

The study which the Shah uses is made entirely of Persian miniature mosaic, walls, doors, ceiling, desk and chair.

The present Shah understandably does not live there but has built himself a nice new modern palace across the road.

We then all drove off in procession to the large and magnificent Officers' Club, which is being used for the meetings of CENTO.

We had a difficult morning for the first item was a highly controversial one, but the Chairman, Tommy White, Chief of Staff to the US Air Force, handled matters very well, and I gave him all the support I could, both at the meeting and behind the scenes.

I had a quiet luncheon with the Ambassador and Lady Harrison, and we returned to further meetings in the afternoon.

TUESDAY, 29 MARCH   The CENTO Military Committee continued their labours from 0930 to 1200.

I had another quiet luncheon with the Ambassador and Lady Harrison and walked in the garden in the afternoon and worked.

At 1600 I went with most of the staff to the Golestan Palace Royal Museum. This is known as the Rose Garden Palace and was built a century ago. This is without question the most vulgar, ostentatious display of bad taste I have ever seen and is worse than the most ornate Maharaja's palace. And yet it has the most priceless and beautiful old carpets.

It has the famous Peacock Throne itself, of solid gold with 4000 precious stones including some big emeralds set in it. It was looted from the Moghuls in Delhi.

The Indian Ambassador, Kaul, came to have tea with me. I was warned he was a snake in the grass, and after I had seen him he apparently went round to the Foreign Minister and told him that I had expressed concern over the political and economic state of Iran. The Foreign Minister mentioned this to our Ambassador, and I am sending him a message to say that I have no knowledge of the political and economic state of Iran beyond that which Mr Kaul volunteered to me, so that I could hardly express concern. I shall report this piece of mischief-making to the Prime Minister of India.

WEDNESDAY, 30 MARCH This was a very exciting and interesting day, for the Shah had invited me to visit him at his palace near the Caspian Sea.

I spent from 1100 to 1230 with the Shah. He walked me round the really exotically beautiful gardens and park and then we sat and gossiped. He paid the most charming and fulsome tribute to Edwina and said how much he had been looking forward to her visit and how Persia mourned her with the rest of the world.

Presently, his third wife, the young Queen Farah Diba, appeared accompanied by the smallest miniature poodle I have ever seen, called Hercules. The Shah introduced his wife by saying, 'You know she was a basket ball champion?'

At 1225 the Shah said, 'Would you and your staff like to stay for lunch, I have a luncheon arranged for you here; or would you prefer to go back in the train? I have also arranged a luncheon for you in the train.' I said I would sooner go by train if he did not mind, and he quite agreed.

TUESDAY, 20 SEPTEMBER. LONDON This is the day of departure for the African tour. The tour was originally planned with Edwina for us to do together at the end of March, but the Prime Minister asked me to postpone it on account of his own visit.*

The general lay-out of the tour was one which included much sight-seeing of the places Edwina recommended, and so I asked Patricia if she would accompany me in place of Edwina. John very generously said he would let her go, and after obtaining Ministerial approval and the concurrence of the Governors, it has been arranged that she will come on this tour with me.

---

* The visit that culminated in the celebrated 'Winds of Change' speech in South Africa.

1960

On Sunday, 25 September 1960 they were in Kenya.

No description we had heard about Royal Lodge, Sagana, prepared us for the fantastic fairyland beauty of the setting, high over a beautiful trout river on the edge of the forest.

Since Lilibet, Philip and Pammy stayed here eight and a half years ago, two important additions have been made. A wing has been built known as the Nursery Wing consisting of three bedrooms, a bathroom and a sitting room, which adjoins Philip's dressing room. Fifty or sixty yards beyond the housekeeper's little bungalow, a new bungalow has been put up consisting of three rooms, each with its own bathroom, and none of them connecting to each other, for the lady-in-waiting, the private secretary and the equerry. Our party of course fills every bedroom to capacity.

TUESDAY, 27 SEPTEMBER. SAGANA At 1215 we drove to the Outspan Hotel at Nyeri, which is only half an hour's drive away. Here we were greeted by Mr Sherbrooke Walker, the owner of the hotel and the creator of the famous 'Treetops'. He has invited our entire party to be his guests.

Sherbrooke Walker enquired after Pammy and gave us a vivid account of the night she spent with Lilibet and Philip at Treetops, and pointed out that Lilibet actually acceded to the Throne while on the top of a huge Mgumu tree.*

The Mau-Mau afterwards burned this tree down but fresh branches and leaves are beginning to sprout from the old stump, so they have not killed it.

The new Treetops is a much more elaborate affair than the old one, and is built on the opposite side of the water-hole to enable visitors to get the favourable sunset light for taking photographs of the animals.

Mr Sherbrooke Walker, the Game Warden, and indeed all the experts, agreed that this was the worst time of year to see animals from Treetops because it is the driest, and this year was the worst year because there had been an uninterrupted drought for four months. No elephant had been seen for eight days, and generally the show of animals had been poor.

With these depressing forecasts for the night, we sat down for dinner. Half way through we were informed that elephants had arrived. We

---

* After the death of King George VI on 6 February 1952.

tiptoed out, making no sound, and found a dozen elephants licking the salt right under us. Hardly had we got over our first intense excitement than one of the elephants made a very soft trumpeting sort of noise, and we looked round and saw another small herd approaching through the trees. Every ten minutes or so another small group of elephants came in until we had counted a total of sixty, all cows, and including over a dozen calves, some of them barely two or three weeks old and busily suckling their mothers.

Although the approaching elephants trod so softly that we had no warning before they suddenly appeared through the little clump of trees on which Treetops is built, once they had joined up with the main herd there were gruntings and blowings and gurglings. Several elephants shook trunks with each other and they generally monopolized the salt-lick and the water-hole to the exclusion of all other game. They went off in turns to drink from the only secure part of the bank.

It was only after well over an hour that our hosts could persuade us to come back and finish our dinner, and then we sat out watching the elephants until midnight when the last of them moved on.

The floodlighting of the salt-lick, and indeed practically the whole water-hole, is magnificent and much better than from the old Treetops. I have not been called so often while turned in at night since I was in command of a ship. Indeed the whole atmosphere was rather like the operations room of a ship, with people brewing hot drinks and writing up their notes.

THURSDAY, 29 SEPTEMBER   At noon we all set off in cars for Nanyuki. At the point where one crosses the Equator, returning from the southern hemisphere into the northern hemisphere, there is a large signpost where we stopped and I took photographs of the party under it.

A hundred yards further on we were stopped by the owner of an hotel built on the Equator, Commander Logan Hook, who was Captain of P.39 when I was First Lieutenant of P.31 in 1918. He is a crank and a bore and I am afraid that when he ended a long monologue by saying, 'Do you know I have actually seen Queen Victoria?' I asked him whether he had knocked her spectacles off her nose as I had.

We then went on to the Mount Kenya Safari Club at Mawingo, which is organized by eccentric American and Swiss millionaires on the most fantastically luxurious lines. We inspected the exotic swimming pool which has a bar below it where you can sit and watch through a large glass window the beautiful girls swimming underwater. They have even built an African village in which they house members of the Meru tribe who perform war dances for the American guests. They put on a very good show for us.

FRIDAY, 30 SEPTEMBER   At ten o'clock Patricia and I rode to one of the African villages where four hundred children were called out of school to be introduced to us on our horses and listen to a speech by the District Commissioner.

The speech in reply by the headmaster said how happy the children were to be given this opportunity by the British to educate themselves. I had thought of asking for them to be given a half holiday, but the District Commissioner explained that the usual form of punishment in an African school is to deprive a child of one day's attendance at school. I then suggested we might give them an extra half day's work on Sunday as a gesture, but he did not think that would be popular with the master!

On 7 October the party arrived at the Victoria Falls.

The Game Warden came to meet us at 1130 and we all drove off to see the Falls from every conceivable vantage point. Owing to the time of year and the exceptional drought, only about one twentieth of the vast volume of water which had been flowing in June was going over the Falls. The great advantage, however, is that when the full seventy-five million gallons a minute are cascading over the precipice, which extends more than a mile in length, and drops over three hundred feet, the resulting mist is so dense that it is extremely difficult to see the Falls effectively. The natives call this place in their language 'The Mist that Thunders', which is a perfect description.

The Warden was fascinating in describing how over the ages the Falls have receded from one gorge to another, and he pointed out the line to which the Falls will have moved in another 1000 years.

I have cruised on the Niger and the Gambia in Africa, but the Zambesi has them both beat. The river is an average of one mile wide, and we passed a place at which it was two and a half miles wide.

10 *October saw them in Nyasaland (now Malawi).*

Patricia and I had only hazy notions about Nyasaland and we could not have been more surprised to find that Zomba was the most beautifully situated city we have seen on our tour, and Government House one of the most attractive, and certainly standing in the most lovely garden and park we have yet seen.

We changed into comfortable plain clothes and had a cosy family luncheon. At 1350 we left to catch the '2 p.m. clock' for the Plateau. The road leading up Zomba mountain is so narrow and twisting that there are notice boards with clocks at each end. One may only pass the post on the way up between the hour and quarter past, and one may only pass the notice board on the way down between the half hour and quarter to.

We came down on the '3.30 p.m. clock'. On return to Government House I changed into Khaki uniform and drove to Cobbe Barracks where a 'tea party' of a couple of hundred European and African ex-Service-men and their wives were assembled, including to my aston-ishment a delegation of the four senior officials of the South African Legion.

They had flown over specially from Johannesburg (more than 1000 miles away) 'to meet the Grand President'. In the course of the speeches we all had to make, the South African deputy president (the president was sick) said they had come to ask me specially to convey a message of loyalty and affection to their beloved Sovereign, the Queen. This statement was received with thunderous applause, coming as it did only three days after South Africa had voted to become a Republic.

Almost equally surprising is that I have received a formal invitation from the South African Government inviting me to come on and visit them officially, but as I am required back for the meeting at Chequers on the 16th, I have of course had to refuse.

I did the usual business of talking individually to as many people as possible, and got off one or two phrases in both Chinyanja and Swahili which went down very well. Once more I was astonished at the high proportion who had served with me in the war.

One of the Chiefs sent me a special gift of a duck. I understand he also sent a duck to Elizabeth the Queen Mother when she was here.

WEDNESDAY, 12 OCTOBER. ENTEBBE   At 1500 we landed at Entebbe airport where there was the usual big reception committee headed by the Governor of Uganda, Sir Frederick Crawford. The Governor drove me to Government House, and I must now revise the remarks I made about Zomba. Government House itself and the grounds at Entebbe are more beautiful and delightful than any we have come across on this tour.

We immediately went into conference with the Governor and his officials to discuss internal security problems if the Kabaka of Buganda carries out his threat to secede.* We also discussed the problem of trouble on the Congo, which is only thirty miles from here.

I received a plaintive letter from the Kabaka saying how anxious he was to return hospitality to me for his visit to Broadlands, and how hurt he had been that the Governor did not include a visit to him at his capital, Kampala, during my stay in Uganda. In fact, Crawford told me that he had personally asked the Kabaka to come to dinner to meet us on Thursday night, but that His Highness had got hurt feelings and refused to come. This is lucky for me, as I certainly do not want to get involved in the political dispute now going on.

The Kingdom of Buganda forms by far the largest part of Uganda, and Entebbe, the seat of our Government, is actually in Buganda. However, I am sure that if anybody could manage the situation Crawford will, as he is so outstandingly good.

Patricia and I feel so sorry for him entertaining us in this huge house so shortly after his beloved wife has died. It must be terrible coping with an official residence and official entertaining without a wife.

FRIDAY, 14 OCTOBER   Patricia and I had breakfast on my verandah in such dramatically beautiful surroundings and in such lovely clear and warm weather that we both felt very sad that this was the last day of our tour.

Funnily enough, we rather felt after Royal Lodge that the rest of the tour would be so hurried and with such a heavy programme that it would all be a terrible anti-climax. In fact the reverse has been the case. Each place we have gone to has been more exciting, or more lovely or more pleasant, or all these things combined, and we agreed that Uganda had been the high spot.

It has been a wonderfully interesting and thrilling trip, which would

---

* Buganda formally declared its independence two months later, but the secession movement eventually came to nothing.

have been very lonely without Edwina, but which the presence of Patricia transformed entirely for me. Not only was she wonderful company and very gay, and obviously enjoying it to the full, but she did a wonderful job at all the official entertainments and functions, besides carrying out her own programme.

1961

*In February 1961 Mountbatten set off on a tour that
was to take him around the world and cover about
35,000 miles. He left London Airport on 8 February
and two days later arrived at the Royal Air Force
station on Gan Island in the Addu Atoll.*

I was still reading my brief on Gan as we landed, and had just read the
Foreign Office view that a request for the US Air Force to land at Gan
should be refused, when I looked up as we taxied in and saw a big
aeroplane with US Navy painted on it. I discovered later that the US
Navy had been operating from here for months in connection with the
Geophysical Year, but luckily the Foreign Office doesn't know it.

Mr Afif Didi, who is the Headman of Addu Atoll, greeted me on the
runway. He is an extremely high-class man and said some charming
things about Edwina. He produces a local paper called *The Times of
Addu*. He also presented me with a local Maldivian knife with a black
coral handle.

Our High Commissioner in Colombo sent a telegram last night to the
Air Vice-Marshal saying he did not want me to see Afif. This was
nonsense as I never had any intention of talking politics with him and I
took no notice of it.

*On Sunday, 12 February Mountbatten arrived in
Singapore.*

My host is the Commissioner General for South-East Asia, the Earl of
Selkirk. He had been away in the Cameron Highlands and only got back
just before me.

MONDAY, 13 FEBRUARY. SINGAPORE Audrey Selkirk drew my
attention to an enormous tent the size of a marquee in which some thirty

Ghurka soldiers were accommodated. She said they had been specially brought in on my account as normally they only had one sentry on at a time. I apologized and said I knew nothing about it.

WEDNESDAY, 15 FEBRUARY   I had breakfast with Audrey Selkirk. She told me that Edwina had slept in the same room as me right up to the moment of her departure for Borneo. Although everybody had thought her programme quite impossible, she appeared on the top of her form, fresh and gay, and looking at least twenty years younger than her age. Her visit had been the most overwhelming success and she was sure that Edwina went away very happy.

At 0900 Dick Hull* came and fetched me, and drove me to Changi RAF Station. We arrived at Don Muang Airport, Bangkok, at 1200 local time.

There was the usual large reception committee headed by our Ambassador, Sir Richard Whittington, and the Chiefs of the Armed Forces. There was a particularly smart Guard of Honour, with band and colours, of the Royal Thai Air Force, and as we had been warned it was an official arrival I wore white uniform and my 'Supreme Commander of the White Elephant'.

A Rolls-Royce driven by one of the Royal chauffeurs, in what appeared to be the full dress uniform of a Siamese Admiral, was placed at my disposal. The Private Secretary drove me in this to Pitsanuloke Palace, which is one of the main guest houses used by the King for his guests.

My own suite is enormous, the dressing room alone being the size of the Wedgwood room at Broadlands.† There are fourteen full-length stained glass windows in my bedroom without curtains or shutters, as I found to my cost in the morning, and a TV set on which we got American films dubbed in Thai.

I went on a round of signing visitor's books. In the King's Palace they seem to keep a separate visitor's book for VIPs because the only other signatures I could see were those of Leopold and Liliane of Belgium.

After this I insisted on trying to find the Palace at which I lived on each of my visits after the war. Nobody seemed to know which it was, but I was able to remember my way through the streets and landed up at

---

* General (later Field Marshal) Sir Richard Hull, Commander-in-Chief of Land Forces.
† Mountbatten's country house near Romsey in Hampshire.

what I thought was the right place. However, Ronnie Brockman, who lived with me in this Palace, seemed uncertain, until the old caretaker came out and practically fell on my neck as he recalled my visits and even pointed out the room I lived in. In fact Patricia and I lived at the Udorn Building of the Amphorn Palace, the rest of the staff living in the main Palace.

I insisted on going to see the white elephant, who was extremely friendly. I tried to take a film but I am afraid it was rather dark in the elephant house.

Shortly before 2000 I drove to the Chitlada Palace where the King now lives. On entering the park I noticed we drove along a fairly narrow footpath which the Rolls-Royce could barely pass along. I enquired if all the guests used this path and was told, 'No, only the King.'

We drove past the Palace, and on to a very dashing modern building a couple of hundred yards away known as the Pagabiron, which I believe means 'recreation centre'.

To my astonishment there were over a hundred guests already assembled, but I was led straight through them to where the King and Queen were sitting by the most luxurious, enormous, illuminated swimming pool I have seen for a long time.

After a friendly talk, they introduced the guests at their own table one by one and they then joined in the circle for drinks. At dinner I sat on the right of King Bhumibol and opposite Queen Sirikit.

The King explained to me that the large hall next to the colossal swimming pool was the gymnasium and badminton court for his school. As a result of questioning it came out bit by bit that he felt it necessary for his children to go to a school, but of course they could not go to one of the schools in Bangkok, so he had built his own school near the Palace, which contained four large classrooms, one for each of his children, with some fifteen to twenty children in each class.

At the end of dinner about fifteen of the male guests got up and moved on to the stage, which was rigged with music stands and instruments. They immediately started playing jazz. His Majesty explained that these were all his personal friends who had learned to play in the band with him, and that they rehearsed twice a week and came to play for big parties on the fairly rare occasions when he gave them.

The King has also organized a party of high-grade crooners, and I could hardly believe my eyes when I recognized Seni Pramoj, who was the Prime Minister when I was here in 1946, among them.

I sat between the King and Queen at a table on a square of red carpet.

The King announced that he had arranged special old Thai dances for me, and sixteen of the most lovely girls I have ever seen then came on in traditional costume and did a beautiful dance in the tradition of North Siam.

The Queen explained that they were all either cousins, ladies-in-waiting, or daughters of high Court officials, as they preferred to have amateur musicians and dancers rather than professionals at their more intimate parties.

The exhibition dancing finished soon after 2200 and then the King went up to lead his band, playing a saxophone, and left me alone with the ravishing Sirikit.

No one danced, and I wasn't sure what the form was, but presently one of the older Princes came up with his wife and introduced her and said, 'You will remember opening the Flower with her in 1946.' I smiled affably as I hardly knew what to say. Then the Prince in a loud whisper said, 'I am sure Her Majesty would like you to open the Flower with her.'

Evidently the Queen had overheard, for she smiled encouragingly, and still not knowing what was meant I said, 'Would you like to open the Flower with me?' She replied, 'I would love to', and got up and walked towards the floor, and it was only then I realized that I was expected to open the 'floor' with her.

The band was playing the most ghastly dead-slow English waltz. The floor was very sticky and no one else danced. The Queen said, 'Do you like waltzes?' and I replied, 'I would prefer a foxtrot.' So she walked over to the King and told him to play a foxtrot. She said 'Is this better?' I replied, 'Not much, it's still far too slow.' So she walked over to the King again, and this time the band played a Charleston so fast that with the sticky floor I could hardly keep up. She said anxiously, 'I hope this is all right now?' and I gently pointed out that we could never get really going until she had some French chalk or powder put on the floor.

A servant was sent for, who disappeared into the ladies' powder room and came back with two tins of Yardley's Lavender Powder which he proceeded to scatter on the floor in the traditional Thai manner, on his knees. This time it really was all right and we got on famously and she was obviously delighted with the result.

An awkward thing about the Court etiquette is that practically nobody asks the Queen to dance except rather boring elderly members of the Royal Family. However, it suited me as I was able to have no less than eight dances with her during the course of the evening, and we got

Savannah, Georgia, 12 October 1959. Lord and Lady Mountbatten arrive
at Hunter Air Force base for a visit to Strategic Air Command.

Salisbury, Rhodesia, 5 October 1960. A call on Sir Roy Welensky.

Mexico City, 28 February 1963. Riding with the *charras*.

on better and better, and she became more and more friendly and amusing.

About every other dance she would call up one of the young girls, who on approaching the Presence, fell on her knees at the edge of the red carpet and advanced the last three or four paces on her knees in full evening dress. The Queen would then say, 'Would you like to dance with Lady Ruda' (or whatever the name was) and I found myself in the astonishingly awkward position of trying to ask a ravishingly beautiful girl to dance while she was on her knees before me.

I noticed that her own cousin, not being Royalty himself, approached her on his knees for a dance, and after the dance remained talking to her on his knees.

The servants were allowed to walk as far as the edge of the carpet on their feet, but had to do the last stretch on the carpet on their knees. This had seemed in keeping with the ancient oriental splendour of the old Grand Palace in 1946, but it was incongruous to a degree in a 1960 Corbusier gymnasium.

I suspect my staff of trying to nurse me, for Audrey Selkirk at the Eden Hall dinner, and now both the King and Queen separately, said to me, 'I know what a very strenuous tour you are undertaking, and how tired you must be. Please choose your own time for going to bed as soon as you like.' To Queen Sirikit I said, 'Why, do I look tired?' to which she replied very candidly, 'Yes.' I then said that I would stay until 2300 and she agreed.

At midnight I said, 'Do I still look tired?' and she laughed back at me and said, 'No, you look wonderful now.' I stayed until after 0100 and never missed a dance.

I cannot remember when I have enjoyed an evening as much as this. Sirikit is the best company and the gayest companion I have met in years and she has pressed me to come back to Bangkok. The King invited me too, though needless to say he did not press me so hard.

Next day the party continued on its way and on 17 February:

We landed at Hong Kong at 2100. It was cold, overcast and drizzly this morning. We were taken to the Observation Post at Crest Hill from which day and night two men observe through binoculars everything the Chinese are doing just across the boundary. Through binoculars I could clearly see Chinese passengers having arrived by train, walking across the bridge over the Shum Chun river and waiting to embark in the British train which was just arriving.

In the days before the war it was possible to go by train from Hong Kong direct to Calais in seventeen days, but now only goods trains are allowed to go straight through, passenger trains stopping at the frontier.

On the East the frontier runs straight through the middle of a village street, rather like between West and East Berlin. This used to be the scene of many troubles, but for more than fifteen months now the Chinese have been extremely amenable.

A short while ago two young bandsmen thought they would like to see what Red China was like and broke out. After being extremely well treated by the Communist Chinese Army they were returned with gifts, including ten dollars of Hong Kong currency each. In fact, relations between Hong Kong and China have never been so good.

SUNDAY, 19 FEBRUARY. NORTH BORNEO We landed at Jesselton at 1520, and were met by the Acting Governor, Mr Turner, and his head people.

We drove up the very steep little hill on top of which the Chief Secretary's house is perched. I gather that it is about the oldest house left in the Colony and completely unmodernized.

Here I met Mrs Turner, and we sat on the lawn in front of the house, and I discovered for the first time that Edwina had not stayed at Government House with the Acting Governor, Turner, because, contrary to usual custom, he never moves into Government House when the Governor is away, and did not like the idea of letting Edwina stay there by herself.

Mrs Turner then asked me if I would like to see her room, and they both took me along through the sitting room to the staircase. We went up four or five steps to a landing, off which led a very small sort of ante-room, and then suddenly I was in Edwina's room. Mrs Turner said very softly, 'We will leave you now if we may.'

I had always visualized that Edwina's bedroom had been in Government House, and I had also thought that Government House had been newly re-built. I therefore imagined a fairly luxurious VIP guest room with a soft light-coloured pile carpet, high windows, full curtains, pelmets, modern painted furniture, built-in cupboards and two rather deep and soft beds.

It was a shock to find that the room was exceptionally simple. It had a bare wooden floor with a couple of small rugs, very simple wooden furniture and very plain beds. It was nice and clean and simple, but somehow the shock of actually being here and finding it all so different was very much more than I could bear, and I was grateful to the Turners for leaving me alone with my thoughts for quite a long while.

I was now also able to visualize the scene described by Irene Checkley,* when Edwina came down for the reception in the garden on the night of the 20th. Miss Checkley had said that she had had difficulty in coming downstairs and that she had had to support her very strongly to get her across the room at all, but that on arrival at the door to the verandah she had straightened herself up and said, 'I am all right now, you can leave me.'

So skilfully did Edwina and her young staff officer manage this whole manoeuvre that Mrs Turner told me she detected no difficulty in coming down the four or five steps, or in walking across the room, and had never before understood what Edwina meant by her remark at the door.

What struck me most about my conversations with all the people was that she had somehow cast a stronger spell over them than ever before, for they had one and all developed a feeling of admiration, one might almost say adoration, which was quite uncanny.

I think myself there was something very special about her in the last few weeks of her life, for I heard rather similar expressions in Singapore and Malaya.

MONDAY, 20 FEBRUARY. DARWIN I was forced to agree to an impromptu press conference, at which I was solemnly asked by the representative of the *Sydney Mirror* whether the statement published in his own paper that the real object of my visit to Australia was 'romantic' was true.

I told him that when I was nineteen years old I had fallen in love with a pretty girl in Sydney, and a pretty girl in Melbourne, and a pretty girl in Brisbane.† When I saw them in 1946 they were all three grandmothers. I expected that they would now be great-grandmothers. He had the grace to blush and apologize; but what a question to be asked on this day of all days!‡

* Edwina Mountbatten's staff officer from St John's.
† When on tour with the Prince of Wales.
‡ The anniversary of the night during which Edwina died.

Next day, 21 February, Mountbatten was in Canberra.

At 1630 I arrived at the Headquarters of the Returned Sailors, Soldiers and Airmen's Imperial League of Australia (commonly known as the RSL) where a special meeting of the National Executive had been called. Representatives had flown in from every State in Australia, including Tasmania and New Guinea. As usual the National President vacated the Chair for me and I took the meeting in my capacity as Grand President of the parent body, the BCEL.* I gave them half an hour's address and then we had a discussion.

Three years ago Australia was our most obstreperous member, but this meeting could not have gone better, and they all swore loyalty, allegiance and financial support. Afterwards I stayed until 1815 for drinks with the delegates.

On my way back I stopped at Capitol Hill to try and find the foundation stone which I watched the Prince of Wales lay 41 years ago. Nothing has been built on Capitol Hill and I had great difficulty in finding it in 1946, and even greater difficulty in 1956, but this time I failed to find it at all. I have now challenged Dallas Brooks† to find it so that I can go and see it again.

THURSDAY, 23 FEBRUARY. CANBERRA   The search for the Prince of Wales's foundation stone is causing considerable excitement. I received a fantastic note from the Prime Minister's Department saying that the Department of Works assured them that there is only one stone on Capitol Hill, and that was the one laid in 1913 to commemorate the naming of the site 'Canberra'. They accused me of confusing this stone with the Prince of Wales's stone. I rejected this.

The Department of Works have now traced the stone to Duntroon Military College nearby, where they say it has been taken to be cleaned! I made it very clear at my press conference that I should certainly expect to see the stone back at Canberra on my next visit.

---

* British Commonwealth Ex-Service League.
† General Sir Dallas Brooks, Governor of Victoria.

Mountbatten continued to New Zealand and on 27 February was in Wellington.

Dear old Walter Nash, who had been Prime Minister until the end of last year, said he wanted a private word with me, so after dinner I went with him to another room. He first of all told me that he thought that Edwina was the most wonderful woman of the century, with which of course I entirely agreed, but he then shook me by saying that after much careful thought he had come to the conclusion that I was a greater man than Winston Churchill. This shows that he is getting softening of the brain in his old age.

WEDNESDAY, I MARCH. WELLINGTON   At 0940 I saw the British officers and other ranks of the United Kingdom Services Liaison Staff and at 1000 I attended a full meeting of the Cabinet which, at my personal request to the Prime Minister, created quite a precedent, since the meeting included the four Chiefs of Staff.

I spoke until 1115 on Defence, without notes, and feel I rather dazed my audience as they seemed to have such very little background knowledge. The questions I was asked surprised me and were not up to the level I expected. I was particularly staggered to be asked by one Cabinet Minister whether I recommended that New Zealand should re-introduce conscription. I replied as tactfully as I could that it was not for me to give them political advice, but I could tell them that we had abandoned it in the UK, and not even the Chiefs of Staff were contemplating asking for its restoration.

At 1230 Steve Weir* gave a luncheon party for Ronnie Brockman and myself and the other Chiefs of Staff at the Wellington Club. I had been warned to look out for their two most prized possessions, nineteenth-century prints of two women in crinolines, stripped to the waist and fighting a duel with rapiers. This is the oldest club in New Zealand, and resembles the most Victorian of the London clubs. I was glad to see some of the pictures, on loan from Admiralty House, London, painted during Captain Cook's voyages to New Zealand.

We got to Government House, Auckland, with barely enough time to change for dinner at 1930. I had not seen this house since I spent a week here in 1920, but so far as I could tell it was quite unchanged.

* Major General Sir Stephen Weir, Mountbatten's approximate opposite number in New Zealand.

There was a large dinner party, among them my late Allied Air C.-in-C. in SEAC, Sir Keith Park. After dinner I had a good talk with the Governor-General, Lord Cobham, about the defence reorganization I had recommended for New Zealand, and was glad to find he was in complete agreement.

He had just been captaining his own cricket eleven against the MCC and was evidently the star performer. His great-grandfather founded the port of Lyttelton, and I was told on all hands he is the most popular Governor-General New Zealand has had.

THURSDAY, 2 MARCH. AUCKLAND   We landed at the big International Airport at Nandi (sometimes spelt Nadi) on the west coast of Viti Levu, the biggest isle of 350 in the Fiji group.

The old Government House was burnt down in 1922, and a very fine new one has been built. My own bedroom measured about 40 feet by 30 feet and is the biggest I think I have ever been in.

There was a dinner party of thirty. Opposite me was seated Lieutenant Colonel The Hon. Ratu Edward Cakobau, who has just been appointed a district commissioner. When the bandmaster came in for his glass of port, Ratu Edward leaned across and said to me, 'The bandmaster comes from the worst cannibal district in the island.'

I asked Ratu Edward if he were a great-grandson of King Thakimbau (though I believe the local spelling is Cakobau), and he replied, 'Yes.' I then asked him whether he knew that his great-grandfather had been to lunch with Queen Victoria in the late 1870s. He replied, 'Yes.' I then told him that the King had sat next to my mother, who, being a very cheeky young girl, had asked him if he regretted having given up cannibalism. She had always said that he had replied, that all he missed was babies' toes.

Ratu Edward was highly amused and said, 'I don't think that can be right, for I always heard my great-grandfather particularly liked ladies' fingers.'

Edward Cakobau was shown the menu on board the ship bringing him back to Fiji recently, and said to the head waiter, 'This menu looks horrible, bring me the passenger list.'

1961

On 6 March Mountbatten was in San Francisco where he attended a lunch of the Bohemian Club.

In the Chair was no less a person than one of the three great surviving national war heroes, Fleet Admiral Nimitz, who is regarded with the same sort of veneration as we regard Winston. He and his wife had visited us in Malta, so we were old friends.

Nimitz told me that 5 star officers in the United States not only remain on the active list for life, like we do, but draw full pay and allowances, whereas we only draw half pay. They are also provided with two serving officers, one as secretary, the other as aide, and an orderly to drive their official Cadillac.

In fact Eisenhower in his request to be reinstated as a 5 star general will be slightly better off, even if he has to give up his pension as a President.

Nimitz told me that when the great General Grant of the Civil War became President of the United States for two terms of office, he retired completely penniless, and asked to be reinstated to the Army List as a Lieutenant General, which Congress refused. He then asked to be made Governor of the Old Soldiers Home in Washington, which at least had a house and a small salary. This was also refused, so as he lay dying of cancer of the mouth he was forced to sell the story of his life for publication. What a shameful episode.

TUESDAY, 7 MARCH. SAN FRANCISCO We landed at Offutt Air Force Base near Omaha, Nebraska, after a three and a half hour flight.

Lieutenant General Griswold* met me and gave me a fascinating briefing explaining how the Joint Strategic Target Planning Staff works. The confused reports in the newspapers had only given me a vague idea and so this briefing was very valuable.

I then got up to go as it was time to take off, but Griswold remarked that he had had another presentation prepared for me on the future of space exploration and defence. This seemed such a fascinating subject that I delayed the take-off by half an hour.

This presentation was quite fabulous and showed the immense scope of space travel which lay within our scientific grasp during the next ten

---

* Deputy to the Commander-in-Chief of Strategic Air Command, General Power, who was away in the Pacific.

years. If there is general disarmament this will be a wonderful age, but if our ability to control space is solely to be used to increase our destructive capabilities then I see little chance of the world surviving.

THURSDAY, 6 APRIL. CLASSIEBAWN I had been spending the Easter holidays with Patricia and John, Norton and Michael-John,* at Classiebawn Castle.† We left on the afternoon of 6 April.

We have been to Classiebawn for holidays every year since the end of the war, but never at any time have the press intruded on our privacy. Last August, however, three photographers and two reporters from London dogged my footsteps for the best part of a week. This time one reporter and one photographer from the *Daily Express* came to the village, but as we had not got the boat out there was not much opportunity for them to catch us. The photographer, however, managed to conceal himself near the beach, and got a telephoto picture of Patricia and me riding.

So it was that we were on the lookout for the press when we left Classiebawn, and Ron Heath (our electrician/driver) had reported that he had seen a car standing at the one part of the road from which the castle is visible, for the whole morning.

When we drove out of the Lodge gates we soon noticed we were being followed by another Ford Zodiac, with two men in jerseys in it.

As we neared Sligo I stopped and waved them on, but they remained stopped behind us. I then drove rapidly on into Sligo, and managed to go up a side turning without being spotted by them. Their car shot on past the entrance, but when we had turned to go out again they had come back, and we met them face to face going opposite ways. However, we got caught in the traffic and they managed to catch us again.

After playing hide-and-seek for a quarter of an hour without success, we dropped Ron Heath off with various samples of things we wanted to order from one of the shops, and then drove on, with the car in pursuit. We managed to get down to the docks and lose them.

We then drove back to a place where there was a yard at the end of a long alleyway. Patricia, John and Norton went off to shop and Michael-John sat with me in the car.

---

* Lord and Lady Brabourne with their two elder sons Norton Knatchbull (now Lord Romsey) and Michael-John Knatchbull.
† Mountbatten's home in County Sligo, Ireland.

They completed their shopping without being spotted by the press, or having photographs taken, but when we left, by sheer bad luck we ran into them again.

John was driving now, and we set off at a good pace. Where the road forked outside Sligo we deliberately took the wrong turning. They hung on to our tail. As we could not shake them off we chose a place where only one car could turn at a time, they had to wait and turn, which enabled us to get a good start on them.

We slipped up a narrow lane, but unfortunately raised a bit of dust, and so the pursuing car eventually spotted us and drove up the lane until our two cars were face to face.

John leapt out, very angry, and asked them what newspaper they belonged to. It then turned out that they were our police escort, but, knowing that I did not like a police escort, they tried to keep their activities secret until we tried to shake them off. Then they felt duty-bound to try and keep on our tail.

They did not think it odd that we were trying to shake them off, because they had been informed that I disliked police escorts.

TUESDAY, II APRIL. WASHINGTON   At 0930 I called a meeting of my colleagues, who were to form the technological panel for SHAPEX.* At 1030, Lemnitzer† took me to call on the President.

What I had understood was going to be a five-minute courtesy call lasted fifty minutes, and was very fascinating. I formed the highest possible impression of Mr Kennedy, who seemed to be realistic and sound on everything we discussed.

After photographers had been and gone, he suddenly said to me, 'Do you remember the party you gave in your penthouse for Sally Norton?' When I replied, 'Yes', he said, 'Do you realize that I was one of your guests?' For the sake of Anglo/US amity I lied and said, 'Yes.'

I then said that I believed that Pammy had been at school with his wife, to which he replied, 'I expect so, I am afraid I married rather a baby.'

Next, Lemnitzer took me over to see Jerry Wiesner, the Scientific Adviser to the President. He talked more staggering common sense than

* An annual exercise conducted by SHAPE – the Supreme Headquarters, Allied Powers, Europe.
† General Lynan Lemnitzer, Chairman of the Joint Chiefs of Staff and soon to become SACEUR – Supreme Allied Commander, Europe.

I ever expected to hear from an American, let alone a man who has the President's ear. As we did not finish talking by the time I had to go and see the Ambassador, he drove with me in the car to continue our conversation.

On Thursday, 15 June Mountbatten paid a brief visit to Bonn.

General Foertsch, the Inspector General of the German Armed Forces, and his three colleagues, the Inspectors of the Navy, Army and Air Force, gave me an official luncheon. During this, without any warning whatever, he got up and made a flattering speech about me in German, to which I had no option but to stand up and reply, also in German.

As a matter of fact I was surprised how quickly my German came back to me. I am never one to lack moral courage in speaking a foreign language!

I arrived at the Ministry of Defence at 1500, where a Guard of Honour was drawn up. This was indistinguishable from a Royal Guard of Honour, consisting of 100 ranks of the German Air Force, the band of the Regiment doing guard duties, and I was received with 'God Save The Queen', and '*Deutschland Über Alles*'.

This does not mean, as we interpreted it during the first war, that Germany should be above every other country. It means 'My father-land comes before everything to me'!

After this the Ambassador joined me for my call on Herr Strauss, the German Minister of Defence, and Commander-in-Chief of the German Armed Forces. We had one and a half hours' fascinating conversation about the world situation generally, and the Berlin situation in particular. We found ourselves in absolute and complete agreement. In fact I thought him a very sensible man.*

---

* Mountbatten had a striking propensity for finding those who agreed with him sensible and intelligent. He was, however, aware of this weakness; there is an element of self-derision in his comment.

1962

In March 1962 Mountbatten visited the West Indies. On Tuesday, 6 March he was in Georgetown, capital of Guyana.

The Chief Fire Officer came to fetch me, and drove me to inspect the appalling fire damage in the very heart of the town, caused by deliberate arson on 16 February, during riots caused by the African supporters of Burnham demonstrating against the Government.* Dr Jagan is the Prime Minister and leader of the People's Progressive Party, which is mainly composed of the Indian community, which exceeds the combined strength of all the other communities.

The extraordinary situation has occurred that the Marxist exponent, Dr Jagan, has had to call in British troops (five Companies) and British ships (at one time five Frigates) to protect him from the fury of the decidedly non-Communist opposition.

Who set fire to the town may never be known, but as it undoubtedly enabled Dr Jagan to get the troops in, there are those who say his supporters did it.

We got back at 1800 to find the Prime Minister, Dr Jagan, whom I already knew, and his key Ministers, assembled for a meeting. This went on until 1920. We discussed the future of troop dispositions, Naval dispositions and internal security at very great length, and I did not hesitate to give them advice as to what I thought they should do.

They finally agreed to take my advice and the suggestions will now be processed through the Governor.

THURSDAY, 8 MARCH. TRINIDAD At 1010 I visited the grave of Digger. This was a truly delightful tame wallaby which was given to

---

* Forbes Burnham's party, the People's National Congress, had recently refused to join a coalition under Dr Jagan.

David (Prince of Wales) in Australia in the early summer of 1920. It became so tame that it would follow us round like a dog, and we used to take him ashore at each Government House for a run round the garden. In Trinidad he ate something that disagreed with him and died. Kenneth Previté, whom I met here and who was the young Marine in the *Renown*, told me he thought we had given Digger too many cocktails.

From 1020 to 1210 I had a meeting with the Senior Naval Officer West Indies, and the Commander of the Caribbean Area, who had come to Trinidad to meet me.

On two occasions during this meeting I broke off for quarter of an hour to meet representatives of the Royal Overseas League and later of the Royal Life Saving Society. My staff were able to carry on with the meeting very usefully during these absences.

At 1210 the Federal Defence Staff gave drinks to our party in the private secretary's bungalow.

At 1230 there was an informal luncheon in the Governor-General's house with no outside guests.

At 1325 I changed into uniform and at 1335 drove to the US Naval Base at Chaguaramas. I was received by an Honor Guard of American Marines and then Captain Luehman drove me round the Base, which is enormous. They are just giving back 1100 acres to the Trinidad Government, but are still holding on to over 10,000 acres. Its wartime capacity is 9000 men, but there are only a couple of hundred there now for maintenance purposes. They have constructed their own very beautiful golf course, and live in the usual luxury.

I called on Rear Admiral Reed, the Commander of the US South Atlantic Force.

At 1515 I called on SNOWI* on board his Frigate, HMS *Londonderry*. She was lying alongside one of the piers in the American base. I addressed the ship's company who were all stripped to the waist and looked very healthy and brown.

At 1545 we drove back to the Governor-General's house and I just had time to change back into plain clothes before the Premier of Trinidad and Tobago, Dr Eric Williams, came to call on me. We spoke urgent defence business for a whole hour. He was wearing a deaf aid, and spoke so low that Dick Ward† could not hear a word of what he was saying and I had to repeat everything to him for the record.

* Senior Naval Officer, West Indies.
† Colonel Ward was a member of Mountbatten's staff.

Patrick Hailes (the Governor-General) had warned me what an extremely difficult man he could be, but he could not have been more charming, friendly, or sensible in his talk with me and we came to some very useful agreements.

I just had ten minutes to tell Patrick Hailes the results of my interview before I had to leave for the new Trinidad Legion Headquarters.

Representatives had collected from all over the Island, and I was presented with the badge of the Trinidad Legion, and had to make a speech. Afterwards I stayed for drinks until 1825, when I drove through the docks and the old part of Port of Spain to the Garrison Officers' Mess.

I got back to Government House at 1920 in time to change for dinner at 2000 with the Governor of Trinidad and Tobago, Sir Solomon Hochoy.

It was a formal party with thirty guests, and took place in the brand new Government House, which was built for the local Governor when the Governor-General took over Government House on the formation of the Federation four years ago; and now the Federation is breaking up.

It is sad from every point of view but heartbreaking for the Hailes's, who have worked so hard to make it a success.

After dinner I had a meeting with the Governor, the Premier and the Minister of Defence of Trinidad, at which we compared the telegrams which we had respectively drafted to the Colonial Secretary and my Minister. We found our telegrams to be completely in step, so we evidently understood one another.

I got back to the Governor-General's house at 2300, and then went through the telegram with the Governor-General.

He told me that when he understood that Patricia and John were coming with me he had proposed for us to arrive on Monday night or Tuesday morning, to see the last day of Carnival.* He said to me, 'Carnival here is something really out of this world.'

He then told me there are 142 steel bands in the Carnival competition. All the bands had followers of at least 100 and some had 800 to 1000, and I believe the record number of followers was 2000 to a single band. They spend the whole year saving up for the costumes they are going to wear.

---

* The Brabournes were unable to accompany him because John, aged thirty-seven, had suffered a severe heart attack.

As Hailes said, the quality of the Carnival could hardly be bettered if the population had been eighty million and rich, instead of eight hundred thousand and poor.

I was about to complain that he might have let me come and see the Carnival by myself, when he took the wind out of my sails by saying, 'Of course I knew that you had only come to work and didn't have any time for the Carnival. So I dropped the idea as soon as your daughter dropped out!' What a lamentable reputation to have. Nearly as bad as Edwina.

Two days later he arrived in Jamaica.

SATURDAY, 10 MARCH. JAMAICA   After dinner was over, the Governor arranged for Sir Alexander Bustamante to sit next to me. He is the leader of the Opposition and seems to think he can beat Mr Manley, the Prime Minister, in the forthcoming elections.* I had met Manley in London, but on this visit he was away electioneering in the North. Bustamante staggered me by asking whether I would be prepared to leave a Company of British soldiers in Jamaica after they got Independence, as an outward demonstration of goodwill and 'To calm the feelings of the ladies'.

SATURDAY, 11 MARCH   At 0930 I saw four excellent young men of the 'Voluntary Service Overseas' organization. They are of all types as far apart as a boy from Eton and an excellent young apprentice from Rolls-Royce. Everyone out here is loud in their praises for what they are doing. The Governor said he would sooner have these four young men than another £4000 on his British Information Budget.

I hear that VSO, with only about 160 young men and women in the field, is doing infinitely better than President Kennedy's vast, and much heralded, 'Peace Corps'.

On Monday, 12 March he was in Belize in British Honduras, though only for three and a half hours.

There had been great excitement because the airfield was only supposed to be capable of taking light or medium transport aircraft, but I

---

* He did, and was Prime Minister himself within a few months.

persuaded the Commander-in-Chief, Transport Command, to let us try it in a Comet, as we should only have seven passengers on board and could fly with minimum fuel. We pulled up with 50 yards in hand.

The airfield was very bumpy, but we didn't burst a tyre, and so did not need the spare wheels we had brought with us.

At Government House I met the Prime Minister, Mr Price, and all except one of his Ministers. The meeting with the Ministers only lasted half an hour, but went off very well.

After the meeting, the Prime Minister asked whether I would be photographed with his colleagues on the steps of Government House. The car in which I had arrived was standing in the way without a driver. The Ministers were very distressed, as they couldn't think of any better place for the photograph, so I got the entire Cabinet round the car and made them push it out of the way. After the photograph had been taken the car was obviously getting red hot in the sun, so I made the whole lot get round the car again and push it back under the porch. Alas, no photographs were taken of the Cabinet all pushing in the same direction for once.

In May 1962 Mountbatten went to Athens for the wedding between Princess Sophia of Greece and Juan Carlos, Prince of the Asturias and now King of Spain. Festivities began at the Palace at 2040 on Friday, 11 May.

The most exciting new acquaintance was Grace Kelly and her husband, Rainier,* who turned out to be much nicer than John had led me to believe. Beautiful as I thought Grace to be, there must have been at least half a dozen young Princesses in Athens who could have given her a run for her money in any beauty contest.

But the most amusing girl I met was Maria Gabriella, the daughter of Beppo of Italy† (I recognized her at once from the pictures in the English papers taken when she was bull fighting) and had an amusing gossip with her.

SATURDAY, 12 MAY. ATHENS   After lunch I went on to the Astir Beach a few hundred yards on round the bay. About 100 of the most

* Prince Rainier III of Monaco married the American actress, Grace Kelly, in 1956.
† King Umberto, who abdicated in 1945.

luxurious, beautiful and delightful cabins have been built here. Each has two foam rubber beds, a little kitchen, shower bath and an open-air dining place, and as springs have recently been discovered there the grass, the flowers and the trees grow in rich profusion.

I went swimming, though the water was cold. The whole of the younger generation of the family were there also. The afternoon ended up with a fight organized by Vittorio-Emmanuele* and Tino,† from two pedalos, which ended up with the throwing of stones and mud and general scrapping, which I evaded.

For the second evening party that night I got Palo's‡ permission to wear plain clothes because my full dress was still wet from yesterday's perspiration!

I danced quite a lot with Grace and a certain amount with Maria Gabriella. She told me about her bull fighting experiences which sounded quite thrilling. It must require great courage to face a bull on horseback and to plant banderillos deep enough into him for them not to come out again.

SUNDAY, 13 MAY   After lunch I invited Grace and Rainier to come round to the Astir Beach and sit on the lawn of our little group of beach huts, with several others. I had a two hours' gossip with Grace and thought she was delightful.

I found we had a free evening and so I got up a party to dine at the King George Hotel and dance afterwards at the Asteria. I invited Grace and Rainier, but they had accepted to dine with Onassis§ at the Yacht Club. I suggested that if they were not too tired, they should come on out after dinner and join my party and they could bring Onassis too if it would help.

That night:

Onassis arrived to join the party. I asked where Grace was and he said that as it was then after midnight and she had to get up at 7 a.m. to get

---

* Crown Prince of Italy.
† Prince Constantine, who succeeded to the throne of Greece as Constantine XIII in 1964.
‡ King Paul of the Hellenes.
§ Aristotle Onassis, Greek shipping millionaire, later briefly married to Jacqueline Kennedy.

ready for the wedding, she was too tired to come on. At the next table to us were Niarchos,* Sonny Blandford† and his new wife Tina, former wife of Onassis!

When the time came to go, Onassis tried to pay the bill but I had great pleasure in absolutely refusing to let him.

MONDAY, 14 MAY   After only five hours' sleep I had to get ready for eight hours of full dress. It was everything and the kitchen stove today. Five British stars, Greek and Spanish stars, the collar of the Garter and three neck decorations!

This was a Spanish occasion. Outside the Cathedral was a large Guard of Honour of Spanish sailors and marines and a band from the cruiser *Canaris*. Inside the Church there were an incredible mass of red and yellow carnations – the Spanish colours. I was in the middle of a pew and could not see much.

After the Roman Catholic service we all drove in procession to the Greek Orthodox Metropole, where I had a splendid view as I was on the outside chair by the centre aisle.

I could see all the processions arrive. The bride was in the State Coach drawn by six white horses with a Cavalry escort and her brother Tino riding next to her.

The Archbishop was supported by no less than twenty-two Bishops in the most fantastic ornate vestments and wearing enormous Orthodox mitres and crowns. The singing here was even better than the Roman Catholic Church; they were evidently vying with each other.

We drove back direct to the Palace whilst the bridal couple did a State drive through the decorated and thickly crowded streets.

Grace came up to me, very contrite, and put both her hands on mine and said, 'Will you forgive me for not coming to your party last night?'

I replied, 'That I can forgive, but I can't forgive you for sending Onassis in your place!'

She was quite horrified and denied having sent him, though she admitted that earlier in the evening she had said that I had invited them all to join me.

---

* Stavros Niarchos, another Greek shipping millionaire and arch-rival of Onassis.
† Marquess of Blandford, now Duke of Marlborough.

1963

On 24 February 1963 Mountbatten left on a month's tour of Latin America.

My party consists of Major Pat MacLellan, Coldstream Guards, my Military Assistant; Squadron Leader Dick Peters, my ADC; Chief Petty Officer Nelson, my Personal Assistant; and Chief Petty Officer Evans, my valet.

I am also taking some people who are not officially attached to my party but are nevertheless accompanying me in this aircraft: Mr Jones of the Joint Intelligence Bureau; Mr Lakin, a Foreign Office representative; and a press party of four. These have been wished on to me by the Foreign Office Public Relations Department, because they have taken over the responsibility of my tour from the Ministry of Defence since the Presidents and Governments of all the countries I am visiting have made me an official guest. Sir Harold Caccia, Permanent Head of the Foreign Office, came over personally to see me to explain why the Foreign Office considered it was necessary that I should take a press party with me. In the face of this request I could not refuse, much as I dislike personal publicity.*

TUESDAY, 26 FEBRUARY. MEXICO CITY   There was a tremendous reception party at the airport, headed by our Ambassador, Sir Peter Garran, who introduced me to the Foreign Secretary, Señor Tello, and a host of VIPs.

The Foreign Secretary then drove me to the hotel. We had a really fascinating drive through a very large part of this wonderful city. As apparently the President has the constitutional right to bulldoze down any houses that are wanted for street improvements, they have

---

* A constant refrain of Mountbatten's, which he neither believed himself nor expected anyone else to.

ruthlessly driven enormous avenues, many of them the size of the Champs Élysées. There are magnificent underpasses and altogether the traffic arrangements are admirable.

I was accompanied everywhere today by police outriders, very smartly dressed in riding boots and gold spurs.

At 1750 the Ambassador called for me and we drove to the Foreign Office to call on the Foreign Secretary.

At the Ambassador's request, I did my best to resolve a diplomatic deadlock which has arisen. The Mexican President* had indicated that he was paying a European visit and would much like to come to London. HM Government had thereupon invited him to come for an official visit early in April. This had been accepted in principle, when de Gaulle invited him to come on a State Visit to Paris, and it then appears that he was having a State Visit in Jugoslavia, Germany and Holland and was no longer willing to accept an official visit in England, for he realized that this was not in the same class as a State Visit.

I pointed out that the main difference between a State Visit and an official visit was that in the State Visit the Queen acted as Host, whereas in an official visit it was the Prime Minister. I said that the Queen would have only recently come back from an exhausting two months' tour in New Zealand and Australia, and I was sure it was to spare Her Majesty that the Government had been unable to arrange a State Visit at short notice. I then suggested that if the Queen were prepared to receive the Mexican President at Windsor Castle, this would be an exceptional honour which I did not remember being accorded to any visiting Head of State. This appealed to the Foreign Secretary, who said he would see whether he could persuade the President to go after all. The Ambassador was very grateful, but I have no idea whether we have resolved the deadlock or not.†

THURSDAY, 28 FEBRUARY Now came the business of getting dressed up as a *charro*.‡ The *charros* had kindly sent me a complete costume made to my measurements which had been provided some weeks ago. The President§ and the Vice-President came round to help

---

* Señor Lopez Mateos.
† They had not. The President never got to London, still less Windsor.
‡ More or less the equivalent of a cowboy, their parades providing opportunities for dressing-up and equine pyrotechnics.
§ Of the *charros*. His wife was president of the *charras*, or cowgirls.

me dress and then we all went off to the *Rancho del Charros*. The arena had been completely cleared and not a soul was in sight. When I was invited to step into the actual arena, at a given signal the *charros* and *charras* rode in to greet me. After this, my horse was brought round, the most magnificent-looking animal, with a fantastically beautiful saddlery, and I was invited to mount. The large and fearsome-looking spurs with which I had been provided were removed. At first I thought they didn't trust my horsemanship, but it transpired that a special set of much more expensive blue steel spurs with silver inlay were provided which went with the stirrups and the rest of the harness of the horse. Having mounted, we then rode out of the arena along a short avenue leading to the boxes in which the steers and horses are kept. I was in the midst of a phalanx of beautiful *charras* and magnificent *charros*. After having ridden all around the precincts, we rode back again.

Riding was rather difficult, for my tight-fitting grey trousers were very right round the tummy. I had to wear an enormous pearl-handled loaded revolver, and between my leg and the stirrup there was a colossal cavalry sabre.

The hat on my head was at least a yard in diameter and beautifully embroidered in silver.

After riding round for about ten minutes or so, I said I wanted to take some pictures myself and this gave me the excuse to dismount. Hardly had I got off my horse than it gave a most vicious exhibition of bucking and kicking; so I can't help thinking it was very lucky I got off when I did.

FRIDAY, I MARCH. VENEZUELA The Ambassador* drove me off in his Rolls up the magnificent new motorway to the capital Caracas. It would be quite a good engineering feat to build a two-lane road up through the mountains to a height of close on 3000 feet, but the Italian engineers called in actually succeeded in building a dual-carriageway with six lanes in all, through tunnels and over viaducts in the most amazing way.

Instead of taking the short cut to the Embassy, our Mounted Police escort led us along the new throughroad through the centre of the city.

This has to be seen to be believed. It is a full-sized motorway running through the heart of the city with flyovers, underpasses, cloverleafs,

---

* Sir Douglas Busk.

and what they here call 'spiders', sometimes on three different levels.

Finally, one comes between the vast new Government buildings which culminate in two tall skyscrapers which are connected together with the main motorway passing underneath.

When one compares the architecture and the road construction with their neighbour British Guyana, the contrast is horribly striking. But then one has to remember that the revenue they make from the oil companies exceeds the equivalent of £40 million a month, so there is plenty of money to spare.

Alas, in spite of this, they have allowed horrible broken-down shanties of rusty corrugated iron to be built round the outskirts of the town, a reminder of the very inadequate distribution of wealth so far achieved.

In the evening the Ambassador gave a dinner party for the Foreign Secretary, the Minister of Defence, the Chief of the Defence Staff and the Commanders-in-Chief of the three Services, and also the National Guard which is under separate command. At least two officers cried off at the last moment, and the Commander-in-Chief of the Army, who had definitely said he was coming, never turned up at all. After half an hour, he was telephoned to and replied quite airily that as he had got back rather late from the office he thought he had better not come.

The Ambassador said that this was nothing compared to what happened during Philip's visit. For the official dinner party, the President arrived twenty-five minutes early, and in the last forty-five minutes five major rearrangements of the dinner table had to be made because some people didn't turn up, some came without wives, others brought wives when they had not said they were coming.

SATURDAY, 2 MARCH. CARACAS It was a lovely morning and we left the Embassy at 0820 to drive to President Betancourt before breakfast. Breakfast was a formal sit-down meal with place cards. I sat opposite the President and had a place card about ten times the size of my neighbour's. The President had completely recovered from the attempt to blow him up two or three years ago, though his hands were still badly scarred from being burnt.

Rather an amusing incident occurred. The Ambassador had warned me not to mention British Guyana in my conversation with the President, as it was a very sensitive subject. However, before going in to breakfast, after the Ambassador and the Minister had gone ahead, the President kept me back and asked me to give a message to my Government to say how grateful he was for the understanding way they had treated Venezuela when they took the boundary dispute to the United Nations. He told me how worried he was about Dr Jagan and wondered whether he was building up an Army. I told him that when I was in British Guyana a year ago, I had strongly recommended both to Dr Jagan and our own Government that he should not try and build up an Army, but should merely increase the size of his police force for internal security purposes. The President was most gratified to hear this.

He asked me over breakfast what I recommended for the modernization of his armed forces. I strongly recommended that the Bofors guns in the British battle class destroyers which they had should be replaced by our new short range missile SEACAT. I also recommended him to buy our vertical take-off aircraft, the P1127. He seemed very interested.

Half way through breakfast, he said to me: 'You remind me very strongly of someone we both knew and liked.' After a pause he went on and said, 'President Roosevelt.'

MONDAY, 4 MARCH. LIMA   The Director of Protocol met us and led us through magnificent corridors and reception rooms to a small ante-room where three ADCs, one from each Service, stood in line and saluted. They then went to the adjoining room and opened the double doors, and in walked the co-Presidents of the Government Junta. These are, in fact, the three Service Ministers: General Lindley, Minister of War; Admiral Torres Matos, Minister of Marine; and General Vargas, Minister of Aeronautics.

Up to this weekend they had an independent chairman, General Perez Godoy, who was President of the Military Junta. But during the weekend the other three considered that he was developing a personality cult, and speaking too much personally instead of only as one of their Committee.

They gave him until 12 o'clock on Monday to resign. Luckily, for the purposes of my programme, he did so without protest. This is made easy in Peru where senior officers receive more retired pay than active pay.

The trio sat together and almost talked together. It is clear they are

74

most anxious that none of them should take the lead and be accused of developing a personality cult!*

TUESDAY, 5 MARCH   General Giriani, who had been the Military Secretary to the former President Prado, gave a dramatic account to us of the arrest and removal of the President by the Military Junta. It appears that if there had still been a President I should certainly have been submitted to a great deal more formality and a white tie banquet. So it seems I have been rather lucky because the military entertainment has been much more light-hearted.

FRIDAY, 8 MARCH. SANTIAGO   The Ambassador and I went in alone to see the President, Alessandri. The call was only supposed to be a formal occasion lasting ten minutes, but he kept me over half an hour discussing world affairs in very fluent French. He explained that Chile was different to all the other South American countries, as they were the only ones operating a democratic institution with non-political armed forces and no fear of a military dictatorship. Indeed, his only fear was that the popular front, in which the Communists have a majority, might seriously challenge his party at the next elections in 1964.†

There is no doubt that the atmosphere in Chile is different to elsewhere. They refer to themselves as the England of South America, and the number of English, Scottish and Irish names to be found is phenomenal. Their great hero is Admiral Lord Cochrane, the first Commander-in-Chief of their Navy.

SUNDAY, 10 MARCH   The air mail edition of *The Times* of 5 March arrived today announcing in fairly sensational terms the Government's decision in principle to adopt my suggestion of abolishing the Admiralty, the War Office and the Air Ministry (and I hope the Ministry of Aviation) to form a unified Ministry of Defence.

It is highly satisfactory to me that this decision has been taken by the Government on my advice but in my absence in South America.

---

* The junta handed over to civilian government after elections held three months later.
† In fact the Christian Democrat, Eduardo Frei, was elected, with an overall majority.

MONDAY, 11 MARCH   We took off at 0700. I was personally very sad to leave Chile, for Philip was quite right that this is the nicest country in South America; at least the nicest we have visited so far.

The clocks were put on one hour and we landed at 1240 local time at Brasilia Airport. Brazil has outdone the other countries in the way of providing me with ADCs. My senior ADC is Vice-Admiral Brasil and my junior ADC is Captain Vasconcellos. The latter turned out to be a wonderful English speaker, in fact bi-lingual. The former spoke volubly to me all day in what he evidently thought was English but which was extremely difficult to understand.

At 1550, we drove to the President's offices at the Planalto. President Goulart is forty-five and an outstandingly strong personality.* In fighting the Parliamentary system to try and get back full Presidential powers, he had been quite ruthless and had brought the country to the verge of bankruptcy during the last year, largely through lack of an efficient form of actual government. However, now that he has won his plebiscite, if he can get on with the business of administration he may be able to straighten out his country's finances, but I suspect he will need a big loan from the United States to tide them over.

The visit was only scheduled to last fifteen minutes, but in fact we went on talking for forty minutes and I found him very interesting.

The project of moving the capital of Brazil from Rio de Janeiro to some neutral inland position has been in the constitution of the country for many years. But it was not until about 1957 that the plunge was taken by President Kubitschek. He selected an area more than 700 miles in a north-westerly direction from Rio de Janeiro. Apart from the President's palace and the first hotel, no buildings had apparently started to be erected until the end of 1958.

The Prefect had very kindly invited the architect of Brasilia, Oscar Niemeyer, to come up and meet me. He had been too busy to come up and meet Philip,† but apparently was prepared to drive twenty hours along the terrible roads to come and meet me, which touched me very much.

We spent the next two hours sight-seeing with the architect and the Prefect and a large company of other people. It is very difficult to find words in which to describe an entirely new experience. Brasilia is so

---

* Strong or not, he was brusquely deposed the following year.
† Mountbatten always recorded with relish any occasion on which he considered that he had outdone his nephew; see, for example, 23 July 1965 (pages 134–5).

utterly different from any other city that I have ever seen that one hardly knows where to start. The city itself consists of one great axis running more or less east and west, and another one at right angles, but swept back rather like the wings of an aeroplane. The east-west axis is very wide and contains all the Ministries and public offices, whereas the two wings, which are each 6 kilometres long, contain the residential quarters, that is to say from end to end there are 12 kilometres or 7½ miles of avenues.

Quite the most remarkable part about the lay-out of the city is that the roads, which are all very wide, never cross each other. There are no traffic lights, no intersections, all roads are one-way and there is no sort of traffic problem or traffic jam, as they all cross under or over other roads.

This did not prevent our police outriders from going round with piercing sirens switched on the whole time quite unnecessarily.

We drove down to the President's Residential Palace, the Palacio da Alvorada. This is a fantastic house with the most extraordinary concept inside. We spent a long time going round this. On our way back we stopped to look at the new cathedral which is ten feet below ground, only the dome showing above ground. The dome consists of a series of arms joined together at the top to form a sort of crown of roses and is quite fantastic.

The architect told me that virtually all the buildings we were seeing have grown up in the last four years. He told me that President Kubitschek was in such a hurry to get Brasilia completed to a point of 'no return' that the architect only had fifteen days in which to design the Houses of Parliament. The President felt that unless he could get Brasilia sufficiently established in the three years left to him of his term of office, the next President might reverse the decision and abandon this great concept.

THURSDAY, 14 MARCH. BUENOS AIRES   The Ambassador* warned me that there was a curious atmosphere and although the Navy had been most excited and enthusiastic about my visit, a number of refusals had been received for various parties from the Navy, which made him feel that they might be thinking of political action.

After calling on the Foreign Minister, we went on to the Town Hall to

---

* Sir George Middleton.

call on the Lord Mayor, and then to the Presidential Palace to call on President Guido,* the stooge whom the armed forces put in when they refused to accept the Peronist victory at the last elections. The hall, staircase and passages were lined with the presidential bodyguard in their 1820 full dress uniforms. They all held their big cavalry sabres at an angle of 45° straight out from their belts, so that one had to zig-zag between them to avoid being cut.

In making conversation, I mentioned my scheme for abolishing the Admiralty, War Office and Air Ministry, and said I was quite glad to have been out of England while the actual decision was made, as otherwise I might have been murdered by the reactionary Admirals and Generals. The President blanched visibly at this and the Ambassador also noticed how worried he was, and explained that he lived in permanent fear of being bumped off by his Admirals and Generals. I understand that the Naval Commander-in-Chief sent his deputy to this meeting at the last moment, which looks ominous!

At 1845, the Ambassador warned me that there were strong rumours that a Naval coup might be staged during the evening, but Captain Lockhart† strenuously denied this.

FRIDAY, 15 MARCH   At 1815 I met 70 representatives of the press, radio and television and had to exchange a few words with each – others nearby listening. It was at this party that poor Philip was caught by his remark that the *Daily Express* was a bloody awful newspaper.

The latest rumour is that the coup has been postponed until Tuesday, as a gesture of courtesy to me!‡

I notice that this is the only Embassy where we have had Army sentries posted as well as police and security guards. Incidentally, the Ambassador's car had its windscreen shattered by a rifle bullet only ten days ago!

SUNDAY, 17 MARCH   At 1545 we flew by helicopter to El Recreo Estancia which lies about 50 miles to the south of Buenos Aires. The

---

* Former Chairman of the Senate.
† The Argentinian naval ADC – *prima facie* a curious person with whom to discuss this hypothesis.
‡ No coup took place. Elections were held some three months later.

owner has had a herd of horses now for over 100 years, and by selective in-breeding he has brought their size down to complete miniatures. The herd is over 400 strong, but he only had time to collect in about a dozen for us to see in his grounds.

I made particular friends with a little chestnut mare called Brandy who stands exactly 18½ inches high and has already had three foals. A speckled piebald called Domino was 20 inches high, but the owner, Don Julio Falavella, said that he had at least thirty smaller in the herd and that the smallest was only 14 inches high. The foals when born weigh about ½ kilo (18 ounces) and stand on the average 6 inches high.

Brandy and Domino followed us into their drawing room for drinks and we measured Brandy's hoof which was 2¼ inches across. The fabulous part about these horses is that they are definitely not ponies like Shetlands, etc., because they have been bred down from big horses, and they are merely very, very small horses. The Ambassador's Alsatian dog stood 11 inches higher at the shoulder than Brandy.

President Kennedy's brother, Robert, recently bought three for his children and flew them back in his aeroplane. If Edwina had been here I am sure she would have bought a couple, as the price works out at only just over 100 guineas. I was photographed carrying Brandy in my arms.

MONDAY, 18 MARCH It has been a fascinating experience to have spent four days in the most sophisticated town in South America, with shops like Harrods, Burberrys and even Nordiska (from Stockholm).

Recently a cattleman made a big sale and brought 5,000,000 pesos in cash into the bank. The doors were open but the clock showed three minutes after closing time. The manager said that he could not accept the cash until the following morning. That night the cattleman sat up over his cash in his apartment with a shotgun. Two intruders broke in – he shot both of them. One was the manager of the bank and the other was the Chief of Police!

FRIDAY, 22 MARCH. BROADLANDS Although this has been a very hectic and high-pressure trip, I personally have enjoyed every moment of it. It has filled in my knowledge of a part of the world I did not know at all, and I have made many new friends among Ministers, Service Chiefs and others.

I have also become somewhat worried and frightened for the future, because so few of the South American countries appear to have any stability. Although many of them have great potential wealth, they are so badly organized and run that there is still a great gulf between the over-rich and the miserably poor.

Democracy is beginning to work under Betancourt in Venezuela, and is not too bad in Chile; but in Peru and the Argentine the Services step in and take over whenever an election shows a left-wing majority.

In fact, democracy just isn't working satisfactorily in South America, and if it can't be made to work the whole continent will become ripe for communism.

I could not put my hand on my heart and recommend any British firm to put any more capital investment into South America, though I certainly think they should sell more goods and send out more technicians and people with brains.

The goodwill to the British is there in good measure. In fact the reception I had from everybody, Presidents, Ministers, Service Chiefs and the crowds, was surprising and at times overwhelming.

It has been an exhilarating experience.

On 26 April 1963 Mountbatten left London to attend the meetings of the CENTO Military Committee in Teheran and then continue to India. He arrived at the first meeting on 27 April.

After I had inspected the Guard, General Hedjazi invited me to say Good Morning to the Guard, which I did by shouting '*Pasdar dorood*', to which the entire Guard shouted back as one man '*Dorood Timsar*' ('Good Morning, Your Excellency').

This incident caused quite a bit of political trouble, because unfortunately the Turkish General was looking out of the window of his office and noted that I had been received by this tremendous shout from the Guard, which had been omitted in his case!

He was told that there had not been enough time to do it in his case! The real explanation, however, is that Hedjazi is particularly anxious to do me honour because, when his sixteen-year-old daughter fell from a second-storey window and suffered a multiple fracture of her jaw, he flew her to London and I was able to arrange an ambulance, a good surgeon and a hospital for her.

In spite of the local forecast that we should require three full sessions to get through the agenda, I had estimated we could finish it in one morning. We did so between 0900 and 1230, in spite of the fact that the Turkish General Sunay was in the Chair and every word he said had to be translated.

General Musa attacked the United States and the United Kingdom violently for giving military aid to India against the Chinese,* and he claimed that by so doing two of the members of the Baghdad pact were strengthening a non-member in such a way that she became a threat to Pakistan who was a member. I told the meeting I was going to India myself and that our only object was to support a Commonwealth country from attack by the Communists, and that I deplored any misunderstandings between Commonwealth countries over this.

At 1815, a Persian General came to fetch me and escort me to the Shah's Palace – not the Marble Palace but the palace in which he is actually living. In the programme I was to have a twenty-minute audience. At 1930 the telephone rang in his study but he said, 'Pay no attention.' It rang again at 1945, at 2000 and at 2015. Finally, I stood up and said, 'I've been here one and three quarter hours and I am sure I have overstayed my welcome. You must be anxious for your dinner!' His Imperial Majesty, however, was reluctant to release me even then and pressed me to come back and stay with him and do some 'hunting'.

I must say we always get on very well together, and this time we got on like a house on fire. He agreed with everything I said and I pretty well agreed with everything he said. He is the only man I have met in Persia who really makes any sense, and on the whole I consider him a pretty high-class statesman, though sometimes weak and jealous.

On 29 April Mountbatten continued his journey and arrived at Santa Cruz airfield, Bombay, to be met by the Governor, Nehru's sister, Nan Pandit.

We had not proceeded more than half a mile before it dawned on me that I was in for one of these unpredictable staggering receptions by the Indian people. The streets were lined on each side by people who waved and clapped and cheered. So I stopped the procession and asked for an open car. They hadn't got one, but they finally produced the police radio telephone jeep. I stood up in the front of this and we then drove on at a much slower speed.

---

* Fighting had broken out between India and China in September 1962. General Musa was the Pakistani representative.

The distance from the airfield to the dockyard is 16 miles. Except in the few spaces where there were no houses or built-up areas, the streets were solidly lined on both sides on an average about two deep, but in places six or seven deep for at least 14 miles. The many apartment houses had their large and long verandahs crowded with people, and so did some of the rooftops.

To the old cry of 'Mountbatten *ki-Jai*' was added 'Mountbatten *Zindabad*'. It was just like the old days. Fifteen years rolled back in my mind as I recalled an almost similar drive with Edwina twice in Bombay. I felt quite emotional, and had to fight to keep back tears as I smiled and waved back to the crowds.

To Ronnie and Vernon* it was just like old times, but to the new members of my staff it was quite a surprise. Vernon and Derek Hodgkinson† calculated that there were 2,000,000 people in the streets to greet me. This I don't believe because Bombay only has 4½ million inhabitants and we certainly didn't see half of them. But the crowd must have been several hundreds of thousands.

On 30 April Mountbatten flew on to Delhi.

At 1530 I drove down to the Parliament building and had a half an hour's private heart to heart with Jawaharlal. We talked about Patricia and Pammy, and of course Edwina. This is almost the first time he has been prepared to talk freely about her, and we both exchanged sentimental memories of the time we were all together in India. He had to take the Chair at a National Defence Council Meeting at 1600, so I came back to Rashtrapati Bhavan.‡ The great State pictures of Edwina and myself by Halliday§ still hang in the position of honour, and I was pleased to see they keep up the pictures of former kings and queens, though they have been moved to less prominent positions. Our marble busts are still outside the President's quarters.

I had to put on my full dress to call formally on the President, my host, at 1630. I must say my old friend, Dr Radhakrishnan, makes a very good and dignified President. He had all his staff present, and a dozen

---

* Colonel Vernon Erskine-Crum, Secretary of the Joint Planners, who had been Conference Secretary in Delhi while Mountbatten was Viceroy.
† Group Captain (later Air Chief Marshal Sir) Derek Hodgkinson, one of Mountbatten's staff.
‡ Former Viceroy's House.
§ Edward Halliday. 'Great' is presumably a judgement based on size rather than quality.

photographers, and received me in the Yellow Drawing Room. When I asked to see my old study and to see if my badges were still in place, he readily agreed and led me down to it.

The furniture has been so completely changed that I could hardly recognize it. Alas, a new set of badges giving the signs of the modern Indian forces have taken the place of my old wartime collection. The President was rather horrified to hear this had been done without his knowledge, and he sent to enquire where my badges were and we received the reply that they had been stored safely. I have suggested they should now be put up in the ADC's room.

WEDNESDAY, I MAY. DELHI   At 1045 I went to the old Commander-in-Chief's room now occupied by the Chief of the Army Staff, my old friend Muchu Chaudhuri. Although I had had five minutes alone with each of the three Chiefs of Staff last night, Muchu had asked to have a further quarter of an hour with me before I met the others to discuss the question of creating a Chairman of the Indian Chiefs of Staffs' Committee.

I was pleasantly surprised that all three of the Indians entirely agreed with my proposal that there should be an independent Chairman appointed for the Indian Chiefs of Staffs' Committee, who might be called Chief of the Defence Staff and be my opposite number. I had originally advised against this post in 1948, saying that at least twelve years must pass until the Navy and Air Force had grown sufficiently in stature to be capable of being considered for the selection of the Chairman. I considered the time had now come and that the emergency with China demanded such an appointment. They all agreed.

After lunch the meeting was with the Military Affairs Committee of the National Defence Council of which the Minister of Defence is normally the Chairman. This time, however, the Minister of Defence had invited the Prime Minister to take the Chair.

Jawaharlal, who had originally written the letter inviting me to attend the Military Affairs Committee, invited me to speak to them as freely, as fully and for as long as I wished.

I took the line that I was speaking neither as a British officer, nor as a representative of the British and US Chiefs of Staff (although I told them I knew their views). I said that I had tackled this task from the point of view of being once more an Indian employed by the Government of India as I was on 15 August 1947. I said that this time I had imagined I was being employed not as Governor-General but as the Supreme Commander of Operations against the Chinese. I pointed out that the war would be largely fought along the same lines of communication as I used in Burma, and I then held forth for 45 minutes.

I had done so much preparation I really knew my stuff, and I think it went over remarkably well. When it was over, the Chief of the Army Staff said [he was] in complete agreement with my estimate of the situation, and to what extent their Army should be built up. The Chief of the Naval Staff endorsed the few remarks I had made about the Navy. The Chief of the Air Staff was rather hurt that I had not stated an adequate requirement for enough modern air squadrons. With the help of Derek Hodgkinson I argued with him, and the general impression appeared to be that the meeting backed me rather than their own CAS.

Questions and discussion continued for nearly an hour, but at 1645 Jawaharlal took me with him to his own room next door, where he showed me an oil painting by the little Indian artist Swamy which he had done of Edwina from a photograph. We both came to the conclusion that although it was a nice picture he had somehow missed the real likeness and that neither of us wished to keep the picture for our own house. We agreed that it might be a good idea to give it to the Edwina Mountbatten Memorial Homes in Romsey, and Jawaharlal agreed that I might take it as a presentation from himself if I wished this. After this we talked about a film which Richard Attenborough wishes to make about the life of Gandhi.*

I then touched on that explosive and unpopular subject, Kashmir. Bit by bit I got him round to listening to me and for the first time in fifteen years we seemed to be making some progress. In fact I think there has been real progress, as we agreed to meet again tomorrow morning to continue our talks. Meanwhile we both had to get away as we were late for our next meetings.

THURSDAY, 2 MAY   At 0845 I went to the Prime Minister's residence for breakfast. I had never seen the scene so often described by Edwina and Pammy of the general public being admitted to see the great man. Various Indians were there bringing all sorts of rather big and boring gifts, all of which he accepted with a gracious smile. Then a very fresh young American couple insisted on photographing him in turn with the other member of the couple.

---

* Which eventually came to fruition in 1982.

Buenos Aires, 17 March 1963. Meeting the miniature horses. Brandy, who is in Mountbatten's arms, stands exactly 18½ inches.

New Delhi, 30 April 1963. With the President of India, Dr Radhakrishnan.

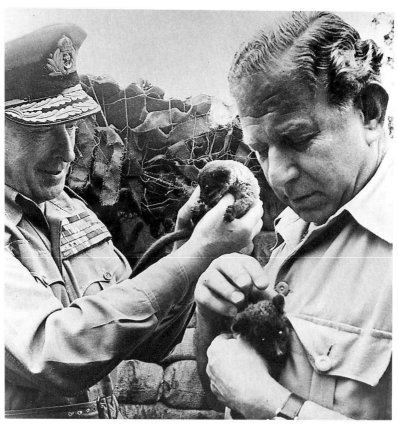

Borneo, February 1965. Petting two baby musangs with Solly Zuckerman.

After this he went on to the verandah where about fifty school-children had come up from Bombay. They were all seated cross-legged, but in turn the Head Girl and the Head Boy came up with garlands which they tried to put round his neck. By a deft manoeuvre he managed to twist the garlands out of their hands and put them back round their own necks. He then addressed a few remarks apparently to individual pupils whom he patted on the head. All fifty children looked at him with rapt attention as though they were regarding their god.

I stayed on and talked with him until after 1000. I found that he had slipped back considerably from the position we had reached the night before. After about a quarter of an hour's talk I got it back again, and so successful was the last hour's talk that he asked me if I would see the Commonwealth Relations Secretary, and the Foreign Secretary. I said I gladly would.

At 1610 Duncan Sandys* and Paul Gore-Booth† arrived to see me and I moved over to the other sitting room with them. Duncan and I then went on to the Parliament House where at 1630 we met Jawaharlal and Sirdar Swaran Singh, the Minister who had been conducting the negotiations in Pakistan over Kashmir. The meeting went on until 1810.

Alas, the rest of my good work appeared to have been undone because obviously other people had been getting at Jawaharlal and telling him not to listen to me. Swaran Singh even went so far as to say that if the Prime Minister did in fact follow my advice, it might destroy him with his party and with the country! I had no idea things had reached such a pass in India.

I dropped Duncan at the High Commissioner's residence where we were both supposed to meet Dean Rusk, the American Secretary of State, to have a talk about Kashmir. Duncan and I agreed that it might cause embarrassment if the press knew that I was taking part in political talks with the Americans on the situation, and so he agreed to report progress personally.

FRIDAY, 3 MAY   The pressure of work here has been quite ludicrous. I haven't been able to fulfil a single private engagement, and the longest free period I had was this morning when I had a quick walk round the gardens. In some curious way I completely recaptured the sense of

* Now Secretary of State for Commonwealth Relations; he had arrived the previous day.
† UK High Commissioner. Later Baron Gore-Booth.

urgency and exhilaration of 1947. In many ways I felt I was back again in that period. I received almost similar treatment everywhere, indeed there were more ADCs to see me off and receive me than in the old days, and certainly the police escort was much greater. It consisted of naval police, military police, civil police, holding up the traffic at every point to a greater extent than I would have permitted in the old days, except for official occasions.

On landing [at London Airport] I found that both the BBC and the ITV television newsreel teams had come down specially for an interview. I was naturally reluctant to give one, but as a matter of courtesy went along to see them. I told them I did not think it would be worthwhile their doing an interview, but they could soon discover by asking me the questions to which they wanted answers.

Needless to say the first one was Kashmir. I replied that this was political and I was not prepared to speak on it. The next question was what advice had I given to the Indians about their forces and equipment, to which I replied this was solely a matter between the Indians and myself. The third question was what did I think of the present state of friction between Pakistan and India, to which I replied this was purely a political matter.

They then thanked me for having saved them from wasting any film and agreed it was not worthwhile having any interview.

1964

Nine months later, on 24 January 1964, Mount-batten was back in Delhi.

Poor Jawaharlal Nehru was still suffering from a slight stroke, so he sent his senior Minister, Nanda,* the Minister of Defence and three or four other Cabinet Ministers to meet me. The High Commissioner and Lady Gore-Booth and many other VIPs were there.

There was a large crowd of pressmen, one of whom yelled out 'Welcome Home'.

SATURDAY, 25 JANUARY. DELHI I rang up Indira [Gandhi] at the Prime Minister's residence to find out if we could come and pay an impromptu visit to Jawaharlal. She told me this must be telepathy because she was just going to pick up the telephone and invite us to come down and see him at his request.

In spite of his slight stroke he was looking better than when I last saw him, largely because of the enforced rest.

He seemed to cheer up considerably at our visit and it was really lovely finding him more or less in his old form.

Indira said that he doesn't really want to read books. All he asks for is to read his files, which is his preferred reading!

SUNDAY, 26 JANUARY Patricia and I had early breakfast and then left in full dress in an open car for the great Republic Day Parade. At the saluting base we were met by the Minister of Defence and the Chiefs of Staff and we sat in the seats of honour: I between the Vice-President and the Prime Minister, and Patricia the other side of the latter.

Jawaharlal had no business to have come really, as it was very cold

* Gulzarilal Nanda, the Minister of Home Affairs.

87

and he limped rather pathetically and had to be supported. But he was in very good form and delighted to be there.

At 1920 V. P. Menon* came to see me for a gossip. We had been advised to keep the wireless on during our talk. What V.P. had to say was absolutely fascinating. I have asked him to let me have some notes in writing at his convenience.

MONDAY, 27 JANUARY Our High Commissioner accompanied me for my call on the Minister of Defence, Chavan. The latter is making quite a good Minister of Defence. In my day he was a *goonda* leading an organization whose object was to kill Europeans and we put a price on his head!

Nan Pandit, who had only just arrived up in Delhi that day, came to Rashtrapati Bhavan for an hour and a half's heart-to-heart gossip. She confirmed in different ways the very sad picture which V. P. Menon had painted to me and filled in a number of gaps.

I had a fascinating hour's interview with the American Ambassador, Chester Bowles. He had been the American Ambassador eight years ago when Edwina knew him quite well, and he was also worried at the state of affairs in India.

He seems a very high-class man and is certainly a good friend of India, and made quite a lot of sense to me.

At 2030 Patricia and I went to dine with Rajkumari Amrit Kaur† at No. 2 Willingdon Crescent. The only other person at dinner was Mac Mathai, who used to be the Prime Minister's Secretary and has remained a great friend of everybody.‡

I had a long talk with both Amrit and Mac and they confirmed in different ways all I had heard before about the state of affairs in India.

The general corruption in higher places appears to be spreading through the country, and with Jawaharlal's illness there is a complete lack of leadership. Everybody is very pessimistic about the future.

---

* V. P. Menon had been one of Mountbatten's most valuable assistants at the time of the transfer of power. He was said to have been disgruntled at not being offered a Provincial Governorship.
† Former Minister and close friend of Nehru. She died unexpectedly ten days later.
‡ M. O. Mathai. A somewhat sinister *éminence grise* who had not remained a great friend of Mountbatten's, whatever the latter might have thought.

TUESDAY, 28 JANUARY   At 1100 I went to the Prime Minister's house where I met Patricia. Jawaharlal had only just woken up from his sleep so I went in alone.

I found him in a most deplorable state, quite different to Saturday. On Saturday he had been looking well and was cheerful and talkative, but now he looked old and sunken and tired, and could hardly take any interest in what I was saying.

I did my best to urge him to shed his day-to-day responsibilities and have someone else become Minister for External Affairs and Commonwealth Relations, to appoint a Deputy Prime Minister, to appoint someone to take over the Atomic Energy Committee, the Planning Commission and Ministerial charge of Parliamentary Affairs. I suggested that he should then remain Prime Minister, only being shown files dealing with high policy.

I told him that he had had a warning as a result of his attack, and, unless he stopped addressing Public Meetings and having endless interviews and dealing with all the details of administration, his health and probably his life would be at stake. He merely looked sad and did not really answer.

Mountbatten continued to Burma and, on 31 January, was staying with the Chairman of the Revolutionary Council, General Ne Win, and his wife Katie at their beach house at Ngapali.

We woke after a really very chilly night to lovely sunshine, blue skies and a flat calm sea like the Mediterranean in July.

At 0830 the General and Katie joined us. He obviously wanted to gossip about old times and his present problems. Patricia and Katie stayed listening attentively, but not interrupting, and presently moved off.

Ne Win really let his hair down and discussed all his problems, and what he was trying to do, and I gave him my views. I had been well briefed by the Foreign Office and by the Ambassador, and with my background knowledge I think I was able to contribute something quite useful to the discussions. At all events the Ambassador thought it had been extremely useful and just what was wanted, because it appears that Ne Win has been so alone and aloof that he has absolutely nobody in whom he can confide, or discuss his plans for the future with, entirely impartially.

*Mountbatten flew on to Colombo, and on
3 February drove up to Kandy.*

We arrived at my old Headquarters, the Peradiniya Botanic Gardens, at
1600. A Curator began by handing us copies of the new edition of his
guide book and catalogue. I had been amused on 21 April 1956, when I
was last here with Edwina, to notice that the only reference to the
Supreme Headquarters of the South-East Asia Command having been
in the Gardens was a statement that the damage which they had caused
was being rapidly effaced. Now even this statement had been removed
and when I asked the author of the book why, he replied that all this had
happened twenty years ago and people had forgotten all about it! There
is, however, one slight reference where it says, 'The short drive turning
to the left leads to the great circle and on the right is the Amherstia
Nobilis planted in 1945 by Lord Louis Mountbatten, Supreme Allied
Commander, South-East Asia.' We visited the tree, which is now nearly
twenty years old, and were all astonished to find that it was not more
than seven or eight feet high, although perfectly healthy.

A few yards further on there was still the carriage drive and circular
approach to my old personal offices, but alas, the woodwork had
become rotten and they had decided, I think quite wisely, to pull them
down.

We walked from here to my old War Room, which had to be built out
of brick because of the many secret maps displayed in it. This still stands
and is used as offices. *

TUESDAY, 26 MAY. LONDON   At 1950 I drove to Buckingham Palace
with a police escort and got there in 8 minutes! I attended the State
Banquet for the President of Sudan.

Philip was wearing a resplendent Sudanese Order and I asked him
what it was called. He replied, 'I asked the President when he invested
me what the name of the Order was. The President replied that he had
no idea!'

After the State Banquet the family foregathered for drinks and I had
a good gossip with Lilibet. I finally got home at 0015 and worked to just
on 0200.

* And still stands today.

WEDNESDAY, 27 MAY   Patricia rang me up just after the 0800 news broadcast which announced that Jawaharlal Nehru was seriously ill. She reminded me of her conviction that when he said goodbye to us in Delhi after our lunch with him on 29 January he knew that he would never see us again. She was convinced then he hadn't got much longer to live, and now she prophesied that he was dying.

I had my hair cut and at 0930 Ronnie Brockman rang through to the barber's to say that Jawaharlal had died, and he had already made preliminary arrangements for me to go out for the funeral which he assumed would be the following day.

I dashed back to the office, Duncan Sandys rang me up to ask whether I would be prepared to go out and represent HM Government, and I said of course I would. I got in touch with Michael Adeane* who told me that the Queen wished me to represent her personally at the funeral.

Meanwhile the Prime Minister† had decided that he would go himself to represent the British Government.

THURSDAY, 28 MAY. DELHI   The Acting Prime Minister, Nanda, and Sirdar Swaran Singh, another of the Cabinet Ministers, were there to meet us. A complete turn-out of British Advisers were there in uniform with their wives and of course the Acting High Commissioner, Belcher.

We drove straight to the High Commissioner's residence. Belcher said to the assembled company, 'I would like to make a speech about today's arrangements.' Alec Home chipped in with, 'It had better be a good speech or I shall fall asleep, I am so tired.'

We were then informed that all of us were being put up in the High Commission. I said that I was sure that I was expected by the President to stay at Rashtrapati Bhavan, and one of the High Commission staff then said that they had taken it upon themselves to ring up the President's staff and say I would be staying at the High Commissioner's residence.

I then asked our Military Adviser to ring up the President's Military Secretary to confirm where we were expected to stay. Back came the reply immediately that the President hoped that I and my party would stay at Rashtrapati Bhavan.

* Private Secretary to the Queen. Later Lord Adeane.
† Alec Douglas-Home.

I therefore sent off Evans with the luggage to get settled in whilst the rest of us had breakfast, and then Pammy and I drove off with a Union Jack on the car to the Prime Minister's residence. We entered by the tradesmen's entrance to the compound and came into the house from the east end door. Pammy and I were immediately greeted by Nehru's sisters, Betty Huthi Singh and then Nan Pandit. They conducted us through to the main front hall where Jawaharlal was lying in state. His daughter, Indira, was keeping close watch by the body, which was being guarded by two Major Generals.

I first of all placed the wreath of Lilibet and Philip in the position of honour over the feet, and Pammy then placed our family wreath beside it.

Seeing Jawaharlal lying there so peaceful and serene was very harrowing, and altogether too much for poor Pammy. On the way out we saw Krishna Menon sitting huddled up over his stick near the body and greeted him warmly, for although I think he has behaved very badly recently he has always been a good friend.*

The Maharaja of Sikkim and his American wife had arrived the day before on a State Visit, and so were occupying our usual rooms. However, we were given the delightful suite of rooms immediately over them and the ones which Edwina and I used to use when staying in Delhi at the time when I was Supreme Allied Commander South-East Asia. At 1030, the President received Pammy and myself, and I had a fifty-five minutes' conversation with him. He told me that Jawaharlal had told him quite recently about my invitation to Broadlands and how he would go for the weekend, for he had been on every occasion of visiting England even though there was a 70-mile motor drive there from London.

He said how delighted he and all of India were that the Queen should have sent me to represent her, and that our Prime Minister should have come in person. He told me that Dean Rusk, the American Secretary of State, was doing his best to get there in time for the cremation, but he, of course, had much further to fly.

With an adequate police escort we were able to get in through the front entrance of the Prime Minister's house this time, but had to get out well before we reached the door on account of the crowds and the troops.

---

* As Minister of Defence, Krishna Menon had seemed to Mountbatten to be insufficiently attentive to British requirements.

We went straight into the front hall where there were scenes of great activity going on. Fourteen of the most senior officers of the Indian services were in there, eight to carry the body personally and six to march by the side as pall bearers.

Madden, Jawaharlal's faithful factotum, went and put a new rose into his usual centre buttonhole where he had always kept one.

It is most disturbing to see an old friend being manhandled, even though it is by Generals and Admirals, in being moved from the lying-in-state position to the traditional Indian litter of bamboos and string on which the officers carried him shoulder high to the gun carriage.

I must say the crowd was quite astonishing, for in the closed Cadillac they all seemed to recognize me at once with great cries of 'Lord Mountbatten' or 'Lord Mountbatten *ki jai*', and sometimes even 'Lord Mountbatten *zindabad*'. I am glad to say Pammy had her own reception. It began with cries of '*Lerki* Lord Mountbatten', which means 'Lord Mountbatten's daughter'. But on two or three occasions men put their heads in at the window and grinning with pleasure shouted 'Pamela'.

I had warned our car to keep as close behind the next car as possible so as to avoid the risk of being cut off by the crowds getting in between. Unfortunately our driver interpreted these instructions so literally that he ran into the police car ahead, damaged our radiator which gave off clouds of steam, and we were brought up to a full stop.

However, the crowd just gathered round and pushed our car along, so we managed to keep up without much difficulty. Then suddenly the two cars ahead did a spurt and got about 200 or 300 yards ahead of us.

Obviously the crowd couldn't push us at that speed, so I decided that we would get out and walk. Pammy and I then processed down a very crowded route and it was a sort of triumphal procession because of course there was no difficulty about the crowds recognizing us from far ahead here.

Finally, we caught up with the President's police car which was completely stopped in a new jam, and Pammy and I managed to pile into this.

The Cadillac had been hot, but the police car was an inferno and we absolutely dripped. The temperature today was about 100°F.

We arrived at the funeral pyre simultaneously with the body. In fact, as we came to a standstill so the body was hoisted up and we all saluted.

We slowly moved round the pyre which was built on a 6-foot-high structure of brick, so that all could see. Finally, we reached the seats allotted to us, and Pammy was enchanted to find that the card on my seat just read 'The Ex-Governor-General'. It was placed next to the President's.

Meanwhile Alec Home and George Brown,* Paul Gore-Booth and others were near us, but hemmed in by the crowd and standing up. I only hope they got seats later. George Brown worked his way across in front of the President, shook me by the hand and said, 'I had to tell you how wonderful you look.' If Pammy hadn't confirmed what he said I wouldn't have believed it.

I had heard that Dean Rusk, the American Secretary of State, was making a gallant effort to get over to the funeral. I enquired whether he had arrived, and was told he had got there about ten minutes before and was among the crowd of diplomats. I plunged into the crowd, and pulled him out and brought him over to meet the President, and we managed to get an extra chair put in alongside Pamela. I felt that if the most powerful nation on earth could send its representative at break-neck speed half way around the world, he certainly deserved a seat next to the President.

We arranged to go down to call on poor Indira, Jawaharlal's daughter, at 1900. She was extraordinarily brave and very sweet. I have never been overfond of her, and yet she certainly seemed wonderful, looking after her father during his illness, and behaved superbly today.

This visit, though it only lasted 27 hours, was even more emotional for me than the former one. India does something to me that is indescribable and the death of dear Jawaharlal made the visit even more poignant. I was quite shaken to find a letter from him dated 24 May on my return, accepting, as usual, my invitation to stay at Broadlands. The handwriting was distressingly shaky.

In September 1964 there was another royal wedding in Athens, this time between the young King Constantine, 'Tino', who had succeeded his father, Paul, and Princess Anne Marie of Denmark.

TUESDAY, 15 SEPTEMBER. ATHENS   I first paid a personal call on General Pipilis† alone and discussed with him the NATO strategy. We

---

* Representing the Leader of the Opposition.
† Chief of the Hellenic National Defence General Staff.

had just got around to discussing Cyprus when the other three Chiefs of Staff of the Army, Navy and Air Force were announced. What had been intended as a purely courtesy meeting, which should have finished at 0900, continued for a total of half an hour and I am glad to say I was able to shift them from their previous view of the military situation in Cyprus to share, or appear to share, my own military appreciation.

At 0915, Pipilis accompanied me to call on the Minister of National Defence, Mr Garoufalias. He had such little English that I decided to conduct our discussion in French. With the agreement of General Pipilis, I gave the Minister a complete account of the previous half-hour's discussion with the Chiefs of Staff. General Pipilis confirmed the accuracy of my report. The Minister was candidly rather horrified, for he said that this was not at all the view that he had formed of the military situation, and he was surprised to hear that his Chiefs of Staff had changed their position and now agreed with my appreciation.

The Minister seemed to be under the impression that the Turkish Air Force could be discounted because of the little damage they had inflicted in their demonstration attack at Mansourah last month. I pointed out that Cyprus was only 40 miles from Turkey and 500 miles from Greece, and that if the full weight of the Turkish Air Force could be brought to bear to support any Turkish invasion in Cyprus, even if the Greeks had 10,000 men in this island as we had been led to believe, they could not possibly stop an invasion supported by so many aircraft, without any supporting aircraft of their own.

It took a surprisingly long while to get this Minister to understand the true situation. Finally, he did understand that the military situation was much more dangerous than he thought, particularly as I warned him the US 6th Fleet would not intervene. We then went on to discuss Makarios, and I told him exactly what I thought of him and found that he thought exactly the same as me.* This I found most encouraging.

*   *   *

Tino and Anne Marie took Gustaf and me round the presents, and I was much touched to find that the silver gilt box which my son-in-law, David [Hicks], had designed, was put in one of the real positions of honour, in what was a very crowded display. It was much admired by Tino, Anne Marie, Gustaf and others who saw it.

---

* Mountbatten's views of Archbishop Makarios evolved, but at this stage he probably considered him a dangerous and self-seeking demagogue.

There was only a short time for us to have a talk together before he had to go off to meet Philip. Long before we had finished talking, an ADC came in and said that Philip's aeroplane was going to land ten minutes early. Tino got very excited, but I told him that he could count on the fact that Philip would never dream of landing early. He took my word for it and continued the conversation. I was absolutely fascinated by all he had to tell me, and deeply impressed by his grip of the situation. However, he hadn't quite finished what he had to say and asked me if I could come back again.

He has so many Kings and Queens coming to his wedding that he seems to have spent his entire time dashing backwards and forwards to the airfield. They are from Denmark, Belgium, Sweden, Jordan, Norway, Netherlands and Thailand. This is not to mention the ex-Kings or Queens of Egypt, Württemberg, Rumania, Italy and Bulgaria. Nor does it include the minor Heads of States, such as Monaco and Liechtenstein.

At dinner at the Royal Yacht Club:

Tino told me that he had arranged a nice surprise for me, for Grace and Rainier were due to arrive rather later that evening, and he would then let Grace sit between Gustaf and me. This seemed an admirable idea.

Meanwhile Charles came to ask me whether I knew Grace and, on hearing I did, said he particularly wanted to meet her and I promised to fix it.

When Grace eventually did arrive, she sat between Gustaf and me and I never had a look in for the first twenty minutes, for they never drew breath talking to each other! Then I had a dance with Grace and finally brought Charles over to sit next to her. They got on like a house on fire, but every time I suggested, in a whisper, that he should ask her to dance he was too shy to do so, and he wouldn't let me help him either. So finally he went away without having asked her.

Tino left Anne Marie sitting next to me for a bit, so I had a dance with the bride, much to my delighted surprise. She is beautiful, sweet and marvellously self-possessed for an eighteen-year-old.* Queen Sirikit was also at our table and so I had a couple of dances with her. Then King Bhumibol came over and I laid the foundation of my visit to Bangkok next February.

There are 180 people in the printed list of Royal Guests, but I think

* Indeed, she had only become eighteen the week before.

there are not quite this number, for several of us appear twice. For instance, I appear under B for Burma and M for Mountbatten! Practically all my nieces and great-nieces and young cousins appear to have turned up. Altogether it was a wonderful evening of happy reunions, and dancing to a wonderful band on a moonlit, warm night, overlooking the Mediterranean. Charles could not get over the magic of it all, and was absolutely thrilled; he explained that he hadn't really travelled much before!

WEDNESDAY, 16 SEPTEMBER   In the evening Tino gave a fabulous party in the gardens of the Palace. There must have been nearly 2000 guests from all over the world. All who had uniforms wore white full dress, but Philip and I decided to wear white ball dress.

I opened the Ball with Anne, who dances very well. I had my first dance with Benedicta of Denmark, one of the only two really professional high school riders in the family, a real beauty and charming. After dancing with Grace I took her to supper and sat next to Alice* on whose other side was Philip.

I met Lemnitzer (SACEUR) and he introduced me to Lynda Johnson, the daughter of the American President, whom she is representing at the Wedding. I had a couple of dances with her, and found her nice and interesting. King Hussein introduced me to his wife, the English Major's daughter now known as Princess Muna.

I had a long and interesting talk with the Leader of the Opposition, Kanellopoulos, whom I knew well when he was Minister of Defence in the old AFMED days. He is quite sound about Cyprus. Makarios was standing in such a position as I walked past that I could not avoid shaking hands with him as he recognized me, but I certainly did not give him any smile!

FRIDAY, 18 SEPTEMBER   The Cathedral was even more sumptuously arranged than for Sophie's wedding, and, of course, there were many more Kings and Queens and important members of the family.

Freddy† carried out the part which would normally have been carried out by Palo, namely the changing over of the rings and the holding of the

---

* Princess Alice of Greece, Mountbatten's sister, and mother of the Duke of Edinburgh.
† Queen Frederica, whose husband King Paul (Palo) had died six months earlier.

Crowns above the heads of the young couple, and changing them over from one head to the other three times. To do this, she had to stand on a specially prepared little footstool as the couple were so tall.

At the end of the ceremony there came a moving moment when Freddy, as the Queen Mother, curtseyed to her son as the King and to her daughter-in-law, as the new Queen. I must say everybody could not help feeling terribly sorry for poor Freddy, for we know what Palo meant to her and the pleasure of her son's wedding must have been mixed with some agonizing memories. However, she was in very good form and with her wonderful sense of humour told me that she had been rather difficult at times with her children, but that my god-daughter Irene had kept her in order with the threat, 'If you don't behave yourself, Mamma, we won't bury you next to Papa!'

In October 1964 Mountbatten visited West Africa,
arriving in Sierra Leone on 5 October.

The arrival was very dramatic in a tropical West African setting, the haze in the background and the rich vegetation all round us. The Guard of Honour of the First Battalion of the Royal Sierra Leone Regiment was mounted with their colourful scarlet waistcoats and tarbushes and band in full dress. They also paraded their Colours. The band played a tune which I was told was supposed to be 'Rule Britannia', but it was difficult to recognize. Half a dozen sergeants of the Regiment, wearing the Burma Star, who had served under me in the 81st and 82nd West African Divisions on the Arakan Front in Burma, were paraded separately.

WEDNESDAY, 7 OCTOBER. FREETOWN   I went to the Sierra Leone television station, where I had very reluctantly agreed to do a television interview. When I heard there were only 300 TV sets in the whole of Sierra Leone, and that they would undertake not to export the film which they made, I could see no harm in agreeing.

A nice Negro asked me a lot of fairly sensible questions, and I suppose we talked together for about a quarter of an hour. During this time the cine-camera which was recording the scene stopped twice. I could hear the sound stop for two quite long periods. I looked at my interviewer, but he did not stop. On the contrary, he went on with his questions while the camera didn't appear to be running.

Afterwards I discovered I was quite right and that, when the camera had stopped, it was because the operator was changing the film and, in fact, they had no film of two parts of the interview. This did not disconcert the interviewer at all, who said, 'We will dub it.' I asked him, 'With what?' He then seemed to realize for the first time that large bits of the interview were missing on film, although recorded on tape, so I suggested he could put on maps, or possibly background pictures, of what we were talking about and he thought this was a brainwave and would probably save the interview. What charming and naive people they are!

THURSDAY, 8 OCTOBER. MONROVIA We saw a fascinating and rather horrifying display given by an old man with half a dozen boys whom he had trained as acrobats. He ended up by producing a very sharp dagger and he let my ADC try the blade and the point which were razor sharp. He then made one of the boys run at him, and as he ran he cut with a knife within an inch of the boy's chest. Each time the boy only missed being cut in half by what appeared a miracle.

He then took the boy and threw him into the air and put the point of the dagger against his stomach, and managed to bring his hand down at the same speed as the boy was falling so that the point didn't penetrate. He did this three or four times, to the frenzied applause of the crowd. It appears that he and his boys believe they have supernatural powers which prevents them from suffering mortal injury!

When we got back to Executive Mansion Mrs Tubman, the President's wife, was waiting to show us round the house as she had promised. We began by seeing the President's study, the offices of his secretaries and then the Cabinet Room. There were two very large waiting rooms each with about 60 chairs in it. His young assistant secretary explained that most of the chairs were occupied by people waiting to see the President. When I asked her how long people waited to see the President, she said, 'Oh, a week or two, sometimes a month or two.'

After a short visit to Liberia, the party moved on to Ghana.

FRIDAY, 9 OCTOBER. ACCRA I drove in a Rolls-Royce straight to Aburi, which we reached about 1740. This is the new personal house of the President of Ghana, Dr Kwame Nkrumah. He has invited me several times to come and stay as his guest. He is a very remarkable man who is now almost deified, and is known as '*Osagyefo*', which, being translated means 'The Redeemer or Saviour'.

I had a charming telegram from him saying that he regretted that the Conference of Non-Aligned States in Cairo had gone on longer than he had expected, and that he had been unable to get back in time to receive me, but would come back just as soon as the Conference broke up, and before I left Ghana.

When Griffiths* was Colonial Secretary he arranged to send young Nkrumah to see me two or three times at 2 Wilton Crescent, with the then Governor, Arden Clarke. I was invited to give him a series of lessons on how to organize the government of a newly independent country and we got on very well together. He got on particularly well with Edwina, who visited him and got to know him well.

We are the first guests he has ever put up at his new house, Peduase Lodge, at Aburi on a ridge of hills 1000 ft high, where the air is crisp and glorious.

It is a very dashing modern house, designed by a young Ghanaian architect, with electrically operated security gates. A smart Quarter guard in scarlet turned out on our arrival. There was still enough light for us to do a complete tour of the entire house and grounds with its vast covered swimming pool. On the floor immediately above us is Nkrumah's private suite which is locked up as he is away and rarely stays there.

MONDAY, 12 OCTOBER We drove from the Naval Base in Takoradi straight on to Sekondi which is a neighbouring town. Here we went to the Regional Commissioner's house for lunch. He met us together with the Paramount Chief of the region.

We arrived at the house at 1230, but we could not persuade him to sit down to lunch before 1320. I sat between the Regional Commissioner and the Paramount Chief who had informed me that he was the President of the Chiefs' Chamber, which has 21 Paramount Chiefs and altogether 400 tributary chiefs under them. He, himself, has 60 tributary chiefs directly under him, Nana Kofi Adianka III.

He asked how the chiefs were organized in England and when I explained to him about the House of Lords, he asked who my mouthpiece was!

* James Griffiths was Colonial Secretary in Attlee's Government of 1951–2.

I then asked him how it was that he was able to speak to me other than through his mouthpiece. He said that this was an informal occasion when they dropped protocol, but on the formal occasion he could only speak through his mouthpiece. I asked how the mouthpiece could possibly know what to say, and received the reply that the mouthpiece knew what was good for the Chief to which I retorted, 'And what is good for the mouthpiece too, I suppose'!

TUESDAY, 13 OCTOBER We were conducted into the presence; a smile lit up Nkrumah's face and he embraced me very warmly, saying, 'My dear, dear friend.' After some exchange of courtesies, he suggested to the others that they might go along to the breakfast room and meet his wife. After they had gone, he said, 'Now we are quite alone and can really talk.'

There followed an absolutely fascinating conversation. All the points that I wanted his approval on for the reorganization of his Ministry of Defence and for the Navy he approved immediately.

He then gave me an account of the Cairo Conference of Non-Aligned States, and again reiterated how heartbroken he had been that this Conference was called after he agreed the dates of my visit, and he assured me that the Conference was so difficult and the part he had to play so important that he couldn't afford to come away.

At about 0915, I suggested that we had better join the others, because I had to get to the airport and leave by 1000. Dr Nkrumah then informed me that he was going to accompany me to the airfield to see me off. I remonstrated that it was somewhat irregular for the Head of State to see off anybody who wasn't a Head of State. He replied that he knew this and he wished to demonstrate his affection and regard in this way.

WEDNESDAY, 14 OCTOBER. LAGOS At 0950 the High Commissioner* collected me and we drove to the Prime Minister's Residence for my official call. Sir Abubakar Tafawa Balewa met me outside his office and conducted me to the Cabinet Room. We talked for well over an hour about every subject under the sun, and I managed to introduce the question of what would happen to the Nigerian Navy if they lost all

* Sir Francis Cumming-Bruce.

their contract-officers as was at present proposed. The Prime Minister immediately assured me that this was very far from the Government's intention, and said it was up to the Commodore to report what contract-officers he wished to retain.

Although this appeared to be a tremendous victory, the High Commissioner warned me that the Minister of Defence, Ribadu,* was anti all foreigners, and had made a declaration that he would have no more white faces in the Nigerian services after the end of the year. Unfortunately Ribadu appears to be in a stronger position than the Prime Minister, and it would be difficult for the Prime Minister to over-rule him. However, as Ribadu had purposely absented himself during my visit, there is a chance that if quick action is taken it may be too late for Ribadu to reverse it when he comes back.

I must say that Abubakar is one of my favourite Prime Ministers. I always find that he is full of common sense and most robust, and indeed he lived up to my idea of him during our long and interesting conversation.

We drove down to the great native markets, to see if I could buy a chameleon. My first request produced some colossal edible snails. Next they produced a dried-up body of a chameleon which is used for making medicine. Finally, they brought a small wire rat cage in which there were two live chameleons. One was the biggest I have ever seen and rather unattractive; the other was one of the smallest and looked rather sweet, so I bought the small one and christened it Abubakar. My Nigerian ADC was quite horrified when they asked ten shillings for the chameleon. He said it was only worth one shilling, and got into a violent altercation with the stall-keeper. It was only with difficulty that I persuaded him that I could afford ten shillings and preferred to pay that than to be the centre of an ever-increasing excited mob.

When I tried to take a photograph of the snails, their owner, a woman, dashed forward to try and prevent me and altogether my taking films in the market was very unpopular because apparently people are apt to think that a camera casts a bad spell on the people or objects photographed.

THURSDAY, 15 OCTOBER   I had an extremely valuable private conversation with the Prime Minister, in which I discussed once more the

* Alhaji Ribadu died the following year.

points I made to him about contract-officers the day before. I also discussed the candidates to become the first Nigerian General of their Army, and he discussed the prospect of a Labour win in the UK.

Abubakar was most robust and said, 'I'm sure the Conservatives will win. In any case I could never work with the Labour Government.' He then told me that the behaviour of the Labour Party over the Chief Enaharo case* was something that no Nigerian could ever forgive. The British had given Nigeria their judicial system and yet the very first time the British had an opportunity of interfering with the course of justice in Nigeria, the Labour Party had done so. Thanks, however, to the Conservative Party's feelings about the Commonwealth, Chief Enaharo had been returned, he had not been hanged, he had been given a fair trial, and had been given a ten-year sentence, which was the minimum possible for his crime.

I pointed out that I did not think Mr Wilson himself had said anything derogatory about the Nigerian Government, and I was certain that he was friendlily disposed towards the Commonwealth in general, and, of course, Nigeria. However, I could not persuade Abubakar that Wilson was not behind the move, or at least had failed to condemn it. I tried to pour as much oil on these troubled waters as I could, but I think that Labour will have a hard time with the Nigerians if they win.†

On 2 December 1964 Mountbatten visited Brussels for discussions with the Belgian Ministry of Defence.

We went to Laeken, which is the Royal Palace on the outskirts of Brussels with a large beautiful park. Baudouin and his beautiful young Queen Fabiola came out of the side door and down to the bottom of the steps to greet me as I got out of the car. Considering it was dark and very cold, and damp, I thought this was exceptionally courteous of them.

They then conducted me into a set of rooms of such magnificence that I assumed it was their own rooms, but Fabiola said, 'I hope you will be comfortable in this suite, may I show you round?', and took me through a private dining room, a large dressing room, a bathroom to an

---

* Enaharo had fought a long legal battle to escape extradition from the UK on charges of trying to overthrow the Nigerian Government by force. The Nigerians resented criticism of their judicial system freely voiced by the British at the time.
† Labour won, with an overall majority of only four, and did indeed have a troublesome relationship with Nigeria.

immense bedroom through to another bathroom and a wardrobe room, which was to be my suite. We three had tea together in my sitting room and a very pleasant long gossip.

I was disappointed to hear from Baudouin that the dinner party he had arranged for the following night was to be all male, so that they could talk NATO business. I had so much wanted to see his beautiful sister-in-law, Paola, that I asked if there was any chance of seeing his brother, Albert. He immediately rang him up and arranged for me to go round and have tea with him tomorrow.

After dinner [at the British Embassy] the ladies left the room and the Prime Minister, M. Lefevre, came and sat next to me. He immediately asked me what I thought of the Mixed Manned Multi-Lateral Force (MLF) and, as I had been warned by Harold Caccia to be careful not to get involved in political questions, I answered only from a military point of view. I told him I considered it the greatest piece of military nonsense I had come across in fifty years, and this seemed to satisfy the Prime Minister.

THURSDAY, 3 DECEMBER. BRUSSELS   Baudouin came to fetch me at 2000 in my rooms and led me down the stairs to the large side entrance where a car was waiting to drive us over to the main entrance. As it only seemed to be a matter of a hundred yards or so, I suggested we should walk. He agreed, but regretted it because it was snowing and we arrived pretty wet.

The Dinner, as he had warned me, was an all-male party and he explained while we were waiting in one of the large drawing rooms that he had done this on purpose so that we could have a good discussion on NATO strategy and the MLF. He even said that he had not invited the British Ambassador, so that I could talk more freely! He had invited the Foreign Minister, M. Spaak,* the Belgian Minister at NATO, the Minister of Defence, the Chief of his Cabinet, and some of the Chiefs of Staff, etc.

Presently, the guests were admitted and he introduced them all to me in turn. Then we went into the State Dining Room, where a very formal dinner was served on silver plate with the servants wearing the full scarlet and gold state liveries.

* Paul Henri Spaak, former Prime Minister and Secretary-General of NATO.

After dinner we all sat round in a circle and had a discussion which lasted for over two hours which was conducted alternately in French and English. It was extremely interesting and very valuable for me. Gradually, everybody seemed to come round to share my point of view and Baudouin said afterwards that he was very pleased with the result.

In December 1964 Mountbatten accompanied the Prime Minister to Washington for meetings with President Johnson. At 1120 on 6 December he reached London Airport.

Besides the Prime Minister, Harold Wilson, we had the Foreign Secretary, Patrick Gordon-Walker, the Secretary of State for Defence, Denis Healey, and all the senior Civil Servants concerned. I sat next to Solly,* which was pleasant. He and I dined at the Prime Minister's table.

MONDAY, 7 DECEMBER. WASHINGTON   At 1100 we all set off in a large motorcade for the White House. Although this was a most formal visit by the British Prime Minister, there was no crowd of any sort outside, though of course there was a large party in the grounds. There were no less than five Guards of Honour, Army, Marines, Navy, Air Force and Coast Guards.

I hung about a bit, but it was made clear that the President wished to see the three Ministers and the Ambassador alone, with just a note-taker on each side; in our case Burke Trend.†

At 1330 there was a large official luncheon party at the Embassy. I sat between the new Vice-President Elect of the United States, Senator Humphrey, and my opposite number, Bus Wheeler.‡ It was a lively and amusing lunch and I got on like a house on fire with the new Vice-President.

After lunch I had a discussion with the Defence Secretary, Bob McNamara, and Bus Wheeler as to whether there should be military attendance at the meetings. Bob thought it was better if we remained available on call, so as to leave the meeting to decide matters on political

---

* Sir Solly, later Baron Zuckerman, Chief Scientific Adviser to the Minister of Defence and later to the Prime Minister. Mountbatten's closest confidant and ideas man.
† Secretary of the Cabinet.
‡ General Earle Wheeler was Chairman of the Joint Chiefs of Staff.

grounds. I accordingly suggested to my own Secretary of State, Denis Healey, that it would be better if I did not attend the meetings unless Bus Wheeler was called in by telephone. Although he said that everything had been arranged for me to go in, he thought it was probably wise to keep out.

I gave him a last-minute briefing on the military points I thought of importance in connection with this idiotic, multi-lateral force of 25 mixed-manned surface ships with 8 POLARIS missiles each.

I might add, in passing, that I have been the arch enemy of this piece of military nonsense from the moment I first heard of it, and have been most outspoken. The chief protagonist, George Ball,* whom I had never met, was introduced to me after luncheon, and referred to my well-known position on the matter!

TUESDAY, 8 DECEMBER Just before dinner, the meetings broke up and Denis Healey gave me an excellent de-briefing of what had occurred, all of which was really very encouraging. The main thing is that it is clear that Wilson and Johnson have hit it off.

* Under-Secretary of State.

1965

1965 was a year of much travel for Mountbatten. In July he ceased to be Chief of Defence Staff and therefore engaged in prolonged journeys of farewell to all parts of the world. Before the date of his retirement had been reached, however, he was conscripted to serve as Chairman of a special Commission to investigate immigration from the Commonwealth, a task which also involved extensive travelling.

MONDAY, 8 FEBRUARY. BROADLANDS I left at 0550 and we reached London Airport at 0730. Our party took off in a Royal Air Force VIP Comet IV for our round-the-world tour. The party [includes] Patricia, Solly Zuckerman, Ronnie and Marjorie Brockman. We have 128 pieces of luggage in all.

FRIDAY, 12 FEBRUARY. SINGAPORE We drove to the City Hall where I was met by Antony Head,* who had been having preliminary discussions with the Prime Minister, Lee Kuan Yew.

After the usual photographs and general talk I asked him if we could go into his office, and Antony and I had a good long discussion with him.

I only know Lee slightly but I have always been deeply impressed by his extreme intelligence, shrewdness, and, I suspect, slyness. He lived up to his reputation.

He conducted me to the main hall itself, where I actually received the Japanese surrender twenty years ago, and had laid out on the table 'flashback' photographs of the event.

* Antony Head, a former Minister of Defence, was currently High Commissioner to the new and brief-lived Federation of Malaysia and Singapore.

The tablet commemorating the surrender which I had given Lee after my last visit was mounted so high up that I asked them either to provide binoculars to read it or have it put lower down. He agreed to have it moved lower down.

We then went out on to the main steps overlooking the Padang from which I read my Order of the Day following the surrender to the assembled Allied forces and vast crowds of citizens.

Lee told the reporters that as a young man of twenty he stood in the crowd and admired the showmanship with which the surrender had been arranged. He ended: 'If it had not been for Lord Mountbatten we should have no freedom today and I certainly would not be Prime Minister.' Not a bad statement from a man who had been suspected of being a rabid Communist!

SATURDAY, 13 FEBRUARY At 2100 the whole of our party went to the fantastic home of Run Me Shaw, the brother of Run Run Shaw of Hong Kong. The story goes that the elder brother used to hang about for messages, saying 'Run run?', and when he had been sent on a message the younger brother would say 'Run me?' At all events they are both multi-millionaire magnates now.

The house is set in an elaborate garden with a large swimming pool, fountains, etc., with continually changing lighting systems. We were shown into an immense private cinema and then with evident pride he said to Patricia, Solly and me, 'Now I will show you my wonderful pink Toyland.'

Solly and I expected to see a display of toys, but in fact it was the most luxurious ladies' loo imaginable with two pink WCs at the far end, indeed a pink toilet.

SUNDAY, 14 FEBRUARY. SARAWAK At 2100 HE* gave a large buffet dinner. I sat next to his wife who smiled charmingly and intelligently at all my conversation until I asked her a simple question, and it was only after I repeated it two or three times that I realized that she had not understood a word of what I had been saying.

The Governor himself had been a fairly lowly employee of the Brooke family formerly. He was very friendly and in fact stood up at the end of

* The Governor of Sarawak was Tun Abang Haji Openg.

dinner and made a charming speech in not very clear English about a charming little lady who had been sitting so quietly by his side and who had come to Kuching to celebrate her birthday. He then proposed the health of 'Lady Patricia Bahbone'. The Deputy Chief Minister, a young Chinese, started singing 'Happy Birthday to you' and I did my best to support him.

THURSDAY, 18 FEBRUARY. BANGKOK   For dinner with the King and Queen that night we were sent *Chao Ban* costume, the traditional Thai peasants' dress. The Queen sent a lady to dress Patricia and the King sent a gentleman to dress me, a complicated procedure, because my 'trousers' consisted of a vast length of silk which had to be folded in many pleats and then passed up through the legs and fastened at the waist with my sword belt, which was then covered by a silk sash.

Patricia looked enchanting in a green blouse, a grey skirt with a pretty pattern and a yellow scarf.

No costume arrived for Solly but I hear there was subsequently a considerable row among the Palace chamberlains at this omission.

We drove off to the *Ruan Ron*, a new wooden pavilion in the Amphorn Palace grounds, fifty yards from our old home, constructed at the side of the ornamental lake on the lines of the very old Thai formal houses.

The King and Queen met us at the entrance. Luckily I knew them well, for they too were disguised in Thai peasants' costume. They led us into the pavilion where the whole of the Thai Royal Family were assembled. I recognized many of them though I couldn't put a name to them; anyway, they recognized me and gathered round with many reminiscences. The Princess Mother, who was away in 1961, was there and just as sweet as ever.

The Royal Family kept themselves to themselves and I was not introduced to any of the other VIP guests, not even Seni Pramoj, who I was told afterwards was there, and had been Prime Minister in 1946.

We were led out of the wooden house to a small wooden open pavilion built over the lake. From here one boat served the drinks and another boat with a charcoal fire produced the delicious Chinese food.

Only six of us were admitted to this little Royal Pavilion and we sat on three adjacent couches; at one end the senior prince, then Queen Sirikit, I next to her on the next couch, which I shared with King Bhumibol and on the next couch should have been Patricia first and then the Princess

Mother, but because the Princess Mother wished to control the food boat they changed places.

The servants as usual served all the food grovelling on all fours, but it was quite clear they were not treated as the slaves of old for they were patted and spoken to kindly by the Royal Family.

The illumination of the gardens was fantastically beautiful and to cap it all the full moon rose over the water.

There was some really lovely classical Thai dancing in the garden followed by such vicious displays of swordsmanship that one young man was dripping with blood before they finished.

Then came fireworks on the water followed by general dancing by all the guests.

The King told me how sorry he was that the Prime Minister had made an issue of treating me as a Government guest on the grounds that the Thai Armed Forces could not allow the Chief of the British Defence Staff to be treated in any other way. The King said, rather sadly, 'If you had remained my guest you would have lived quietly with me and been spared the guards of honour, official banquets and all the other things that the Field Marshal intends you to have.'

MONDAY, 22 FEBRUARY. HONG KONG   I spent the morning with the three services. I first went at 0900 to the excellent new Naval Base, HMS *Tamar*, which I had seen under construction in 1961 and which is now complete.

It is the most modern and I believe the finest Naval Base we have, and I had a good look at it. The Commodore told me that 138,000 British and 420,000 American Libertymen landed from warships during 1964. He told me that he had entertained 86 different American Admirals in his house and with repeat visits the numbers were well up in three figures.

I then went in the Admiral's barge to RAF Kai Tak and spent from 1015 to 1100 looking at the RAF Station. They only have 4 Hunters (of 28 Squadron) and 4 Austers (of the Army Air Corps) so the overheads are very expensive.

At 1100 Rory O'Connor* fetched me and we drove up the centre road to the north of the New Territories through Kowloon. I have never seen such fabulous development as is going on here. Mountain tops are

* Lieutenant General Sir Denis O'Connor, Commander, British Forces.

being pushed into the sea and skyscrapers are being built on the reclaimed land and on the flattened hills. The average number of new apartments or homes being built in this one small colony is 400 a day.

THURSDAY, 25 FEBRUARY. PORT MORESBY, NEW GUINEA I told them how disappointed I had been when on the Prince of Wales's staff in 1920 our visit to Port Moresby had been cancelled on account of quarantine.

I mentioned that from 15 August 1945 until I turned over New Guinea to the Civil Administration, it had been under my Supreme Command, and I also mentioned that Edwina had bought Ticket No. 1 to fly as the first passenger from Australia to England, and that I was proud to be passenger No. 1 to alight at Mount Hagen airport and to declare the aerodrome open.

This was then translated into Pidgin English for the crowd, after which we went round the fabulously decorated warriors.

The Chiefs or head men were all assembled in one long line with fantastic Bird of Paradise plumes in their head-dresses and faces painted in every imaginable colour, except red, which was reserved for the women.

In their noses they had long feathers or quills, or mother-of-pearl discs. One man had a small china saucer attached to his nose with the factory mark clearly visible.

A couple of men were trying to smoke cigarettes out of the extreme corners of their mouths, to keep clear of the discs and quills.

From the back of their waists hung branches of green palm leaves by way of a sort of tail. They carried long spears or bows and arrows and battleaxes with green stone blades. Occasionally one saw a steel axe marked 'Made in Sweden'.

Many of them came from more than 100 miles away and had to start walking three or four days ago to get here.

I was told that a 'Sing Sing' of this nature was dying out, and that in five or six years they would all be wearing shirts and trousers and would disdain their centuries old dress, which is rather sad.

FRIDAY, 26 FEBRUARY At 2115 we drove out of town, south along the Kuta road for a couple of miles until we reached a long house which had been specially erected for the occasion. Here our host, Chief Wamp, received us.

We then entered and I don't think any of us will ever forget the sight we saw. This was the famous native courting ceremony, only rarely held nowadays, none having been seen in the district for six years. The Roman Catholic Bishop was furious that the DC arranged this as he has been trying to stamp it out.

Sitting in long lines, as far as the eye could see through the smoke, were pairs of natives, highly decorated. The men's faces were basically painted in black and yellow patterns and the young girls in bright red. To the beat of the long tom-toms the rhythmic movements were going on frenziedly.

Each couple squatted on the floor and sat up erect, placing their noses and foreheads together and doing a rapid rock backwards and forwards three times. They then plunged their heads down to almost floor level and rocked again three times, and then came up erect together and repeated the performance. Their faces remained firmly pressed together and they moved as one.

Their feather head-dresses had a cooling, fanning action on our feet.

I was afraid Patricia would get her dress burnt, for the old women sat in the middle keeping torches alight and acting as chaperons.

The performing girls were all unmarried and quite young. The men were either bachelors or married men seeking their second, third or subsequent bride.

After doing the whole tour we staggered out blinded and coughing, but very excited.

TUESDAY, 2 MARCH. CANBERRA   At 1630 I arrived at Parliament House to attend a press conference. There was TV, radio and about fifty correspondents including national papers from Sydney and Melbourne. I made a prepared statement and spent half an hour avoiding answering very hot political questions.

I began by saying that I had written out a statement and sent it home from Hong Kong for Ministerial clearance and that this had now come and copies of my statement were handed round.

The Times correspondent, before he had touched his copy, stood up and said, 'Please say whether you have added anything to this handout since Hong Kong.' I replied, 'You have not seen the statement yet, how can it matter?' He came back with, 'Before I accept this statement I want to know whether it will include the results of your Defence talks in Canberra?' I finished with, 'It does not and so you don't need to accept the statement!' He sat down amidst laughter and this helped to get me off to a good start.

WEDNESDAY, 3 MARCH   At 0955 the Prime Minister and Dame Pattie Menzies arrived by air from Melbourne to come and see me off. In fact Bob Menzies, Bill Oliver* and I had a forty-minute tête-à-tête conversation which was the best value of any meeting I had in Canberra, for I was able to put over all the points to him which I put to his Cabinet and Chiefs of Staff, and found him in complete agreement.

In fact, over the proposal of sending a permanent representative from the Defence Intelligence Staff to sit with their JIC he said, 'This proposal has a ten yards start in a hundred yard race so far as I am concerned.'

FRIDAY, 5 MARCH. WELLINGTON   A disturbed and distressing night. At 0145, while I was still working on papers and speeches, MacLennan† came in to say that a local newspaper had rung up to say that Louise was suffering from a heart attack.‡

At 0730 a rather more reassuring message came from him, followed at 0900 by a telegram from Gustaf himself saying, 'Louise had sudden severe attack thrombosis of right leg early this morning. Immediate major operation necessary and has been successfully carried out and was well stood but condition serious for the next few days.'

I replied, 'Patricia and I deeply distressed to hear about Louise's illness and operation. We are in New Zealand half way through world tour but will of course cancel this and fly back if she would like this. Please give her our most heartfelt and affectionate love and say we are thinking of her and you continuously. Naval Attaché can arrange to pass immediate messages to me.'

I went at 0925 to call on my old friend, Mr Dean Eyre, the Minister of Defence, in Parliament House. He told me he had carried out all the things I had suggested to him in 1961: the creation of a CDS, the creation of a Secretary of Defence, the creation of a small inter-service

---

* Lieutenant General Sir William Oliver, UK High Commissioner.
† Sir Ian MacLennan, UK High Commissioner.
‡ Mountbatten's sister, Queen Louise of Sweden.

Defence Staff, etc., and was keen to have my next proposals. We discussed them and he asked me to repeat what I had said to him during the subsequent two meetings that were to follow this morning.

I went with Eyre and the High Commissioner to call on the Prime Minister* and the Defence Committee of the Cabinet. We had the best part of an hour's vigorous discussion, at the end of which I felt I had really interested the New Zealand Government in a full and proper reorganization of their Defence.

At 1300 a luncheon was given by the Prime Minister in the Members' Dining Room of Parliament House, to about 100 Ministers, Members of Parliament, Ambassadors, High Commissioners and Service Chiefs.

In my speech I quoted attending identical lunches with Mr Peter Fraser and his Deputy, Walter Nash, in 1946; with Sid Holland in 1956 and with Kiwi Holyoake in 1961. I gave an account of the New Zealand Brigade attacking Malerne Airfield after *Kelly* and *Kashmir* had given them covering bombardment, and incidentally given their lives in their cause. I went through the complete Maori *Haka* I had learnt in 1920, and I feel it was a notable occasion. Certainly the only survivor among my earlier hosts, Walter Nash, wrung me emotionally by the hand after it was over.

SUNDAY, 7 MARCH. OTEHEI BAY, NEW ZEALAND   At 0300 Ingrid† came through on the telephone loud and clear with the disturbing news that Louise had had to have a tube put in her throat to relieve her breathing and was still very weak. No one was allowed to see her.

Gustaf had been put to bed with a temperature but he wished me to know that it was pointless coming back, at all events for the present, as there was no chance of my being able to see her unless she took a decided turn for the better. Ingrid said, 'We have not given up hope by any means.'

At 2100 Ingrid rang up again from Stockholm with the devastating news that Louise's recovery, about which they had been hopeful, had had a severe set-back. In fact she prepared me for the worst by saying that she was now in a coma and the doctors did not think she would ever come out of it again. She said that she had asked the doctors to give her love from Patricia and me when they saw her, and she thought they had been successful in getting her to understand this.

We went to bed very gloomy.

* K. J. Holyoake, Prime Minister 1960–72.
† The Queen of Denmark, King Gustaf's daughter by an earlier marriage.

MONDAY, 8 MARCH At 0030 Peter* woke me up with a 'Flash' report from the news-agency to say that darling Louise had died.

At 0300 Stockholm came through again, this time remarkably clear, and Ingrid broke the news to me afresh with a lot of sad but interesting details.

Gustaf then came on the line personally and told me that for some weeks now he had a feeling that she was sinking, and that her strength would not be sufficient to withstand a further attack.

We commiserated with each other, for I must have been nearly as fond of her as he was. I told him that had she rallied sufficiently for me to speak to her, even for only five minutes, I would have flown home at once. I was quite ready to cancel the tour and fly home with Patricia for the funeral on Saturday.

He said that he and the Swedish people would very much welcome my presence, but on the other hand he and they would entirely understand our not coming back from the furthest point in the world in the middle of an official tour.

At this point he had difficulty in hearing and turned the telephone over to Bertil.† I asked him to try and obtain guidance from Gustaf and the others as to whether it would do if Pammy went and represented us, or whether they really thought we should come back.

After some consultation they finally agreed that Pammy should go and we should carry on with the tour, and I made arrangements accordingly.

SATURDAY, 13 MARCH. TAHITI I woke up feeling very sad for today was the day of Louise's funeral.

Patricia and I got hold of one of the police Jeeps and drove to a charming old Protestant Church just beyond Bali Hai. By an extraordinary coincidence it was painted in the Swedish colours, blue and yellow, and was deserted but open.

We went in alone together to pay our own private tribute to her on this day.

THURSDAY, 18 MARCH. LOS ANGELES We landed at 1650. We taxied to a private hangar where John, who had arrived a couple of

---

* Squadron-Leader Peter Lithgow, Mountbatten's ADC.
† Prince Bertil, third son of King Gustaf and uncle of the future King Carl Gustaf.

hours before from New York, was awaiting us, together with our host and hostess, Mr and Mrs Mike Frankovitch.*

The British Consul General and Mrs Dalton were also there and various members of the Columbia Company, which is Mike's company.

I told our Consul General that when I was met by his predecessor, in October 1941, on my arrival at Los Angeles from Pearl Harbor, he had handed me a telegram from the Prime Minister saying that he wanted me urgently for a completely different job. This spoilt my visit to Los Angeles and upset my plans, for it took me away from the command of the *Illustrious* and recalled me to Whitehall to take over Combined Operations.

Mr Dalton replied, 'I am afraid I have got exactly the same sort of telegram for you from the Prime Minister again.'

In fact, the telegram stated that the Prime Minister was sending his Principal Private Secretary, Derek Mitchell, on a direct flight over the Pole, arriving at Los Angeles the following afternoon, to discuss a very urgent matter with me.

As I am due back in England on Thursday morning, I simply cannot imagine what horror the Prime Minister has in store for me.

FRIDAY, 19 MARCH   We got back about 1810. Mitchell, the Principal Private Secretary to the Prime Minister, had arrived direct from London.

Patricia, John and I had been tremendously intrigued as to what the proposition could be. After all, I am due back in London on Thursday morning. It must be hard for the Prime Minister to be able to spare his 'Chief of Staff' for the three days needed to accomplish this mission.

We started wondering as to whether I was going to be sent off to Vietnam to investigate the situation for the British there, or whether I was to be sent off to see President Johnson to talk to him about the situation, or what it could possibly be.

In the event, it turned out to be an invitation to be the Chairman of a special Commission to investigate immigration in the Commonwealth. This will involve visits to places like India, Nigeria, Canada, the West Indies, Cyprus and Malta to get a preliminary report ready before the Prime Ministers' Conference in June.

However, a letter from Denis Healey indicated that, much as he

___
* President of Columbia Pictures.

Borneo, February 1965. With a forward company of the Argyll and Sutherland Highlanders.

Port Moresby, 26 February 1965. The famous 'courting ceremony'.

March 1965. Patricia Brabourne and Solly Zuckerman aboard the Comet.

Bangkok, 18 February 1965. In traditional peasants' dress for dinner at the Palace.

Canberra, 3 March 1965. Being seen off by Sir Robert Menzies.

would miss me, he felt this must have priority and he hoped I would be able to do it as well as remain Chief of the Defence Staff.

I told Mitchell I would think it over and let him have my answer in the morning.

Mike and Binnie [Frankovitch] had very kindly invited Shirley MacLaine to 'balance' me at the dinner. I drove her in my car to Jack Warner's dinner, at which only a few outsiders were present. After dinner we saw the new Columbia film *The Collector*, perhaps the gem of the psychological horror films; I only hope it will be a box office success. *

I drove Shirley back in my car – she certainly is a very sweet girl.

SATURDAY, 20 MARCH   At 0930 I had a meeting to work out how I could possibly fit in the extra visits to Commonwealth countries required by the new assignment, if I accepted it. When it appeared it could be done with some difficulty, I accepted to head the Commission enquiring into Commonwealth immigration, subject to obtaining the prior agreement of the Leader of the Opposition and the Leader of the Liberal party, and clearing up any difficulties with Pakistan.† Derek Mitchell dictated his telegram to the Prime Minister, it was typed and then he went off with it.

After that I went to 'Pickfair', the home of Mary Pickford,‡ now Mrs Buddy Rogers. She had fallen and broken two ribs and was unable to come to my dinner, and had written to ask if I could come and see her. This I was glad to do because I wanted to see the house again in which Edwina and I spent part of our honeymoon in 1922, and in which we attended a dinner party together in 1941.

It brought back poignant memories of very happy times and I was sad to see Mary Pickford, the one-time 'world's sweetheart' who must now be in her seventies, had become very plump and dumpy, but still very sweet.

We had two and a half hours in Disneyland from 1445 to 1715. Walt Disney was unfortunately away himself, but he sent his representative, an assistant, a hostess and a photographer, and we were taken around the various shows by-passing all the queues.

---

* A film based on John Fowles's novel, which was a resounding box-office as well as critical success.

† Mountbatten was *persona non grata* in Pakistan because of what they believed to be his pro-Indian policies as Viceroy and Governor-General.

‡ And previously of her husband, Douglas Fairbanks Senior.

The best show of all, undoubtedly, was a cruise down an African jungle river with the most realistic life-sized models of elephants squirting water on themselves, various forms of big game, lions, etc., and crocodiles, and, above all, hippos, which were unbelievably realistic and reminded Patricia and me very much of seeing them in Uganda.

Time was getting on so we cut out everything in Tomorrowland, except the trip in the wonderful new Monorail train which runs right throughout the whole of Disneyland. On our way back to the main entrance we did a trip in the ancient Santa Fe and Disney Railroad through a remarkable diorama of the Grand Canyon.

It is difficult to do justice to the imagination of Walt Disney in producing such a charming afternoon's entertainment for young and old alike; it could not have been a more fascinating afternoon and we all enjoyed it immensely.

We got back to the Frankovitchs' house just before 2300. They had asked back Cary Grant and his girl friend Dyan Cannon, as well as the original party.

Mike did some really brilliant conjuring tricks, and after that he tied up couples together to see if they could get free. Derek Mitchell and Claudia Cardinale were I think the funniest, and he resolutely refused to be untied before he had found the solution. John and Dyan got tied together and Patricia and Cary Grant were tied up, and I was tied up with Shirley MacLaine. Finally the party broke up into small groups of couples gossiping together until about 0140.

I must say Shirley is a very sweet and amusing girl and we got on like a house on fire.

In April 1965 Mountbatten began the round of travel relating to the Immigration Mission, combining the visits, so far as possible, with his farewells as Chief of Defence Staff.

WEDNESDAY, 21 APRIL. MALTA   At 1030 there was a Plenary Session at the Prime Minister's* official residence, Auberge d'Aragon, which started with the usual photography. There were 20 round the conference table, and it lasted until 1215. I explained the object of my Mission and the difficulties which faced HMG. The Maltese explained their position and I am sure this meeting was very valuable.

* Dr G. Borg Olivier.

Except for a visit with Edwina when I was First Sea Lord to the old Admiralty House about eight years ago, I have not spent more than two or three hours re-fuelling in Malta.

This time I have had time to poke my nose into all my old haunts in glorious weather and have found it all not only nostalgic, but painfully disturbing. I started my tour memories at 52 Strada Mezzodi (now South Street), which was my father's old house where we lived in 1901 and in 1907. From then on, I progressively visited all our old haunts tearing my heart strings more and more in the process of doing so.

TUESDAY, 27 APRIL. LONDON   At 0930 Dr Eric Williams, Prime Minister of Trinidad, called on me to discuss the Immigration problems of Trinidad. Within half an hour we had virtually reached a complete understanding of principles, but it was agreed that the officials of the Mission should visit Trinidad to fix up the details.

I said to Dr Williams, 'I presume you won't require me to come in person now that you and I have fixed up everything', but he said that the Governor-General, Sir Solomon Hochoy (whom I knew), and many others in Trinidad would be deeply disappointed if I did not come; and so I have now got to go and do an extra visit really for the sake of 'face' in Trinidad.

MONDAY, 3 MAY. DELHI   Although I had asked for a very informal arrival at Palam and had arrived after dark in plain clothes, there certainly was a remarkable gathering at the airport. Swaran Singh, the Minister of External Affairs and one of the most senior Ministers of the Cabinet, was at the head of the receiving line, and Indira, now Minister of Information, was also there. I was surprised not to see Nan, but received a pathetic letter from her to say that she was no longer sufficiently important to come out to the airfield and it would have upset Protocol had she come, and so I have asked her to dine with me tomorrow night.

TUESDAY, 4 MAY   At 1800 I invited the ten members of my Immigration Mission and my staff to have drinks in my sitting room. I then took them on a personally conducted tour of the big house. I was fascinated to see that not only are all portraits of our Kings and Queens still up, but they have now added a portrait of Queen Victoria which I have not seen before, and the State portraits of King George VI and Queen Elizabeth which were painted, of course, against the background of the interior of Viceroy's House.

WEDNESDAY, 5 MAY We had a Plenary Meeting on immigration with the External Affairs Minister, Sirdar Swaran Singh, which ended at 1040 when the officials remained behind to continue their deliberations. They are also to meet tomorrow.

Muchu Chaudhuri, the Chief of the Army Staff, called and I saw him with Ronnie. Ronnie had told me in London that Muchu hoped to be able to arrange for me to be made Colonel of his old regiment, the famous 61st Cavalry, during my visit; but he explained now that he was sure I would understand that this was not an auspicious moment to raise it with his own Government.

I had to admit it, because it has become only too clear to all of us since our arrival that the feeling towards the British has undergone a sharp and sad decline. This is, I think, largely attributable to the fact that the Pakistanis had unquestionably invaded Indian territory in the Rann of Kutch, which I turned over to India at the time of partition and as part of India.

Instead of the British immediately supporting India and denouncing Pakistan as aggressors, they feel we have failed them and this has deeply offended the Indians.

In any case, after seventeen years changes were bound to happen, particularly after Jawaharlal's death, but it is tricky that I should come out for my farewell visit at the precise moment when this misunderstanding has occurred.

The result is that the whole idea has had to be postponed to happier days, when Muchu promised that he will immediately raise it. However, if it ever comes off it will be a wonderful excuse to come to India again and a great thrill for me.

THURSDAY, 6 MAY At 1100 I went with Solly and Ronnie to call on the Minister of Defence, Chavan, and the three Chiefs of Staff. Although they had been individually most forthcoming when any of us three talked to them alone, I sensed at once that in Committee they were going to be appallingly difficult.

It required all my diplomacy to keep the conversation going to the full time allotted. At one stage when I said, 'Would you like to hear about our War in Borneo which I have just been looking at?', the reply was, 'No, we are too engrossed in our own War in the Rann of Kutch.' I then asked, 'Would you like to tell us about your War?', and got an abrupt, 'No'; this from Muchu who had given me a very full and frank account informally the night before!

In the past they have always wanted help over arms or aircraft, but now their line was that they would follow our example and buy the best equipment available regardless of whether it was made by the British!

After an hour of persistent blandishments I finally got them relaxed, and they started to smile and later laugh. So it broke up with good feeling and having achieved precisely nothing.

How sad the situation is since Jawaharlal's death. Our failure to state publicly that the boundaries I laid down on behalf of the British in 1947 showed quite clearly that Pakistan had invaded Indian territory, even though that territory in itself was largely swamp, has caused great sadness and umbrage. I shall have to see what I can do about it when I get back with Solly.

After lunch Indira drove me to the old Prime Minister's residence, which has been turned into a museum for Jawaharlal. I don't really know how she could have the courage to take me round, for I found it almost unbearably painful to see his bedroom as it was when Patricia and I sat talking to him during his illness, and to see his study where Edwina and I had so often gossiped with him, entirely unchanged with all his personal things still lying about. It was an uncanny and distressing experience and I was glad when I got to the end of the tour.

FRIDAY, 7 MAY   At 1045 the High Commissioner* came to pay his farewell call and at 1120 I went to pay my farewell call on the President.† It was fascinating because he was so candid about what was going on in India, and it is clear that he is the strong man who is holding the position with much difficulty.

The President ended by saying, 'Of course you must promise to come back and visit us all soon.' When I pointed out to him that this was my farewell visit, he laughed it off by saying that my next visit would be

---

* John Freeman, former Labour Minister and editor of the *New Statesman*.
† Dr Radhakrishnan.

much pleasanter for me because I could come in plain clothes and relax in his garden. 'Bring your two daughters,' he said, 'sit in the sun, spend a fortnight and refuse all engagements.' He then urged me to come in February 1966 or in October 1966 or at the very latest in February 1967, so I settled for February 1967 provisionally!

What a very emotional and disturbing visit this has been. The atmosphere has been almost as electric as during the communal disturbances of 1947. I was in charge then and could do something about it, but I felt such a helpless spectator this time, but in spite of feelings in the press, on the radio, in Parliament and in gatherings, the personal friendship shown to me was just as strong and affectionate as ever, which somehow made it all the worse.

I hope that better times may prevail and we shall be able to go back in 1967, perhaps to receive the Colonelcy of an Indian regiment; who knows, or some other distinction which the President hinted at.

THURSDAY, 13 MAY. LAGOS   At 0815 we held a full-scale briefing meeting between the whole of my Immigration Mission and the High Commissioner* and his staff in the Residency.

At 0930 the High Commissioner took me for a private interview with the Prime Minister, Sir Abubakar Tafawa Balewa. He received me with amazing warmth and friendship. We talked intimately about every sort of interesting problem.

When I told him I was going to retire on 16 July he said, 'You will never retire. You can't be allowed to retire, and I am sure you have no intention of retiring.'

I called on the new Chief of the General Staff (or GOC Nigerian Army as he is still called), Major General Aguiyi Ironsi. Though I do not admire his character, or ability, he is extremely cheerful and listened to all the advice I gave him with every appearance of being genuinely interested.†

I now took my own small party with me to the bazaar, which always fascinates me, to buy another chameleon. In fact, I found three very attractive ones and bought them all for 5/- apiece.

At 2015 we went to the Prime Minister's house for the official banquet. And it really was a banquet. There were over fifty people

---

* Sir Francis Cumming-Bruce.
† He was to head a military government after Abubakar was killed in a coup in January 1966, only to die himself in a counter-coup six months later.

present including all the Cabinet Ministers and senior officials on both sides.

I sat between the Prime Minister and the Minister for Trade * and we had a most interesting conversation.

The Minister for Trade was a very jovial man who spoke on the following lines, 'When I first heard that Lord Mountbatten was being sent travelling to a different Commonwealth country each week, I thought to myself, how can they treat an old man like this? Now I see you young and vigorous and I can't understand how you could have been Churchill's Principal Military Adviser during the war, or how you could have been Viceroy of India in 1947.'

Abubakar enquired after Pammy and sent her his best regards, and asked me why I hadn't brought her with me this time. He also enquired after the chameleon which he remembered I had bought. I told him it was very well and had been called after him. He said that was politically most unfortunate because he never changes his colours!

We got back fairly early after the Prime Minister's dinner, for he follows the Koran which says, 'After a feast disperse at once.' It's a pity this rule isn't observed at all dinner parties.

THURSDAY, 20 MAY. OTTAWA   At 1630 I went with the High Commissioner[†] to meet the Prime Minister, Mike Pearson. From 1630 to 1655 I put over four separate points I wished to discuss with him. Then we had ¼ hour top-level discussion on immigration which went very well.

The Prime Minister kept a Cabinet Meeting waiting for ¼ hour to complete our discussion. On the way out, the High Commissioner said, 'That was the most rapid machine-gun fire I have ever seen at a high-level conference. However, every bullet went home.'

FRIDAY, 21 MAY   At 0930 I had an hour's meeting with Paul Hellyer, the Canadian Minister of Defence. This was fascinating because he gave me his views on the reorganization of the Canadian Armed Forces, which he is carrying through. I told him he is going too far too fast, but, in principle, I admired very much what he was doing.

* Dr K. O. Mbadiwe.
† Sir Henry Lintott.

From 1030 to 1215 I met what would have been the Chiefs of Staff but now consisted of the CDS, VCDS and the Chiefs of 'Personnel', 'Logistics, Engineering and Development', 'Operational Readiness' and the 'Controller'. They gave me an excellent briefing on the far-reaching reorganization which they are carrying out and all seemed very enthusiastic.

I gave them a very brief description of how far we had gone, and, in answer to questions, admitted that after I had gone in July the forces of reaction would almost certainly be able to slow up any further advance.

MONDAY, 23 MAY. NEW YORK Lydia* has shown me a book called *The Mountbattens, the Last Royal Success Story* by Alden Hatch. I have never met him, and refused to authorize the book when he wrote or to give him any co-operation.

It is an immense glossy book, close on 500 pages, which luckily sells at over $9 (with tax) and is therefore unlikely to have a considerable sale. Hutchinsons had already asked whether I minded them publishing it in England, and when I said it was unauthorized they turned it down. I hope it never is.†

TUESDAY, 25 MAY. WASHINGTON At 0800 I spoke on the trans-Atlantic telephone to Godfrey Hobbs.‡ It appears that the *Sunday Express* are now going to serialize that wretched book *The Mountbattens, the Last Royal Success Story*, and I have asked Godfrey to let the editor know that I do not know Mr Hatch and do not approve of the book. Godfrey said he would gladly do so, but thought this would make the *Express* all the keener to publish it!

WEDNESDAY, 26 MAY. NEW YORK At 0925 Lord Caradon (Edwina's friend, whom I remembered as Sir Hugh Foot, Governor of Cyprus), who is now our Ambassador to the United Nations, called to drive me to the United Nations Building.

I had a meeting with U Thant, the Secretary-General, which I thought

---

* Mountbatten's hostess, Mrs Lydia Melhado.
† It was – by W. H. Allen in 1966.
‡ Brigadier Hobbs was Director of Public Relations in the Ministry of Defence.

was very valuable, and I was able to put over my ideas on the military organization he ought to have to be able to run peacekeeping forces much more efficiently than happens now. He told me that he had written a book on Burma's post-war history, of which the first chapter was largely devoted to me. It had never been translated, otherwise he would have sent me a copy. I asked him to send me a copy in Burmese for my archives and he promised to do so. He was most upset when I was not able to accept his invitation to luncheon or dinner, but I assured him I had very important engagements.

The American Ambassador to UNO, Adlai Stevenson (who twice just missed being President of the United States), had asked to call on me, but as I had no appropriate place to receive him, I said I would go and see him. Before this call, Hugh Caradon took us round the whole of the main assembly halls of the UNO building, which I had seen before, but was glad to see again.

Adlai Stevenson was very polite and insisted on meeting me at the lift and finally conducted me out to my car in the street. We had three quarters of an hour on every sort of subject. I was astonished to hear he never knew that Truman and Attlee had divided French Indo-China at the 16th Parallel, leaving me in charge of the South and putting the Generalissimo in charge of the North. He sent a bad Divisional Commander to Hanoi, who was soon swamped by the Communists.

WEDNESDAY, 2 JUNE. CYPRUS   Although I had made it clear that I was coming in a civilian capacity, wearing plain clothes and in a commercial aircraft, Archbishop Makarios had insisted on mounting a Guard of Honour and Band, a somewhat incongruous arrangement. They had chosen the Cypriot Commandos with green berets in my honour, and the procedure was, of course, like a Greek Guard of Honour with the Band playing and the Guards presenting arms the whole time.

I gave a press conference in which I made a great point that I had not come to discuss anything but immigration, for the papers had been full of rumours that I had really come on some mission to try and settle the Cyprus crisis! I was driven in Makarios's sumptuous Cadillac, with outriders and police cars and sirens, to the Presidential Palace, as Government House is now called.

I was greeted on arrival by the President, Makarios, and 20 photographers with flashlights. After we got rid of them we had a preliminary talk. I congratulated him on his English which I said was entirely due to me. He asked, 'How?', and I told him that I was the man who had provided the frigate which took him to the Seychelles where he learnt his English. He smiled.

I then told him that I was at a Chiefs of Staff meeting when an official from the Colonial Secretary came to ask if I would provide a frigate to take him to the Seychelles. I replied, 'Certainly, how long do you want her to stay there?' The Colonial official was taken aback and said, 'Why should she stay there?' I replied, 'To save fuel, because you cannot get any settlement until you bring Makarios back again.' This delighted His Beatitude.

He told me that he had specially opened the Palace for me as he did not live there himself and hardly ever invited people to sleep there.

He insisted on taking me upstairs and showing me my rooms. He pointed out with pride the air conditioning which he had specially installed for me, and on which electricians were still working. He showed me where the bathroom was, where the bells were and the light switches. He asked me what time I wanted to be called and what I wanted for breakfast.

I congratulated him on being the 'best hostess' I had ever met, and he laughed.

THURSDAY, 3 JUNE   At 1145 I went with some of my Mission to call on the Vice-President, Dr Kuchuk, who is also the leader of the Turkish Community. It was an eerie experience driving across the Green Line, past the strong sandbag posts of the Greek Cypriots through no-man's-land, which was being patrolled by Danish and Canadian armoured cars of the United Nations, and through the sandbag posts held by the Turkish Cypriots.

I got back to the Presidential Palace in time for the great banquet of 60 served in the enlarged dining room at one long table.

The photographer wanted to get a photograph of Makarios with me, so I caught the Archbishop before he came in to lunch and asked if he would agree. He was delighted and said, 'But I must dress up for this.' He then went back and put on his robes, his big gold chain and cross and his hat and we were photographed outside his office.

FRIDAY, 4 JUNE   The afternoon paper had stated yesterday that in spite of my statements to the contrary, I had come to bring pressure on the Cyprus Government for a political solution. This was clear as I was visiting Cyprus first, while there were other more important countries in the Commonwealth, and as I would stay here for two days while in the other countries I would only stop for a few hours. I replied that, in fact, I visited Cyprus last and not first, and I had already spent four days in India and Canada, three days in Malta, two days in Jamaica, etc., but had only managed to spend one day in Cyprus.

Another paper had said that it was a scandalous act to visit the Turkish Cypriot leaders when I was a guest of the President. I pointed out that in every country I had visited the opposition, and had, of course, seen Dr Kuchuk with the full acquiescence of the Cyprus Government.

The reporters took my strenuous denials in very good part, but it remains to be seen how they handle these in their papers.

SATURDAY, 5 JUNE. LONDON   At 1400 we drove to Battersea heliport where Sir Norman Hulbert* and a friend were awaiting us with two helicopters in which we flew down in company to Broadlands.

We arrived at 1520 to find the final preparations for the great farewell garden party in full swing.

Although the morning forecast had been very bad, and forecast heavy thunder showers during the afternoon and evening, the latest forecast said that there would in fact now be no rain.

By this time, of course, the decision had been made to leave all the marquees up, instead of taking them away as was the intention had the weather forecast been good in the morning. In fact another big marquee had been put up to make sure we could accommodate all the 1400 guests under cover if it should rain.

I now decided that three of the six bars were to be moved out into the garden round the fountain and this was very willingly undertaken.

One by one the various service units came and joined my staff. First of all four Warrant Officers of the Life Guards arrived and were shown upstairs to change into their red full dress. They acted as announcers and looked after the guests as they arrived.

Next, 25 of the Royal Navy turned up, 9 stewards and 16 Wrens. They were followed by the Royal Air Force who were to man one bar. Then 25 Sergeants of the 5th Battalion of the Hampshire Regiment

* Member of Parliament and authority on civil aviation.

came; to help with the bars and to have one in each room to show the guests around.

Although guests had not been asked until 1730, the first ones arrived at 1645 saying they had misjudged the traffic. In fact by 1730 there must have been the best part of 100 people in the garden.

Patricia and Pammy helped me to receive the guests and, except for one moment when the receiving line became too long and I arranged to let guests break off and get a drink and then come back to shake hands, we met everybody as they came in. Just over 1400 people came.

The weather got finer and finer and the sun came out and it was really lovely.

At 1830 the high spot of the evening occurred when the massed bands of the Royal Marines of the Portsmouth Command Beat Retreat. There were 114 in the Band and they carried it out on the green lawn in front of the orangery. Everybody agreed that they had never seen a finer performance by the Royal Marines in their lives. I certainly hadn't.

They had really gone to town and had practised and rehearsed. They had written a fanfare, the 'Broadlands Fanfare', especially for the occasion and had scored a march version of tunes from *Camelot* and *My Fair Lady* at my request.

Indira came with the High Commissioner of India. Rex Harrison and his wife, Rachel Roberts, stayed on after the party but left before supper.

TUESDAY, 13 JULY   The Prime Minister surprised me by saying that he was extremely distressed that he was going to be in Birmingham on Friday and would thus be unable to be present in person to bid me farewell on behalf of HM Government. He said, however, he would send his wife to represent him. I told him I knew nothing official about my farewell as it was supposed to be a surprise, but it had been leaked by Chapman Pincher in the *Daily Express*.

I had been rather put out because at the end of last week I instructed the Defence Services Secretary, General Sir Rodney Moore, to apply for an official audience with the Queen for me to take leave as Chief of the Defence Staff, only to get a reply that the Chief of the Defence Staff was not one of those entitled to see the Queen at the end of his time.

I told him to go back again and ask that this should be reconsidered, as the appointment of Chief of the Defence Staff was really quite new and I thought it should definitely be one of those to have that privilege.

On Monday I heard that the Queen would see me at 1015 on Thursday, and so when I saw Lilibet in the Waiting Room at Victoria I told her how glad I was that she had over-ruled her staff and was going to allow me to bid an official farewell on Thursday. She smiled and said she was particularly happy that I was coming then.

At 1445 I took the Chair at my last Chiefs of Staff meeting. It was a particularly important one as we took the Defence Planners' 'Capabilities Studies'. It really was the fruits of all the labours in the Ministry of Defence over the last months.

By this time I had quite forgotten that this was going to be my last meeting with the Chiefs of Staff, and I was genuinely surprised when I got up to go and David Luce* said, 'One moment; I have a piece I want to say.'

He then made a farewell speech to me (rather like General Rambert, the President of the Military Committee of NATO, had done in Paris when I attended my last meeting with them on 18 June). This time, however, it meant much more to me. Already, when the normal tea and biscuits were served, in place of biscuits there was a lovely cake with icing and with 'Farewell CDS' written on it in sugar.

Now they flashed on our two screens at the end of our room a picture on the left taken of me as a small Naval Cadet in 1913, and a picture on the right of me as an aged Admiral of the Fleet taken in 1965. David then made a long and extremely flattering speech about the whole of my career, and paid a tribute to how much help I had been to the Chiefs of Staff, particularly to the present generation.

This was particularly generous of him because I have been aggravating them by trying to get a further step in the Reorganization of the Ministry of Defence through before I go.

Finally, iced champagne was brought into the Chiefs of Staff meeting for the first time in history and they all drank my health. It was a very moving moment. Although I have had some very trying meetings over the last ten years, and particularly during the six years I have been Chairman, in retrospect I have enjoyed every moment of the Chiefs of Staff Committee and, including my time during the war, I have actually done a total of twelve years on the Chiefs of Staff Committee, which is definitely a record.

---

* Admiral Sir David Luce, First Sea Lord.

WEDNESDAY, 14 JULY   This morning I started my farewell interviews, saying goodbye to the different members of my staff. From 1100 to 1215 I ran the first Defence Presentation in peacetime given to the Leaders of the Opposition, Alec Douglas-Home, Christopher Soames (for the Conservatives) and Jo Grimond (for the Liberals). I had been trying to get all-Party discussions on Defence for at least six years, and it was a great personal pleasure to me to have been able to organize the first presentation before I left.

The Prime Minister was in the Chair and Denis Healey on his left. After that there were only the four Chiefs of Staff, Solly and people concerned with the Presentation. I introduced the Presentation and I summed up.

We had taken a great deal of trouble over this, in preparing everybody's scripts and all the photographs, maps and diagrams which were shown up on our screens. After preliminary rehearsal with my staff, I had held another one with Denis Healey and the Chiefs of Staff, so that the final presentation really went extraordinarily well, and I was very happy with it.

At the end of questions, Alec Home caught my eye and remembered my having prompted him to ask the question, 'How is Defence Reorganization getting on?' I looked at Denis Healey, who said, 'I hope to have a firm pronouncement on one specific improvement next week.' I imagined he was referring to the integration of Defence Intelligence, and indeed when I asked him about this afterwards he confirmed it and said that he had just signed the necessary order to integrate Intelligence. This is one scheme which has been very near to my heart from the beginning, and it would have been a great blow if this had been turned down before I left. It, however, does not go nearly far enough, and I must still work hard to get functionalization through eventually.

From 1630 to 1800 I had my official 'Turnover' interview with Dick Hull.* It was mainly talking to him about personalities and the state of play in some of the most controversial problems.

In particular I told him that I was deeply distressed to find that, after I had gone off on my round-the-world tour, answers to questions asked by the Secretary of State about the future of aircraft carriers and island bases with long-range RAF aircraft had caused such profound ill-feeling between the Naval and Air Staffs that the matter was really quite serious.

* Field Marshal Sir Richard Hull, Chief of the General Staff, Mountbatten's successor as Chief of Defence Staff and bitter opponent of all his plans for Defence reorganization.

I told him that I had come straight back and had to go on Immigration, and had not been able to do much about it myself. In any case, it seemed to me that a Field Marshal was a much better impartial person to try and get these two staffs together again than an Admiral of the Fleet.

The fact that such ill-feeling could arise within the same building only shows that we have not gone nearly far enough in our reorganization.

THURSDAY, 15 JULY I had a haircut and went straight from Toppers to Buckingham Palace for my official farewell call on the Queen.

When I came in Lilibet said to me, 'You think you have come for your farewell call? Well, as a matter of fact I have got something else for you.' She then handed me the Military badge of the Order of Merit. This really was an absolutely wonderful gesture on her part. The Order of Merit only has 24 members and usually is given to great authors like Thomas Hardy or poets like Rudyard Kipling or scientists like Rutherford, and, as far as I know, has only been given once before to a sailor for work in peacetime and that was the great Admiral Jackie Fisher in the early 1900s. In the First World War Beatty and Jellicoe got it, and in the Second World War A.B.C.,* Chatfield and Pound. So far as I know, I am only the seventh sailor to get it. The other two living military members of the Order are Field Marshal Lord Alexander and Marshal of the Royal Air Force Lord Portal.†

I must confess this has been a real thrill to me, particularly coming at this moment at the end of my 52 years in the Navy.

After lunch I had my farewell interview with the Secretary of State. Denis Healey was extremely kind. Then I took Ronnie with me to the House of Commons to see the Prime Minister in the Cabinet Room. We discussed the idea of informal private conferences between the leaders of thought in the various Commonwealth countries, on the lines of those carried out in Western Europe and North America by the Bilderberg Conferences presided over by Bernilo of the Netherlands.‡

We agreed now that we should go ahead with Philip to be the President, myself to be the Chairman and Ronnie Brockman to be the

---

* A. B. Cunningham.
† Mountbatten's historical exposition was off the mark. Kipling refused the OM, and eleven sailors had received it before him, seven of them for work in peacetime.
‡ Prince Bernhardt.

Director. We decided on broad policy on what steps to take next, and that a good name would be the 'Windsor Conference'.

As we were saying goodbye, the Prime Minister shook me by the hand and made warm references to what I had done for the country, etc. I took the opportunity of having him alone to ask him whether he intended to re-shuffle his Ministers, so that the three Ministers of Defence for the Navy, Army and Air Force would be dispensed with and in their place there would be two Deputy Secretaries of State for Defence, one to deal with Personnel and Logistics and the other to deal with Research, Development and Production. He told me that he was still very keen on this idea, which had been discussed between him and Denis Healey and me when I had asked Denis Healey to take me to see the Prime Minister because I was so dissatisfied with the progress of Defence Reorganization.

I told him that if he really meant this, it would mean that my last Defence Council meeting would be much easier as I wouldn't have to make an issue of reorganization. He ended up by saying that he was as keen on doing this as I was, which is really extremely encouraging, particularly at this moment.

FRIDAY, 16 JULY   I found to my surprise that every Admiral, General and Air Marshal, at least 60 or 70 of them in the Ministry of Defence, had brought in uniform and had changed into uniform to see me off and were standing on the steps. So I shook each of them by the hand to say goodbye. I had a look at the family who were in a special enclosure with Mrs Harold Wilson and Marjorie Brockman and had a very brief word with them. I then got into the car and drove away to the strains of 'Auld Lang Syne' and to the accompaniment of three cheers given by all the Admirals, Generals and Air Marshals.

It was an emotional moment for me and I wondered whether ever before an officer had received three cheers from so many Flag, General and Air Officers in uniform. The whole of the Richmond Terrace side was packed with crowds, certainly several thousands of them and all the windows of the Ministry of Defence contained men and women waving as I left. The crowd even extended into Whitehall where the police were holding them back as I drove away.

*The official jollifications in London did not bring to
an end Mountbatten's cycle of farewell visits. On 20
July he was again in Addis Ababa.*

The Guard turned out as we came in and when we drove up to the Palace I was delighted to see on two special pedestals at the porch of the Palace were two glorious tame cheetahs.

I had been told that one of them had savaged the Japanese Ambassador when he attempted to make friends, so I thought I would be one up on the Japanese by going up and scratching its head, which it accepted very graciously.

We went into the Palace and found that the ceremonial had been considerably relaxed. For instance, Patricia and I only had to make one bow and curtsey and another one when we met the Emperor, whereas the middle bow and curtsey half way down the long hall had been cut out. Patricia did not have to wear a long dress with long sleeves and a tiara.

THURSDAY, 22 JULY. ADDIS ABABA I had difficulty in getting in to the City Hall because the drive-in had been blocked by tar barrels. There were other obstructions which had to be removed and finally, with the help of our five police outriders, we managed to get the car up to the main entrance, where we were clearly not expected for there was nobody in sight except workmen. After a few minutes they found the Lord Mayor, a cheerful fat man, who apologized for the lift being so new that it was not yet working, and we climbed up four flights of stairs, at the end of which it was clear that his object was to show me the TV studio.

I explained to him I had been there the night before, and then he suggested as an alternative we should climb the remaining flights to the roof garden to which he had taken Lilibet to see the unrivalled view of Addis Ababa. When we got to the door of the roof garden it was locked. He then sent for the key. It didn't arrive. Other messengers were sent; panic stations ensued, but no key could be found.

I noticed that the bottom right-hand panel of the door was missing, and although it was a fairly small opening, I knelt down and put my head through and found that by twisting my body I could just get my shoulders through and crawl through the empty panel. I shouted back suggesting that nobody should follow me, but I maliciously hoped that they would and they did. Next came the Ambassador,* who was fairly agile, followed by my ADC General, then Peter Lithgow crawled through and finally with much struggle and pushing they got the Lord Mayor through the hole.

While we were looking at the view, the latter was in a frenzy to get the door open because he didn't fancy having to crawl back through the hole. Carpenters arrived, they tried to unscrew the door and then to get it off its hinges. Finally, the Lord Mayor came up himself and rattled the door and bashed it and very nearly broke it down. While he was doing that, I quietly crawled back through the hole and the whole party had to crawl back again on their hands and knees. It was all most entertaining.

Back at the Embassy:

The poor Russells were driven nearly mad because one member of the Imperial Family had asked if she could bring her son, a special place had to be made for him and then he didn't turn up. Meanwhile Princess Sophie, who had accepted, rang up just after 2000 to say that she couldn't find a suitable dress. The Lord Mayor came without his wife. He said she was feeling rather poorly and would have been no addition to the party. So we all had to wait while the table was rearranged.

As it was the eve of the Emperor's birthday, the Russells had the happy thought of bringing in a birthday cake borne by two little eight-year-old Ethiopian boys dressed up in scarlet turbans: a tape recorder was switched on and we all sang 'Happy Birthday'. It was a bit of a mouthful getting in the last line 'Happy Birthday your Imperial Majesty', but we could hardly sing 'dear Haile'. Then champagne was served and he was obviously greatly moved. He said to Aliki Russell, '*Personne n'a jamais fait ça pour moi.*'

FRIDAY, 23 JULY   After all the nobles and VIPs of the land had collected in the Throne Room, and there must have been several hundreds of them, the Minister of the Court collected us and we were ushered in, in procession. After we had all shaken hands with the Emperor, an official appeared bearing a large silver tray on which there was a green box. The Emperor took the box and handed it to me to open. It contained the insignia of the Order of the Seal of Solomon

---

* Sir John Russell.

which he conferred upon me, in front of the assembled multitude. This decoration is apparently extremely exclusive. The Crown Prince informed me later that there are five Orders in Ethiopia: (1) the Seal of Solomon, (2) the Order of Sheba, (3) the Order of the Trinity, (4) the Star of Ethiopia and (5) the Order of Menelik. Each has several classes, except the Order of the Seal of Solomon which has only a broad ribbon and a solid gold star and badge ('like the Garter,' he said). This is confined to the Imperial Family and Crowned Heads. The Crown Prince said that the Emperor and he had the Order, which had also been given to President Eisenhower and President de Gaulle and to the Queen. When I asked, 'What about Prince Philip?' he replied, 'HRH was given the Order of Sheba.'

On 26 July Mountbatten was installed as Governor of the Isle of Wight.

I had breakfast with Lilibet and Philip in their verandah at 0900. They left the Royal Yacht at 1000 and proceeded in the Royal Barge escorted by two of the *Britannia*'s boats up the river Medina to Newport. On landing here they were received by the Lord Lieutenant, Lord Ashburton, and the Guard of Honour was provided by the 4th/5th Battalion of the Royal Hampshire Regiment (TA) of which I am the Honorary Colonel.

On our way back to the *Britannia* we visited Queen Victoria's old residence, Osborne House, which Lilibet had apparently never seen before. We drove past our old house, Kent House, and then went to see the hovercraft at Saunders Roe in East Cowes. Then we re-embarked in the *Britannia* and immediately weighed and sailed for Ryde. During the trip we had luncheon on board and at 1415 we landed in plain clothes at Ryde Pier.

I introduced the Mayor and then the Civic festivities started. After country folk-dancing by children at Ventnor Park, we drove on to the Winter Gardens where a schoolchildren's choir sang songs. Afterwards we drove on to the top of the Shanklin Cliff lift where we were taken down to see the recently unveiled plaque commemorating the fact that PLUTO (Pipe Line Under the Ocean) had its terminal at the base of the present lift.

We next proceeded to a dais overlooking the sea front where aquatic sports were held. I found the most interesting one was a demonstration by two men who were on water-skis and held kites which lifted them up about 15 or 20 feet into the air and brought them down again at will.

From Shanklin we drove on to a dais at the pier and then our cars were sent away, but a fresh procession of cars was formed for Philip who was going to go by helicopter. This and a motorcoach bringing up police reinforcements effectively blocked the processional route in front of the dais. After some movements, they managed to get a military band to march past leading floats, each carrying a carnival queen.

The Queen of Ventnor took first prize by taking her crown off when she passed the real Queen. We then walked down the pier and embarked in the Royal Barge and went back to the *Britannia*, which had come round in the meanwhile. We were a bit late so we came back at 20 knots and anchored at Cowes at 1815.

Then Philip arrived and picked us up and we all went to the Royal Yacht Squadron for a Cocktail Party. This was the first time I had ever worn Royal Yacht Squadron buttons and cap badge because, although I was a fully paid-up member for some years and am still a naval member, I never saw any reason why I should wear their uniform. However, now I am Governor of the Isle of Wight, I feel that I mustn't be silly about this and I am now so doing.*

This has been a wonderful and exciting day. Not only did I originally think up the idea of having the Installation Ceremony and inviting Lilibet to perform it, but I had, more or less, devised the ceremony and procedure and rehearsed it, for which I came over twice to the Island by helicopter. It all passed off without a hitch, and after that the whole day going round the different towns of the Isle of Wight went off equally well.

TUESDAY, 27 JULY. *Britannia* Lilibet and Philip departed at 1040 in the hovercraft which was to take them to Chichester Harbour and so up to Goodwood. I heard later that the hovercraft broke down when only 100 yards from the landing place!

This ends what will probably be the last 'tour diary' I shall keep. They have been fun but also rather a sweat. I don't suppose they will be of any interest to anybody, except me, for at least another hundred years.

---

* Mountbatten had been blackballed from the Squadron in 1926 and again in 1931 and had never quite forgiven it.

1966

It was not long before Mountbatten concluded
that his life was still sufficiently interesting and
his tours sufficiently extensive to justify continuing
with his diaries. On 10 January 1966 he was at
Sandringham:

I was just going with the Queen and her party after dinner to the cinema
when her Private Secretary, Michael Adeane, came out of his office and
spoke to the Queen. He broke the staggering news to her that the new
Prime Minister of India, Lal Bahadur Shastri, had just died of heart
failure at Tashkent in Russia, after having signed an agreement on peace
with Pakistan.

We stopped to have a brief discussion. She asked Sir Michael Adeane
to draft a message of condolence to the President, and we then discussed
representation and she asked me if I would represent her at the funeral.
I, of course, agreed.

TUESDAY, 11 JANUARY. LONDON We boarded the Comet 4 at
1100, and took off.

The party on board consisted of Pammy, David, Ronnie Brockman,
Simon Cooper,* Evans, Barratt,† Trooper Malpas, Sen Gupta of the
new Commonwealth Secretariat in London, Sir Paul Gore-Booth, Head
of the Foreign Service and the previous United Kingdom High Commissioner in Delhi, and His Highness of Sikkim.

George Brown only had his Private Secretary, John Burgh, with him,
but then he is not representing the Queen and ceremonial is less
important for him on this occasion.

---

* Mountbatten's ADC from the Life Guards.
† John ('Jack') Barratt, Mountbatten's private secretary who was to stay with him till the
end.

WEDNESDAY, 12 JANUARY. DELHI   I am in the room which Patricia had last time because Mr Kosygin* is in the big bedroom which I usually occupy. However, I much prefer the smaller room, which is the one I used when I first came out as Viceroy. The house is pretty full. They have George Brown staying here and the representatives of other Governments.

At 0830 George Brown went off to lay the British Government wreath, and at 0900 our party of six went in two cars behind the President's car to the Prime Minister's residence where we struggled through the crowd and I was able to lay the Queen's wreath in a prominent position on the bier, while Pammy laid a wreath on behalf of myself and my daughters immediately after me.

I had a long and interesting interview with the President,† and at 1100 our party drove off again in procession with the President to the cremation place, which is a bit further on from the place where Nehru's body was burned. The crowds were nothing like as dense as at Nehru's funeral, but the Police arrangements were better. The result was that our procession drove by at such speed that it was impossible to exchange greetings with the crowd as we did on the last occasion.

I sat immediately behind the President and at one time, wishing to talk to him, leaned forward and got hold of the little sofa on which he and the Vice-President were sitting to pull myself forward and tipped it back so that they very nearly fell off backwards; a proper Charlie Chaplin situation.

At 1900 I called on Kosygin. There was an extremely good interpreter. I told him about my lecture at the Royal Institution on the selective dissemination of information and, as I suspected, he boasted that Russia was well in advance in this field. I then asked him if I sent a copy of my lecture would he send me all the latest information in Russia, and he promised to do so if I wrote to him personally. This is a fine breakthrough, as so far we've got nothing out of the Russians on the subject yet. We talked about the war and my meetings with Stalin, and briefly about my time in India which he seemed to know about.

I then told him of my various ancestral relations who had married Emperors of Russia. He countered by saying that I evidently had a long ancestry of people who didn't have to work, but that he had a long line of ancestors who had had to work hard in St Petersburg. I then told him

---

* Alexei Kosygin, Chairman of the Soviet Council of Ministers.
† Dr Radhakrishnan.

how lucky he was to have come from a long line of workers as it was easy for him to work himself, and how much more difficult it had been for me to come from a long line of people he evidently thought did no work to have to start to learn how to work myself. This went over very big and he laughed a lot. I told him I might visit Russia one of these days and he said I would be a very welcome visitor. I then pointed out that if I came I wanted to come as a tourist and not as a Government guest, and he said I could, of course, please myself in this matter.

THURSDAY, 13 JANUARY I had a good gossip with Indu, though she seemed rather sleepy. She explained that she had had 'flu, but had felt it necessary to get up to take part in the funeral and had meant to take a 'pep' pill but, in fact, had taken a sleeping pill and was having difficulty in keeping awake.

However, we had a very friendly conversation reminiscing about old times and discussing the political situation in India.

She had been made the second senior Cabinet Minister after Nanda, who was now the Acting Prime Minister. Nanda is a nice man but, in my opinion, quite disqualified from being the regular Prime Minister because he always consults a personal tame astrologer as to whether the stars are in favour of any decision he makes.* I do not think Morarji Desai has a real chance because, although he is extremely able and clever, he is really one of the old capitalist class and rather out of date in India. T. T. Krishnamachari has probably blotted his copy book and had resigned or been thrown out of the Government shortly before the Prime Minister's death. Apart from Indu, the only other contender appears to be Chavan, the Minister of Defence.†

I like this man and he is gradually developing into quite a good leader. Nevertheless, he was a *goonda* when I was Viceroy and as far as I remember I had a price on his head!

I had a feeling that this left Indu as favourite in the field for Prime Minister, but was very careful not to refer to this in my discussion with her, of course.

I was distressed to find the feeling in India so very bitter about the British. This appears to be largely directed personally against Mr

---

* He remained in the Government as Minister of Home Affairs when Mrs Gandhi became Prime Minister.
† He continued as Minister of Defence.

Harold Wilson for having written an unfriendly letter about India's case to Mr Francis Noel Baker, which has got published far and wide throughout India.* The President said that only a personal visit by the Prime Minister to Delhi could put matters right.

On 17 February Mountbatten paid a brief visit to Monaco.

On arrival at the Palace I was shown straight up to the Prince's private apartments where Rainier and Grace were waiting to receive me. I stayed and gossiped with them for an hour or so, and then, as Grace had to have her hair done, I went down to the aquarium.

In the evening there was a dinner party of eighteen. After dinner a film was shown in the large room converted to a theatre. The film was *Lady L.* The original book in French was excellent, but this film was spoiled by a perfectly ridiculous Hollywood ending with Lady L's anarchist lover acting as her aged chauffeur, instead of being a corpse in the ornate trunk left unopened in the summerhouse for forty years. After the film we played with Rainier's marvellous toys, his super-Scalex and a form of computerized bowling alley.

FRIDAY, 18 FEBRUARY. MONACO   At 1100 Grace showed me all round the Palace, including the very fine museum of Napoleonic relics and the State Archives. I must say she has done a marvellous job in doing the Palace up, although the Grimaldi family portraits are hideous.

Rainier drove us up to lunch at the Grill Room at the top of the Hotel de Paris. He had to go back for an audience, but Grace and I decided to walk back in the lovely sunshine. It took us forty minutes on foot and we had a delightful gossip. In the evening we all went to the great centenary gala, 'Le Bal de la Rose', at the Winter Sporting Club. The whole place had been specially decorated with thousands of fresh roses and looked lovely.

SUNDAY, 20 FEBRUARY   The famous Commandant Cousteau, who really invented Aqua-lung diving and whom I know, is the Director of

---

* Wilson was not alone in annoying the Indians by seeming to give equal weight to India's attack on Pakistan in September 1965 and Pakistan's infiltration into Kashmir the previous month.

the International Marine Institute here and came to see me in my sitting room. We had an hour's extremely interesting talk about all his developments, and he showed me from the window of my bedroom his underwater house, which had been lifted out for docking and refitting. It is, of course, made in the form of a large sphere.

He told me he thought he was still five or six years ahead of the Americans, although they were now spending a fortune to try and catch up. Funnily enough, various European countries were giving him financial and active support, but so far he had had no support from the British. This appears to be largely because he has not asked for it! I offered to help.

In May Mountbatten with his two daughters, visited Stockholm to stay with his brother-in-law, King Gustaf. It was his first visit since the death of the Queen, his sister Louise. On 10 May:

We had supper at 1845 and drove off at 1935 to Drottningholm to attend the gala performance of Mozart's opera *Cosi Fan Tutti* given by the Viennese Opera Company to celebrate the 200th anniversary of the opening of the Drottningholm Palace Theatre. It was a superlative performance in a real 'old master' setting, even the Orchestra and attendants being in eighteenth-century costumes with powdered wigs.

In the interval Gustaf presented the famous Prima Donna, Elizabeth Schwarzkopf, with the Swedish Medal for Literature and Art. At the end of the performance we went round to the rest of the cast with whom we conversed in German. They were wildly enthusiastic about the wonderful old theatre. Fräulein Schwarzkopf remarked that it was 'like singing inside a violin'.

WEDNESDAY, 11 MAY. STOCKHOLM   After tea Gustaf took us up to Louise's Ulriksdal Library where he invited us three to take any books we liked. Louise, herself, had marked several shelves containing our Parents' books with chits saying, 'For Dickie'.

This brought back rather poignant memories of my visit here just two years ago when she had tried to make me sort out what books I wanted after her death. I found it all too sad and embarrassing at the time and she had concluded by saying, 'Very well, you will have to come back here and sort them out after my death!'

FRIDAY, 18 MAY   At 1030 Gustaf took us from the Palace on a walking tour of the old city which is on the same island as the Palace. The present houses are all sixteenth-century, and the cross streets or lanes so narrow one can hardly walk two abreast through them. We ended up at the magnificent Storkyrkan, the Church in which Louise's funeral service took place, which Pammy and David attended.

We admired again the fine wooden life-size polychrome equestrian statue of St George slaying the dragon which was carved in 1485. There is a full-size reproduction in metal outside the Church which includes details not possible to carve in wood, such as the foot-long spurs, although the originals may have been in metal.

After an hour and a half we four were more than usually exhausted, but eighty-three-year-old Gustaf remained fresh and gay. Patricia, who against my advice wore high-heeled shoes, complained that the cobble-stones had corrugated the soles of her feet.

THURSDAY, 19 MAY   Gustaf had broken a tooth last night, the first tooth he has ever damaged, and went to the dentist. The rest of us, including Christina, went to Rosendal, the lovely little *Directoire* Pavilion in the Djürgarten Park built by the first Bernadotte King, Carl XIV Johann, in the early nineteenth century. We got there at 1100 but Gustaf only joined us at 1150.

At 1415 Gustaf drove us to Arlanda Airport where we caught the 1500 BEA Trident, which reached London at 1725. It must have been the first time a reigning Monarch has seen his brother-in-law and nieces go up the tourist gangway of an aeroplane.

We were all really sad at leaving, but I feel Gustaf was the saddest of all. He made us promise to come back with John next year, as he is obviously very lonely without Louise and loves having the family with him.

For some time after the beginning of October Mountbatten's trips abroad were largely concerned with the making of the television series based on his life. On 9 October he set off for Malta.

Evans drove me up from Broadlands to London Airport where I met Pammy and David and all the TV team except the Producer, Peter Morley, who has gone ahead. Commander Robin Bousfield, who is the

biographical assistant to Alan Campbell-Johnson, has been working on
the script with John Terraine* and accompanied the party.

MONDAY, 10 OCTOBER. MALTA   At 0930 we started filming on the
Upper Barracca. The Italian Rear Admiral Giometti was one of my
NATO Commanders in 1953, and Peter and John had snapped him up
to do an eye-witness account of what HAFMED† was like when it was
first formed.

SATURDAY, 15 OCTOBER   We started at 0800 filming on the Commander-in-Chief's landing stage. They tried to make me say something
I found rather difficult which produced a sort of psychological block,
and I had to be re-filmed seventeen times. Finally they gave up the
unequal struggle and filmed it in two parts. I am told that this can
happen to the greatest film stars!

At 1000 we went down and re-filmed the sequence at the Marsa Polo
Club because the weather was so much nicer; but they said I looked so
exhausted that they may decide to use the first sequence after all.

At 1215 I joined David and Pammy at the colossal wedding reception
for the Prime Minister's‡ daughter. Pammy and David had been to the
actual wedding at the Cathedral in Medina which I had luckily missed.
However, it was a chance of seeing many old friends.

I was interviewed by the local Malta Television Service. The interviewer said, 'Lord Mountbatten, I understand you are here in Malta in
connection with making a television serial entitled . . .' Then he pulled a
bit of paper out of his pocket and read the title '"The Life and Times of
Lord Mountbatten". Is this correct?' I replied, 'Yes.' He then startled
me by saying, 'Could you tell me what part you are playing in this
serial?'

---

* Distinguished author, who as well as the scripts wrote a book related to the series, *The
   Life and Times of Lord Mountbatten* (1968).
† Headquarters Allied Forces, Mediterranean, the NATO Council of which Mount-
   batten was C.-in-C.
‡ Dr G. Borg Olivier.

1967

Early in 1967 Mountbatten and those concerned
with the television series left London on a long
filming trip around South-East Asia. On 30 January
the party arrived in Colombo.

The Ceylon *Daily News* had this to say about my arrival: 'Lord Louis
stepped quietly and unobtrusively off the BOAC airliner at Katunayake
yesterday.' It lists the people meeting me, then goes on: 'He posed for
photographs without a trace of impatience. Equally quietly he stepped
into a Queen's House Austin Princess and drove away in the wake of the
fussy Police pilot car.' I never realized what a reputation I must have had
as Supremo and perhaps as CDS for flamboyant arrivals and impatience
with the press!

WEDNESDAY, I FEBRUARY. KANDY We spent the whole day filming
round the King's Pavilion which was very convenient. The weather was
as glorious as ever, blue sky, bright sun, and not too hot.

I find I am getting better at learning the scripts and I think John
Terraine is getting better at writing the sort of scripts I can easily say. At
all events we completed the whole schedule right up to date, and had
time for one of Friday morning's sequences as well.

THURSDAY, 2 FEBRUARY I had been told by John Terraine that he
was worried that he had too much stuff to shoot in the jungles of Burma,
and I was also worried that the jungle near Mandalay which they had
chosen didn't in any way resemble the wild creeper jungles of the North
of Burma. I couldn't help feeling that the jungle at the back of the King's
Pavilion resembled what I remembered of the North Burmese jungles
much more than the jungle around Mandalay. I therefore persuaded
Peter and John Terraine that we should do a bit of shooting in the Kandy
jungle on the following day.

Today we received copies of *Weekend* of 2 February. The heading is:

SUPREMO TO ACT WITH SEX-BOMB

The article opens with the following statement:

> Former Supreme Commander of South-East Asia Admiral of the Fleet the Earl Mountbatten of Burma will co-star with the most talked-of woman in the film world, sex-symbol Raquel Welch, in a film that is to be produced by a top-ranking organization in Britain. It is expected to be the most authentic war film ever to be made. Some scenes will be set in Ceylon to take in the former SEAC headquarters in Peradiniya. It will have no connection whatsoever with the present film that is being shot for purposes of TV.

The story was written by one of the reporters at the Charity Ball. He seemed such a stupid man that I had to dictate the essential parts of my speech to him and he took it down in long-hand.

Briefly what I said was:

> I have started the 'British Commonwealth Ex-Services League Welfare Fund' and, as Grand President, have attended various functions in aid of the Fund around the Commonwealth. I have attended dinners in Nassau and Montreal and a film première in Malta. Besides this Charity Ball I am attending one in Delhi and a film première in Singapore.

On being asked what the film was I said it was *One Million Years BC*. I was asked who the film star was and I said 'Raquel Welch'. I was asked if I knew her and I said I had never met her, but understood she was very attractive as a semi-nude cave woman. That is all there is to this fantastic story.

FRIDAY, 3 FEBRUARY   We started especially early this morning at 0830 doing the last of the scenes to be shot in the King's Pavilion grounds. We managed to get through by 1130.

Then we transferred to the 'jungle' locations I had chosen near the little lake in the sanctuary which were really sensational. Here we did some successful shooting, then we all came back to the King's Pavilion for a quick lunch.

In the afternoon we went back again to shoot the episode where my eye was nearly put out by a bamboo.* Since no bamboos were growing anywhere near a jungle track, a dozen gardeners dug up an entire clump of bamboos and planted them in a suitable position on a track for me to be able to demonstrate how it happened, with a real jeep in the background.

Unfortunately it started clouding over and it was touch and go whether there was enough light to take the film. However, they took the first part and then the rain came down and we were prevented from taking the second part. However, they think they can do the second part all in close up elsewhere.

We moved back to the King's Pavilion because the rain had stopped, but the background noises of the King's Pavilion were so different to the jungle that they wouldn't shoot it, so we shall have to do it again on some suitable occasion later on.

On 4 February the party continued to Singapore.

There was some mail waiting for me and a splendid telegram from John which read: 'As requested have signed contract for you to co-star in Life and Times of Raquel Welch.'

THURSDAY, 9 FEBRUARY. SINGAPORE   Poor Peter had had the entire night up on the telephone to London and was very worried by what had happened about the developing of the colour film. They are using the very latest American particularly fast colour film, which previously had to be developed in New York. Not long before we set off on this tour a British laboratory was set up and tested very fully by Peter to see whether they could handle the new film for him. They passed the test with flying colours and so the films taken in Kandy and on Tuesday at the Istana were sent back to London and developed by them.

The first hint of trouble was a telephone message to Kandy that the film was coming out under-exposed and not very well focused. However, matters came to a head last night when they telephoned to say that the films taken here in Singapore were 1½ stops under-exposed and consequently not sharp enough for showing!

Until we know what the trouble is every single shot is to be taken twice, with two different film magazines. One of these will be sent to

* When visiting Stilwell's headquarters in Burma in 1944.

London to be developed and the other will be sent straight to New York to develop. This will enable a comparison to be made to see whether the trouble lies in the laboratory.

They have already checked over the projector as fully as possible and they think the trouble must lie in the English laboratory.

The bore is that quite a lot of the film already taken in Ceylon will have to be shot again in some other suitable location.

FRIDAY, 10 FEBRUARY Peter Morley had had another sleepless night on the telephone to London, but had been much cheered by a conversation with John who reminded him of the bad preliminary reports he had had from London about his tiger in his film *Harry Black*. However, Peter Morley and John Terraine had had a big discussion, and they came to propose to me this morning that we should re-take virtually the whole of the scenes which we had shot in Ceylon.

I had no option but to agree. Peter said that John had remarked that I didn't look particularly well in my brown shirt and trousers, and so we decided to shoot all wartime scenes in my old green bush shirt which evidently looks better. I was able to cheer them up by saying that now I had got into my stride I was sure I would put up a much better show; and learn my pieces much quicker.

SATURDAY, 11 FEBRUARY The Prime Minister, Lee Kuan Yew, was on the top of his form and a splendid host. He provided us with a really fine Chinese dinner with something like eighteen courses served by some beautiful Chinese girls.

I had written to him to ask whether he would kindly reverse the decision of his Minister for Defence and the Interior, who had written a curt note declining any aid for the Singapore Ex-Services Association. He promised he would, indeed, reverse this and quite understood that they were well worth supporting.

I feel I must record a most astonishing statement which Lee Kuan Yew made to me after dinner. So near as I can remember, this is what he said:

> Singapore will never forget you. There will always be a Mount-batten Road. Indeed you may have noticed we are greatly widening and improving the existing Mountbatten Road. The plaque commemorating your taking the surrender at the City

Hall has been put into a very important position. I am not at all sure that we oughtn't to put up a statue to you in Singapore, not only in personal recognition of what you did but what the British have done for us.

(I here interposed that I wasn't much in favour of the statue, and in any case it would probably be pulled down again one day!)
He said:

I am not one of those who under-estimate what the British have done in developing their Empire and turning it into a self-governing Commonwealth. The other day I was having a conversation with the Governor of the World Bank, Mr Eugene Black, an exceptionally high-class American. I told him if he and UNO would stop always trying to use international teams to run their projects, and just use the British as their agents, everything would go much better. The British would do it with half the manpower, twice the efficiency and at one-fifth of the cost!

The British ran India with less than two thousand civil servants. Now there must be tens of thousands of civil servants, none of whom gets an adequate salary or has any sense of loyalty or feels his job is worthwhile. This is very sad. India should have been the greatest case of democracy functioning efficiently in the East and it is heart-breaking to see it running down to the present deplorable state.

On 14 February the party moved on to Kuala Lumpur, capital of Malaysia. Meetings of the Ex-Services Association and Royal Life Saving Society – both interests of Mountbatten – were followed . . .

. . . by a big Reception to which all the High Commissioners of Commonwealth countries came and most of the Ministers and senior officials too.

At this party a really extraordinary thing happened. There has been a long argument with Peter Morley and John Terraine as to whether it was possible for me personally to give the account of how I nearly lost my eye in the jungle when accompanied only by two members of the Chinese Army. They said it was too much of a Walter Mitty story and

Stockholm, April 1965. A visit to the Wasa Museum with his grandsons Norton and Michael John.

London, 30 March 1965. Mr and Mrs Denis Healey at a Defence Council
Reception for the CENTO ministers.

that unless I could get an eye witness they couldn't use it. This grieved me very much because I thought it was such a good story.

Well, the million-to-one chance came off, because a cheery-looking man called Dara Singh came up to me and said, 'Lord, do you remember me? I was one of the two men in the jeep with you when you nearly lost your eye!'

It turned out that Dara Singh is a Malaysian subject of Indian origin who had joined up with the Chinese Army and held rank in the Chinese Army, and that is why he was in the jeep with me and Captain Yung of the Chinese Army. He remembered the whole incident very clearly.

Simon Cooper immediately rang up Seremban to tell Peter Morley and John Terraine that we had found the eye witness they had asked for. Needless to say a message came back that they didn't believe me!

The Prime Minister* gave a big dinner party at his residence which was really magnificent, even for him. I don't think I have ever eaten such good food with Chinese, Malaysian and European dishes and with such an entertaining company.

At the end of the dinner the Tunku made a presentation to me. He said he knew I had a wonderful collection of weapons and that last time he had given me an old and historic Malayan *kris*. This time he proposed to present something which he was quite sure I didn't have in my collection, a Malayan *susohayam*, which being translated is a Malayan cockspur.

The blade is only some 3 inches long and curved into the shape of a very sharp pointed sickle. The metal handle terminates in a ring which is slipped over the little finger. This fearsome weapon is then held concealed in the hand and is used for cutting people's throats. He said it was popular 150 years ago for Malayan women to slit the throats of their husband or lover as they lay together unsuspectingly, and he presumed also for husbands to cut their mistresses' or wives' throats! At all events it is a fascinating addition to my collection of swords.

On 17 February back in Singapore the charity showing of One Million Years BC *took place:*

A series of the most ridiculous local advertisement films were shown and some very bad trailers of Chinese films. It was at least half an hour before we got through the advertisements and were able to start the main film.

---

* Tunku Abdul Rahman.

However, when the main film came I am not sure that the Chinese advertisements weren't more entertaining. The beautiful Raquel Welch only made a few grunts, as it was the era before human beings had any language. Apart from some really stupendous trick shots of dinosaurs fighting each other it really was rather schoolboy trash.

On 20 *February Mountbatten proceeded to Bangkok where he went straight to the Palace.*

An Admiral and two Chamberlains, all three of whom I remembered, were most apologetic when they said that it would be against protocol for the King to grant an audience in the garden, and that we would have to go and see Their Majesties in the Audience Chamber. However, lights had been installed to enable the television film to be made there. Peter Morley had a look at the lights and then reported that they were not nearly powerful enough for colour television photography and insisted that it could only be done in the garden.

The Court officials were most apologetic but said it was quite out of the question for the King to go to the garden, and that they had already consulted His Majesty who had decided that he would not go into the garden. Tony Rumbold* then told me that unless I could work a miracle there could be no filming!

However, when we were admitted to their presence and had exchanged greetings I explained to the King and Queen exactly what the TV serial was all about, and how important it was that Siam should appear in the film. I told him that we had already had people like Eisenhower and the Duke of Windsor taking part and that we were not proposing to take a sound record but only a film.

The King was polite but firm, and said that he regretted it was out of the question his leaving the Audience Chamber to go into the garden. I then asked the Queen if she would come out with me and she said, 'Certainly I will', and stood up. I stood up. The Rumbolds stood up. But the King remained seated obstinately.

I then appealed to him. I said, 'Surely you won't wish me to go out and be photographed alone with the Queen. Why won't you come with us?' And then the Queen took him by his sleeve and gently forced him up and with great reluctance he went to the door. Then at the door I had to ask Their Majesties to stop while Peter went out ahead to photograph us

* Sir Anthony Rumbold, the British Ambassador.

coming down the stairs. We walked along in front of the Palace. The Queen all radiant smiles and the King with a face like a boot.

However, he relented sufficiently to say, 'I am afraid my park is not as beautiful as your park at Broadlands', and then suddenly cheered up a bit. He started to take part in the conversation. We came round to the main entrance where the King suggested that we should go in. But Peter was signalling that he wanted us to walk back again. With some difficulty I persuaded the King to walk back via the garden to the other entrance.

We then returned to the Audience Chamber and completed the audience with the King in quite a good temper again but the courtiers still full of consternation at this breach of protocol.

The same day they went on to Rangoon.

I had telegraphed to the Ambassador* to know whether Mike† could get out so that my landing in Burma could be filmed but got an urgent telegram back asking that this should not be done.

When we arrived I saw the reason for standing at the foot of the ladder was the great General Ne Win himself. I hardly had time to talk to our Ambassador before I was whisked away in the General's own Mercedes. He insisted I should sit in the seat of honour on the right and I found my feet on top of a Tommygun, with two more in the front seat. We had a heavily armed escort in front and behind us.

WEDNESDAY, 22 FEBRUARY. RANGOON At 1520 Patricia and I went to the Shwedagon pagoda. The magnificent covered staircase entrance nearest to the State House has been ruined by the addition of a hideous modern lift. We went up by the lift but came down by the staircase.

Patricia was enchanted to see a notice at the entrance to the lift: 'NO FOOTWEARING'.

So we duly took our shoes and stockings off.

The ground was, of course, very hot round the pagoda, but we had luckily brought two or three mats on which to stand for the filming.

I had a particularly embarrassing and agonizing piece to say amidst

---

* Mr Leonard Wakeley.
† Mike Rhodes, the lighting cameraman.

so many Burmese: 'I knew that the Burma National Army had co-operated with the Japanese; and of course I knew that some of them had committed some atrocities at that time.'

Finally I got Patricia to take the Burmese Captain attached to the TV unit out of earshot and John Barratt walked away with my ADC. The rest of the crowd were kept at a good distance and I don't suppose they understood English anyhow.

SATURDAY, 25 FEBRUARY. MANDALAY   In the afternoon Patricia came with me when I had my third shot at filming the so-called 'hump' sequence.* We had first done the whole thing in Kandy, and then because the film was bad we did it again in Singapore. Then because we found Dara Singh who was able to tell the story of the actual damage to the eye in the jeep, he was filmed in Seremban, and now I did my third attempt to tell the rest of the story against a group of Basha huts that looked rather like the American 20th General Hospital at Ledo in Assam, where I went with my bad eye.

I was congratulated all round on the speed with which I completed the task with practically no re-takes. Everybody attributed this to a very flattering telegram from John saying that the shots he had seen recently were the best yet.

SUNDAY, 26 FEBRUARY   We started filming again in the grounds of the old Palace at 0830 and Patricia came with me. I had one of my usual small arguments about the script with John Terraine and warned Patricia that he was sure to see me off. Needless to say he did, though I was able to get my own back by pointing out a grammatical mistake, which I insisted on correcting as I had told him I wanted to speak like an educated man!

That thrust got home, I hope; because when it comes to the actual text of the script I always feel I have to give way; and I must be honest and admit he is usually right.

THURSDAY, 2 MARCH. RANGOON   The General and Katie came for an hour's gossip before lunch, and during lunch we had

---

* The 'hump' was the mountain range dividing Burma and China over which all supplies to China had to pass in 1943–5.

two hours' fascinating gossip all about past events and the future of
Burma.

He said that the Burma National Army had been fully prepared to
fight the British if we showed no wish to give them independence, and
they had been tremendously surprised to find that the Supreme Commander was prepared to do this. Katie said, 'You must have been very
unpopular with the old-fashioned people in England for being instrumental in giving away so much of the Commonwealth!' Anyhow,
it's clear that we were saved a serious civil war as the result of the policy
I pursued.

FRIDAY, 3 MARCH. DELHI   At 2030 Patricia and I dined with the
Prime Minister, Indu, and her son Rajiv. After dinner John Terraine
joined the party to discuss Indu's appearance as an eye witness in the TV
film.

She has completely recovered from having her nose broken by a stone
during the election riots, and seems to have developed a quiet and rather
charming self-assurance, and to have lost that rather cynical aloofness
that she used to have. It was a very pleasant evening gossiping about her
father and about Edwina.

SATURDAY, 4 MARCH   The *Hindustan Times* of the 3rd had this
delightful paragraph:

> Lord Mountbatten is being accompanied by his eldest daughter,
> Lady Brabourne, who also spent some time in India as the Bengal
> Governor's wife in the mid-thirties.

The *Hindustan Times* of 4 March has an amusing cartoon of a
Congress leader having fainted with a newspaper in his hand bearing
the headline 'Mountbatten here to re-enact Viceroy's role'. His son is
saying to him, 'Wake up, Dad – it's nothing to do with our search for the
new President.'

SUNDAY, 5 MARCH   We are all very worried about our visit to Jaipur.
In Rajasthan there was a deadlock with the Congress Party having 90
seats and a coalition of the minorities having 90 seats. Then two Inde-
pendents decided to join the Opposition giving them a majority of two,

who went along to the Governor and gave this to him in writing. The Governor, however, decided to nominate the Congress party as the Government and this has led to demonstrations in Jaipur. There have been *hartals* (strikes) and processions with black flags, with our hostess, Ayesha Jaipur, walking in the procession. All the Opposition leaders have been arrested except Ayesha and the situation is tense and difficult. I only hope we shall be able to go and do our filming there without causing any trouble.

The obvious way from our suite to the main door is to go out by Patricia's room and down by the lift which is opposite it. However, she insists that we should always go out through my sitting room because outside that room stand two of the Body Guard in full dress waiting to salute me. She feels it's a great disappointment to them if they don't have an opportunity from time to time to salute me going in and out, so we do a circuitous route to please the Body Guard, or rather Patricia.

When, however, I am dressed for sun-bathing then she insists I should not go out that way. She thinks it inappropriate to be saluted in shorts.

Nan said that she had recently heard a Minister saying to several people, 'After all, we used to be better off under the British.' She was indignant.

THURSDAY, 9 MARCH. JAIPUR   In the morning we did some shots against the dramatic background of the whole height of the Palace. We drove back at 1245, leaving the rest of the team to have their lunch there. The curfew was now on and the intensely busy streets were completely deserted. It reminded one of the scene in the film *High Noon*. There was something almost uncanny to know that in every house the population was bulging at the seams, but no one was allowed out.

THURSDAY, 14 MARCH   Ayesha told me of an *Alice in Wonderland* situation which occurred during the curfew. The Manager of the Union Bank, one of the most respected citizens of Jaipur, was working late with three accountants in the Bank and thus missed getting home before the curfew. They had no passes so he rang up the local Superintendent of Police who volunteered to drive them home himself. He arrived with a loaded revolver in his hand. The Manager pointed out that it was against the Law of India to enter a Bank with a revolver in one's hand, whereupon the Superintendent of Police had him seized by his men, taken out and beaten up so severely that his arm was broken. The three accountants very gallantly came out and rescued the poor Bank Manager and the police drove off.

The Manager then rang up the Deputy Inspector General who sent a car to collect them and take them home and instituted an inquiry. The Superintendent of Police's defence was that on the moment of entering the Bank he had had a black-out and remembered nothing since that time! This tragi-comic story shows the appalling state of neurosis in Jaipur.

THURSDAY, 16 MARCH. DELHI   An astonishing piece of luck has occurred; my successor, the great Rajagopalachari,* who is in his ninetieth year and only comes up from his home in Madras to Delhi once a year, has arrived.

It is true I had written to ask him whether he would take part in the film, but I had told him that if the trip to Delhi was too much for him the team would fly down to Madras to film him. However, he very gallantly has come up and made his visit to coincide with political affairs and the filming.

He was due to arrive at 1600 but Patricia wisely made me come down at 1550 with her to await him. We arrived at the President's front door simultaneously with the drawing up of his car and fell into each other's arms. What a dear old boy he is, and how very lively at the age of eighty-nine.

The President† wanted to meet him but the doctors didn't want him to come downstairs, so we took Rajaji up in the lift to see him. A lot of photographs were taken of the historic meeting of the three surviving members of the four Heads of State India has had since independence.

He made some wonderful cracks. For instance when I told the President that my old *khitmagar*‡ had been to see me the day before, and was anxious to have a house and a job for his son, the President

---

* Mountbatten's successor as Governor-General.
† Dr Radhakrishnan.
‡ Footman.

replied, 'All these jobs around here are hereditary.' Rajaji quick as a flash said, 'Including that of Prime Minister.'

He then asked the President how he got on dealing with his Prime Ministers, and the President ruefully said he always had difficulties. Rajaji said he had always had difficulties with his Prime Minister. He then turned round and said, 'Dickie Mountbatten is the only man who ever kept Jawaharlalji in order. While he was there his feet were on the ground.'

What a scoop to have had India's first Indian Head of State on the film. He is the only one of the old leaders with whom I had dealings left alive.

FRIDAY, 17 MARCH At 2020 Nan Pandit came to dine alone with Patricia and me. She was in wonderful form and said some most marvellously illuminating things about the situation out here. I also got confirmation about how very unhappy Jawaharlal Nehru's marriage had been, and what an unsatisfactory wife he had. This must have made life difficult for their child, Indira.

I persuaded Nan to accept the position of High Commissioner in London if I could persuade the new Prime Minister to give it to her.*

TUESDAY, 21 MARCH At Patricia's suggestion I had invited Krishna Menon to come and have breakfast with us at 0830. He turned up at 0815 while I was still in my bath and said he had misunderstood the time. We had him for about an hour. He looked physically well and was quite cheery but was more bitter and cynical than ever.

When I asked him why in the world he chose such an utterly unsuitable man as General Kaul to fight the war against the Chinese, he replied that this man was thrust on him and he had no option. When I think of all the efforts that I know were made to prevent Krishna from employing Kaul in this way, and how he insisted that he was the only man he could trust, I was really rather sad to find him trying to bluff it out with me.

---

* Mrs Pandit had been High Commissioner in London from 1954 to 1961 and the post was not offered to her again.

*In July 1967 Mountbatten, with his daughter
Patricia Brabourne, went to Canada for the
Centenary celebrations and in particular to open the
Calgary Stampede. They arrived in Calgary on 5 July.*

I was extremely interested to hear that the man who had suggested that I
should be invited to open the Calgary Stampede was Doug Harkness,
the previous Minister of Defence whom I knew quite well. After the
invitation had been despatched to me and the day after they received my
acceptance, a message came from the White House that President
Johnson would be very happy to open the Stampede in Canada's
Centennial Year if invited. They had replied that they had already
invited me, and the strong pro-British faction in Alberta were apparently
delighted.

THURSDAY, 6 JULY. CALGARY   At 1400 we moved over to the actual
Rodeo grounds to witness the Stampede. I had seen Rodeos before but
nothing I have seen quite prepared me for what we now found.

In the arena there was a continuous stream of cow-boys riding
bucking broncos with saddles, or bare back, or roping calves, or
wrestling with steers, or milking unwilling cows. Every half-hour a flat
race of horses took place between the arena and the grandstand; to cap
it all on the stage, which was between the racecourse and the grandstand, various entertainers appeared who spoke to us over the microphone. It reminded me of a three-ring circus but was really rather
more exciting and bewildering.

The President told me that the Stampede, started in 1912, has been
growing every year, and in 1966 during the six days that it lasted no less
than 650,000 people attended. As they think they can get more people
by increasing the number of days, it has been increased to nine days this
year and they think they may get up to 900,000. This is truly remarkable when you think that the entire population of Calgary is only
335,000.

At 1530 we were driven over to the small Indian Reservation in
Victoria Park where the Chiefs and Representatives of the four local
tribes were gathered: the Blackfoot, Peigan, Sarcy and Stony tribes.
Occasionally one or two of the tribes honour some VIP by making him
an honorary Chief of their tribes. Very rarely three of the tribes have

joined together; this was apparently the first time all four tribes had decided to make a Chief and I was the lucky one chosen.

I was first invited to sit cross-legged on a bear-skin rug opposite the Medicine Man, Chief One Gun, who appeared only to speak the Indian of the Blackfoot tribe – he occasionally used a few English words to me to indicate what I was to do. After appropriate incantations he produced a little bag with bright yellow powder which he proceeded to smear across the bridge of my nose, from a corner of each of my eyes to my hair, and from each side of my mouth to the end of my jaw. My wrists were also circled in yellow.

After this the huge magnificent feathered head-dress of the Chief was placed on my head, to the accompaniment of ritual drumming. More incantations and speeches in Indian were pronounced. After this I joined in a tribal dance with the Chiefs of the four tribes, One Gun, Ben Calf Robe, Joe Bear Robe and Rosary Duck Chief. The dance was very simple and consisted of bobbing up and down in time to the drums, but then the Medicine Man took me by the hand and danced round the circle with me in a very graceful, dignified manner. After this the two senior Squaws, Mrs Calf Robe and Mrs Bear Robe, took me one by each hand and danced three times round a tree.

I only learnt two words in Blackfoot: *moximum* which apparently means 'bad' or 'naughty', and *mistaput* which apparently means 'beat it'. With this vocabulary I feel capable of dealing with any obstreperous Blackfeet!

I then asked if I might introduce Patricia, and explained that she was much more of a Red Indian than me as through Edwina she was a descendant of Princess Pocohontas and Rolfe. I later made the joke that I had now made an honest Injun of 'Papoose Patricia'.

FRIDAY, 7 JULY We took off at 0930 and landed at Edmonton at 1010. This is the capital city of the Province of Alberta. We drove with a large police escort, five motor-cycle outriders, and two police cars to the home barracks of the Princess Patricia's Canadian Light Infantry.

We walked over to the Regimental Museum; it was a wonderful way of learning all about the history of the Regiment. It was raised at the beginning of August 1914. The Governor-General, Uncle Arthur (the Duke of Connaught), appointed his own Military Secretary to be their first Commanding Officer.

As far as possible they only recruited ex-soldiers, that is to say regulars who had served mainly in the British Army and had emigrated to Canada. The result was that they were formed into an effective force so quickly that they actually got into the fighting in France before the end of 1914, the only Canadian Regiment to do so. They claimed to be the proudest Regiment in Canada and one of the greatest in the British Commonwealth, and I am sure they are right. They are colloquially known everywhere as the 'Patricias'.

Of course they were fascinated to find that Patricia was a god-daughter of their Colonel-in-Chief, Patsy Ramsay, and that she had the same two names as Patsy, that is Patricia and Victoria, as these initials and coronet form the Regimental badge.

I was taken to a private room for discussion about the future of the Regiment. I gave them messages from Patsy and they gave me messages back for her.*

There is no doubt the Regiment absolutely adore their Colonel-in-Chief; Patsy has been Colonel-in-Chief now practically since the formation, 53 years ago, of the Regiment which bears her name. At lunch I made a small speech conveying the good wishes of their Colonel-in-Chief and told them I had seen her only two and a half weeks before at her home in England. I promised to give her a report of our visit on return.

[Back in Calgary] we went to see a most staggering motor-car. It was a large open white touring car which might have been designed by Lady Docker† if she had been a cow-girl. Across the entire front of the radiator there was a vast pair of bull's horns probably from some West Highland cattle. Twenty-one rifles and revolvers were placed all round the car. The door handles each consisted of pistols. Five hundred and eighty-six solid silver dollars were attached to every part of the inside, and between the two front seats was a saddle covered with silver dollars. The wing driving mirror was held up by a large spur; ammunition belts were slung across the back of each seat.

The owner showed us round with great pride, and then threw a switch upon which sounds of a whinnying horse and lowing cattle emerged from loud speakers through the radiator; not into the interior of the car but out into the street like a traffic horn. How mad can you get?

---

* This was eventually followed by the appointment of Patricia Brabourne as Colonel-in-Chief of the 'Patricias'.

† Wife of Sir Bernard Docker, the industrialist, and herself a flamboyant socialite.

TUESDAY, 11 JULY. TORONTO   Our High Commissioner, Sir Henry Lintott, rang up. He had just seen the revised ending of my speech for tonight and wanted me to cut out all reference to the Commonwealth White Ensign. This I refused to do, having had the reference cleared by letter from Michael Adeane written from Canada on 5 July. I did, however, agree to cut out a reference to the fact that Canada was the only country that did not yet use the Commonwealth White Ensign.

We had been bullied into agreeing to give a press conference at this time. Patricia went into her bedroom with one of the women editors, and I went into the sitting room where there were two reporters and two television teams complete with lights rigged up. I pointed out that the only reason I had accepted the press conference was to be able to answer questions about the Empire Club Dinner that night, and I certainly didn't intend to have a television film taken of me before the Dinner as I realized that if they did so they would use that interview and not the speech at the Dinner.

The CBC cameraman then spoke up very strongly and said that the arrangements made in the great room in which the Dinner was to be held were entirely inadequate and that they wouldn't be able to film there. He said he had been in the Navy in Combined Ops and knew that I would wish to be told the truth.

On this I insisted on going down to the room itself with the team to see what could be done about it, but the team from the local TV station melted away and lost interest.

When we got down we found that it was a vast room where twelve hundred people were going to dine, and the platform for the TV cameras was so far away that they wouldn't get a worthwhile picture of the speakers.

When I suggested we should move the TV platform nearer to the head table, the CBC reporter pointed out that unless they finished filming by 2130 they could not get their film developed in time to put out on the 2300 news.

The speeches were unlikely to start before 2130 and there was no hope whatever of getting my speech over before 2230 at the earliest. When I suggested they should use the speech the following day, the CBC reporter objected violently that it would no longer be 'news', and that anything I had said of interest would have been reported in the papers and would not be worth picking up on television later on.

It happened that there was one passage in my speech which I particularly wanted to have put on television exactly as I said it, and so I offered to go and put on my dinner jacket and medals and come down and do any passage of the speech they selected from my script for them at 1815 – an hour before the guests arrived. This was agreed to, and I handed them a copy of my script so as to let them choose what they wanted to record.

They chose the wrong part and I then had to draw their attention to the part I wanted recorded and agreed to record both parts on condition they did not leave out the bit I wanted. This was agreed to and the recording was made. They promised also to come and take a general view of the Dinner beforehand, so as to make it appear that the speech had been recorded at the Dinner.

The section of the speech which I wanted to be shown on TV referred to the fact that the title of my speech was 'The Unsinkable Commonwealth'. I ended up as follows:

> To carry the analogy further, if the Commonwealth is an unsinkable ship this is because the ship herself is constantly undergoing changes, being refitted and modernized, in such a way as to make her more and more unsinkable.
>
> And talking of ships, my personal contribution to the outward and visible symbol of unity among the Commonwealth Navies has been to advocate that in addition to flying their National Flag in the bows of their ships, they should fly a Commonwealth White Ensign at the stern.
>
> This consists basically of the flag of St George, white with a red cross, but has the National Flag of the country concerned in the upper corner.
>
> Let us not forget that it is at sea that the forces of the Commonwealth most frequently meet.
>
> I am therefore glad that as well as Australia and New Zealand, the Navies of the other Commonwealth countries such as India, Pakistan, Malaysia, Nigeria, Ghana, Jamaica, Trinidad and Ceylon fly this White Ensign.

I had originally meant to include one more sentence but this was the sentence I cut out at the request of our High Commissioner: 'There is only one Commonwealth Naval Power which does not yet follow suit and that is Canada.'

1968

After a holiday in the West Indies and a brief visit to Mexico City, on 28 February 1968 Mountbatten arrived in Acapulco. From there he continued to the United States, his visit being on behalf of the charitable organization Variety International.

SATURDAY, 2 MARCH. ACAPULCO The houseparty drove down to the most magnificent private villa. This is the fabulous home built by Merle Oberon who appears to be the uncrowned Queen of Acapulco. She had invited ex-President Miguel Aleman to the dinner and I had a long conversation with him and his principal aide. The latter asked me whether I was going to write my memoirs and when I replied I wasn't, President Aleman urged me to do so as he thought it would be of great interest to Mexico!

This gave me a wonderful opening and I told him about the TV serial, but presumed that that would be of no interest to Mexico. He replied on the contrary, he himself was the man who controlled the Mexican Television Company and if I would send him particulars he would be very interested indeed to consider it for the Mexican Television.

Claire Luce, the famous widow of Henry Luce, proprietor of *Time* and *Life*, had just arrived from New York. I had missed being introduced to her and wondered whether she would remember me. I sat myself down on a sofa between her and Mary Lee* in a rather dark part of the garden before dinner. She said to Mary Lee, 'Who is this? I am so blind now without my spectacles that I can't recognize people.' She then went on and said, 'I hear Dickie Mountbatten is here tonight and hope to meet him again. I haven't seen him since I was the Ambassador in Rome ten years ago.' She then told Mary Lee that the two most handsome men she had met in her life were Lord Mountbatten and Lord

---

* Mary Lee Fairbanks, wife of Douglas Fairbanks Junior.

Ribblesdale! As he was at least forty or fifty years older than me this seemed a good spread. When finally Mary Lee re-introduced us she tried to pretend she hadn't known it was me sitting alongside her! A really marvellous diplomatic reunion.

Luckily Bill Paley* had reminded me that he had been at the dinner at which I had first met Merle in London in 1942 when she was the wife of Sir Alexander Korda. I said I did not remember the occasion, which surprised him because he said the effect had been electric. At all events I got good marks from Merle by recalling the occasion, which appeared to please her for she said she had been knocked all of a heap and had remained so for a long while! She reminded me that I offered her a lift home in my little 10 HP Ford but that Alex Korda had forbidden her, saying that I had 'too much bludy gold lace on my uniform to be safe for her'!

SATURDAY, 9 MARCH. MINNEAPOLIS   We left the Sheraton-Ritz Hotel at 1030 this morning and drove out in a big procession to the General Mills headquarters. This is a gigantic Company with an annual turnover of some $800,000,000.

We drove past the Betty Crockett's kitchens. There are seven of these each experimenting with a different form of cooking and different food, and then went to the J. F. Bell Research Centre which has just been set up by General Mills nearby.

The first thing that fascinated me was to find a very large, modern, experimental establishment built entirely of brick. I asked how they could afford to lay such a quantity of bricks. They explained that they laid them in vast forms on the ground, the average form being some 20 by 30 feet. At the bottom of the form there was wet concrete, and over the top was placed a large wire mesh guide and into each space a brick was dropped. After this liquid mortar was automatically poured into the gaps between the bricks, and when the whole thing was set it was turned up vertically to form part of the wall.

This has various advantages, not the least of which is that the Bricklayers Union in the States prohibit more than a certain number of bricks to be laid in one day by any bricklayer, but this method does not count as bricklaying as it is unskilled and automatic work.

When we got inside, all the head scientists and key people were on duty and I then realized with horror that when I changed the pro-

* President of the Columbia Broadcasting System.

gramme from Friday to Saturday I had inadvertently chosen the weekend holiday. They were quite prepared to have all their workmen called in on that day, but unfortunately they had contracted to have the plant renovated and painted by contract labour. As it was we had quite a lot of people on duty.

·However, they had a series of excellent coloured slides showing the process throughout the experimental factory, so when we went round to see the machinery the fact that it wasn't running didn't matter. First we were given a lecture on what they were doing in this vast experimental establishment. They had come to the conclusion that domestic animals were thoroughly inefficient converters of green food into meat containing proteins and calories. They carried out experiments with soya beans. When they fed these to cattle the conversion efficiency was 7 per cent, to chickens it was 12 per cent and to pigs 15 per cent.

They therefore conceived the idea of converting the soya beans synthetically and chemically instead of through a living animal, and were able to achieve an efficiency of 80 per cent, an average of nearly ten times as much. They showed us the end product which was a series of thin fibres which they plaited together in the form of a rope. Although you could eat the rope raw or boil it or mash it up, it was unpalatable and nobody would eat it. The next step was to give it synthetically appropriate tastes. So they put in the necessary chemicals and spices to turn the fibres into synthetic bacon, synthetic beef, synthetic chicken, etc. They were even able to imitate the appearance of beef if it was desired to serve a whole slice.

We were then served with plain chicken, a chicken rice curry, a large hamburger, bacon, etc., and I must confess the foods were all delicious and were really indistinguishable from the original animal foods.

Not only is this a cheaper way of producing food in any country but when it comes to the under-developed countries of the world they can so easily grow vast quantities of soya beans, ground nuts and local seeds and then process them into foods. Furthermore they can give the foods the particular taste that the people like. For the Indians they could reproduce the taste of chapati with its appropriate filling, for the Muslims they could produce beef, and there would then be no limit to the amount of food which could be produced and made palatable for the local population. This they think will solve the world food problem and they may well be right. At all events it was an incredible experience and I was given a complete set of samples to take home with me, as one of the advantages of this type of food is that it lasts for several months.

The party proceeded to a private house overlooking Lake Minnetonka.

Although it was a lovely warm day and the sun broke through while we were there, the Lake itself was still frozen although beginning to thaw. On the Lake ice yachts were travelling at high speed in every direction. I expressed a great desire to try one. The Polks' yacht was out and at that moment had a broken stay. However, they went out on a sort of ice motor bicycle and repaired it.

I just managed to squeeze in with the man who had been handling it, although there was barely room for two grown men, and after two runs he got out and left me alone.

One lies full length, feet forward. The tiller works in the reverse direction, that is to say it is pivoted at one's feet, and when one turns the tiller to port the boat goes to starboard. This was a very small yacht with a single leg of mutton mainsail and fairly simple to operate. The wind was strong and gusty and presently I found myself going at a tremendous speed, the windward runner began to lift and I tried to luff, but of course put the tiller in the wrong direction. The wind now really caught me and we listed right over, going faster and faster, and I felt that at any moment we were going to turn over so I in desperation let fly the sheet and we came back on an even keel. I went about and then saw to my horror a really large ice yacht with a jib as well as a mainsail turn completely over on the ice at high speed. I realized what a lucky escape I had had and tried to proceed at a more leisurely pace. However, it was very difficult to avoid suddenly going very fast so it was all very exciting.

I discovered afterwards that they can get up speeds of 140 miles an hour, though they doubted whether I had done more than 40 or 50 miles an hour. It certainly seemed like 100 to me.

MONDAY, 11 MARCH. WASHINGTON   At 1115 I had half an hour's gossip with Pat Dean.* He then drove me to the White House at 1200 where we first met Walt Rostow,† the Principal Adviser to the President, which was absolutely fascinating. The President‡ was very caught up and we got in to him rather late. He looked remarkably fit and

---

* The British Ambassador, Sir Patrick Dean.
† Professor of Economics and History and formidable polymath.
‡ Lyndon Johnson.

relaxed and gave me an overwhelmingly friendly reception. I handed him an invitation from Variety International to attend one of their Dinners and talked about some of the problems which face the British and Americans, notably naval ones.

We finally got out of his room at 1310 which made me very late for luncheon with Arleigh and Bobbie Burke at their delightful house in Bethesda in Maryland. In fact we did not get there until 1345 instead of 1300. He had asked two former Chairmen of the Joint Chiefs, Admiral Radford and General Nate Twining of the Air Force, and their wives. I was astonished how much they all detested President Johnson.

MONDAY, 18 MARCH. NEW YORK   At 1000 Sir Leslie Glass* came on behalf of Lord Caradon, our Ambassador to UNO, to collect me. He had been one of my ICS boys and I had seen him on and off since then. At 1020 General Rikhye, the Secretary-General's Military Adviser, met us and I had a ten-minute interview with him from which it appears that all my efforts to build up his military staff had been in vain, mainly on account of Russian opposition and also because Ralph Bunche† is so bitterly opposed to the military.

At 1030 U Thant, the Secretary-General, came out of his office to greet me and take me into his conference room. He had asked to entertain me but I had no space in my programme and I offered to call on him instead. He undertook to take a personal interest in Variety if they would subscribe to UNICEF; a great triumph.

We discussed the Paper put up by the Maltese Ambassador on the need to control the sea bed. As this is a subject I have long been interested in, we had an animated discussion and U Thant invited me to come down to the conference room to hear him open the first meeting of the *ad hoc* committee on the sea bed.

At 1750 Darryl Zanuck came to fetch me and drove me to the CBC studio where I had agreed to take part in the 'Tonight' TV programme with the famous Johnny Carson. It was quite an experience. There was a large and hilarious audience and it was a sort of knock-about turn rather like David Frost but more hilarious and sexy.

---

* Deputy Permanent UK Representative to the United Nations.
† Bunche, an American negro and Under-Secretary-General at the United Nations, doubted the advisability of the UN building up its military staff, let alone its own army. On the way to this meeting Mountbatten passed a portrait of the first Secretary-General, Trygve Lie. 'My God, not Noël Coward here!' he commented.

I had twenty difficult minutes with him but it went off well. I particularly asked that I shouldn't have questions about Vietnam but needless to say he insisted. 'What advice would you give to the President on Vietnam?' he asked, and then followed it up with, 'If you were President of the United States what would you do about Vietnam?' I replied, 'I'd tell the English to keep their noses out of it.' This brought the house down and turned the tables on Mr Johnny Carson.

Though this visit was on behalf of Variety International, Mountbatten was already taking a keen interest in the affairs of the Atlantic Colleges, soon to be re-christened United World Colleges.

WEDNESDAY, 20 MARCH. NEW YORK   I went on to 444 Madison Avenue which is the *News Week* building, and was conducted to the top floor where Mr Malcolm Muir, the Chairman of *News Week*, was waiting to receive me.

He had summoned a meeting of the newly created US Commission for the Atlantic Colleges. Ten people attended, including the famous Dr Kurt Hahn* himself who was on a visit. I had told them I had been so recently appointed as Chairman of the International Council of the Atlantic Colleges that I had not had time to have a proper meeting with anybody, and I invited them to brief me. It soon became pretty obvious to me that they had not really cleared their own minds about what they were going to do, and how they should set about it, so I am afraid I rather told them what I thought they ought to do and they seemed to accept it. Anyway, it was very good value making contact with them.

TUESDAY, 26 MARCH. LE HAVRE   Jimmy Carreras† had arranged for the *Sun* to send a special team to produce an article publicizing my tour on behalf of Variety, so a journalist and a photographer from the *Sun* duly boarded the ship in France to come back with us.

I was rather dreading this but the journalist turned out to be an absolute honey. She was an extremely attractive young woman, an American whose family own the *Baltimore Sun* and who had married

---

* German pedagogue, founder of Gordonstoun and inspiration behind the Atlantic Colleges.
† Chairman of Hammer Films and Variety International.

Anthony Crosland, the President of the Board of Trade, whom I knew. I let Ronnie bombard her with propaganda before lunch, and then we gave her lunch and it was a hilarious luncheon party at which we got to know her quite well. I used the luncheon to interview her and get the story of her life, and in the afternoon I answered her questions. She seemed charming and intelligent but it remains to be seen what sort of a fist she makes of her article.

THURSDAY, 28 MARCH. LONDON I had an appointment with Susan Crosland at 1115 but she only turned up at 1130. I then found that she had in fact rather double-crossed me by making the whole interview about me and very little about Variety. I wouldn't accept this and she said she would have difficulty with her Editor, who wasn't interested in putting in anything much about Variety but wanted as much as possible about me. I told her the price her Editor was paying for an interview with me was advertisement for Variety. She would have to guarantee to insert a lot more stuff I was going to give her about Variety and take out some of the stuff about me, otherwise I wouldn't go on with the interview. She capitulated but it delayed me getting to Television House.

On 24 April Mountbatten visited St Donat's College in Wales. This was the first Atlantic College to open, the second being Lester Pearson College in Vancouver, Canada.

We drove to Llantwit Major and then straight on to St Donat's Castle where we were met by Rear Admiral Desmond Hoare, the Headmaster. Desmond had been on my staff when I was Commander-in-Chief Mediterranean as my Fleet Engineer Officer and had got special permission to retire from the Navy to take on this very exciting job. We were taken on a conducted tour of the Castle and the various school buildings which have been erected outside it.

I remember very well old William Randolph Hearst reconstructing this castle for his girl friend, Marion Davies. It appeared that Marion and he came down for the first visit during really bad weather and she said she didn't like Wales and wanted a castle in California. So he built her St Simeon. Marion had often asked us to go and stay there but only

Edwina had managed to accept. At all events all this was lucky for the Atlantic College, as they found a ready-made place to move to.

I found they had some 210 boys between sixteen and eighteen from 37 different countries, and that by the end of the year they hoped to have up to 280 boys from well over 40 different countries.

Desmond Hoare told me that the idea was originally conceived by Air Marshal Darvall when he was Commandant of the NATO Staff College in Paris. He was so amazed at the results achieved with all the different NATO nationalities so quickly that he thought even better results could be achieved if one could get youngsters together in the same way. He talked about this to Kurt Hahn who immediately became fired with the idea and together they started working on the scheme.

They had the good sense to persuade Desmond Hoare to participate and get himself released in order to take on the Headmastership. He told me that he virtually had no bosses at all and had had to do everything for himself. He had to find the place and he chose St Donat's; he had to advise what buildings he needed; he had to select his own staff; make arrangements for the selection of the boys, etc. He said that although he was a great admirer of Kurt Hahn and Darvall, the amount of administrative ability these two had between them wouldn't fill a teaspoon!

After I had been round all the classrooms and laboratories we had lunch in the Headmaster's delightful rooms, and I had a fascinating conversation with Mrs Hoare. She described to me conversations which the boys had among themselves; when the German boys asked the British, 'Why do you hate us?' and finally disentangled the facts that both sides had inflicted grave injury on each other and were only just beginning to get over it.

She told me that in class quite often a boy of one nationality would stand up and object to history as it was being taught, and said that was not how they were taught it in his country. He would then send away for the history books of his own country. They now appear to have come to the conclusion that most of history was a biased account according to what the historians in their own country wanted to put out.

I had agreed to be interviewed on television and on radio about the Atlantic College and the future of the international scheme. The BBC behaved well, but the ITV man from the new Harlech Company behaved disgracefully as without any warning he started asking me questions about whether I thought that the threat by students against Prince Charles was really worrying him and whether it was serious, etc.

However, I stopped all that by saying into the camera, 'You asked to interview me about the Atlantic College; you have twisted this interview round and I have no intention of playing your game', and I then shut up.

Then I went into the Common Room where there was a press conference at which most of the National newspapers were represented, and I explained the whole scheme of the Atlantic Colleges which seemed to be news to most of them.

It is going to be quite a job trying to help with the International Atlantic College scheme, but certainly very thrilling and worthwhile.

The outlook for the next ten days is rather bleak as I shall have some eleven major speeches to make, among them the Burma Reunion at the Albert Hall; the Commando Reunion at the Porchester Hall; the opening of the new mathematics building and computer centre at the Queen Mary College of the University of London; the opening of the Brighton College of Education; and the Degrees Ceremony at the Brighton College of Technology; the opening of the Lymington Marina; and the presentation of the Mountbatten Trophy to No. 3 Wireless District at Gaydon. Altogether I am still making many too many speeches in much too short a time; I feel I ought to have my head examined!

1969

The television series The Life and Times of Lord Mountbatten *was shown in twelve parts early in 1969.*

WEDNESDAY, 19 MARCH. LONDON   I went along to have dinner with Philip and Lilibet, and afterwards we saw the last of the television series of my *Life and Times*, Programme 12, together.

I was rather apprehensive about this programme. It was not the usual straightforward television history of the other eleven programmes, but an attempt by Peter Morley, the producer, and John Terraine, the script writer, to analyse my personality. However, it went off much better than I thought it would, largely due to the excellent part Philip played in it. At all events they seemed to like it, though I liked it the least of the twelve.

At the end I was very touched when Lilibet said that she would not know what to do with Wednesdays in future, as she had booked every Wednesday from the 1st January to see the television series. She also congratulated me on the success of the series and said that she had liked Programme 8 the best.* Finally she told me she had had a certain amount of 'fan mail' herself. When I asked her what she meant she said that people had written to her to say how good they thought the series was. True praise indeed from the Queen.

THURSDAY, 20 MARCH   I walked to Television House where I met Peter Morley and John Terraine for a discussion before we recorded an interview.

At 1130 we three went to the studio and were interviewed jointly by Eamonn Andrews and Geoffrey Golden. They asked a lot of questions

---

* The programme about India.

171

about the series and voiced the criticisms which various newspaper critics had raised, and invited us to answer them. On the whole I think we got away with it pretty well, especially as Golden turned out to be aggressive and persistent and not very bright.

The following day Mountbatten and Prince Charles flew together to Sweden.

SUNDAY, 23 MARCH. STOCKHOLM   Another lovely day with cloudless blue sky and hot sunshine on the snow. Charles went off for the day with Carl Gustaf on a long car expedition to his new country house at Stenhammar. He feels Carl Gustaf's English is still not fluent enough to make worthwhile conversation easy, but he is much more sure of himself and boisterous than he was in the *Bloodhound* and at Balmoral.

Incidentally, Carl Gustaf depressed me by saying that most of his student friends are on principle 'Republican' and he fears for the future of the Monarchy. I tried to buck him up by saying that as he developed and became better known agitation for a Republic would die down.

I spent the morning in bed working on my next two speeches. I went to see Gustaf just before lunch and said I wanted to have a private word with him, and he turned round and said he wanted to have a private word with me.

Being a King he got his word in first. He told me that he and all the family were very worried about my overdoing things and exhausting myself; I tried to do many too many things – I must remember I was an old man almost seventy and I couldn't go on like this, etc., etc.

I then turned round to him and said that funnily enough the reason I wanted to see him was to tell him he was doing too much and that all our family were very concerned about it. I thought it was a case of the pot calling the kettle black, because I was only sixty-eight and he was eighty-six and still doing too much. Finally we both agreed we were both doing too much and we promised we would both see if we could do less.

FRIDAY, 28 MARCH. BROADLANDS   Just before 1900 I was rung up to be told President Eisenhower had died and that the Queen wished me to represent her at his funeral.

I had been warned about this at the time I was at Classiebawn when he had been so ill, but I was now told that as all the other Heads of States were going in person, e.g., de Gaulle, Baudouin, the Shah etc., the Foreign Office had tried to persuade her to nominate Philip. But she stuck to her guns and thought I was more suitable, and I was warned to leave tomorrow afternoon, so I spent the rest of the evening cancelling and rearranging my programme.

SATURDAY, 29 MARCH   At 1245 I drove in a Royal Marine car to London Airport North which we reached at 1425. We went straight to the Queen's VIP room where I found the rest of the party. They consisted of Marshal of the Royal Air Force Lord Portal, Sir Alec Douglas-Home, Major General Sir Kenneth Strong and Brigadier Sir James Gault.*

SUNDAY, 30 MARCH. WASHINGTON   At 1415 I drove with Denis Healey and a State Department man to Washington National Cathedral. Here the Heads of State, their representatives and members of the family were assembled. Indeed, Denis wasn't supposed to come to this but as he had been made to fly over urgently through a misunderstanding in London they let him come.

I met so many old friends it is difficult to enumerate them all. I did take the opportunity of introducing the Shah of Iran to a number of people he didn't know, including many of the senior military wartime Commanders.

After a long delay the President† arrived with Mamie Eisenhower and the family. His daughter is married to Ike's grandson, so he is a member of the family.

After the service Mountbatten continued to the Capitol.

The others were kept outside but I was brought in with the Heads of State and stood in the front rank. On my right was the Vice-President Agnew, then the Shah, then myself and presently Mamie Eisenhower

---

* Sir Kenneth Strong, first Director General of Intelligence, had been head of Eisenhower's Intelligence Staff from 1943 to 1945. Sir James Gault had been Eisenhower's Military Assistant while he was Supreme Commander in Europe from 1951 to 1953. The party was later reinforced by Field Marshal Viscount Alexander of Tunis and Denis Healey, the Minister of Defence.
† Richard Nixon.

came in, but in the meanwhile a private soldier was positioned to be ready to support her and stood right bang in front of me.

However, I got a good view and was very near the President when he delivered his splendid eulogy; too near, in fact, because the echo was such that I couldn't understand what he was saying.

After a curious ceremonial which included the lifting of a cellophane cover off the National Flag on the coffin, President Nixon read his eulogy. There was a very short blessing by a priest, and then it was all over.*

We trooped out and drove back to the Embassy. Here I got out of my No. 3s and decorations, and put on a monkey jacket with medal ribbons only, and went back again with the whole British Delegation to pay a special tribute and to sign the book. There was no book, but the press expressed great appreciation that we should have come back twice, so we got some good marks.

We had a very pleasant dinner at the Embassy and I sat next to Mrs Graham, the owner of the *Washington Post* and *News Week* and some television stations in this area. She offered on her own to help try and get the television series of my *Life and Times* shown on the CBS network. I suggested she should ask the Ambassador first, and John Freeman was really staggeringly polite about the whole series which he said was absolutely magnificent and just the thing for America.

Apparently, one Wednesday night in London when he couldn't avoid an official dinner, he started fidgeting at 8.55 and his neighbour said, 'Are you thinking about the Mountbatten series?' When he admitted he was, she said, 'So am I, I never meant to come to this dinner!'

MONDAY, 31 MARCH. WASHINGTON   The Heads of States were to call on Mrs Eisenhower at 1300. As I had been bidden to lunch at the US Senate at 1300, I asked whether I could come earlier and this was agreed. I arrived at 1250 and jumped the entire queue. I got in while Mamie was telephoning her grandson, David Eisenhower, at the White House (he is Nixon's son-in-law) to congratulate him on his twenty-first birthday.

About ten minutes later President Bourguiba of Tunisia came in. He spoke French to Mamie and I acted as an interpreter. When I came out

---

* Mountbatten does not mention the immense yawn he gave at one point in the proceedings, which was captured by the television cameras. The significance of this gesture was exhaustively analysed by Professor Cohen in the *Bulletin de Psychologie* (1969–70, 281, XXIII, No. 4–5).

there was quite a queue waiting, Johnnie Luxemburg, Bernilo of the Netherlands, the Shah, etc., so I was lucky to have got in ahead.

I then drove down to the old Senate Building where my host had already gone ahead to the luncheon room. Here the guests were Gina Liechtenstein and Senator Edward Kennedy.

At lunch Teddy Kennedy, the younger brother of President Jack Kennedy and Senator Bobby Kennedy (who were both assassinated), told me that he is now the Chief Whip of the Senate and as such was responsible for getting the Senators down to the Cathedral that afternoon.

He had been told that they were supposed to be down by 3 o'clock and the Heads of State by 3.30, but as they had been kept waiting an hour and a half the day before at the Rotunda he thought he would get them down at 4 o'clock, which would be plenty of time as the service wasn't timed to start till 4.30 at the earliest. In view of this I decided to disregard the instructions I had received to leave the Embassy at 1515 to be at the Cathedral and in my seat by 1530.

I got dressed into full dress and arrived just ahead of the buses containing the Senate and Congress party, and got into the Cathedral exactly at 1600. I was amused to find all the Heads of States already seated. The front row was de Gaulle, President Bourguiba, Baudouin of the Belgians, etc. I bowed graciously to them and most of them looked rather sour, as of course they had been sitting there for at least half an hour by this time. I saw Tino of Greece and waved to him, and had a word with Bernilo of the Netherlands.

I was much amused to see that they had sergeants of Marines and enlisted men of the Navy to act as 'escorts' to the important ladies. This they did by pushing aside their husbands and taking the arm of the lady concerned. I was particularly amused by the slight struggle which a young sailor had to push President Johnson out of the way and take Lady Bird Johnson on his arm and conduct them to my pew.

The coffin did not arrive until 1645 – quarter of an hour late – and the service did not really get started properly until just before 1700. It finished at 1730 but then the coffin, the family and the President had to go out first.

I said to Morarji Desai, who was representing the President of India, that I wanted to get out past him. He managed to make way and I got one of the Security men to guide me behind all the pews to the main entrance. I reached it just after President Nixon had left and three Marine sergeants shut the door in my face. It took a little tact to get them to open it again. As soon as I got outside Alistair Donald* was waiting for me. Apparently they thought he was the Shah's ADC and were treating him with great respect.

He waved to the Embassy Rolls which came up outside the rank of cars and past all the cars of Kings and Presidents. I got away with a police escort and reached the Embassy well before the sirens indicated the departure of the first Head of State.

WEDNESDAY, 17 APRIL. LONDON   At 2000 I arrived at the Swedish Embassy for the big dinner the new Ambassador was giving in my honour. Sam Elworthy (the present Chief of Defence Staff) was there and told me that he had been in America when the funeral arrangements were announced, but as he had not been told to stay he felt he ought to go and thus was in New York when the body was moved to the Rotunda. He happened to switch on the TV set in his hotel at the moment that it showed me coming into the Rotunda and the commentator said, 'Lord Louis Mountbatten arriving attended by his Royal Marine and civilian aides.' These were Alistair Donald and, joy of joys, Denis Healey! I told Sam I hoped he would tell Denis of this and he promised he would.

A few days later Mountbatten returned to the United States, inter alia *to promote the United World Colleges and the sale of his television series.*

WEDNESDAY, 23 APRIL. NEW YORK   I went to 30 Rockefeller Plaza and in room 610 met three of the four head people of one of the three big television networks, the National Broadcasting Company. These were Bobby Sarnoff, whose father I had known quite well. He is in fact the head man, being the President of the Radio Corporation of America who own NBC. Walter Scott, the Chairman of NBC, was there, and Mort Werhner, the Director of their television programmes.

The meeting lasted a full hour and was an absolute eye-opener to me. Walter Scott gave me the most astounding explanation of why, however much they might like the programme and think it was worthwhile, and however great its success in other parts of the world, they would not be able to fit it in. He told me that over the years the three networks had

---

* Major Alistair Donald, Mountbatten's Royal Marine ADC.

come to an arrangement by which they decided on their programmes throughout the year at least a year ahead. At all the prime times they already had programmes running.

He told me that twelve one-hour programmes was the worst possible proposition for them. They could deal with a single programme of 90 minutes – they might possibly be able to manage about three of 50 minutes, and they could certainly manage 26 half hours and preferably 52 half hours. What they could apparently not manage was twelve one hours.

I put a hypothetical case. I said if God the Father had miraculously produced a television series of the Life and Times of Jesus Christ and had offered it to NBC, what would they do about it? They said that if it consisted of twelve one-hour programmes this would place them in a very embarrassing position because they would feel that they really ought to take it, but they wouldn't know how to fit it in.

I then remarked that they appeared to be the prisoners of their own traditions and rules and regulations they had drawn up. I pointed out that in the Navy for hundreds of years all big Fleets were built round the battleship; I claimed to have been probably the first man in charge of a Navy to have abolished battleships altogether and actually sell them, for today there was not a single battleship in any Navy except the odd one or two being used by the Americans for shore-bombardment in Vietnam.

I suggested that we were more flexible in the Navy than the networks appear to be in their own organization, and that if they went on like this the networks organization would probably break down within five to ten years, and I thought it was time they should take a new look.

The only man who made any sense in this party was Bobby Sarnoff himself who was very friendly, and admitted perhaps that I had a good point and that he thought they really ought to look at themselves to see whether they couldn't do a bit better.

SATURDAY, 26 APRIL. NASSAU   Christina and Henry Ford II came for the day. I recounted my meeting with Neil McElroy,* who had promised to go into the question of Procter and Gamble sponsoring the series, but [said] that I understood from Bobby Sarnoff that sponsors

---

* Chairman of Procter and Gamble, the giant manufacturer of soaps, washing powders, etc.

could not interfere with a programme, and indeed McElroy had confirmed that even if they put up the money the network could still refuse to show the series if it did not fit in with their pattern of ideas.

I then said, 'It looks as though the networks won't take this type of series, even if the sponsors are willing to put up all the money.' Henry Ford now chipped in with a very pregnant remark, for he said that his company actually owned a weekly hour on the American Broadcasting Company's network. He went on to say they had the absolute right to choose the programmes they put on themselves and that ABC could not interfere.

I asked him how this came about and he said that ABC was the weakest of the three networks, and were keen to get support built up by Fords, and had therefore come to an agreement which no other network had ever made.

Henry Ford then went on to ask more details about the series and I gave him the best picture I could. I told him of its success when networked in the UK and that it had been booked for Australia and New Zealand, and was coming on in Canada on 8 June for twelve weeks. This made him prick his ears because he said that in their house near Detroit they were able to get Canadian television so that they would be able to see the series then.

He then said that he thought it was time that the American television switched off sex, violence and undue introspection and took some interest in history and the sort of series that made people proud to be patriotic. He said he would be very interested in this series and might decide to take it for Fords when they came to the end of their current programme on the FBI. He said he would like to see one or two programmes and I suggested Programmes 2 and 8 to give him a full spread. He asked how soon he could see them as he was off to Toronto the next day.

I told him that Dave McLaughlin* lived in Toronto; that he would see him the following evening at the Royal York Hotel and would have available Programmes 2 and 8 from then onwards any time he liked to see them. He was obviously impressed by the efficiency of the arrangements, although it was a pure coincidence he was going to Toronto, and said he would look into the matter personally as he didn't want any of his subordinates to handle a matter of high policy like this.

Whether he takes it or not remains to be seen, but if he does it will be

---

* Representative of Associated British Pathé.

the one great breakthrough on the American networks – the showing of all twelve programmes.

He said he had bought a new house in Shepherd's Market and was thinking of getting a man called Parr* to decorate it. I told him that the firm of David Hicks & Parr had broken up and that the man with the interior decoration creative genius was David and not Parr. He laughed and said he would remember that.

FRIDAY, 2 MAY   Sir Harold Christie† drove me to the airport at 0945 and we flew in his delightful old Catalina flying boat to Rock Sound Airport in the south of Eleuthera. We drove in two taxis to Windermere Island which is a property being developed by Harold Christie, which I visited last year. Almost the first plots of land had been bought by my daughters and their husbands in a very advantageous position near the Windermere Island Club.

John and Patricia have decided to build their house actually on the beach so that it will be possible to step down off the platform round the house on to the sand. I have seen the design by Stokes and it consists of lovely long windows from which one can see the beach from the sitting room and two main bedrooms, and a further room above the others giving an even better view of what must be about the finest beach in the world; four miles of white sands. They are not yet developing their plot of land on the other side of the road away from the beach.

Next to them is David and Pammy's house 'Savannah'. This is the extreme opposite in concept. It is built as far away from the beach as possible on their plot of land above the road, and as originally designed it had absolutely no windows whatever overlooking the beach. I understand that David's argument was that having spent the day on the beach the last thing one wanted to do on coming up to the house was to go on looking at the same view.

However, as Harold Christie has undertaken to let the two houses, which have been built with the grandchildren's trusts for their benefit, he insisted that there must be some view of the beach from the house. Two fairly narrow high windows have been put in, one each side of a very large brick fireplace, so it is possible to see the beach from the sitting room. One of the bedrooms has a corner window about 18″ each

---

* Thomas Parr, David Hicks's partner, eventually joined Colefax and Fowler.
† An eminent figure in the economy and government of the Bahamas.

way, but it will not be possible for the occupants to turn their beds to see the beach for the beds have been put against the blank wall next to the window, with a concrete dressing table with electric leads let into it between them, so that the beds cannot be moved.

The other room which has a slight view over the beach has been turned into a kitchen so that people living in the house will have the minimum chance of actually seeing the beach.

Instead of driving in from the front the drive goes round the back of the house, and, indeed, the back of the house appears to be the front. Having said all this I must admit it is a very attractive house indeed, somewhat reminiscent of an Egyptian temple on the Nile.

John and Patricia's house is far too conventional in outlook ever to hit the newspapers; and indeed I am sure they don't want it to.

On the other hand, for an interior decorator like David it is essential to get the maximum publicity, and he is absolutely bound to get this, having built the first house on Eleuthera as far from the beach as the plots permit and facing away from the beach with practically no view of it. I hope this will help to continue to build up David's growing international reputation.*

WEDNESDAY, 7 MAY. ST LOUIS   Fulton is 110 miles away along a marvellous motorway so we arrived at 1000 and then were directed to the house of the President of Westminster College, Davidson.

Here an 'Honor Guard' of soldiers was drawn up on each side of the short walk into the house. Outside the house my old friend General Mark Clark was waiting to greet me in full dress white uniform. The President had been unable to come at the last moment and had therefore sent Clark as his personal representative and to greet me. He had a military staff with him also in white full dress.

President Davidson took me up to a bedroom where I changed into blue No. 5s – then we all drove to the campus for the press conference.

The public ceremonies were run by the Master of Ceremonies, beginning with an invocation from the Bishop of Dover, followed by the singing of the American and British National Anthems by Mr Gene Boucher, the New York Metropolitan Opera star who was a graduate of Westminster College. Then the President of the Student body welcomed us.

---

* A year later Mountbatten commented: 'I must say it is absolutely charming – far, far nicer than I thought it was going to be.'

New Delhi, 6 May 1965. Visiting the newly opened Nehru Museum
with Indira Gandhi.

Nicosia, 2 June 1965. Calling on Archbishop Makarios during the visit to Cyprus of the Commonwealth Immigration Mission.

London, 16 July 1965. Mountbatten leaves his last Defence Council meeting on his retirement as Chief of Defence Staff.

Next Averell Harriman* spoke. He was due to speak for between seven and ten minutes; in fact he spoke for something like twenty or twenty-five minutes. It was all good stuff but was delivered in a flat and boring way – I couldn't arouse any enthusiasm even when he said nice things about me.

Then the Westminster College choir sang the 'Battle Hymn of the Republic' in a very moving way from the street itself. President Davidson gave us all our Fellowships – he hung a large Fellowship medal round the necks of Mark Clark and myself.

After this John Freeman was invited to introduce me. He said that he understood I had been asked by the Queen to go to the funeral of the President of India, but as this would have clashed with this occasion I had asked for special permission to keep to my programme and the Duke of Kent had gone out instead. This was received with tremendous applause.

The proceedings had now been going on for an hour and ten minutes in the street and for half an hour before that in the church and I thought that most people would be practically asleep.

I based my speech partly on what I had said before about Winston, but of course I introduced the fact that he had made his famous Fulton speech on 5 March 1946 here in Fulton, Missouri. This had really put the little town and small college of 800 students on the map in a big way and it had become internationally famous.

As I went along I suddenly felt I had the whole vast multitude under control. They laughed when I wanted them to laugh; they applauded when I hoped for applause; and I have plenty of evidence to show that when I wanted them to weep they wept.

Item 13 on the programme was 'Comment' by the Governor of Missouri. He was supposed to comment on my speech; luckily he thought it was good! After this a new item was introduced as General Clark spoke in place of the President and made, I thought, an excellent speech.

THURSDAY, 8 MAY. NEW YORK I promised that I would meet Paul Mellon in his house to try and interest him in the United World

---

* President Roosevelt's special representative in London during the war and currently US Ambassador-at-large. Mountbatten in fact spelt him Averill, Averil or Averel, but never as above.

Colleges. He was taking the Chair at one of his Foundation meetings and couldn't see me until 1600, which was unfortunate because Julian Goodman, the No. 2 of NBC, had invited me to a drinks party at 30 Rockefeller Plaza at 1700 and had suggested I should come along at 1630 if I would like to discuss the TV series first.

I couldn't leave Mellon until 1630 when I had got his agreement to come and visit St Donat's Castle. By the time I got into Julian Goodman's office it was 1650. I apologized for being so late when he had been kind enough to make time available, and he said that if we hadn't finished talking business he could make his guests wait a bit for us.

I told him I did not think this would really be necessary as I presumed he had the same outlook on the television series as his three colleagues Bobby Sarnoff, Walter Scott and Mort Werhner. He regretted he shared their views and hoped this would not upset me too much.

To this I replied that I didn't really mind because the sad thing to me was that the American people were going to be denied seeing a television series which the rest of the world found sufficiently interesting and unusual to take. If it was merely that NBC thought the series too bad for the American market, or insufficiently interesting, that would be one thing, but they had none of them seen any of the programmes and merely said on principle they wouldn't take a programme which consisted of twelve one-hour parts.

Mr Goodman then admitted that, although they had not yet seen any of the series, he could not see why the American people should be expected to be interested in my life. He said, 'I freely admit that next to Sir Winston Churchill you are by far the best-known Englishman in America, and the only Englishman for whom they could show any interest, but even so let us take the reverse case. The British people were very fond of General Eisenhower. Do you suppose that if he had made a twelve one-hour programme of his life and times for TV that the British would take it?'

I admitted that the BBC might not take it as they had not taken my TV series, but I did think that Independent Television probably would. I pointed out, of course, that Eisenhower's life started when he was fifty-two years old and became a Major General, and by the time I was fifty-two years old and Commander-in-Chief of the Mediterranean ten one-hour programmes had been completed of my *Life and Times*.

I ended up by saying, 'As none of you have seen any of the series I presume you are turning it down on principle and, however worthwhile it is, you won't look at it.' He said that since my last visit in April they had had quite a number of talks, and in fact they had tried to get hold of a couple of programmes but were told that they were being sent to Henry Ford to see. I made no comment on this beyond saying that Henry Ford was probably seeing them in the coming week, and after that they could see them at NBC if they were really interested, but if they were only doing this as a gesture to me then they were wasting their time.

I made a final comment on the American television scene. I said that in England we were apt to think that American television was the finest and greatest in the world, but when one came to America and switched over to the various channels either one heard 'Bang, bang; bang, bang' as some Western was going on, or else there was fornication or violence but no interesting worthwhile adult programmes. I added that I thought their colour compared badly with the British colour. This horrified Goodman, who called upon his people to put the best possible colour picture they could show me on his monitor. A picture came out of Dean Martin looking like a beetroot, and I told him we wouldn't tolerate so bad a coloured picture anywhere in England, let alone on a network monitor.

On 2 July 1969 Prince Charles was invested Prince of Wales in Caernarvon Castle. Mountbatten joined the Royal Train the night before.

During the night there was a false alarm when a policeman patrolling the line found what looked like a time bomb which turned out to be a packet of clay with an alarm clock. However, the delay did not worry us because we were all asleep and knew nothing about it. During the night the train stabled in a siding near Caernarvon.

The rest of the family on board the train are Elizabeth (the Queen Mum), Alice Gloucester and her son Richard, Eddy and Katherine Kent, Alexandra and Angus Ogilvy, and Michael Kent.

This is the biggest Royal Train within memory with some fifteen coaches. I am very well off as I have a large bedroom with a chest of drawers, wardrobe, armchair and my own bathroom. Unfortunately the water tank in my coach is leaking and my bath had to be filled with buckets of water from the next coach.

The family had breakfast at 0900 in the Royal dining room. I gave Charles a really charming pair of cuff links with the Prince of Wales's Feathers in enamel, which had been given by his great-great-grandfather, Edward VII, to his great-grandfather, my father, about a century ago, probably after the *Ariadne* trip of 1869.

At 1330 we all went to change into our finery. The ladies were all simply dressed without decorations, but the men got into full dress. I wore Admiral of the Fleet's uniform with diamond Garter and GCVO stars, and the diamond Grand Master's badge of the Star of India – in fact I had it all on except the kitchen stove, but this was a great occasion and a collar day too.

At 1325 the Royal Train moved off and arrived punctually at 1400 at the Ferodo Works. Here a special platform had been erected, and their normal car park had been turned into a parade ground on which were drawn up a Royal Guard of Honour of the Royal Welsh Fusiliers with the Queen's Colour and their goat and the band and drums of the Royal Regiment of Wales.

At 1410 the Royal Family motor-car procession took place. I travelled in the fourth car with Alexandra and Angus, and we arrived at the Water Gate at 1420. A Guard of Honour of the Welsh Guards was drawn up in front of the Water Gate and the whole route was lined by the three Services from Ferodo to Caernarvon Castle through the town.

We were then all taken into the Eagle Tower where a number of key people were already assembled.

At 1430 members of the family who had come in the motor-cars moved in procession to their seats which were in the front row of the main block. I waited for the Queen's procession.

At 1435 the Prince of Wales's carriage procession arrived escorted by the Prince of Wales's Escort of the Household Cavalry. At 1440 Charles went in procession from the Eagle Tower to the Chamberlain Tower. As he entered the Castle the assembled company sang 'God Bless the Prince of Wales'. This reminded me of the 1920 Prince of Wales tour to Australasia. There was always a bit of argument when we should have the 'God Bless' and when the 'God Save'. I was told that in Canada they used to sing 'Oh! let the Prairie Echo' for 'Oh let the Prayer re-echo'.

Meanwhile at 1450 a small procession with Elizabeth, Margaret and Anne moved to their places and at 1455 the Queen's procession moved off; it included, I am glad to say, the four Chiefs of Staff, the Lords Lieutenant of the Counties of Wales, the Constable of Caernarvon Castle, Tony Snowdon in an elegant green uniform he had designed himself, the Kings of Arms, the Earl Marshal, the Lord Great Chamberlain and the Sword of State. Then came the Queen with Philip on her left, and I had the privilege, as her personal ADC, of walking immediately behind her, while the Mistress of the Robes, Fortune Euston, walked behind Philip.

Just as we were about to move off a pin which had been left in Lilibet's dress moved and started to prick her. The Mistress of the Robes was then called upon, probably for the first time in history, to adjust the Queen's robes just before the procession moved off!

There were many trumpeters on different parts of the battlements sounding fanfares at appropriate moments, and it was a very moving occasion as we moved into the great courtyard of this magnificent old Castle. The lawns were lovely and green and the grandstands had been put well back against the walls.

The decorations were excellent, and had been carried out under Tony Snowdon's direction as Constable of the Castle and has earned him the GCVO. The ceremonial was impeccably organized by Bernard Norfolk, the Earl Marshal, as always.

Fortune and I broke off as the Queen and Philip went up the steps to the Royal dais, and I had a wonderful view just behind and to one side of Anne. Next to Anne were Elizabeth, Margaret and Tony Snowdon. The rest of the Royal Family were in the main stand behind us.

The ceremony began by the Queen commanding the Earl Marshal to direct Garter King of Arms to summon the Prince of Wales. Charles then came out in a special procession of his own with five Welsh peers carrying his regalia.

On arrival at the dais he knelt on a special cushion in front of the Queen. The Letters Patent were delivered by the Lord Great Chamberlain to Her Majesty who handed them to the Home Secretary (Jim Callaghan) to read the English text, and the Welsh text to the Secretary of State for Wales (George Thomas). While the Welsh version was being read Lilibet invested Charles with the insignia of his Principality and of the Earldom of Chester. First the sword, then the gold ring, then the very modern dashing and heavy coronet, then the golden rod, and finally the rather short mantle.

Whilst still kneeling Charles paid homage on behalf of the Principality of Wales and the Earldom of Chester by placing his hands between those of the Queen and declaring, 'I Charles, Prince of Wales, do become your liege man of life and limb and of earthly worship, and faith and truth I will bear unto you to live and die against all manner of folks.' The Queen then raised him up and they exchanged the kiss of fealty. I confess I was immensely moved and I suspect that the 500 million people watching on TV must have been moved too.

When they came to the top of the steps Charles and his parents halted for the presentation to the people in the lower wards of the Castle. They were just going to move down the steps when the Earl Marshal shook his head violently to the Queen and she hesitated and stopped, not realizing that she still had to wait for another fanfare. However, I don't think anybody else noticed.

I formed up immediately behind Charles with the two Mistresses of the Robes on my right and left. Behind them came the presentation procession, and after that came the rest of our own procession headed by Gold Stick-in-Waiting and the Master of the Horse.

A really complicated manoeuvre carried out entirely from written instructions, as I had not been present at any rehearsal, and very effective.

We then processed between the stands and the lower wards which had vast crowds in them full of the wildest enthusiasm; staid people like General Sir Hugh Stockwell, who was with me in Burma, went wild. He took off his uniform cap and waved it as he cheered lustily. The leading part of the procession went on ahead and entered the Eagle Tower.

Finally we all went into the Eagle Tower, I following immediately behind Charles who had begged me not to step on his mantle! We waited for a few moments, and then Charles and his parents went out for the fly past in close formation of the Royal Air Force Squadrons from Strike and Air Support. Everybody went into the train for final farewells and then Charles and Anne departed. First Charles was given a Royal Salute by the Guard of Honour of his own newly reconstituted Regiment, of which he is Colonel-in-Chief; then he inspected them. Then he and Anne got into the big State Rolls-Royce and drove off in fine style. It was quite an emotional moment and I turned to Philip and Lilibet and said, 'This must make you feel very proud and slightly old to see your two grown-up children going off on their own to the *Britannia* for their subsequent tour of Wales.'

After getting out of our finery we had a very gay party gossiping and laughing and a tremendous family dinner.

On 28 July 1969 Mountbatten accompanied the Queen and the Royal Family on their visit to the Western Fleet.

The Commander-in-Chief of the Western Fleet, Admiral Sir John Bush, paid his official call on the Queen. The Queen asked him officially in a signal in her capacity as Lord High Admiral to carry on with the administration and control of the Fleet. This is a new departure which I instituted after reorganization at the Ministry of Defence had caused the Queen to take over the office of Lord High Admiral herself.

We found on board the *Britannia* the First Sea Lord, Admiral Sir Michael Le Fanu, and the Minister in attendance Dr Owen, the Under-Secretary for Defence, Royal Navy.

At 1115 I went with Lilibet and Philip in the Royal Barge to the *Hampshire*.

Every time I visit one of the County Class guided missile destroyers I get a renewed thrill, for these certainly were the children of my imagination when I became First Sea Lord.

The first demonstration they put on was moving the Wessex helicopter into its hangar. I remember when I decided that these ships were to have a Wessex helicopter I was told that there was no possible place in which a hangar could be provided. I went down myself to Bath and helped to find a place which turned out to have only 3 inches to spare. I said that was enough, and it was proved today for they managed to wheel this great monster into the hangar quite easily with the help of guide rails.

At 2000 we arrived alongside the *Eagle*, the great 50,000-ton aircraft carrier which is the biggest ship we've ever had in the Royal Navy, a sister ship of the *Ark Royal*. Both have recently been modernized at a cost of £30 million and could continue well into the 1970s but for this tragic decision of the Government to abolish them in their prime of life and kill off the Fleet Air Arm, which is probably the finest flying service in the world today.

This decision effectively destroys the homogeneous Task Force I had designed with the Commando Carriers, amphibious ships, guided missile destroyers and nuclear submarines. Furthermore it means that the carriers will be irretrievably finished before the new form of naval aviation by vertical take-off Harriers can be developed.

TUESDAY, 29 JULY. *Britannia* I had breakfast with the family on the verandah deck. During breakfast Bennett, the Queen's Page, came in with a message from the Flag Officer of the Royal Yacht to ask whether the Queen would mind leaving at 0953 instead of 0955. She replied that two minutes strict timing was nonsense and that they would go when she was ready. I discovered afterwards that poor Admiral Morgan had sent no such message which had come through a misunderstanding.

WEDNESDAY, 1 OCTOBER. LONDON   At 1230 I went with John Barratt to the Dorchester Hotel to attend a Foyle's Literary Luncheon for the launching of Oliver Warner's biography of Charles Lambe entitled *Admiral of the Fleet*. I made what was virtually the only speech to a record audience of many hundreds, and took the opportunity to launch a very strong attack on the new Government policy of scrapping the aircraft carriers.

I had written out this particular section of my speech in full, and had sent the script to the Prime Minister who had passed it on to the Secretary of State for Defence, Denis Healey, who passed it on to the First Sea Lord who wrote and said that Healey had no comment but asked me to say that not £66 million but only £30 million had been spent on modernizing the carriers.

Shortly after I got the letter came a telephone message to say that instead of it being worded that, 'The Secretary of State for Defence wished me to change this', it was 'we' who wished it changed. Thus Denis Healey didn't want to take the blame for what he must have known was a very incorrect request.

However, I adopted this suggestion and the speech appeared to go over very well. At all events the press appeared to like it.

I gave Michael-John dinner at the Royal Thames Yacht Club and then took him to see *Conduct Unbecoming* – an entertaining play about a cavalry Regiment of the Indian Army in about 1870.

THURSDAY, 2 OCTOBER   I was much amused to see that the *Daily Express* in reporting my speech said I was wrong in quoting £30 million as the cost of modernizing the carriers as it was well known to have been over £60 million. So Denis Healey did himself a disservice by his interference.

1970

*On 16 February 1970 Mountbatten was in Paris for
the dubbing of the French version of* The Life and
Times of Lord Mountbatten.

The trouble is that French is a language which employs at least 30 per
cent more words to say the same thing in English. This means that I
would have to speak tremendously fast and enunciate very clearly to be
understood at all. My aim was to find the words which could be omitted
without damaging the sense too much. Only I could make this decision,
as frequently it did slightly alter the context.

The next difficulty is that syllables with consonants like P in them
have to come at exactly the same moment as when a P was used in
English.

The film is run over on a screen in front of a desk on which stands the
microphone. The finally approved translation is written on a loop
which goes horizontally across from right to left, and at the moment
that the actual word, or indeed the actual syllable, which has to be
pronounced passes an arrow one has to say it.

It is quite difficult enough synchronizing in this way, but on top of
that one has to act it. So one has to hear the English version two or three
times to get the intonation and the mood in which the words are said.
One way and another it is an art which requires one's maximum
concentration.

On top of this I had to work on the actual scripts which were being
written for the commentary. The problem here is that the English
version consisted of twelve programmes of fifty-two minutes each, a
total of ten hours and twenty-five minutes. The French are cutting this
down into six hours made up of four programmes of one and a half
hours each. It means very considerable cutting and alteration; they were
anxious I should approve everything.

*   *   *

I wrote a letter to the Editor of *The Times* in support of a point made in Lord Wigg's article on 'The Perils of Defence on the Cheap', in which I pointed out if tactical nuclear weapons were ever used it could only end in escalation to total global nuclear destruction, and for this reason nobody in their senses would ever use them.*

SUNDAY, 22 FEBRUARY. PARIS   I dined alone with David (Duke of Windsor) at 4 Route du Champ d'Entraînement. Wallis was away 'resting' so David and I had a delightful evening entirely to ourselves.

We seem to have caught the old spirit really even more than in the 1930s, and I must say I thoroughly enjoyed the evening. His eyes seemed all right again, but his hip gives him trouble with arthritis though he can still play nine holes of golf.

MONDAY, 2 MARCH   David Windsor was very keen I should come round to see him; he told me that although Wallis was back she was not feeling well and would not be down for tea, and suggested I should come round and have tea. So I went round and had an hour's further gossip and tea when he repeated for the third time how much he had enjoyed the dinner with me.

> On 4 March Mountbatten spent a day visiting the Swiss army and airforce and then continued to Berne:

I was very gratified that the Ambassador had asked Prince Sadruddin Aga Khan to come up from Geneva and that he had accepted. He is the United Nations Commissioner for Refugees and is widely tipped as being a likely successor as Secretary-General of UNO when U Thant retires in a couple of years' time.† I knew his father, the old Aga Khan, very well, and we got on like a house on fire. In fact, I invited him to come and join our luncheon party at the Geneva Airport the following day to continue our discussion and he accepted.

I had a most unexpected success with Gnägi.‡ After a lot of polite

---

* The letter was published on 20 February 1970 and caused a considerable stir, more because of the authorship than the contents.
† The tip did not come home. Prince Sadruddin remained Commissioner for Refugees until 1977.
‡ Swiss Minister of Defence.

remarks in German on the effect of my visit to Switzerland, and expressing his deep regret that he only learnt French, Latin and ancient Greek at school and couldn't speak English, we discussed education in general and I found that he was really interested in this subject and also in international education.

I then turned the full blast of propaganda about United World Colleges on him and he responded magnificently. He asked me if he could help me, and I told him it was my intention to come over next year to Switzerland when the International Baccalaureate had been accepted by St Donat's and try and form a Swiss National Committee with a view to getting money for scholarships, possibly a teaching fellowship, and a Selection Committee for selecting young Swiss.

I told him I wanted to get the new President of Switzerland to be the Patron, as other Heads of States were becoming so in other countries. He then told me that next year he would in fact be the President of Switzerland himself and that he would be prepared to come to Geneva to take the Chair at a meeting to form the Swiss National Committee. I couldn't get over my good luck and thanked him profusely.

When Sadruddin heard of my success with Gnägi he was overjoyed and expressed his very strong support for the whole United World Colleges scheme. He promised to go down to St Donat's and to take a personal interest when he came over to England. He offered to put me up at his own house when I came over to Geneva next year to start the first National Committee.

MONDAY, 27 APRIL. NASSAU Jeffrey Archer* called me at 1100 from London to say that as a result of tremendous negotiations with Eric Morley, who is running the 'Miss World' contest at the Albert Hall, and Jimmy Carreras, he had managed to get the Albert Hall clear for 16 November for the Frank Sinatra/Bob Hope concert† and he wanted me to ring up and fix the new arrangements with Mike Frankovitch.

This I did after lunch and had endless trouble getting through because I was first connected to Hollywood in Florida not realizing that there were two of them.

---

* Jeffrey Archer had been elected to the House of Commons four months earlier but continued to work in public relations.
† In aid of the United World Colleges.

TUESDAY, 5 MAY. PUERTO RICO   At 1740 we drove in to San Juan. I went to a meeting with Mike Frankovitch and Jimmy Carreras to discuss the concert.

They convinced me that Jeffrey Archer's idea of getting Richard Burton and Elizabeth Taylor to do pieces at the Festival Hall while Bob Hope and Frank Sinatra had to struggle in the Albert Hall was not really sensible. Mike said that he thought the reason Leonard Bernstein had found it inconvenient to come on 16 November was because he heard that he was going to be a rival show to the Frank Sinatra/Bob Hope concert. He feared that when Sinatra and Hope heard there was going to be a rival show the same night they would start trying to get out of their engagement.

We all agreed that there could only be one main show but there would be no harm in having closed circuit television at the Queen Elizabeth Hall as we had already secured this hall. This means having now to send a long and grovelling telegram to Eric Morley who has given up one of his rehearsal days for the 'Miss World' competition at the Albert Hall on 16 November.

They also thought it was wonderful to get Leonard Bernstein conducting the Vienna Philharmonic Orchestra in the spring as this would be an even greater success than the previous Bernstein proposal.

FRIDAY, 8 MAY   It was the night of the great Humanitarian Award of Variety International. I have been selected for this honour, the fourth Englishman to be selected since the Awards started more than forty years ago; the other three being Philip, Winston Churchill and Sir Alexander Fleming (penicillin).

The VIPs had drinks in a special room where I had been photographed in front of an over life-size bust of me made of lard by a young chef; not a bad effort either.

Thank God dinner took place first this time, and as soon as it was over the Governor was called upon to make a short welcoming speech. He spoke for nearly quarter of an hour giving nothing but the most boring statistics about infant mortality in Puerto Rico, etc. A thoroughly damping beginning for the evening, though, of course, it was a great thing having the Governor there to make the opening speech.

After this the great surprise of the evening, at least it was supposed to be a surprise for me, took place. Mike Frankovitch was Master of Ceremonies and began by standing up to announce that I was to get the

Humanitarian Award, and then began, 'Lord Mountbatten among other things is a Colonel-Commandant of the Royal Marines – march on the Royal Marines!' The band struck up 'The British Grenadiers' and the Sergeant Major and twenty men from the *Sirius*'s Royal Marine Detachment marched on in blue uniform and white helmets.

Although it was a hot night they volunteered to put on blue because they thought they would look nicer, and indeed they did. They marched behind the dais on which the top table was erected – it was a long top table so that the twenty marines just about spanned the back of the dais on the ground floor level. At the order 'Royal Marines left turn – one pace forward march', the twenty men took a step forward and up about two foot on to the dais appearing suddenly as though by magic, which had an electric effect on the large audience who clapped madly.

It appears they had got John Terraine to write a special script for the occasion. It turned out to be too long and had been cut short by Mike. It was arranged that Cary Grant would speak one part, Johnny Mills* the second part, Mike Frankovitch took the third part and the fourth part was taken by Rocky Wilkins, a survivor of the *Kelly*. It was a beautifully organized show and apparently they had spent the whole day rehearsing it. Even I was moved and apparently people in the audience were in several cases reduced to tears.

I could only detect one line which I am sure John Terraine never put in. Cary Grant said to Johnny Mills something like, 'He is a man you can never say "no" to – I only arrived last night and he had a thousand dollars subscription out of me for his Patrol Life Membership scheme right away. Did he sting you too?' Johnny Mills replied, 'He stung me two days before that for a thousand dollars.'

It was a great honour Cary Grant coming over because he still is the No. 1 pulling star of the films and was absolutely mobbed by the crowds wherever he went for his autograph, etc., while in Puerto Rico.

I was then given the framed Gold Heart of the Humanitarian Award for which I had to return thanks.

I had taken a lot of trouble about my speech and was told it went very well. At all events it produced a tremendous ovation from the nine hundred in the hall, largely helped by the fact that there were a hundred and fifty of the *Sirius*'s ship's company there to add to the noise, making over a thousand.

---

* John Mills had made rather a speciality of nautical roles (including a part in *In Which We Serve*) and was also active in the affairs of Variety Club.

A rather dramatic incident occurred after I had been speaking for ten minutes. One of the Royal Marines fainted and fell face down, heels together, on to the dais. Nobody moved. I then drew the audience's attention to the fact that such was the *esprit de corps* and discipline in the Royal Marines that although he couldn't help fainting he had fallen strictly at attention and nobody had moved.

I then said we had better get him off now and that there was only one way to do this. That was for the Sergeant Major to give an order to march off. So the Sergeant Major gave the order, 'Royal Marines Detachment left turn, quick march', and the marine who had fainted pulled himself together, stood up and marched off with the others to great applause.

Increasingly Mountbatten recorded in his diary events of particular interest, whether or not they took place on tour. In June 1970 a joint seventieth birthday party for Mountbatten, the Queen Mother, the Duke of Gloucester and the Duke of Beaufort was held at Windsor Castle.

FRIDAY, 19 JUNE. WINDSOR Elizabeth, the Queen Mother, has been very kind and is lending Royal Lodge for selected members of the family for the birthday party tonight, because she and Margaret and her staff are in fact living at Windsor Castle because it is Ascot Week.

Ascot Week this year has carried on one day longer into Saturday because of the election which took place on 18 June when, to nearly everybody's surprise, the Conservatives won.* Incidentally, Lilibet told me I was almost the only person who gave her an indication that there was a good chance that the Conservatives might win. I felt this in my bones during the last few days of the election.

After lunch I drove in Elizabeth's car with her and Anne to the point at the edge of Windsor Great Park where we all changed into the landaus for the carriage procession. I went in the second carriage again with Elizabeth and Anne.

The drive lasts about twelve minutes – it was a lovely day and great friendly crowds were out lining the route and the course itself.

I had not been to Ascot for many years because racing bores me.

* By 37 seats. Edward Heath replaced Harold Wilson as Prime Minister.

Every year Lilibet has been trying to make me go, but last year matters came to a head. I arrived after the Trooping the Colour to stay over for the Garter Service two days later and then leave before the Ascot Party really came. The Sergeant Footman met me and followed me up the staircase in the Augusta Tower. He remarked that I was the first member of the Ascot Party to arrive and I told him he was wrong as I always left before Ascot. Unfortunately Lilibet was standing just out of sight at the top of the staircase and said, 'I heard that! Next year you must definitely come to Ascot.' I solved the problem this year by going to one day of Ascot without having to spend the whole of the week going to the races every day. However, it was really quite a thrill driving down the course and seeing the wonderful new stand which has been built at Ascot.

I saw a lot of old friends and didn't take much interest in the racing or in the betting, and as soon as Lilibet and her staff left I took advantage to drive back at 1730 to Windsor Castle, where I picked up my Jaguar and drove myself down to Royal Lodge.

Poor Lilibet had to go off very late that day to see the outgoing Prime Minister, Harold Wilson, at about 1800 and then to ask the new Prime Minister, Ted Heath, to form a Government at 1830.

Ted amused her by asking whether he might still come to the party to which he had been invited. She replied she would be delighted and, in fact, he did turn up later on that evening. He came straight up to me and said, 'I have come to congratulate you on your seventieth birthday', and I replied, 'I hope you have come to receive congratulations on your victory.'

I then took the chance of telling him that he must do something about saving the aircraft carriers *Ark Royal* and *Eagle* right away, so as to be able to send at least one mobile flexible task force to the Middle East and Far East when necessary. He agreed he would have it looked into as a matter of urgency. To be honest this was my main reason for wanting the Conservatives to win this time. Denis Healey's decision to abolish the carriers was such a blatantly dishonest step.

The party itself started at 2230 and Philip and Lilibet received all the eight hundred guests themselves. St George's Hall was laid out with one long immense buffet table and on the opposite side there must have been a couple of dozen round tables.

Dancing took place in the Waterloo Chamber appropriately darkened with one vast pyramid of flowers floodlit in the middle. There were two bands, Joe Loss and a pop group, who played between them continuously. The room was never uncomfortably full but was always gay and crowded.

I met innumerable friends but I had nominated about 150 of my personal friends and relations to come to the party.

I have never seen the Castle look so beautiful. The towers and battlements were floodlit, and not only were all the State Apartments open but Lilibet had kindly left the main corridors in the private wing open so that guests could come and have a look at the wonderful pictures in the corridors, and see some of the great drawing-rooms which were not, of course, open to the public with the State Rooms.

The party had originally been thought up by Philip and Lilibet for my seventieth birthday and they asked me when I would like to have it. I asked for the Friday before my birthday so that various relatives coming from abroad could come over for the dance at the Castle, then come on down to Broadlands for the weekend.

After this had all been agreed Lilibet remembered that 1970 was the seventieth birthday of other members of the family who were also born in 1900, notably her mother in August, her Uncle Harry Gloucester in March and Master Beaufort* in April. So finally it was agreed to be a general family seventieth birthday party, and we were each allowed to send in a list of names. Lilibet, Philip, Charles and Anne put in the remainder so there were well over eight hundred people at the party, and it was extremely gay.

About 0200 I became rather sleepy and asked Lilibet if I could go to bed. She replied, 'Certainly not – this is your party, you can't go yet.' She saw me again at about 0300 and said I could go to bed now. But by this time I didn't want to go to bed – I had got my second wind, and I stayed on until after 0330.

I have no doubt that it was by far the most fabulous and enjoyable party I have been to for at least thirty years – how sweet of Lilibet and Philip to have taken all this trouble.

I tumbled into bed about 0400, not really feeling tired at all.

SUNDAY, 21 JUNE. BROADLANDS I have had a fabulous lot of presents. Tino and Anne Marie† have given me the most delightful matching clock, which strikes ships' bells and barometer inside the

---

* The Duke of Beaufort, so-called because he was a great hunting man, Master of the Beaufort Hunt and Master of the Horse from 1936 to 1978.
† The King and Queen of Greece.

steering wheels, which I am putting up in the bar of the swimming pool. Juanito and Sophie* gave me a lovely little gold electric clock. Peg† has given me that charming picture of my father aged forty-four by Kaulbach and a miniature of my grandfather. The Hohenlohes‡ have given me one of my Grandfather Alexander's guns, a hundred years old, which they bought out of the collection at Kranichstein. The Sopwiths§ have given me a hand-painted Minton breakfast set for fourteen people. The De Passes¶ cut glass tumblers for the cocktail tray.

Lilibet has given me the photostat copies of my mother's pre-marriage letters to Queen Victoria, bound. Charles has given me a miniature radio set, etc. But the most magnificent present of all really is two silver models of the Viceroy's Body Guard mounted given me by my children and grandchildren which I am thrilled to have. Previously I only had a small silver horse given by the members of the Body Guard themselves.

SUNDAY, 28 JUNE. WINDSOR   My great friend the Maharaja of Jaipur had died suddenly in between chukkas at a polo match in Cirencester last Wednesday. Charles had rung me up from Windsor to ask if I would give a two-minute tribute on the loud-speaker system to him. I agreed to do this, and the two teams taking part in the Jaipur Trophy match lined up in front of the stand while I gave the address.

I then sat with Lilibet and the others. She had the agonizing experience of seeing first her son knocked down and heavily rolled on by his pony, but Charles being only twenty-one jumped up, shook himself and carried on. In the next chukka Philip was badly crossed and came down very heavily and lay quite still. The doctor ran out to see him. It was evident he was in pain and the doctor wouldn't let him go on playing. They put in a substitute and Windsor won the match.

Meanwhile I suggested to Lilibet that she should try and control Philip and make sure that he had an X-ray and went to bed. She said she wouldn't be seeing him for at least three days, as he was leaving from the polo ground on a tour to the West Country and Scotland. She wished me luck to see if I could stop him. I went down and had a show-down

---

* The King and Queen of Spain.
† Princess Margaret of Hesse and the Rhine.
‡ Princess Margarita of Hohenlohe-Langenburg was the Duke of Edinburgh's eldest sister and Mountbatten's niece.
§ Sir Thomas and Lady Sopwith, Hampshire neighbours.
¶ Commander and Mrs Robert De Pass.

with Philip. He promised to go and at least have an X-ray taken at the local hospital but would not undertake to cancel his visit to Bristol to see the 127-year-old ship Brunel's *Great Britain*, as he had been instrumental in getting her back; nor his visit to Scotland.

I then got hold of his detective and in Philip's presence said, 'Take His Royal Highness to the hospital. Have him X-rayed. Look at the X-ray with the doctor, if the doctor thinks he isn't fit to go on tour lock him up in the jug and ring me up and I will come and release him and take him back to Windsor Castle.' Philip had the grace to grin and said he certainly would treat the matter seriously.

I was very much gratified to find that in fact my advice had worked to the extent that he cancelled his trip to Bristol and delayed his trip to Scotland. Nothing is broken but he has torn some ligaments in his shoulder which must be very painful.

THURSDAY, 2 JULY. LONDON   Today was the State Opening of the new Parliament by the Queen after the Conservative victory.

It was my turn to be the Gold Stick-in-Waiting but I had received a message from Sir Michael Adeane that Her Majesty particularly wished me to carry the Sword of State. This is a great honour for next to the Crown it is the principal piece of regalia at this State function and is traditionally carried by a five-star officer of the Services and, wherever possible, of course, a wartime leader.

In the past Bill Slim, Bruce Fraser and Peter Portal have been among those who have carried it,* and quite recently it was carried by Monty, who found the weight of the Sword too great for him and had to give up and retire to avoid fainting.

However, Monty is at least twelve years older than me and so the ordeal held no terrors for me. In fact it was rather exciting.

I wore naval full dress uniform with orders and decorations, and then had to put my peer's parliamentary robes over that with the collar of the Garter. I had some difficulty in hitching up my own sword.

The Sword of State arrived with the Crown in a special coach with its special escort of Household Cavalry. The Gentleman Usher to the Sword of State carried it up into the gallery where, in front of a large crowd, the ceremony of it being turned over to me took place.

In the Queen's procession I took precedence over the Earl Marshal

---

* Field Marshal, Admiral of the Fleet and Marshal of the Royal Air Force respectively.

and the Lord Great Chamberlain, who preceded the Queen walking backwards up the staircase which was lined by the Life Guards and the Blues and Royals. I walked forwards behind them but immediately in front of the Queen.

We separated when the Queen and Philip went to the robing room for the Queen to put on her Crown and Robes. Philip, instead of being in full dress uniform, was in a morning coat because his injuries from his polo accident were so bad that he couldn't bear the weight of the heavy full dress. He just put on his Duke's robes over his morning coat. Charles and Anne accompanied their parents.

I found it all very exciting and dramatic and felt very well. Then, as the Queen began to read her speech I suddenly started to feel faint. It was a hot day. Especially powerful lights were on for colour television, and I could feel I was sweating freely. Then I suddenly found the ground was starting to come forward in waves and I realized I was very near fainting.

At that moment the Earl Marshal, the Duke of Norfolk, signalled discreetly to one of the Ushers who came across and offered to carry the Sword. Although it is a heavy Sword and has to be carried in an upright position in front of the face aided by a strap and embroidered bucket, it annoyed me so much that I told him to get the hell out of it. I then started a battle of mind over matter and thank God the mind won and I lasted out. As soon as we moved off I completely recovered and felt quite well again.

After the Gentlemen Ushers to the Sword of State and Cap of Maintenance had removed them from myself and Peter Carrington respectively, he came over to enquire how I felt.

He told me afterwards that when he met the Chiefs of Staff they enquired after my health and his reply was, 'When I went over to ask Dickie about his health, before I could get a word in edgeways he turned round to me and said, "What are you going to do about the aircraft carriers?"'

I met the Bishop of London before leaving and he told me that all the Bishops on their bench had prayed for me when they saw how ill I suddenly looked. He then added, 'May I be allowed to say that I thought it was a wonderful exhibition of guts.' To this I replied, 'I thought you were going to say it was a wonderful demonstration of the power of prayer.'

At 1640 Noël Coward came to tea to discuss the part he is to play in the great 'Night of Nights' performance when he is going to introduce

Frank Sinatra and Bob Hope at the Royal Festival Hall at the 7.30 and the 11.30 p.m. shows.* He brought with him his seventieth birthday present to me consisting of a delightful modern painting of a crowded beach scene which he had painted himself.

I then drove to the Royal Overseas League London Headquarters where at 1800 I met the Queen in my capacity as Grand President. Philip should have come with her but he had to go for medical treatment, so I followed round in his place.

Lilibet was most concerned about my health; she said that she was so horrified at seeing me swaying in front of her that she tried to read her speech from the Throne more quickly so as to give me a better chance of surviving! She told me that Anne had been sitting with her hands held ready to receive me if I fell.

Patricia had been staying with Pammy at Britwell† and they watched the Opening of Parliament on television and were horrified at what they saw. Apparently the BBC kept their cameras on me expecting that at any moment I might collapse altogether. My daughters made me promise to go and have a medical check-up as soon as possible.

FRIDAY, 17 JULY. BROADLANDS After a ride in the morning I drove over to the Royal Naval Hospital, Haslar, for the promised medical check-up. This took quite a long while – it was very thorough including electro-cardiograms.

When it was all over Surgeon-Commander Preston, who had been in principal charge of the check-up, made the following statement to me. He said, 'I can only hope that when I reach the age of seventy I will be in the splendid all-round physical condition that you are now in, but I am slightly worried about your ECG, and I would like you to go and see Lawson MacDonald who is a heart specialist in London as soon as you can.'

On further enquiry he explained that the ECG showed that the blood supply to my heart was not as adequate as it should be through the narrowing of one of the main arteries in the heart – in fact in one of the coronary arteries.

He assured me there was nothing for me to worry about and I need take no special action before seeing Lawson MacDonald.

---

* A last-minute attack of pleurisy prevented him playing any part. Grace Kelly stood in.
† The Hicks's country home.

MONDAY, 20 JULY. LONDON At 1800 the new First Sea Lord, Peter Hill-Norton, came round for an hour's talk about the future policy for the Navy and Defence generally. He was brought in quickly to succeed Mike Le Fanu when he [Le Fanu] became so seriously ill. Mike was supposed to relieve Sam Elworthy as CDS, and now Sam has been made to stay on for nine months while Peter has a crack at the Navy and then goes on to relieve him as CDS. I am sure he will do the Navy and, indeed, Defence a great deal of good, particularly with Peter Carrington as the Secretary of State for Defence.

Geoffrey Archer* came in for a discussion about the great 'Night of Nights' on 16 November, and then at 2030 Peter Carrington came for a drink and I took him to the Royal Thames Yacht Club for dinner. We had an excellent talk on Defence policy. It is all a question of whether they can raise enough money to keep both the *Eagle* and the *Ark Royal* and, incidentally, enough men. At all events they have pretty well undertaken to keep the *Ark Royal* in commission for at least another ten years until the new type of carrier or 'through-deck cruiser' for vertical take-off aircraft can take over operating fixed-wing aircraft.

FRIDAY, 24 JULY At 0930 I went to see Dr Lawson MacDonald in Wimpole Street. He is a famous cardiologist who served in the Navy during the war. He told me that my electro-cardiogram had deteriorated considerably in the week since it was taken at Haslar, and that the constriction in my heart artery was more serious and that he must take immediate action to arrest it developing into a dangerous situation.

I asked him what I had and he said that I could call it 'pericarditis'. He then told me that I must cancel all my engagements and go straight to a hospital and to bed for at least a fortnight.

I then said I must now go to the Guards' Chapel in Wellington Barracks to deliver the address on the Maharaja of Jaipur at the tribute which I got the Life Guards to arrange as he had been an officer of the Regiment. Lawson MacDonald said I couldn't do it and I must go straight to bed.

I replied that even if it killed me I must carry out this last duty as he was such a great personal friend, and he rather reluctantly agreed.

So I drove round to Ayesha's flat in Grosvenor Square to collect her

---

* Mountbatten was inconsistent in accepting that Mr Archer spelt his name 'Jeffrey'. He had similar trouble over Nehru.

and her son, and other members of the family, and take them to the Guards' Chapel for the service.

After the service I drove back with her to her flat and had a long talk about her future and offered all my help. She is such a beautiful sweet woman whom I have known so well over thirty years, it is heartbreaking. The life of a widow in India is so difficult, even though the British have stopped them committing suttee (i.e., jumping on the funeral pyre of their husbands).

After this Tony drove me straight back to Broadlands where everything had been arranged for me to go to bed. I turned in with much relief and suddenly felt very tired – I slept soundly.

THURSDAY, 13 AUGUST. BROADLANDS   Lawson MacDonald has made it clear to me that I must keep out of circulation for about three months, but can start doing things again about the end of October. He wants me to cut my commitments by at least 50 per cent. This isn't going to be easy because I belong to over two hundred organizations and, indeed, I am the President or Chairman of forty-five of them, many of them international or Commonwealth wide which take a lot of personal attention.

He particularly wants me to cut out public speaking, and lectures. This has meant that I have sadly had to cancel the rather exciting lecture tour which had been laid on by the United States Naval Institute for a month from mid-September, visiting all the important Service Colleges in the United States. A couple of years ago in October I made twenty-eight speeches in thirty-one days, and he wants me to cut this right down, and I will.

My mail has been becoming rather unmanageable and has grown up to fifty letters a day. This has now been cut down by dint of my staff sending out cards to say that there can be no reply for a couple of months, and indeed in some cases sent a note to say the letter can't be shown to me at all at present but if they wish to follow the matter up they can write again in two months' time. I hope this is going to work.

There is no doubt I am beginning to feel better and better. People say I look better than I have for years which is very encouraging. The ECG which was taken on my return showed I was back to the same state I was several years ago when an ECG was taken for an insurance medical examination.

Really the incident at the Opening of Parliament has not been a bad thing because I don't believe I would have ever taken this pull if I hadn't had this providential warning.

On 5 November 1970 Mountbatten was in Washington for a meeting of the US and Canadian National Commissions of the United World Colleges.

When Charles and Anne were staying at the White House in July I had sent him a telegram through the Foreign Office urging him to ask President Nixon to give me some support for the United World Colleges in America. Charles was so successful in talking to the President that he offered to give a dinner for it.

At first the dinner was planned to take place during my lecture tour of the Service Colleges in the United States, but then, when the doctors prevented my going, the dinner was put off; in the meanwhile the President had to do a tour himself and he finally chose a most inconvenient date – the 5th November – because I had to get back for Gustaf's arrival at Broadlands the following day which required quite a bit of organization.

First of all we heard he might ask twenty American guests to meet me. I then got the Ambassador to send a message to say that we had a number of names of both Canadians and Americans who ought to be present if possible, and with some reluctance the White House thought they might go up to forty for dinner, which was an unusually large number for a private dinner.

I must say to my utter amazement the President suddenly turned it into what John Freeman called 'a complete State Banquet'. The President met me half way down the front porch steps, and conducted me to the place in the hall to receive musical honours. They had asked whether I would like to be received with 'God Save The Queen' and I had asked that they should play 'Rule Britannia' instead, as this was the personal salute of an Admiral of the Fleet. The White House had agreed. When the President and I stood opposite the band, it turned out to be the famous Red Coat Band of the United States Marine Corps Headquarters and after the musical honours there were a lot of TV films and photographs taken.

The President then conducted me into the big Ballroom where the party was lined up. The total number at dinner was ninety-six. I was told the maximum they could get in was a hundred – four people had fallen out at the last moment otherwise it would have been a hundred. President Nixon introduced each guest to me personally and I was surprised that I knew more than half the people pretty well and some of them very intimately.

He had included six of his Cabinet Ministers, the Chiefs of Staff, and most of the wartime leaders who were still in circulation. Then we moved off to the State Dining Room in which the whole party was seated at one long top table with three arms to it. I sat on the right of the President and on my right was the Secretary of State, Mr William Rogers.

Half way through dinner twelve men came in dressed in the Red Coat uniform of the British Army of two hundred years ago. They played 'The British Grenadiers' on fifes and drums, and did a sort of parade round the dining tables which reminded me of the Scots Guards' pipers going round at State Banquets at Buckingham Palace! The President told me it was the first time he had tried this idea and he hoped I didn't find it too theatrical.

A little later on about thirty or forty of the special Glee Party of the United States Army came in and proceeded to sing appropriate sea shanties, as well as 'Hearts of Oak' and 'Rule Britannia'.

During dinner I was able to talk to the President a bit about both Tino and Juanito to try and put over their respective points of view about Greece and Spain, and how I felt that the United States could help them.* The President appeared to be so interested that he called over to his Secretary of State to join the conversation and we had a three-cornered conversation lasting about twenty minutes.

Then came the moment for the speeches. David [Hicks] who was present told me that everybody all round him was deeply impressed with the fact that they had never seen the President make such a human and natural speech before!

In my reply, which lasted about twelve to fifteen minutes, I was able to reminisce a bit about the times I was over in the White House with Roosevelt, and I talked about Churchill. I said that a big dinner by the President of the United States in the White House was one of the greatest civic honours in the world, and that I now had had it twice as fifteen years previously Eisenhower had given a dinner at which he asked all our colleagues of the war to be present. I thanked the President

* Mountbatten was constantly urging the merits of constitutional monarchy in both Greece and Spain.

for having asked the surviving colleagues who were here now, but pointed out that there were practically none of the old party of fifteen years ago. The oldest person I recognized was General of the Army, Omar Bradley.

After coffee was over we moved into the Ballroom which had been rigged for a cinema, and here we showed the United World College film of St Donat's. The Ambassador thought that I ought not to speak for more than five minutes as the President would then want to go away. However, I am afraid I over-ran my time quite a bit, and the President himself asked questions and kept the thing going.

I had been worried that it would be against US Protocol to invite the President to become Patron of the US Commission of the United World College, and it might be counter-productive to ask him. I chanced my arm and did ask him. To my great surprise and joy Mr Nixon accepted; not only that but he made a statement in favour of the United World Colleges and announced to the whole company that he had accepted the position of Patron for the USA.

A general discussion followed and continued until 2330, at least forty-five minutes later than I had been told the President would be prepared to stay up.

1971

TUESDAY, 2 FEBRUARY. LONDON At 1610 the Maharaja and Maharani of Dhrangadhra and their son came to talk to me about the future of the Princes in view of the forthcoming election in India. I was deeply impressed by his statesmanlike and sensible approach to the whole question, and all the more disappointed in the way that Indira Gandhi has been treating them. What her father would think of her breaking the promise which he and Vallabhbhai Patel gave to the Princes, and which was enshrined in the Constitution, I cannot imagine. However, it is encouraging for the honour of India that the Supreme Court has reversed the crazy decision by the Prime Minister to try and de-recognize all the Princes separately under a section of the Law intended only to de-recognize a single Prince at one time, if he had committed a criminal offence and should have his privileges removed to enable him to be tried.

FRIDAY, 5 FEBRUARY. PANAMA The *Britannia* sailed at 0700 flying Philip's standard for the Pacific Cruise. He had invited the following guests to accompany him: Alexandra, Angus,* Patricia, John, Solly Zuckerman and myself.

After dinner the Galapagos films made by Anglia TV under the direction of Aubrey Buxton were shown. This gave the party a foretaste of what was to come.

SUNDAY, 7 FEBRUARY. *Britannia* GALAPAGOS ISLANDS At 1015 we arrived for our week's visit to the Galapagos Islands, which I for one had always longed to visit since the accounts of Philip's visit to them in 1964. John maintains he had been hoping to visit the Galapagos Islands ever since he read about Charles Darwin's visit one hundred and thirty-five years ago.

* Princess Alexandra and her husband, Angus Ogilvy.

206

From the moment of our arrival life became exciting. Several sea lions who had been basking on the lava rocks slid lazily into the water and then instead of diving and making off swam up to the boat to see what we were up to. After a steep 100 ft scramble up the lava rocks, we stumbled on to a fascinating plateau of lava sand on which a lot of peculiar small trees or large sparse bushes were growing. They were called *Palos Sanctos* – or Holy Poles – and some of them appeared to grow out of cracks in lava rocks with no visible earth to support them. But what made one feel one had arrived in Alice's Wonderland was the fact that on the branches of almost every little tree there sat a large exotic bird. There were frigate birds, some of them displaying for the mating season by blowing out a large scarlet bladder covering their neck and chest; there were red-footed boobies sitting on branches and masked boobies on the ground beneath. But what I found quite unbelievable was their splendid air of indifference. They took no notice of us whatever and in trying to persuade one to fly off John had practically to push it off its branch with the lens of my cine camera which he had borrowed.

Philip, the old campaigner, led the way far too quickly for my liking, while Patricia and I dallied to study these large, extraordinarily tame birds. Finally we broke out of the miniature forest in the sandy glade and arrived on a bare plateau of broken slabs of lava. Here there was the excitement of spotting our first marine iguanas. They are hideously attractive lizards but are only 1 to 1½ feet long on Tower Island, which breeds a particularly small species. They too were tame and only moved out of our way slowly and reluctantly.

No descriptions or films really prepare one for the miracle of walking among exotic animals and birds which are entirely unafraid, indeed unmoved, by human beings. We all agreed it was an unbelievable experience.

MONDAY, 8 FEBRUARY In the evening it was decided to have a barbecue ashore. We had a magnificent feast and then the full moon came up and bathed the beach in a suffused light. Patricia came back from a walk on the beach and talked of seeing many sea lions, so Solly and John and I set off. There were several groups of three or four each on the beach, but when we turned inland an astounding sight met our permanently astonished gaze. Two hundred yards back, down a reverse slope, there was an extensive mangrove swamp and on this reverse slope there were herds of sea lions. The normal family harem consists of a bull with about ten wives and some babies. But now they were in what Solly described as 'loose association'. I counted 40 in the first group. Solly estimated there were at least 100 more.

Most were asleep and took no notice of us until we were right on them, but the bull in each case leapt to their defence and with much bellowing advanced to the attack. We had heard that recently an imprudent photographer had been bitten in the leg by an enraged bull, so we beat a hasty retreat whenever a bull came for us. There was a peculiar smell, as strong as any fox, which emanated from the sea lions. Solly said that not only had he never dreamt to have the luck to see so many herds in 'loose association', but he wondered how many people had ever had the luck to see such a sight.

THURSDAY, 11 FEBRUARY   The Royal Yacht had moved the evening before to Academy Bay on Indefatigable/Santa Cruz Island. At 1050 we proceeded in the motor cutter to the Port, hardly more than a village, called Puerto Ayora. Philip was bunched by some local girls with lovely flowers in plastic bags. Finally, after a lot of argument, it was agreed that Solly and I should accompany Philip in the only serviceable vehicle to the Charles Darwin Research Station, whilst the rest re-embarked and went round by sea.

We drove direct to the Darwin Staff Dining Hall, erected in a pleasant modern style of stone two years ago, and waited for all the others to join us. Then we walked past the Director's charming house to the new circular tortoise-rearing house, which has just been erected at the expense of the rich San Diego Zoo.

A tall bearded young man from Belfast was in charge of the tortoise/ turtle department. Solly put him firmly in his place by asking, 'How many oviducts do the tortoises here have?' The poor young man obviously didn't know the answer but retaliated by saying he was the son of Professor Pritchard, whom Solly knew. But Solly's judgement was that this only made his ignorance less excusable.

Five of the fifteen species of giant tortoise are apparently already extinct, and until yesterday only seven of the dramatically different Hood Island tortoises were known to have survived. They are very distinctive as the carapace round their necks has grown up high like a tall narrow Elizabethan ruff. The Darwin team had left two on Hood

Island with slender hopes that they might produce young ones as they didn't even know their sex. They took off the other five, one male and four females two years ago. In the first mating season nothing happened and they were terrified that if their only male proved sterile this fascinating breed would die out.

This year eggs were laid which proved infertile, but then another lot of eggs appeared and to everyone's intense excitement six of them in the special incubator hatched yesterday, thus practically doubling the known population of the Hood Tortoise overnight.

In the evening Philip gave a dinner party of 36. The Royal Marines orchestra played and several of the guests expressed their thrill at attending such a wonderful banquet in the Galapagos Isles. I sat between the wives of the Minister of Defence and the Commander-in-Chief of the Navy,* which was rather heavy-going as the latter spoke only Spanish. The footman's face was a study when Granda Garces,† on unfolding his napkin, blew his nose in it.

FRIDAY, 12 FEBRUARY   The Royal Yacht proceeded to the small island of Plaza, just off the east coast of Indefatigable Island. Our party went in the motor cutter to the narrow passage between the islands.

Plaza was not in our programme, but I expressed such disappointment to Harris‡ at not having really seen any land iguanas that he recommended going there. A small, rough jetty had been built on the main island to which tourists were regularly taken. As he wasn't going to be there I asked, 'How do we find the land iguanas?' He replied, 'Take a bunch of bananas and walk inland and they will find you.'

We found four large sea lions lying, one on each step, at the end of the jetty. They were reluctant to move and only made way as we actually came alongside. In an adjacent, shallow pool there were over a hundred sea lions disporting themselves, with a couple of old bulls bellowing defiance from the seaward side.

The others immediately went to the pool, so I went on alone into the cactus grove of small opuntia trees. They had prickly pear flowers and fruit, too high for the iguanas to reach. I called 'Iguana! Iguana!' and shook my paper bag of over-ripe bananas, without any apparent result.

* Don Acosta Velasco and Vice-Admiral Benavides Chavez of Ecuador.
† An Ecuadorian friend of the Minister of Defence.
‡ Dr Michael Harris, an Englishman working with the Darwin Institute.

Presently I heard Philip shout, 'Look behind you', and there they were, three gloriously coloured, big land iguanas, following my footsteps in single file.

I stopped and held out a banana, which they immediately seized and devoured. By now the iguanas were appearing from all directions from the cactus grove, well trained to answer the tourist's call. The rest of the party came up and I shared my bananas with them. One impatient reptile even tried to climb up my leg to get at my bananas and more than once they had real fights over them.

They were uglier and fiercer but more fascinating than their marine counterparts. Their tails were shorter and fatter and their bodies bigger. Several exceeded four feet in length. They had bright yellow heads and red, green and grey bodies. When we ran out of bananas we picked the prickly pears – rather a painful process – and these proved equally popular with the growing pack of land iguanas.

THURSDAY, 18 FEBRUARY At 0840, Patricia called us to the veran-dah deck to look at Easter Island as we steamed down its western coast in bright sunshine and a mill pond sea. Through our binoculars we could see a row of seven of the famous Easter Island giant statues and herds of wild geese.

> *The party landed and drove to the slopes of Rano Raraku. Mountbatten was accompanied by Edmundo Edwards, grandson of a former Chilean Ambassador in London.*

During the fifteen-mile drive, we got Edwards to explain to us his version of the history of Easter Island, and we all continued discussions with him throughout the rest of the day. I must admit at once we were impressed by his honest and un-doctrinaire approach. He began by saying that he had unfortunately only arrived in Easter Island a couple of months after the Norwegian Expedition had left, but the natives openly admitted that they had given Heyerdahl* what he wanted. He arrived determined to find proof that Easter Island had originally been settled direct from the South American continent. He showed the

---

* Thor Heyerdahl, of *Kon Tiki* fame, who sought to demonstrate that the Polynesian Islands and other Pacific settlements were colonized by Peruvian Indians.

Mayor pictures of the sort of carvings to be found among the relics of the Inca civilization, and was delighted when Pedro Atan said that he had just that type of carving in his family cave, but was not allowed by his Aku-Aku to show them to anyone. Other natives who co-operated with Heyerdahl also 'recognized' the pictures. After considerable delays because of the opposition of the Aku-Akus, the spirits of the ancestors, bit by bit carvings were produced from three people's caves bearing a remarkable likeness to the Inca pictures. Heyerdahl was delighted, but in his book admitted he was disturbed by the newly washed appearance of the objects. The natives explained that once a month, out of respect for their ancestors, they cleaned and scrubbed all the artifacts in their family caves, and this apparently satisfied Heyerdahl.

In fact, Edwards did not oppose the possibility of an early settlement coming from South America, particularly if it were via an early settlement from the East in the Marquesas, he merely stated that there was not one valid scrap of archaeological evidence which had so far turned up to support the theory of direct settlement.

Edwards produced as evidence against a settlement from the East the fact that the Incas, and all Central and Southern American natives, knew of a special way to sharpen obsidian (the brittle, hard, volcanic stone) into daggers and spear and arrow heads effectively. This method had never reached Easter Island. But Philip, with fair-minded impartiality, refused to accept this as proof of no direct arrivals from the East, as those who came in rafts might have been peaceable, with no knowledge of how to handle obsidian. Edwards accepted this objection and rested his case on there being no positive evidence available.

He stated that the theory accepted in Easter Island itself was that a number of Polynesians arrived in large rafts, probably from the Marquesa Islands between 500 and 800 AD. In the ninth century there is evidence that they started cutting the relatively soft tuff from the great natural quarry of Rano Raraku, with basalt implements.*

A gorgeous yellow canvas tent had been erected on the beach for the ladies to change in. The men undressed on the beach. I could not find my bathing bag and asked the Governor† to get it. John remarked cynically, 'It takes a former Viceroy to send a Governor to fetch his bag!' The bathing was delightful. After we had dressed again we looked at the

---

* The Duke of Edinburgh warned Solly Zuckerman, who had by now left *Britannia*, 'Dickie, having studied the problem "in depth" is quite ready to explain it to anyone whether they are prepared to listen or not.'

† Of Easter Island.

foundation of one of the canoe-huts. Slabs of dressed stone were placed in the shape of the deck plan of a huge canoe. The stones were pierced with holes into which used to be set the framework of ti-branches or sugar cane bent like a canoe's ribs. The roof was made of totora reed matting covered with grass. The low, hull-like shape enabled those huts to withstand gale-force winds.

Then we all drove down to the nicest house of all, that of the Captain of the Port. A feast had been laid out in his garden to which several officers of the Yacht had been invited. Lamb had been cooked in the traditional Polynesian way. A pit had been dug in the earth, a fire lit, stones placed on top of the embers, and when the stones were hot, the lamb, wrapped in banana leaves, was placed on top and then covered with earth. Two hours later the meat was cooked to a turn.

Philip claims he had pork but the rest of us certainly had lamb as there are thousands of sheep on the island. In fact sheep farming is their main activity. The horses have run wild for years and there are now 5500 – five times more than the native population which is only 1060. There are another 500 Chilean officers, service personnel and engineers.

A group of native women of all ages, some in grass skirts, some in costumes made up of white sea-bird feathers, performed traditional dances and songs. Alexandra accepted an invitation to join the dances and did so with her usual grace. Philip declined the invitation with the excuse that he was suffering from archaeologist's feet! The entertainment ended with more garlands of shells and flowers and an exchange of presents accompanied by much kissing. I was given a charming reproduction of a rongo rongo and a carved walking stick which I passed on to John.

SUNDAY, 21 FEBRUARY. *Britannia* PITCAIRN ISLAND   No sooner had *Britannia* anchored than two white long-boats carrying vast Union flags put out from the tiny harbour in Bounty Bay and before long Philip was shaking hands with the Chief Magistrate, Pervis Young, and the members of the island council.* These were followed by families of Christians, Youngs and Warrens, varying in age from eighteen months to about eighty. Patricia, John and I joined the receiving line at a discreet distance. The visitors were entertained to 'High Tea' to which they did

---

* Pitcairn Island was populated by descendants of the mutineers from the *Bounty*, led by Fletcher Christian and Midshipman Young.

Addis Ababa, 20 July 1965. Mountbatten proudly (if a little gingerly) pats the imperial cheetah which had recently savaged the Japanese Ambassador.

Romsey, 20 July 1965. The King and Queen of Thailand visit Broadlands.

splendid justice. One man who looked exactly like 'Pop-eye the Sailor man' polished off 12 mince pies at one sitting. Then they all settled down to enjoy a concert by the Royal Marines Band.

MONDAY, 22 FEBRUARY All small island communities have a character of their own. The people of Pitcairn are no exception. Considering the problems of making a reasonably civilized existence on an island 2 miles long by 1 mile wide which rises to over 1000 feet and on which there is no flat space big enough for a tennis court, it needs a people with fairly exceptional qualities to survive 180 years.

Our day ashore began with the arrival of the long-boats to take us into the diminutive landing place barely sheltered from the heavy Pacific swell. The people – some 68 out of a possible total 83 islanders and 9 expatriates of all ages – were seated in rows on benches in the blazing sun on the village square facing the white Court House. Lying on its side under the House verandah was the black painted anchor of HMS *Bounty*. A speech by the Chief Magistrate, Pervis Young, was reminiscent of the immortal Sam Weller when he bade us a 'Wery warm welcome to our Village'! He referred to His Royalty Highness who had brought members of His Royalty family with him, Sir Lord Mountbatten and Mrs Lord Brabourne. Philip made a really excellent extempore reply. Then everyone present shook us all by the hand on their way into the Court House for morning refreshments. Cakes, sandwiches, biscuits, water melon both red and yellow, and soft drinks were attacked with vigour before the guests set off on a tour of inspection.

The Islanders have nearly all become Seventh Day Adventists and are allowed neither liquor, nor, regrettably, any of the wonderful crayfish which are only used as bait. We then visited the white wooden church and looked at the *Bounty* Bible.

We visited the Dispensary run by the Pastor's wife who is a trained nurse, assisted by a volunteer island girl.

The dentist Elwyn Christian works in one corner of the Dispensary. His most successful activity is pulling teeth out, but he also does fillings which were reported as notorious for their insecurity. He makes dentures which are reputedly ill-fitting and alter the outward appearance of the mouth grotesquely.

Next to the Dispensary is the Library and then the Post Office which is certainly the island's most important source of income. The last mail into the island produced over 100 letters from philatelists all over the world asking for stamps and all the other things collectors need. By the time the Postmaster had completed all *Britannia*'s demands, even his horny hands were rubbed sore by his franking stamp.

Norris Young, aged eighty-three, greeted Philip with, 'Of course you remember me. I was the man standing on the street corner in Auckland when you and your missus drove by. I was the man who had one foot in the air as I was about to step off the pavement and you waved to me.' At the end of the visit he held me by the hand and said to Philip, 'I hope your grandfather looks after you well.'

TUESDAY, 2 MARCH. *Britannia* SAMOA   In the following account of our visit, I have as usual made free use of Philip's excellent SITREP. He begins by quoting Rupert Brooke:

> You lie on a mat in a cool Samoan hut, and look out on the white sand under the high palms and a gentle sea, and the black line of the reef a mile out, and moonlight over everything –
> And then among it all are the loveliest people in all the world, moving and dancing like gods and goddesses.
> It is sheer beauty, so pure it is difficult to breathe in.

Actually, it wasn't quite like that when *Britannia* arrived in Apia. For one thing, it's the rainy season and a two-day torrential downpour only just stopped before *Britannia* went alongside.

Philip has, understandably, tried to keep the ceremonial down during this cruise, but realized he could not get out of wearing uniform for the official arrival here. He tried to suggest 'White Bush Shirt', but the Samoans asked for 'Full Dress' and to my dismay he yielded. I had not been expecting this and, although I had a white tunic onboard with medal ribbons and aiguillettes, I had not brought my medals or decorations.

Philip arranged for his Valet to let me look through anything he had to spare. Luckily he had two sets of medals and I found I was entitled to every one, including the Greek War Cross and the French Croix de Guerre, so I borrowed the spare set. Philip agreed to wear his GMBE neck badge and lent me his OM. He also lent me a spare Garter Sash, but without the Lesser George or Star. The PMO lent me his sword and undress slings. With all this borrowed plumage I felt somewhat embarrassed, but Patricia assured me I looked all right.

WEDNESDAY, 3 MARCH   We arrived a quarter of an hour before they expected us at the Race Course sports ground to watch Samoan cricket being played. They call it Kirikit and that is not the only change they've made. Teams are merely limited by mutual agreement and on this occasion each side mustered 10 players. Bats are more like three-sided clubs, the ball is made of natural rubber and the pitch is 22 yards of concrete.

The ball is bowled from whichever end it happens to end up after the previous ball was bowled. The two umpires carry red flags to signal 'out' and white flags to signal 'not out'. Batting is exclusively aggressive and more in the baseball technique. The next two batsmen, bare-footed and without any padding, wait at about 'point' for the next wicket to fall, which occurs fairly frequently. If the batsman connects, the ball usually travels a long way, but anywhere on the compass and from vertical to horizontal. The rain had left a number of large puddles on the field and any fielder keen enough to dive for the ball almost had to swim to get out.

Batsmen were caught, bowled or run out, in that order of frequency, and each wicket to fall was greeted by a short chant and dance of victory by the fielders. Each team wears its own distinctive pattern of lava-lava or cotton skirt, and their greens, blues and brilliant reds add colour to the scene of continual bustle and activity. Meanwhile, each team is encouraged by its own group of singers and dancers, who keep up a continuous performance throughout the match. A score of 39 runs for 14 wickets would probably look a bit odd at Lord's, but then the Lord's game is not kirikit. However, the Samoans can also play the MCC rules and defeated the *Britannia*'s cricket team today, though our soccer team beat theirs.

Samoan racing resembles European racing in much the same way as kirikit resembles cricket. The principles are the same, but the practice is rather different.

The average age of the jockeys would appear to be about eleven and most of the horses looked about the same age. The youngest jockey was only eight. In the main race for The Duke of Edinburgh Cup, one jockey had boots and breeches – but he didn't win – and three sported crash helmets. The remainder rode in jeans, bare foot, though one had spurs on his bare feet. The recent heavy rain had made the going rather muddy so many of the colours were not immediately recognizable. As batting in kirikit, the riding was aggressive with the result that the pace had slowed down considerably by the end of the 11 furlongs or just over twice round the course.

Betting appeared to be moderate, but the noise at the end of a race would have done credit to a close finish at Epsom. The bar, meanwhile, was doing the same sort of trade it does on all race courses all over the world. We followed Philip on a tour of the paddock, weighing room, bar and Tote. As we came back to the 'grandstand', a wooden platform raised about 4 feet off the ground, we were astonished to see a lot of people crouching on the grass underneath our stand. Apparently, the front of the grandstand is always kept clear and so they get a fleeting view as the horses flash by.

Mountbatten left Britannia *on 8 March and after visiting Australia arrived in Mauritius on 12 March.*

I had twice planned to visit Mauritius because of its big and important naval wireless station and also because its beauty was so renowned. At last I had this unexpected chance to come, and I was particularly delighted because I have always had a special interest in Mauritius as it was the scene of the most remarkable demonstration of *Nauscopie** in the eighteenth century, when it was still a French colony.

A French naval official, named Bottineau, evidently developed human powers which produced results never again achieved for 180 years when radar was discovered. He served in the island for twenty years from 1764 and developed the astonishing ability of detecting an effect produced in the atmosphere by the presence of a ship at sea. He could not only detect the presence of a ship when it was below the horizon, but up to distances of 100, 150 and occasionally 200 leagues, that is one, two, three or even four days sailing away.

In 1780 Bottineau wrote to the Minister of Marine in Paris announcing his discovery. The latter instructed the Governor of the island to enter his announcements in a register and compare them with actual arrivals. This had already been started, and between 1778 and 1782 he had announced the arrival of 575 vessels, many of them up to four days before their arrival.

The dilatoriness of the French Ministry of Marine, and the confusion caused by the revolution, meant that this fantastic discovery, proved by the official trials in Mauritius, was never followed up or explained. It remains one of the world's great unsolved scientific mysteries.

I was quite horrified to hear from the Prime Minister's official

---

* In its English form, 'nauscopy'. 'This pretended art was invented by a M. Bottineau from the year 1782 to 1784' – OED.

Secretary that I was expected to go to the State Banquet that night which I was told would last until nearly midnight; that all arrangements had been made and it had been announced in the papers. I pointed out that I had not got a dinner jacket with me and that I had already refused the invitation in London.

The Prime Minister's Secretary confirmed that the High Commissioner for Mauritius had sent a telegram to say that I would not wish to accept an invitation for the dinner, and he was quite sure the Prime Minister would understand if I didn't come. It was a great relief as it would have been very exhausting particularly with the change of time.

At 1915 we went to call on the Governor-General. He and Lady Williams were very friendly and charming but it seems a pity our Labour Government should have selected a couple that cannot speak French, for although English is the official language French is the spoken language to this day among all the natives.*

At 1945 the Prime Minister came to Government House, Le Réduit, to call on me. He is a charming man of about seventy called Sir Seewoosagur Ramgoolam. I had sat next to him at a Buckingham Palace Banquet for a Commonwealth Prime Ministers' Conference some two years ago and had made quite good friends with him. At all events he received me as though I was a long-lost friend, grasping my hands in both of his and repeatedly saying how pleased he was to see me.

The Prime Minister expressed his disappointment that I was not coming as his guest to the State Banquet for the Independence Day Celebrations. I told him that his High Commissioner in London had promised to send him a telegram saying I could not accept. He admitted receiving it but went on that his High Commissioner had added words to the effect that, 'Lord Mountbatten is a very sympathetic and kind-hearted man and I am sure if you press him hard when he arrives he will agree to come.'

I explained how tired I was, particularly with the eight-hour change in time, and I did hope he would forgive me if I didn't come. He said sadly that he would. Nevertheless the papers had already had my name among the list of guests so no doubt they would report my presence the following day.

SATURDAY, 13 MARCH. MAURITIUS A glorious sunny morning and we had breakfast on the verandah at 0830. At 0900 we drove into the

---

* Sir Arthur Williams's previous experience had been confined almost entirely to Labour politics in Yorkshire.

capital of Mauritius, Port Louis, to call on the Prime Minister. He had agreed last night that we could wear informal attire, and I warned him I should be in red trousers and a blue Tahiti shirt and he said that that would be quite all right. So we went to call on him dressed like this.

We went round to a side entrance where the Minister for Finance, recognizing me, came over and greeted us, and led us in to the Government offices and showed us where the Prime Minister's office was. When we arrived at the office we caused great consternation because the reception party had been out at the main entrance waiting for us. However, we came in and many photographs were taken with the Prime Minister including TV films. It must have been the most unusual dress for anybody calling on a Prime Minister to be filmed in!

After a gossip he offered to show us round the building, which we gladly accepted because it was of such historic interest. We saw all the State Rooms including the Throne Room with all the pictures of our Kings and Queens, and we were shown the new Council Chamber as well.

TUESDAY, 16 MARCH. LONDON   At 1830 the Spanish Ambassador, the Marques de Santa Cruz, had asked to see me. He brought a lot of copies of press cuttings from America saying how very successful the visit of Juanito and Sophie (the Prince and Princess of Spain) to Washington and New York had been. He complained bitterly that the British papers hadn't given adequate and favourable publicity. He also showed me an excellent photograph taken and published in Spain of Juan* and Juanito being reconciled in public with Sophie looking on smiling.

He then urged me to pay a visit to Madrid and stay with Juanito this year. I said that fortunately I had the excuse of going to see him on United World College business, as he is the Patron of the Spanish National Committee, and I would now go ahead and fix the visit in the autumn.

On 6 May 1971 Mountbatten flew to Brussels.

Baudouin had brought one of the rare giant 'Heads of State' Mercedes to meet me, exactly the same as the car we had been lent for our tour of

---

* Don Juan, father to the future King Juan Carlos of Spain, made heavy weather about renouncing his title to the throne in favour of his son.

Germany. Robert Blackburn,* who had gone ahead to make the arrangements, met me, and Baudouin very kindly gave him a lift back to the Palace.

Baudouin asked me what I would like to do, and I said I would like to have a look at the park and gardens. I reminded him that when I was here in the early spring of 1964 there was snow on the ground and one couldn't see very much; also, I was so busy visiting his Army, Navy and Air Force I didn't really have much time.

So off we set to walk through the truly magnificent park. It is 450 acres, completely isolated from the town which surrounds it. There are the most lovely ornamental lakes with exotic birds on them. There are many different trees which are quite lovely. All the blossom was out as well as the azaleas and rhododendrons. There is a series of vast conservatories about the size of the Crystal Palace running out from one wing of Laeken, including one which houses the tropical vegetation from the Congo.

But the really remarkable thing was a vast dome-shaped glasshouse which turned out to be the swimming pool. The pool itself was surrounded by tropical sand and tropical trees and shrubs, and laid out with little inlets. It was, without doubt, the most astonishing swimming pool I have ever seen. He offered me a bathing costume or as an alternative to go and see the rest of the park. I said I would like to see the rest of the park.

Baudouin insisted on coming along to my suite to fetch me for dinner and conducted me along the long corridors through the State Dining Room to the great domed Reception Hall. It was a small informal party of intimate friends, chiefly what he called 'hunting people' – it turned out they really all shot, except for the lady next to me who didn't like shooting and liked hunting on horse-back in the true sense of the word. He had a professor friend from the University of Louvain and made me tell him across the table in the middle of dinner all about St Donat's which enabled me to do good propaganda.

Following the continental custom, after dinner the ladies sat at one end of the big saloon and the men gathered at the other end. I was put in a chair at the head of two sofas where the other men gathered; I was then bombarded with questions about the world in general and India, and nuclear warfare in particular. One of their best-known Ambassadors, who I gather was head of the Foreign Office, led the

---

* One of the senior officials of the United World Colleges.

questioning which everybody took part in. It was very lively and interesting.

About 2230 Baudouin came along and spoke in a low voice to me. I thought he was to say it was bed time, but not at all, he asked if I would like to see the hot houses. I said 'Of course' and he replied, 'It will take a few minutes to get the lights turned on.'

In due course we all trooped off on a tour of the famous hot houses. They are like a collection of Crystal Palaces placed end to end with large glass passages. When we came to the first one we almost gasped it was so lovely, and then we went on to more beautiful flower arrangements through tropical trees and vegetation brought from the Congo jungle. Here some of the palm trees were growing so high they reached the roof, although the roof itself must have been about 100 ft high.

Fabiola showed me how they were preventing them from going through the roof by digging down into the earth round the tree a big hole, so that the tree had in effect to grow downwards instead of upwards!

After we had spent about half an hour admiring the great greenhouses in the first group, we came to a large staircase leading up to a higher level. Fabiola said, 'Would you like to see the best display of all, but it is a long walk.' I accepted with pleasure and indeed it was a long walk. The ADC who accompanied us said that the total walk was over a kilometre long through glasshouses and galleries. Every hundred yards or so a side gallery opened with a vista of another magnificent garden, wonderfully laid out, and very ingeniously lit to give the impression of bright tropical sunlight or soft mellow light, according to what was in the garden.

Finally we came to the great azalea display. There were so many hundreds all crammed together that I have never seen such a splash of colour in my life. A sandy twisting path led between these banks of azaleas. I was told that every one was brought in a pot and the pots were jammed together so that the whole effect was a blaze of tightly packed colour and quite unlike any azaleas growing in the open.

They told me that Leopold II had created this form of crystal palaces, and that traditionally they were always open during the month of May to the citizens of Brussels. They come in their thousands every day so that it is impossible for the family to make use of them in the day at the best time of the year. For this reason they had arranged all this wonderful lighting so that the family could enjoy the hot houses in the evening after dinner.

FRIDAY, 7 MAY. BRUSSELS Breakfast was laid out in my dining room at 0800. I have never seen such a spread for one man even in India. There were eleven dishes and plates, eggs and bacon and a variety of wonderful cold meats; a variety of cheese; all sorts of toast, bread and cakes; croissants and petit pain, jam, honey and marmalade and coffee with hot cream; as the coffee was very strong, I asked for some hot water; this created consternation and they finally brought it in a cup; evidently they had not been asked for it before.

All the dishes like, indeed, all the dressing table fittings, looked as though they were solid gold but I presume they were silver gilt. The coffee service itself was laid out on a vast gold or gilt tray with the Belgian Arms in the middle. Hollywood could not possibly have done better.

WEDNESDAY, I SEPTEMBER. CLASSIEBAWN This is the last day of the family holiday. I had six of my Security Guard in for drinks and small farewell presentations at 4 p.m. They have been most discreet; I have had a total of four uniformed police and eight Special Branch Detectives, of which three have been on round-the-clock duty in the house, besides two police cars for escort duties. I think the Irish Government were afraid the IRA might try to kidnap me and offer me in exchange for some of their leaders who are now in internment in Northern Ireland. However, we had no trouble at all and it has been a very pleasant stay without any undue police activity.

I invited those on duty tonight to come in and see Programme 12 of the television series of my *Life and Times* which is being shown again. It was great fun having some of the grandchildren present in the room at Classiebawn Castle seeing the twenty minutes of film taken of us all on holiday at Classiebawn Castle about five years ago. It was astonishing how much they have all grown, perhaps the most of all Michael-John.

SUNDAY, 5 SEPTEMBER. BROADLANDS The Lord Chamberlain wrote to me officially some time ago to say the Queen wanted my views on my own funeral and I promised to write my suggestions. One of the things I had to decide was where to be buried. I have had long discussions with the family about this in Ireland. My ancestors have, of course, been buried for seven centuries in Hesse and for several centuries before that in Brussels and all round in Lorraine.

When my father took British nationality and sold our castle in Germany, Heiligenberg, in which there was the mausoleum and graves of his parents, he obviously had to find a new place. As my mother had inherited Kent House from her great-aunt* Princess Louise, Duchess of Argyll, who had inherited it from her grandmother the old Duchess of Kent, Queen Victoria's mother, the obvious place was to be buried in the Isle of Wight.

Whippingham Church was built by Queen Victoria to use when at Osborne House. It had a small chapel known as the Battenberg Chapel in which my Uncle Liko, Prince Henry of Battenberg, lies in a sarcophagus as he had been Governor of the Isle of Wight. The ashes of his son, Drino Carisbrooke and the latter's wife, Irene, are in the Chapel, and I have lodged the ashes of my nephew, David Milford Haven, there also. There are memorial tablets to my brother Georgie, and sisters, Alice and Louise.

Outside in the churchyard nearby there is a lovely grave which my father and mother share, with a wonderful small replica of the giant golden cross over his parents' grave at the Heiligenberg. I find there is room for a plot for me to be buried there and have started negotiations with the vicar. However, the family are all determined that I shall be buried at Romsey and so I undertook to follow this up.

On 9 September 1971 Mountbatten and Solly Zuckerman flew to Stockholm to attend a meeting of SIPRI, the Stockholm International Peace Research Institute. He combined the visit with doing propaganda for the United World Colleges.

We had a fifty minutes' first-class discussion in which I think I was able to shift the Prime Minister† from his preconceived socialist notion that the United World Colleges were just places for bringing up the children of the élite. I told him that 70 per cent of all our places at St Donat's were from scholarships and that Sweden was the only one of the four Scandinavian countries which did not give Government scholarships and fellowships to teachers, with the result that it was only in Sweden that we had to look for the children of the élite. Even here we still had up to five scholarships given by Foundations but we wanted Government

---

* In fact, aunt.
† Olof Palme, a wealthy Socialist.

support. This went surprisingly well for I had been warned beforehand that there was little chance of changing the Prime Minister's mind.

After that I told him that we were discussing that very afternoon the possibility of having an associate United World College in one of the four Swedish Government sponsored boarding schools. He showed great interest in this.

SATURDAY, 11 SEPTEMBER. STOCKHOLM At 0940 Solly and I drove in one of the Royal cars to the Park Hotel where the meeting of the Scientific Council of SIPRI is being held. We were met by the outgoing British Director, Robert Neild, and his successor, Frank Barnaby. They and Solly between them introduced me to all the other members of the Council so that I knew them all by the time we sat down at 1000 in a very fine dark wood-panelled Conference Room.

There were twenty of us sitting round the room with opposite us the officers of the Institute, that is Professor Gunnar Myrdal,* Neild, Barnaby. The first thing we did was to elect a Chairman and we unanimously elected that delightful Ghanaian, Dr Robert Gardiner.† I must say he controlled the proceedings with much tact and skill.

Neild gave me his progress report since the last meeting of SIPRI which was also the first in 1967. SIPRI does a most amazing job with a staff of some thirty-six people and another half dozen consultants. They have produced a lot of really excellent books. First of all the great *SIPRI Year Book* which has now won an international reputation for accurate information on armaments and peace endeavours, etc. They have produced several large volumes on the problem of chemical and biological warfare, but their latest book is probably the most interesting on the arms traffic and consists of some nine hundred pages. I will give them all to St Donat's on return.

A great many Governments, including the British, refused to pass on any information to SIPRI but they wormed it out for themselves in any case. Solly made an excellent contribution, and after about half a dozen people had spoken I thought it was time I introduced myself.

I said that honoured as I was to have been elected to the Scientific Council of SIPRI, I thought it was very sensible that they should at last have somebody who knew something about the art of making war instead of only about the art of discussing how to avoid it. For the same

* Swedish economist and itinerant sage.
† At that time Visiting Professor of Economics at the University of Strathclyde.

reason I strongly urged them to accept at least half a dozen carefully picked Naval or Military Officers of about Captain's rank from the major powers who could help the staff work of SIPRI in all its departments, and at the same time would learn a great deal about problems which would be of use to them when they went back into their own Service Ministries.

To my surprise this was extremely well received. I pointed out that at present they only had one Military Officer in the whole organization and that was a Swedish Colonel whom I knew, and I hoped that this would be a good move.

On 25 September he was in Switzerland.

I only got to Les Avants at 1105. We had some difficulty in finding where Noël Coward lived because of course we pronounced the name 'Coward' as in English. Noël later explained to me that his house was called the 'Chalet Kohvah' which is how they pronounce his name in French.

He had the Lunts staying with him and Charlie Chaplin and his present wife, Oona, had come over from their place, twenty minutes away, to meet me. It was really an extraordinary meeting. When I came in Noël leant forward, put both his hands on the arms of his chair and made a motion as though he was going to get up. I asked him not to get up and he replied that he couldn't anyhow even if he tried – he was merely trying to look polite; Noël seems in a really bad way. However, he was spritely compared with Charlie who sat on the sofa by me and practically never uttered or moved.

Alfred Lunt was gay, wearing very dark glasses, but I discovered he was completely blind. His wife, Lynn Fontanne, was really the only hale and hearty person, and of course she is getting pretty old too. So I set about reminiscing which went very well as they remembered the reminiscences and joined in. Luckily I had put off lunch from 1230 to 1315 so I was able to stay an hour and a quarter, but at the end of that time when I wanted to go they wanted to have photographs taken; so we practically carried Noël and Charlie out on to the verandah while poor Alfred felt the way round the walls with his hands. Here a series of snapshots were taken and books were signed.

1971

*After a brief return to England he flew to Madrid on
16 October 1971.*

After tea at the Embassy the Russells* drove us down to the Royal Park
El Retiro where we got out and walked along the ornamental lake. We
then drove back to the Embassy where the Prince of Spain, Juan Carlos
(Juanito), was to meet us.

I had arranged some weeks previously to stay with him and his sweet
wife, Sophie, sister of Tino of Greece, but the Shah's two thousand five
hundred year celebrations in Iran clashed and Juanito said he could not
get back until the Sunday. For this reason it was agreed that Pammy and
David and I should stay at the Embassy until the Sunday. The next thing
I heard was that he couldn't get back until the Monday.

He rang me up just before he left for Iran to say that he really couldn't
face missing us for two days, and he was therefore cancelling the second
part in the main official jollifications at Persepolis so as to get back to
meet us. I did my best to dissuade him but he said he wasn't really keen
on going to Teheran in any case. At all events he arrived at the Embassy
at 1920 having flown from Shiraz that day.

At dinner they both let their hair down and gave us a blow-by-blow
account of events in Persepolis. Juanito explained that the heirs apparent or consorts such as himself, Philip and Bernilo, were received by a
Guard of Honour at the airfield at Shiraz without being invited to
inspect it. They were then each driven in armed procession to Persepolis;
a trip which took me three quarters of an hour when I was there in 1963,
took two hours because there were so many people on the road in
separate processions each with three armed jeeps.

A tremendous tented compound had been put up, the five radiating
avenues being named after the five continents with five tents on each
side of each avenue, making fifty in all. Each tent had a large sitting
room, two bedrooms and an annexe with folding beds for the servants.
Apart from their own suite they had an Iranian Colonel and Lady-in-
waiting and French servants specially flown over from France at a wage
of £50 a day.

Sovereigns, including Tino, were met by a large Guard of Honour,
which they inspected, at Persepolis where the Shah received them
personally and then conducted them to their tent.

Juanito and Sophie persuaded Hussein, the King of Jordan, and his
wife, Muna, to come with them ahead into Tino's tent to await their

* Sir John and Lady (Aliki) Russell had transferred from Addis Ababa to Madrid.

225

arrival. When the Shah conducted Tino and Anne Marie to their tent, he threw open the door and said, 'This is your home.' He was taken aback to find four grinning people already in the sitting room. He was quite put out and didn't really like it.

The banquet of six hundred people took about two hours, with every sort of fantastic delicacy like quail's eggs and Imperial caviare, stuffed peacocks with quails round as the peacock isn't really edible. The wines were the finest obtainable each worth £40 or £50 a bottle.

Maxims in Paris had been given the contract and they brought the staff of the Palace Hotel in St Moritz and the Principal Hotel in Monaco who cooked and served the meal, which was delicious and hot.

SUNDAY, 13 OCTOBER. MADRID   We drove to Aranjuez. This was at my suggestion as I remembered going there with Alfonso and Ena when Edwina and I were staying with them, and we had both been immensely impressed by the beautiful Palace and the surroundings.

We drove along with two car-loads of security men following us, and every three or four hundred yards there were members of the Guardia Civil. Juanito told me he was unable to stop this because this was the procedure whenever Franco drove out and he had been granted the same privileges and could hardly decline them. He said, however, that when he became King he intended to cut that out, as it was entirely unnecessary and very unpopular with the unfortunate police.

Aranjuez has been wonderfully maintained ever since the days that Alfonso spent so much money on it, and it is open to the public except between 1300 and 1500. Thus we arrived when the public were not there. I must say wherever we went that day the public in the park gathered in little knots to clap loudly to show their enthusiasm for Juanito and Sophie. When we walked among them they all dashed forward to shake them by the hand and obviously they are very popular.

We spent about two and a half hours going through every room in the Palace, one being more beautiful than the next. Franco had given instructions that there was to be a special section showing the clothes and uniforms of Kings and Queens down to Alfonso XIII. It is now ready but he said it was not to be opened to the public until Juanito had given his personal approval, so our visit was in the nature of an approval and most interesting.

We had dinner just before 2100 and afterwards had another film in the delightful little cinema – this time it was *The Killing of Sister*

George. I am afraid it shocked Sophie immensely seeing Lesbians behaving in a very unashamed way in the film, and Juanito found it rather dull.* I personally found it entertaining.

After the film Sophie showed us the marvellous jewels she had taken to Persepolis, which included the famous original Pellegrino. Ena had told me theirs was the original and that the one Richard Burton gave to Elizabeth Taylor was not the famous original one.

---

* In his bread-and-butter letter Mountbatten thanked Prince Juan Carlos for the 'fabulous caviare' and 'the delightful cinema with its shocking Lesbians'.

1972

Mountbatten was in Paris on 4 February 1972.

We drove to 4 Route du Champ d'Entraînement. Here I called at 1630 on David and Wallis Windsor. I was shocked at his appearance; he seems to have aged by ten years since I saw him last, and was hobbling about on a stick. He told me that the deep X-ray treatment of his throat had arrested the growth there but he now had a hernia and was worrying about an operation.

I asked them both whether they had any idea of the amount of unfavourable publicity about the film being made by an American television company of their life called *The Woman I Love*, with Faye Dunaway doing the part of Wallis. They said they had never been consulted, had never given their authorization, and had already written a lawyer's letter to the American Broadcasting Corporation asking them to stop it. This had been passed on to the television film company that was making the film but without result.

I urged them to take immediate action. I persuaded David to ring up our Ambassador, Christopher Soames, and ask him to send his Press Attaché down to see him at once. Christopher agreed. I then drafted out a statement which I suggested David should read out at a press conference sitting together on a sofa with Wallis. I suggested they should have the conference as soon as possible, and that after having read out their statement they should withdraw and leave it to his Private Secretary and the Embassy Press Attaché to answer further questions. I urged them to allow photographs to be taken to get the maximum publicity for their repudiating this film.

As their lawyer said there was no chance of stopping it in America, I suggested they should concentrate on an appeal to the British and Commonwealth television companies not to embarrass them by showing a film of such atrocious bad taste in their countries.

They liked the idea and appeared to be very grateful and are following it up, but whether contrary advice will prevail remains to be seen.

1972

David Windsor rang up from Paris to say he and Wallis had both been thinking over my advice to give a press conference denying that they had authorized the film being made of them, but that their solicitors in America had advised against this, saying it would only give a great deal of publicity to the film without stopping it. They had talked to our Ambassador, Christopher Soames, who agreed with this advice.

I told him that I thought this would be all right provided they prepared statements to give the press in reply to any questions asked, making it quite clear that they had not authorized this film in any way. This he agreed to do.

In February 1972 Mountbatten, accompanied by the Brabournes, visited Burma and Singapore and then joined the Royal Yacht, Britannia. *He arrived in Rangoon on 9 February.*

The Ambassador* had warned me that the plan for the General to come round with us had been changed, nominally because he had to have meetings with the Prime Minister of Malaysia, and other conferences, but in fact he thought it had all been changed because within the last three or four weeks he and his sweet wife, Katie, had broken up.

Nothing was known officially but they had not been seen together in public for four weeks, and obviously it would be too embarrassing for him to come round without his wife on a conducted tour with such old friends. We felt terribly sad about this and slightly embarrassed not knowing what to say. However, he was very cheery and cheerful and full of apologies at not being able to come round, and asked us to come back early to Rangoon so that we could come and see him for a gossip before the Union Day dinner.

Having received a letter from U Nu, the former Prime Minister of Rangoon,† written ostensibly from the North Eastern area of the country and claiming still to be the Prime Minister, saying that he and his forces were about to start an invasion of Burma within the next hundred days, I was slightly worried and asked some questions about U Nu. It transpired that he in fact was living in Thailand and had less than

---

* Mr Edward Willan.
† [*sic*] Presumably Burma was meant. U Nu had been ousted in a military coup in March 1962.

a thousand followers and was really giving nobody any trouble. This was what the Foreign Office had told us so we stopped worrying.

FRIDAY, 11 FEBRUARY. RANGOON   We got dressed in lounge suits to call on the Chairman of the Revolutionary Committee and Prime Minister of the Union of Burma, in other words our old friend General Ne Win. He received us in his own house which he built after the war on Inya Lake, and very charming it was, much smaller and more compact than the real State House. We had a ten minutes friendly talk about every sort of matter, and then suddenly he turned round and with charming candour told us the sad story that he and Katie were divorced. He said it had happened about a month ago and was a great shock to him, but matters had arisen which he could not disregard. They remained good friends but now lived apart. He had given her one of his houses and the children were divided between them. We expressed our great sadness at this news and I asked him if I might write a line to her and the General agreed.

After this we all three had a long discussion about the United World Colleges trying to persuade Ne Win once more to let us have a boy or girl from Burma. This time he was much more sympathetic, as he said that the Burmese level of education had recently risen to the required standard, but he still was worried about American influence if there was American money behind it. I suggested he should send his Ambassador with some of the people from the Embassy to pay a visit to St Donat's, and this he agreed to do and I said I would arrange it. It looks like progress at last for Burma.*

At 1855 Ne Win drove us in a great procession with the usual armed guard to the old State House. (I might add that we have our own police escort and we have our own soldiers in Rangoon this time.) The occasion was the annual celebration of Union Day, and in fact the Silver Jubilee of the date on which various tribes and districts of Burma agreed to come together and form a union in 1947. I recalled having seen the late Major General Aung San at our house in Chester Street just before I went out to India while he was having his discussions with Attlee. The result was that their Independence dated from January 1948 but the Union from February 1947. Patricia and I had been to the Twentieth Anniversary five years ago but this was even more splendid.

---

* Mountbatten was over-optimistic. Ne Win never changed his view that the United World Colleges had little to offer Burmese youth.

None of the Corps Diplomatique, nor indeed any foreigners are invited, but Ne Win said everybody regarded us as honorary Burmese.

There were four thousand guests from all over Burma in traditional dresses, and something like eight hundred people sat down to a served dinner at tables, and the other three thousand odd collected their meal themselves and sat at small tables. There was a magnificent band and a large collection of artists who sang and entertained us during dinner. There were splendid illuminations, more than ever before, having myriads of lights in all the trees.

We left at 2230 and said farewell to Ne Win, whom I gave a gift as usual in recognition for all he is doing for us on this trip.

MONDAY, 14 FEBRUARY. MAYMO   I went with the Station Commander, Colonel Tun Aung Gyaw, to visit the Burmese Defence Services Academy which is under his command. In fact he has a large command of over five thousand soldiers.

Incidentally it seems quite odd that with an army of over 120,000, about two thirds the size of the British Army, they have only one or two Brigadiers, and all the rest are Colonels when they would be at least Lieutenant Generals or Major Generals in our Army. In fact the only General is Ne Win himself, who is also Chief of the Defence Staff, and presumably because they do not want to give an impression of too much militarism they have kept the senior ranks down drastically in all three services. The three Chiefs of Staff are of Brigadier or Commodore rank.

This Academy is fairly new and some of the buildings are only two or three years old, though it was founded here in 1958. The complement is just over 400 cadets who spend four years there and take a concurrent civilian degree of Rangoon University, who send up lecturers as part of the staff. Round about 10 per cent each year is taken for the Navy, and another 10 per cent for the Air Force; as these are all volunteers they are usually the best of a good bunch. On an average they get about 5000 applications each year which they reduce to 500 by going through their school records, and the 500 are each brought in in groups for a week to be tested and finally they pick the 100 best to enter. So they are getting a pretty good stamp of officer.

I was shown their dormitories and ante-rooms. In the library they showed me a book about myself called *Mountbatten of Burma* by

George Baker, a book which I hardly remember having seen before.* I found they hadn't got John Terraine's *Life and Times* so I offered to send them a couple of copies.

Then they produced the Burmese translation of my *Report to the Combined Chiefs of Staff* on the campaign in Burma.† I was so fascinated by this that they gave me a copy, and I said I would accept it in exchange for the two books I was going to give them.

I went and saw some of the classes at work. It was amusing to see a mathematics class having simultaneous equations written on a blackboard and the physics class doing applied mechanics; the language of instructions being Burmese except where the terms are too technical when they have to use English.

Finally we went to the Officers' Mess. The Director of Studies, Commander Mya Aung, is a fine old Naval Officer who knew all my old Burma Navy friends. The Director of English, who is a Lieutenant Colonel, joined him in telling me that the teaching of English was greatly hindered by not having up-to-date equipment. The British Council had helped them with some tape records from the BBC but they really want a proper language laboratory, and I undertook to try and see if I could get the British to cough up enough money to provide them with one. The Commander suggested that as I had been able to get a large ocean mine-sweeper *Marina* given to the Burmese Navy free, it shouldn't be too difficult to get a language laboratory!

SATURDAY, 19 FEBRUARY. SINGAPORE   I had arranged to call on the Prime Minister and was interested to see he had abandoned his offices in the old City Hall and had moved into what was the Governor's Secretariat.

This wing has been completely redecorated and altered in a very modern and dashing style with a new lift. Harry Lee Kuan Yew was as charming and friendly as ever and I had about ten minutes' business talk with him about the United World Colleges project.

In the course of this I asked him whether he would now agree to become the Patron of the Singapore National Committee for the United World College when it was formed in a few months' time. He was very

* The book, published in 1959, was one of a series of 'Red Lion Lives' to which Mr Baker had also contributed volumes on the Duke of Edinburgh and Peter Scott.
† Published in English by the Stationery Office in 1951.

diffident about this, and when I explained to him exactly what I wanted he said he was not worthy or qualified or fitted for the job. I heartily agreed that he was entirely unfitted and unworthy but nevertheless I still wanted him to be the Patron, and he laughed and said when the time came he probably would accept.

He told me he had a great scheme to create a display in the room in the City Hall in which I had taken the Surrender, and they wanted to have full-scale reproductions of the Allied Commanders and the Japanese Commanders, probably with waxwork likenesses, or at all events some adequate form of representation. After a lot of research had been done, he said that he was very disappointed that the Japanese refused to co-operate and pretended they couldn't remember the names of the Generals who took part! I suggested to him that it would be very remarkable indeed if the Japanese should have co-operated in a permanent memorial to their own defeat.

MONDAY, 21 FEBRUARY. *Britannia* Cabin 'A' (normally used by Charles) which I am using is really splendid and comfortable and light, though not quite so big as the cabin I usually have. We spent the day cruising idly in the Straits of Malacca so as to give Lilibet and the others a rest from their strenuous tour. We stopped off [at] an island where tents were erected for a picnic party, but Lilibet felt too tired so we remained on board. I have breakfast and tea with the family as usual, but all of us have lunch and dinner in the dining room with the Household.

TUESDAY, 26 FEBRUARY At 0930 *Britannia* berthed alongside the new quay at Port Klang. This is the new local name given to the famous old Port Swettenham.

At 1800 Tony Duff* drove me in the Rolls down to the Morib beaches which are only some six miles south of Klang. The main part of my ZIPPER Force consisting in all of some quarter of a million men, to the best of my memory, was planned to land in assault craft across the Morib beaches when we invaded Malaya in September 1945. In fact the dropping of the atomic bomb ensured that there would be no opposition, but the beaches turned out to be treacherous and soft in places so

---

* Antony (later Sir Antony) Duff. Deputy High Commissioner, Kuala Lumpur.

that the tanks and most of the lorries got bogged down and had to be pulled out by the Beach Recovery Organization.

I mentioned to three of the guerrilla officers present at the luncheon the bad intelligence they had given me about beaches, and they laughed and said that when I went down I would find out how deceptive they were. They pointed out to me in any case they had done a successful deception operation which had moved the bulk of the Japanese forces to the north, leaving only one battalion covering the Morib beaches area which we could very easily have knocked out with our overwhelming infantry which landed without difficulty.

Tony Duff and I arrived to find a most magnificent long beach, even more splendid than Ngapali, and an even more gradual slope so that at low water there is a very long stretch of beach. We walked right out to the water's edge and the sand appeared to be exceptionally firm. Only in two places was there any sign of softness, and then we didn't sink in above the soles of our shoes. I suppose there must be some crust formation with soft sands underneath which give way, but there was certainly no indication now and I can hardly blame the people who gave me the intelligence.

At all events the story that we could have been defeated on the Morib beaches is actually nonsense because of course we would have got the troops ashore; all that was delayed was the tanks which could have fired from the beaches. I feel a great deal better about it now that I have seen the notorious Morib beaches for myself.

MONDAY, 28 FEBRUARY   We sailed in the night, escorted, as usual, by our frigate *Cleopatra* and four patrol boats of the Royal Malaysian Navy. We arrived alongside at 0930 at the old Port of Jesselton, now re-christened Kota Kinabalu, capital of the state in the northern extremity of the great island of Borneo, the biggest island in the world.

At 1000 the Royal Party disembarked and after being received by the Governor, the Chief Minister and other notables, we set off in the usual motor-car procession. We reached the Queen Elizabeth Hospital at 1030 where an inspection tour was carried out. This was the first of the nostalgic rather painful memories for me, for it was here that Edwina carried out her last hospital inspection the day before she died.

The Eye Specialist of the hospital was attached to me and explained that he was the Commissioner of the St John Ambulance Brigade and had helped look after Patricia and me when we were here in 1964. He told me that the state of the hospital had got more decrepit and dirty than could possibly be imagined. When they knew that Queen Elizabeth was coming to see the Queen Elizabeth Hospital the Government gave an immediate grant of $93,000, with the result that the hospital now looked like new and they were particularly grateful for the Queen's visit.

We then walked back to the Officers' Mess and joined the Royal Party for morning refreshment. I asked Lilibet, Philip and Anne if they would like to come over and see the room where Edwina died. They said they would, and we all set off on foot much to the consternation of the officials who had a motorcade set up with police outriders who blocked the way down to where we were trying to walk. Luckily, however, the press had left by this time, so we were spared twenty journalists with thirty photographers who would have made the visit to the old Chief Secretary's house quite intolerable.

As it was we went entirely alone and the only person who was allowed in was the Army photographer in uniform to take one picture. We four went into her room very silently and sadly.

A Reception was held on board at 1900 at which rather a wonderful and exciting event occurred. The Chief Minister told Philip and me together that it had been decided to name the road off which the house in which Edwina had died stands 'Lady Mountbatten Road'. I was deeply touched and I think Edwina would have been too. The High Commissioner, Sir John Johnston, when informed expressed the greatest surprise and pleasure as he said the whole policy in Malaysia, particularly Sabah, was to get rid of all the English names and substitute Malaysian names. This was the first case he had heard of during his time of an English name being introduced.

TUESDAY, 29 FEBRUARY I feel I ought now to explain my position on this cruise. When Lilibet very sweetly said I could come for the cruise, and to do what I liked about landing or not with the party, I had originally suggested that I should remain on board the whole time. The first place at which this became impracticable was in Sabah, because of course I wanted to be there when we went and saw the room in which Edwina had died, and half the effect of the trip would have been lost if I hadn't stayed with the Royal Party.

In Brunei the situation was quite different for Sir Omar was an old

friend of mine and told Philip Moore* when he came on the reconnaissance trip that he particularly wanted me to land with the Queen and
take part in all the events with the Royal Family. So Lilibet sweetly
agreed I could land there, and after that it was agreed I should land
everywhere. However, one effect of this very recent decision is that
practically none of the printed programmes have my name in them
anywhere and I have to play it more or less by ear after landing.

Since my last visit to Brunei with Patricia in 1964, the old Sultan, Sir
Omar, abdicated in favour of his son who has just completed his
training at Sandhurst and has an Honorary Commission in the
Coldstream Guards.

So it was that the young Sultan, I suppose about twenty-seven, did all
the honours today with his young wife; met Lilibet and Philip on
landing and conducted them to where the rest of the Brunei Royal
Family were drawn up, among them Sir Omar and his wife. I followed
immediately after Anne, shaking hands with the family. We were all in
full dress. I had had to telegraph for my Garter sash which had been
forgotten because I found that Philip had no spare sashes on board this
time.

One of the Gurkha Battalions with the British Army is kept in Brunei
in rotation. The Sultan pays the expenses of stationing the Battalion
here, realizing that it was due to the Gurkhas that he did not lose his
throne in the rebellion in 1962.

There followed a fantastic procession through the streets of Brunei.
There were about two hundred and fifty men carrying either different
coloured umbrellas or ceremonial silver spears with coloured silk
streamers attached to them. Then followed the golden chariot which
was used for the coronation of the young Sultan. It is 18 feet long and
has seats on three different levels; on the top level there is the throne
which was occupied by the Queen and the Sultan; on the intermediate
level sat Philip and the Raja Isteri, the Sultan's wife; on the lowest level
there were four seats occupied by Anne, Sir Omar and Suri Begawan
Raja, his wife, and finally one of his daughters, Princess Masna, to
balance Anne. Equerries and ADCs walked on each side of the chariot,
which was drawn by 120 men by means of wooden bars fixed across the
shafts.

Lilibet and Philip both enjoyed the trip very much as the chariot went

---

* Sir Philip Moore, who had been Assistant Private Secretary to the Queen since 1966,
  succeeded Lord Charteris as Private Secretary in 1972.

smoothly and comfortably on rubber wheels. They were high enough up to get a good view of the enthusiastic crowd. Immediately behind the golden chariot there was a large car carrying the traditional band of ancient instruments; then came the motor-car procession headed by our High Commissioner and myself, followed by other members of the Brunei Royal Family, and finally the rest of the court officials.

We drove by car to the Sultan's Palace, the Istana Darul-Hana. Philip, Lilibet, Anne and I went to a new wing which has been built for the Royal Visit, really beautifully constructed and furnished but apparently only completed 48 hours ago as the whole place still smelt of paint. My ADC then came to tell me that Sir Omar wished the Sultan to present me with 'The Most Esteemed Family Order', the same as Lilibet, Philip and Anne had received. I pointed out that I should have to get permission for this, as I had to refuse at least a dozen Orders all over the Mediterranean and in South America through not having the Queen's official per-mission. I asked Lilibet and she said I could accept this because it was given during one of her official visits.

Meanwhile Lilibet, Philip and Anne got themselves decked out with the new Order, whereas I was kept in a state of suspense as obviously the Orders had to be worn at the State Luncheon. Just before lunch there was an exchange of gifts in Lilibet's sitting room, and at the end of this the Sultan came and presented me with the large box containing the Order. I dashed outside and with the help of my Leading Steward we tried to get myself fixed up in it. There wasn't time to get it properly done as in Philip's case, but what I could do was to hang the collar over my shoulder straps and push the pin of the star through my white tunic. All was well while I walked slowly in a dignified manner in the procession into luncheon. But when I tried to pull up my chair and leant forward and gave it a jerk, the whole decoration slipped round my neck and hung down below my belt. However, it wasn't noticeable at lunch and I managed to adjust it before we left.

At 1615 we left to go back to Pangkalan Batu where a large bamboo band was playing. The Governor and his wife saw us off and we embarked in the Royal Barge and the escort boat and went down the river for just over a mile escorted by the famous Dragon boats. These boats are forty to fifty feet long manned by up to twenty young men, each rowing with a short paddle and very quick stroke, very gaily dressed, each crew in similar uniforms. There were some sixteen of these boats paddling very fast and very close to each other. There were also two large decorated boats, one with a large Chinese Dragon.

All this went well, until the police launches started coming up too fast and their wash swamped one of the Dragon boats which slowly sank as the crew jumped out. (Needless to say this proved to be the only item picked up by the press, who really seem to concentrate on things going wrong. For instance, we found that the *Daily Mirror* made a great story of the unfortunate tribesman in Sabah who was unable to blow the dart out of his blow-pipe.) When the Dragon boats broke off we still had quite a long way to go round the bend of the river to get back to the place we landed in the morning; and then we went on to *Britannia*, the whole trip taking just under one hour. It was very high water and the banks were completely hidden; the palm trees on the edges appeared to grow out of the water.

SUNDAY, 5 MARCH. SINGAPORE   The Prime Minister of Singapore has been most co-operative about this return visit to Singapore, and accepted that this would be entirely to the British Commonwealth Forces and nothing to do with the Civilian Authorities in Singapore.

It was a nostalgic, and in a way sad, day for me. Having seen the great Naval Base started in 1922, almost completed when I was out in 1934 in the *Daring*, and finally having had to restore it after the damage by the Japanese in 1945, and having again seen it in full working order as First Sea Lord and then as Chief of the Defence Staff, and having had my final television series filmed in the Naval Base in 1967 when we had a magnificent Far Eastern Fleet and many troops and air forces, it was a great blow to me when the Labour Government suddenly decided in 1968, three years after I had left, to withdraw the whole of our military forces from the Far East.

I was delighted when the Australian and New Zealand Governments said that they would at least each keep a battalion, some aircraft and a frigate there, and the very moment the Conservative party won the election they announced that they were going to participate in a Commonwealth Force. This Force known as ANZUK (Australia, New Zealand, United Kingdom) took over on 1 November 1971 when our Far East Command Organization was dismantled.

Unfortunately we had given over the whole of the Naval Base and the British airfields, barracks and facilities to the Singapore Government, though Lee Kuan Yew was bitterly opposed to the removal of our Force. So new negotiations had to take place to try and get back from the Singapore Government the facilities that were wanted. So less good arrangements could be made than would otherwise have been possible. However, it was exciting to see an inter-Service/inter-Commonwealth Organization thoroughly integrated on the lines I have always advocated.

MONDAY, 6 MARCH. *Britannia*   We anchored off Malacca at 0930. Lilibet and Philip did a very successful 'walkabout' as far as the Dewan Perbandaran, that is the Municipal Offices. Here she was received by the Commissioner of the Malacca Municipality and led into the main hall, where a most original performance had been prepared for us showing a traditional Malay and a Chinese wedding. The Malay ceremony was held in accordance with the Hindu custom, which was adopted by the Malays in the fourteenth century before the coming of Islam to this part of the country. The bride's wedding dress was in magnificent gold brocade and embroidery and she looked beautiful.

The Baba of Peranakan wedding is a cultural heritage of the Straits-born Chinese of the former British Colony. Every movement of the feet of the bride and bridegroom had a significance, and the bride had to keep her hands completely hidden inside an elaborately embroidered cover rather like a muff.

Both bridegrooms were attended by a sort of best man, and both brides were attended by an elderly woman, apparently a professional 'marriage arranger', who looked after the bride and kept arranging her clothes.

Lilibet, Philip and I went up afterwards and spoke to the brides and bridegrooms and were startled in the case of the second couple to be introduced to their child, a five-year-old girl, for they had been married for six years; and the other couple had been married a year or two. They were just going through the form of ceremonial again for our benefit.

After this we had to attend a reception given by the Chief Minister which was tiring and boring; in fact I really felt very tired, and went out and sat down outside to rest for a bit. Lilibet, who misses nothing, spotted this and tried to arrange for me to be driven straight on in the car when they did their next 'walkabout', but I felt better and in fact followed walking behind them which gave me an excellent chance of seeing their excellent technique.

At 1240 we arrived at Sri Melaka, the former Residency of Malacca. It is a delightful and typical British Official house, where the Governor gave a large luncheon party.

We were allowed a rest period and Philip insisted on my lying down, and even went and produced a cushion to put under my head. It was hot and I suppose I looked a bit tired, but I am being careful, and am well looked after.

In the evening there was a full dress State Banquet on board for Their Majesties. Philip wore a white tie and decorations, and the staff wore their Household coats. I hadn't got a tail coat onboard and so wore mess dress, but I hadn't got a Garter dinner sash and so I had to pin my full dress sash on with safety pins. Philip was wearing the Garter and not the local Malaysian Order which Lilibet had on. He explained that Lilibet had refused to give the Queen Consort an Order, and her husband had refused to give Philip one!

Philip told me that the unfortunate Australian Rear Admiral who commands the ANZUK Force had had his request to be allowed to call on the Prime Minister, Tun Razak, turned down on more than one occasion and hadn't yet been received by him. It appeared to be an intentional form of slight and Philip was worried about it. I promised to try and fix it.

I got hold of my old friend Tun Razak and talked about our recent visit to the Commonwealth Brigade, and got him to agree that it was an excellent thing to have kept this Commonwealth Force as the British presence in the Far East. I asked him if he had yet met the charming Australian Admiral in Command and when he said he hadn't, I implied it was very remiss of the Admiral not to have come to pay his respects and asked the PM if he would like me to fix it. He had practically no option but to say 'yes', upon which we immediately sent a signal telling the Admiral to go and call on him. Philip was delighted about this and so was the High Commissioner. I hope it works.

WEDNESDAY, 8 MARCH   The *Britannia* berthed at Swettenham Pier at Penang at 0930.

The Malay population, which is in a considerable minority in the city, produced Kompang performers beating many drums very hard. They made up in noise what they lacked in numbers.

We had left our cars at the Supreme Court, a delightful old Colonial type building, and now walked to Dewan Sri Penang. Here the Government of Penang had arranged a special exhibition of the products of Penang. I was astounded at the vast range of manufactured goods, not only the traditional woven fabrics but highly sophisticated things like electronic equipment.

When a man in charge of one stall proudly showed me his printed circuits, I said to him, 'These are out of date, you should be having miniaturized integrated circuits.' He then took me to the next stall where they had micro-miniaturized circuits and had microscopes to enable one to see the detail. They told me that their electronic equipment, including the latest stereophonic car radios and tape players, were sold at a lower price than the corresponding Japanese goods.

It took us half an hour to reach our destination because we had to drive slowly as almost the entire route was lined by crowds, mostly school children highly organized with paper flags. They were almost delirious with excitement and pleasure, for, being in the second car, I could see their faces transformed with smiles, grins and laughter as they hopped up and down and often hugged each other in sheer delight.

After lunch there was another rest period when I used the bed again. As the time came to go down Philip left, and presently there was a knock at the door and Lilibet came in and told me I couldn't go down in my condition because all the white fluff off the bedspread had come off on my clothes. She then took the only available brush, an elaborately embossed silver hair brush, and proceeded to brush my clothes down. Philip came back to see what the delay was and helped by pulling the fluff off with his fingers. It would have been entertaining to have had this item put in the programme as 'Her Majesty will brush Lord Mountbatten's suit with a silver hair brush!'

THURSDAY, 9 MARCH   It was really a lovely day, hot and calm. It is delightful to think we are going to have four quiet days at sea to recover from all these activities.

We had dinner on the verandah deck again as it was so calm and lovely. It is much more friendly sitting close together round a well-lit table with darkness all round one and the sea breeze stirring lightly. The band played on the Royal Deck just above us and made it all very romantic. I keep asking why we can't have the music of *The Tales of Beatrix Potter** and I am told the explanation is that all the music programmes are selected and printed before the Yacht leaves England

---

* A musical taste explained in part by the fact that this film had been produced by John Brabourne and Richard Goodwin.

and so they can't be altered. So they always play 'Beatrix Potter' whenever there is a Reception on board without a printed programme, but one can't hear it so well.

After dinner all of us except Lilibet, who said she wanted to work, went to see an old James Bond film, *From Russia with Love*. Although I had seen it before I had practically forgotten it, and found it just as exciting and entertaining as the first time.

FRIDAY, 10 MARCH   Another lovely day at sea. I sun-bathed systematically, and after tea I was reading *Victoria R.I.* by Elizabeth Longford in my bunk when there was a knock at the door and Lilibet came in and called me to come and see some Russian ships. I dashed up and there was a 5000-ton Russian submarine tender of the DON Class followed by two old submarines at one-mile intervals. It really is rather frustrating to see the Russians with a Navy so big that their ships are roaming the Indian Ocean where the Royal Navy used to 'rule the waves'. Our escort, the *Arethusa*, has been sent to take off some Maldivians who had got adrift in their boat and had been picked up by HMS *Hydra* on her way to Singapore. So *Arethusa* was told to take them over and deliver them to the Maldives.

Then on top of this the wife of the Engineer Officer of the Blue Funnel Line had a heart attack, and so the *Arethusa* went off to her at high speed and sent her Doctor over by her own helicopter. Thus we had no escort with us, whereas on several occasions we had two frigates and four motor-launches. Lilibet was quite put out that the Russians should see the Royal Yacht without any escort at all.

SATURDAY, 11 MARCH   At 1215 I accepted an invitation to have a drink in the Junior Ratings' Recreation Space. I really felt rather proud to see the way they take their beer very cheerily, and apparently have no cases of drunkenness, because I was the person mostly responsible for getting beer on board ship. How much better than that dreadful old rum for youngsters.

SUNDAY, 12 MARCH   Still at sea. I read the Lesson in Church and at my request they played two of my favourite hymns, 'I vow to thee my Country' and Rudyard Kipling's 'Recessional'. There was a great argument about what tunes should have been used after the Service and we tried four or five different tunes over. Philip heard the other tunes being tried and he came back and immediately guessed what was up. 'I

bet you're trying to find the right tune for your Memorial Service!' is
what he said, and he was quite right.

MONDAY, 13 MARCH   I sun-bathed in the morning and we anchored
off the island of Male, capital of the Maldive Islands, in the afternoon.

We set off on a drive through the little town. We had been told that
the population of Male was now close on 14,000. There were such
immense crowds on the streets that I commented on this, and Mr Didi*
explained that at least another 6000 had come in during the last 48
hours from all the nearest Atolls by boat, and were living in their boats,
to see the Queen. He stressed what a great occasion this was to the
Maldives, for in all their history they had never had a visit from a
reigning sovereign, let alone from the Queen who had been their
protecting power for so long.

I did not ask him why they decided not to join the Commonwealth
because I knew of the bitter disagreement over the three southern
Maldive Atolls; at the time they wanted to break away in order to get
special terms for our using the island of Gan. However, it is clear that
this visit is being used to make a great effort to re-establish really
friendly relations. There were banners up everywhere with 'Firmer
Friendship with Britain' or 'Maldivian-British Goodwill', and even
'Peace, Prosperity and Progress for Britain'.

TUESDAY, 14 MARCH   We entered the great anchorage inside Addu
Atoll, and anchored in the Lagoon at 1145.

At 1300 we had lunch in the Mess. A beautifully prepared and bound
programme of the visit had been fortunately sent to us at Male because
Lilibet actually read Annexe D which gave the luncheon menu. She was
horrified to find that this was practically the same menu as she decided
on for dinner that evening, and so she luckily had time to change our
menu on board.

I sat next to the President of the Mess Committee who told me that
they had had a complete dress rehearsal of the entire visit on the 9th
March. As the only woman on the island, a member of the WRVS, had a
part to play they borrowed a Wing Commander of the WRAF, on
passage, to take the place of the Queen. At the luncheon the Maldivian

---

* Mr Hilmi Didi, Minister of Fisheries.

waiter who had the privilege of waiting on her was so overcome with enthusiasm and loyalty that he gave her no less than four separate pork chops on her plate.

Philip let me have a very welcome parting present in the form of a draft written by himself agreeing to take over from me as Grand President of the British Commonwealth Ex-Services League in 1974. He has been refusing to do this now for months. In return I gave him one of my only two pocket combs with a clip which is so difficult to get nowadays!

SUNDAY, 19 MARCH. NAIROBI   After forty minutes all passengers boarded the aircraft and should have left punctually, but then I was told that only 99 out of 100 passengers had reported back and the new Captain who had taken over refused to fly on. So I asked him to see me, and he said he had had instructions that his aircraft was under special security rules and he didn't dare take off without all the passengers or having the luggage checked. I asked him why he thought there were special security rules and he quite openly admitted it was because I was on board. So I complained I was being made to suffer by my own presence for the long delay.

He pointed out that if there were 100 passengers at the Seychelles and one left Nairobi without coming back, he might have a bomb in his suitcase on board. Anyway, the Captain decided to have all luggage put on the tarmac; everybody had their hand-baggage searched; everybody had to get out and identify their luggage and put it back. It took the best part of an hour. In fact we left Nairobi extremely late. I then took a sleeping pill instead of eating a large meal and slept for about five and a half hours until we reached Nicosia, where I woke up drowsy, but I dozed again after we left Nicosia.

Mountbatten was almost immediately on the move again, this time to the United States.

FRIDAY, 24 MARCH. NEW YORK   At 0845 I went up to have breakfast with the new Secretary-General of the United Nations Organization, Kurt Waldheim. A surprising group of TV camera men and still camera men were there with lights to record our first meeting, and then we went with one of the senior staff officers in to breakfast. We got on extremely

New Delhi, 16 March 1967.
At Rashtrapati Bhavan, with
Patricia Brabourne, the President,
Dr Radhakrishnan, and Mountbatten's
successor as Governor-General,
C. R. Rajagopalachari.

Calgary, 6 July 1967. The Indian
tribes unite to create Mountbatten
an honorary chief.

Lake Minnetonka, 9 March 1968. Embarking on a trip by ice yacht.

Washington, 11 March 1968. A call on President Johnson. The British Ambassador, Sir Patrick Dean, is at the other end of the sofa.

well and I liked him very much. I told him all about the United World Colleges and invited him to come to St Donat's and he accepted.

When at about 0930 I thought I ought to go and made a move he said he wanted to discuss the world situation with me; he wanted particularly to discuss the situation in the Middle East and in India, so we had half an hour's very interesting talk together on these subjects. He certainly is very impressive and seems to have all the right ideas.

On 25 March Mountbatten flew on to Las Vegas.

We were met by Mike Frankovitch and the owner of the Riviera Hotel, who lent us his enormous Mercedes car. I must say by day Las Vegas is not at all that impressive; it is built in the middle of the Nevada Desert. I had flown over it at night when I was doing my tour with the American Navy in 1958. We refuelled here and all my staff went in and amused themselves, but I refused to go for fear of adverse publicity interfering with my tour as First Sea Lord. I have always wanted to come because I was told a visit here is a real experience.

At midnight we went into their fascinating auditorium [of the hotel Caesar's Palace] based rather on the principle of the old London Casino or the Talk of the Town in London. There were tables for supper for about a thousand people. Two extremely comfortable tables with high horse-shoe shape backings were put at our disposal.

We saw the Alan King–Lena Horne show, which is proving such a great success here. I have never met him but I have known Lena Horne since she first came to London twenty-five years ago. She is now a most alluring grandmother and sings more superlatively than ever.

After a further walk round the gambling tables and one-armed bandits, we went off at 2200* on a night tour. We drove down town which is really a separate town about three miles away and was the original Las Vegas. Here a different clientele live in the hotels and gamble at a much lower rate from the millionaires up town.

It was fascinating to see the difference in the dress and behaviour of the people at the gambling tables, and rather pathetic to see housewives who were obviously gambling what they saved out of the house-keeping money without much prospect of really winning. Apparently about 30 per cent come from all over the States and about 70 per cent from California and Arizona.

---

* [*sic*] Since Mountbatten did not get to bed till three-thirty he presumably means 0200.

I was staggered to see a number of places called 'Wedding Chapels'; some have subsidiary titles like 'The Hitching Post'. Here a couple can go in without giving any notice at all and a Justice of the Peace is in permanent session to marry you at once. The price is $9; however, for a few dollars extra you can have wedding bells and the Wedding March in potted music; you can borrow flowers which you return; you can hire a tuxedo for the men and a wedding dress for the ladies for an hour; and then you can have a room in a motel to consummate the marriage.

If in the morning it hasn't worked out you can go and get a divorce for about $20. This is a most lucrative business for we saw at least half a dozen of these wedding chapels and I am told there are more.

MONDAY, 27 MARCH. LAS VEGAS   We packed and left the Riviera Hotel at 1030. At Palm Springs we found Cary Grant who had flown in another of his aeroplanes. Frank Sinatra had sent his new Rolls-Royce to meet us.

Palm Springs is an extraordinary place because it is right in the heart of the desert, indeed like Las Vegas except that there are no real hotels. There are many millionaire villas in their own grounds. There is plenty of water under the ground, and wells only have to be put in and water has to be piped and the desert sands produce fertile growth of palm trees and grass.

Frank Sinatra's house is charming and in good taste. He himself lives in a little central house alone with just a few reception rooms. In front of it there is a swimming pool, and round it there are two or three guest houses. There is also a big so-called play room which has a cinema in it.

An old railway carriage in the grounds has been converted into a sauna bath and gymnasium, but it is all quiet, nice and cosy. He proved a most pleasant host, very attentive and personally introduced me to all the guests who included Sherrill Corwin, the International President of Variety, who had come up to welcome me as a Gold Card member. Most of them I already knew but others were new to me. At lunch I sat between Ginger Rogers and Rosalind Russell. These were actresses I used to admire very much in my youth, but I must say that although they were gay and amusing they have lost their figures and their looks.

I asked Frank if I could see him alone with Mike after lunch and he said 'certainly' and took us into his little study where we had twenty minutes very valuable talk. He told me that he hopes to go to England this summer to direct a new film *The Little Prince* on the well-known

French story, the music of which has been written by Loewe, who wrote *Gigi* and *My Fair Lady* and who was at lunch.

Sinatra promised to come down for one weekend at Broadlands and another weekend in St Donat's Castle to see the place towards which his charitable performance contributed so much. I had an offer from the *Sunday Mirror* of £40,000 to the United World Colleges if Frank would give them four interviews. But he asked to be excused, for this was against his policy, and I readily understood that. However, he made it pretty clear that he had not lost interest in the United World Colleges and was likely to be able to help us in other ways later on.

I told him I wanted to see Walter Annenberg's* house and he rang up and laid it on. He himself had to fly off to Florida to play golf with the Vice-President of the United States. We drove all round the Annenberg property which is fantastic. A few years ago it was an absolute desert; now it is an enormous green park with an eighteen-hole golf course; a very modern house with a glorious swimming pool and garden, and is really rather unbelievable. He had asked us to go and stay there but I have not been able to go. I was told he failed to get elected to the local golf club because of their anti-Jew attitude, so he built a better eighteen-hole golf course for himself.

Mountbatten continued to Toronto where, on 30 March, he took the salute at a parade of Sea Cadets.

Then came my great problem, how I was going to have any effect on this crowd of young Canadians. I had absolutely refused to stand on the dais and address them fallen in. When they agreed that I could move them forward to gather round me for the address, they wanted me to stand at a desk which was on the same level as the boys, so I had to move all the microphones back to the dais to speak from there. I had to persuade them to let the Guard ground arms, and finally I persuaded the band to move with much difficulty.

Having got them all round I started to speak but soon realized that they were not accustomed to an English voice, so I spoke more slowly and carefully. I made my first joke and it fell absolutely flat. I was told afterwards that this was out of respect for they didn't think they ought to laugh in my presence, but I suspected that they had not understood what I was saying. So I spoke more slowly and distinctly, and bit by bit I got them. Bit by bit they started laughing, and jostling themselves, and

---

* At that time American Ambassador in London.

at the end they were very cheerful and I had three really good laughs out of them.

The whole of the ceremony took over an hour, and then I went up to the Ward Room for drinks and to meet the guests. There was a Judge of the Supreme Court, who surprised me by being one of those who wanted my autograph; as it was I was inundated with requests for autographs, and was quite glad to escape to visit the Chief Petty Officers. I was piped as though for rounds on my way to their Mess where I met a typical crowd of delightful old Chief Petty Officers. Many of them claimed to have served with me or to have known people who had served with me and they could not have been more friendly. I was given the last tot of rum in the Royal Canadian Navy as the rum issue stops at midnight and forever, like in the Royal Navy.

I was horrified to find that the name was no longer Royal Canadian Navy but something like the Canadian Armed Forces Sea Wing. The various officers, including the Admiral, wore a sort of dark green uniform with one thick gold stripe and then military bands of rank on their shoulders. The whole thing is rather sad and ludicrous and has gone far beyond anything I had ever envisaged for unification.

By 7 April 1972 Mountbatten had arrived in Detroit to stay with the Fords.

It was very hot in Miami, about 90°, but when we got to Detroit the temperature was down to 20° and there was snow; in fact the weather was so bad that the helicopter couldn't come to fetch us. Our host, Henry Ford II, had driven in to meet us and took us straight off in his car; our luggage was collected in another car. We drove through the city on a great motorway and then came down to Grosse Pointe which is divided into a number of small towns.

The Fords live in Grosse Pointe Farms. The French names owe their origin to a French priest who discovered this area from Canada which is only a couple of miles away across the water. I gather the town was called Detroit from '*d'Etroit*', the straits on which it lies. Many of the streets had French names.

We reached the Ford House, 457 Lakeshore Drive, shortly after 1730 after a fifty-minute drive. It is a charming house built in 1929 of red brick on a Regency pattern. It is curious that such a large and expensive house should stand only a hundred yards back from the main motorway along the shore of the lake and that the garden should only be a few acres at the back. However, the house is extremely tastefully decorated and very comfortable and well run and well organized. Henry and his wife, Christina, were in the house and an hour later Henry's daughter, Charlotte, arrived for the weekend. She made the appalling error of marrying Stavros Niarchos because she was having a baby by him. The marriage broke up immediately afterwards. She now calls herself Mrs Charlotte Ford.

SATURDAY, 8 APRIL. DETROIT   At my request, Henry's Public Relations Chief, a man called John Morrissey, had been bidden to luncheon and to meet me. At John's [Brabourne] suggestion I had telegraphed to Henry about a week ago asking whether it would help if I did TV interviews to boost my TV series being shown on the Indianapolis programme at the Henry Ford House. I spoke to Morrissey the night before and he said he had written out the scripts for three short pieces to say before his programme, but I had urged that I should do an ordinary general television interview with a proper interviewer. He told me he had now got up the principal interviewer from the Indianapolis station for TV and another man to do a radio interview. I told him I did not like working from a script and certainly wouldn't use the teleprompter which he had organized.

At 1510 Henry took me to the Ford Library where John Morrissey awaited us with some twenty men in television teams with lots of lights and cameras.

The first struggle I had was to cut out the teleprompter team he had brought. I explained that I didn't want to use his scripts but if he told me what he wanted me to say I would say it in my own words. We began by the sound radio interview, then I said I was prepared to do the television interview first go, straight off without any rehearsal. This surprised them; however, I carried on an interview with quite a number of unexpected questions for twenty or twenty-five minutes.

After this I did introductions to the first three programmes to be shown and a general introduction to subsequent programmes, and finally when they wanted me to do the whole thing again in case the time of the programme was changed from 7 to 6 p.m. on Sundays I merely did a little tail piece of five seconds saying, 'Correction, I have just been told that the time is 6 p.m.'

THURSDAY, 25 MAY. LONDON   Lilibet told me on the telephone that the 'news from Paris was very bad' and that her Uncle David had become unconscious and could not live more than another two or three days. She confirmed he was going to have a private funeral at Windsor and that she would invite Wallis to come and stay at Buckingham Palace. She said that she relied on me to give her as much help as possible as I was the only member of the family who really knew her.

Lilibet was very worried about her Birthday Parade as she said it would be impossible to have the funeral before the Trooping the Colour, and so she felt it would have to be cancelled. She realized what a disappointment this would be to all the troops on parade, and to the thousands of people who had bought tickets, as it could hardly be laid on again later.

I immediately suggested that far from cancelling it, it should be turned into a tribute to David, the colours and drums should be draped in black, officers should wear black mourning bands, and a special tribute with a roll of drums should be paid at the commencement of the Parade in her own presence. She thought this was a wonderful idea and said she would follow it up.

SUNDAY, 28 MAY   At 0730 Eric Penn, the Comptroller to the Lord Chamberlain, rang me up with the news that David had died and that the Court would wear mourning for a fortnight, that was until midnight on Saturday, 10 June. He said that the Queen was sending the Kents to meet the coffin when it flew in an RAF aircraft to Benson on Wednesday, but that if the Duchess was not well enough to fly with the coffin she wanted me to meet her on her behalf. I, of course, readily agreed.

MONDAY, 29 MAY   Harry Middleton of the BBC rang me up to ask if I would pay a tribute to David at the Lying-in-State at Windsor. I refused as this was against all precedent; I pointed out that I had not done anything of that sort for King George VI when he died and he also had been a great friend. Middleton then made the point that the Royal Family had not paid any adequate tribute to the former King Edward VIII, certainly nothing comparable to the tributes paid by other Heads of States, like President Nixon and President Pompidou, and that it would be taken very much amiss by the public as a whole and the many great admirers of the former King if none of the family said anything about him at all.

So I agreed to ask Her Majesty's Private Secretary for official approval and I rang up Martin Charteris. Martin was against it until I used Middleton's arguments, and then he changed his mind completely and said he thought it was essential I should do it. Later on he rang up to say that the Queen, after considerable thought, had approved provided I spoke about him in a balanced way.

THURSDAY, I JUNE. BROADLANDS Eric Penn rang up to confirm that the Duchess of Windsor had been too distraught and ill to come over with the coffin, but that an Andover of the Queen's Flight was being sent to Paris to collect her and I was asked to meet her. She was still in great doubt whether she would come. I told Eric that I thought it was absolutely essential that she should be brought over, and that he ought to get in touch with her Secretary and say that whatever happened they had to try and bring her over as she herself would be miserable if she missed the funeral, and the result on public opinion here would be disastrous.

FRIDAY, 2 JUNE This is the day that Wallis flew over from Paris. I had agreed to meet her. The sketch plan of the complicated arrangements for finding one's way to the temporary VIP Reception Lounge at Heathrow was sent to me but unfortunately I only started looking at it just before I was due to leave in the car. It was so complicated that John Barratt and I spent more than ten minutes finding our way on the map into London Airport. The result was that I left ten minutes late at 1010 and drove myself up in the Jaguar.

I had put the red crown up so as to have no trouble with the police and drove at very high speed, so much so that I reached the outskirts of old Windsor in just over one hour. I was taking my wreath up to St George's Chapel and wanted to drop it there on my way, but as I turned off the A 30 I heard an ominous bump, bump, bump and stopped. Denis* got out and reported that the main silencer had broken at one end and was dragging along the ground. With great courage he lifted it up in spite of its heat and put it back. I drove on carefully and then bump,

* Denis Chalk. Naval steward/footman at Broadlands.

bump, bump. He looked again and explained to me that it wasn't dragging along the road but the front end was broken and was digging into the road like a plough.

I got out and looked at it – it looked rather dangerous but we managed to get it up once more out of the way. I drove on very slowly, then again bump, bump, bump. However, it was absolutely essential that I should get to London Airport on time so I drove on very slowly and carefully to the nearest garage where a mechanic pulled the whole silencer off. I then drove on at high speed through the Frogmore Gate to St George's Chapel where I deposited my wreath and had a quick look at the Lying-in-State which was going very well. The scene was wonderfully dignified – very moving. I wished I could have stayed longer and was determined to go back later.

I then drove as fast as I could to the VIP Lounge at London Airport and managed to find it without any difficulty. The crown of course helped us and various police on the route waved us in the right direction.

The Andover arrived extremely punctually and I went on board to greet Wallis. She had brought with her a great friend, Grace Dudley (widow of the Earl of Dudley), Mary Soames, the wife of our Ambassador in Paris, John Utter, the Private Secretary (whom she had attempted to dismiss only ten days before but who, on Lilibet's insistence, remained to help make the funeral arrangements), David's American doctor, and a former equerry to David.

I helped Wallis down the ladder as she was very frail and nervous. I took her straight into the waiting Rolls-Royce. I had arranged for a Life Guards driver to come down with the Royal car to drive my Jaguar, as Denis Chalk has not yet got his driving licence.

Her first question was, 'Have you seen David?' I was luckily able to say I had just come from St George's Chapel where his body was lying in state with a large crowd already filing past. I described the scene with the four officers of the Guards in full dress standing on guard at each corner. She reminded me that David and his three brothers had stood Guard round the coffin of King George V when he died in January 1936 and she had seen it.

Then we talked of David's illness and she admitted that they had both told me how much better he was when I saw him in February. In fact they thought the cobalt treatment had cured the cancer of the throat. She said David never really knew how terribly ill he was and she only realized he was going to die two or three weeks before his death.

The anticipation made it worse for her and it had been a terrible shock.

She said how extremely nervous she was of having to confront the whole Royal Family without David to support her. She had only seen them once before briefly at the unveiling of Queen Mary's Memorial at Marlborough House, and then he had been with her. This was going to be very different and she was really apprehensive.

Wallis was particularly worried about Elizabeth the Queen Mother who, she said, had never approved of her. I was able to set her mind at rest for I told her, 'Your sister-in-law will receive you with open arms – she is so deeply sorry for you in your present grief and remembers what she felt like when her own husband died.' I explained I was able to tell her this because I had dined at Clarence House as recently as 29 April when she knew that David was dying and had expressed her warm feelings towards Wallis. This comforted her a lot.

Then she began to reminisce about our early meetings and her early life with David. I told her that Lilibet had given me permission to record a tribute to David which was going to be heard on television that very night. I warned her that I would say everything that was in my heart which was very nice about David, but I was bound to state how much I disapproved of his abdication. She said to me, 'You are quite right. I disapproved of it too. I spent a long time over a very bad telephone line from France begging him not to abdicate. I went so far as to say if he abdicated I wouldn't marry him.' Then she turned round to me and said, 'When are you going to see David?' I had luckily been warned that her memory was failing so I started off again very patiently explaining I had seen him that morning at the Lying-in-State.

SATURDAY, 3 JUNE. LONDON   We drove to the Deanery and I arrived just before Charles who walked over from Windsor Castle where he is staying with the family, whilst Wallis came down from Buckingham Palace with her little party.

We went to St George's Chapel. She told me that she was feeling very ill and sad so I gave her the support of my arm. However, she left me to go to the head of the coffin and stand for a few moments alone, her head bowed in grief. Then I helped her again to walk round the whole Chapel which took a long time, at least 7 or 8 minutes. At the end she stood again looking at the coffin and said in the saddest imaginable voice, 'He was my entire life. I can't begin to think what I am going to do without him, he gave up so much for me and now he has gone. I always hoped that I would die before him.'

Then Charles and I saw her off. She kept on telling me what a charming young man Charles was and what a comfort. Charles certainly was splendid in supporting her.

MONDAY, 5 JUNE. WINDSOR When Wallis arrived she looked very sad and somewhat embarrassed, so I went up and took her by the arm and escorted her round to every member of the family explaining who everybody was. Many she knew, but not all. Then Lilibet, Philip, Charles and Anne and also Elizabeth arrived, and they went up and were very sweet to Wallis. The ladies were then taken to their seats and the men formed a procession and walked behind the coffin as it was carried from the Albert Memorial Chapel round to the bottom of the nave, and up between the congregation into the choir where it was placed on the trestles facing the altar.

I was amused to find Lilibet standing at the door of the usual family drawing room and looking through a crack. As she saw me pass she opened the door and beckoned me in. She said, 'I am trying to avoid too many people coming in here, the rest are going down to the Green Drawing Room.' I then warned Patrick Plunket* to tell Patricia I wanted to see her. He met her with a broad wink and said, 'Your father wants to see you in that room', so she got in among the 'sheep' while the rest went on to the 'goats'.

Wallis rested a bit and came at the last moment and was conducted by Lilibet down to the main room where we had drinks and further talks. Lilibet asked me to take charge of Wallis and take her over to the sofa and sit with her.

When we went in to luncheon, at which there were five tables of about eight each, I found that Wallis had been placed between Philip and me so I was able to give her my support at luncheon as well. I must say I am desperately sorry for her – she is so lonely and sad, and yet kept saying how wonderful the family were being to her and how much better the whole thing had gone than she had expected.

After luncheon a very small number of the most immediate members of the family drove in cars the short distance to Frogmore where we drove into the Mausoleum grounds. Here a plot had been prepared for

* Lord Plunket was Deputy Master of the Household.

David and a space left for Wallis to be alongside him in due course. I fear now it may not be very long, as she is so frail.

I had rather hoped that I would be asked to take Wallis back to London Airport, as she was leaving immediately, but on enquiry I found that the Lord Chamberlain had been appointed by the Queen to represent her on this occasion. As he was new, and would obviously be upset if I tried to take his place, I didn't.* In retrospect I think it was a mistake as quite a number of the papers commented that no member of the family had gone to see her off at the airport. It would have been very easy for Patricia and me to have done so. As it was we drove back to London direct.

Looking back I feel that on the whole everything went as well as could be hoped. The great thing was that Lilibet, Philip and Charles were able to go and see David during their State Visit to Paris, while he was still well enough to be able to get dressed and see them upstairs in his bedroom. Wallis told me what very great pleasure this had given to him, and obviously to her too. Then the friendly reception which Wallis had from the family healed the breach.

SUNDAY, 30 JULY. BROADLANDS At 1520 I drove the Jaguar to Gosport where the Royal Barge was awaiting me. The plans for embarking in the *Britannia* had had to be changed because of the national dock strike, otherwise I should have gone on board very comfortably in a quarter of an hour from Broadlands right alongside the ship. Because of the dock strike the *Britannia* had been sent to anchor off Spithead, and Lilibet's train had been diverted to Portsmouth, taking a very long time, and we all had to go out by boat.

Anne arrived on board about 1720, having found her own way down to Portsmouth by car after taking part in a jumping competition. She made the most astonishing statement – she had got so fed up with her horse which was conceited, playing the fool and not paying attention, that to punish it she let it go without any aid or help from her – she fully expected that the pony would take a frightful smash and fall on its face, and didn't seem to mind falling on her own face to teach it a lesson. As it was it hit the jump extremely hard but didn't actually come down, so the punishment worked out quite successfully.

---

* Lord Macleod had become Lord Chamberlain the previous year.

MONDAY, 31 JULY. *Britannia* We entered Dartmouth at 0900 in quite good weather. We were due to land at 1035, but at 1030 it came on to rain extremely hard. Philip and I had some difficulty in persuading Lilibet to wait until the shower cleared off, but she finally agreed and we landed at 1043 in sunshine.

I had a letter from a very loyal couple who said that they would be looking out for us at their house in Victoria Road and we should recognize them because they would hold up their Pekinese dog. I had just told the occupants of No. 2 car about this when we all saw them, and we all waved madly at them and they were overcome with excitement. We stopped before the Captain's house and walked up through his garden so that Lilibet could later make a more ceremonial entry on to the Parade Ground through the main College doorway.

TUESDAY, 1 AUGUST At 0400 as we rounded Land's End we ran into quite a storm, with winds up to 30 and 40 knots, the sea had got up and the swell was heavy and the ship moved quite a lot. Lilibet and Anne remained in bed for breakfast, but Anne got up for lunch.

The wind and sea dropped and by the evening the ship was hardly moving at all. Lilibet turned up for tea in good form and everybody was together again for dinner tonight.

It is very sad to think it will be my last dinner in this ship for quite a while, as she goes in for her long refit after this when she is going to be modernized and all the lower-deck accommodation really brought up-to-date. This will just about double the length of her life.

Philip and I reminisced over the origin of the name STC. When I came to the Admiralty as First Sea Lord there was great consternation because the Treasury had refused the money to buy new sailing yachts to replace those taken over from the German Navy at the end of the war called the 'Windfall' Class.

I decided to let matters rest for six months, as the old yachts could carry on, and then I started a completely different approach; instead of referring to 'yachts', we started on the need for more practical training in seamanship for the College and put up various suggestions and among them we said we must have six properly designed 'Seamanship Training Craft'. The Treasury immediately approved the project, hence the name STC.

1972

WEDNESDAY, 2 AUGUST   At 0900 we entered the Bay of Douglas, the capital of the Isle of Man. Before landing we were handed a lot of literature, including a pamphlet called 'General Information Digest'. At the bottom of the index on page 1 we discovered a new cult in the Isle of Man for it listed 'Places of Pubic Worship'.

We landed at 1015 and were received by Sir Peter Stallard, the Lieutenant Governor, and Lady Stallard. He introduced the members of the Legislative Council and their wives beginning with the Bishop of Sodor and Man. I asked him afterwards what 'Sodor' stood for and he said it was the Western Isles. I noted that this was where the whisky came from and wondered why he didn't call himself the 'Bishop of Whisky and Sodor'. The first Deemster was next introduced, he is the Chief Justice of the Island. Afterwards the Speaker and the Members of the House of Keys and their wives were introduced. This is the local parliament.

On our arrival at the dais the Manx Festival Chorus sang 'God Save The Queen' and on our departure 'Oh Land of our Birth', the local anthem of the Isle of Man. A large banner announced WELCOME TO THE LORD OF MANN. After a 600-yard run we dismounted and went to another dais, but this time the Mayor of Douglas did the honours and introduced the Members of the Corporation. Then we did a 'walkabout' to the cars which were waiting some 80 yards away.

We drove through the town of Laxey and saw the famous Water Wheel which is immense. I asked my companions in the car if they knew what the famous product of this town was. None of them knew, and when I said it was 'tives' it took them some time to see the point.

SATURDAY, 5 AUGUST. CLASSIEBAWN   It really is wonderful the family being back here at Classiebawn Castle again after all the excitement and worries about whether we should come. The Police Security Guards seem adequate, and very inconspicuous and co-operative, and it is lovely seeing the old staff here again.

At 1130 the whole party went out in my old Irish fishing boat *Shadow V*; we dropped our eight lobster pots. We caught some mackerel and pollack and got back at 1400 for late lunch.

Most of us had a rest after lunch and slept; Classiebawn is always a good place for sleeping; I suppose it's part of the holiday atmosphere.

MONDAY, 7 AUGUST   The tide was right this morning and we had a prawning party. Patricia, Amanda, Phi, Timmy and I set out at 1115 and later Norton* came and helped me with my bucket from the pier. We prawned for an hour and a half and got two large dishes full of prawns.

At 1530 most of us except Patricia went out in *Shadow V* again but Amanda and Phi rode. We got lots of lobsters and crabs again. Patricia came down to the harbour to pick up John and they both drove to Sligo station to fetch Dodo† who was coming from Dublin. The train was twenty-five minutes late.

Sacha‡ and I went for a ride, she on Paudeen, I on Lucky Streak and Phi came as usual on Timmy. I find it very confusing having two grandsons called Nicky and Timmy and two ponies called Micky and Timmy.

11 TO 31 AUGUST   I have only recorded the first week of our four weeks' stay at Classiebawn, as this week is typical of the remaining three, and indeed our annual family holiday at Classiebawn every August. The Castle is always crammed full with my daughters, their husbands, their ten children, two nurses, and, over the last two years, my great-nephews, Georgie Milford Haven and Ivar Mountbatten.

There is plenty for everyone to do. Some go riding, some go out in the pony cart. Quite a number go out in *Shadow V*, and on the 25th the whole party went over in her to see the seals lazing on the rocks at Bomore Island and to visit Inishmurray. We had a picnic lunch on board in the little harbour and then we took Solly round the ruins of the ancient Cashel, which fascinated him.

We played with the children on the beach, making dams and canals in the sand. We had several successful prawning expeditions in and round the harbour. We got a total of 55 lobsters in our Swedish lobster pots. In the evening some lay puzzles, others play card games or read. It is all very relaxing, uneventful and fun; but one day John did a hole in one at the Bundoran Golf Course. Michael-John determined to equalize and landed within two yards of the hole! If he'd pulled it off what a sensation that would have been.

---

* Norton, Amanda, Philip and Timothy Knatchbull were among the children of Lord and Lady Brabourne.
† Doreen, Dowager Lady Brabourne.
‡ His god-daughter, the Marchioness of Hamilton (later Duchess of Abercorn).

1973

After a short visit to Luxembourg, Mountbatten continued to Paris. On 8 February 1973:

The Embassy car came to fetch me at 1645 and drove me to tea with Wallis Windsor at the nice house in the Bois de Boulogne. I knew she had been in hospital with a broken leg and I was quite surprised to see her walking very slowly down the staircase, supported by a nurse, evidently much better.

She came to me quite radiant and obviously pleased to see me and said, 'Have you seen David yet?' This shook me. However, I said, 'How nice that you feel he is so close. I share your feelings that he is very close to us now. Isn't it sad to think that he is now actually dead and gone?' She sadly shook her head and said, 'Yes, I suppose he has gone, but I feel he is always with me and I can keep close touch with him.' After that we had a more or less normal conversation which contained some further surprises.

I thanked her for having taken my advice in having sent all David's uniforms, decorations and official things, including his papers, to Windsor for the Queen to dispose of as appropriate. I told her I thought Sir Godfrey Morley, her English lawyer, had done a very good job. She then said that she had sad news for me because her French lawyer, Maître Blum, a woman whom she had had for thirty years and whom they both had liked very much, had bowled out that he had been incompetent about a special private 'tax' company that had been set up for them. When Madame Blum had disagreed with him he had got a second French lawyer in who had proved equally unsatisfactory.

At all events she had been advised by Madame Blum to get rid of the other two and this had been awkward. Finally she said that she didn't want three lawyers and had therefore paid Morley and his French friend off. There had been quite a row about it but she didn't think she could have done anything else. As she seemed so absolutely insistent that

Morley had done badly I thought it was useless to try and argue about it, beyond saying that I couldn't believe that he could intentionally have done anything wrong as he was much too high-class and honourable.

I let that go for a bit and then she fortunately consulted me about whom she should give the various little boxes and important souvenirs to. We agreed that any form of souvenir which had the Prince of Wales's Feathers, the Imperial cypher 'ERI' or even the Duke of Windsor's personal cypher 'E' should all be handled in a very circumspect manner.

She then astounded me by telling me that she had absolutely no members of her family whatsoever surviving. I asked about her intimate friends the Rogers, with whom she lived in the South of France when she left England, and she told me they were both dead. She then said she had absolutely nobody at all because naturally she wasn't on happy terms with any of David's family except myself.

She admitted that she was worried that Morley had had to be removed as an Executor of her will when his firm was paid off. I then said that although I was far from wanting to volunteer for any more work, as I had too much to do already, if it was of any help to her, and she wanted at least one member of David's family, I would volunteer my services as Executor. She appeared very grateful.

Then I said that I thought that she should ask Charles, as the next Prince of Wales, to be responsible in choosing whom the various objects should be given to if she couldn't make up her own mind, and if she liked I would help him with advice even though I were not an Executor. She thanked me for this as well.

Then I tried to persuade her to leave souvenirs to George Kent's children because they had been such great friends; at all events I suggested that every box or souvenir that had been given by George should be given to one of his children. This she agreed to.

Finally I tackled the sixty-four-dollar question of an English solicitor. I told her it was unthinkable that a former reigning King of England should have the whole of his vast affairs settled for his widow on her death only by a French firm of lawyers. I said the very least she ought to do was to have another English firm, and I would gladly try and find a lawyer who was associated with the Royal Family.

To my relief and surprise she agreed to this and I said I would follow it up right away. I asked if I might talk to Lilibet and Charles freely about this and she said I certainly could. I said I would also like to talk to

Martin Charteris* and she also agreed to this. In fact it all went quite well.

At this moment there was a telephone call for me. The sister who was looking after Wallis said that Wallis's doctor, a Frenchman called Thin, was a connection by marriage of Stuart Wyatt's, and he would like to send a message through me to Stuart Wyatt.† So I obtained Wallis's permission to go to the telephone in the next room.

After a preliminary talk about Stuart Wyatt, Dr Thin surprised me by saying that at last he had found somebody he could talk to about Wallis's health. He said, 'I have discovered she has no members of her own family living and she doesn't want to deal with her late husband's family, but apparently is friendly with you.' He then asked whether I would accept his communicating with me about her health and seeking general advice.

With some reluctance I said I supposed I would have to agree, but that I had no official standing. I asked about her health, and he said that her mind was rapidly deteriorating and it would not be very long before she would be incapable of making any decisions, though her physical health was quite good and she might live quite a while.

This proved to me that it is necessary to move quickly to get an English lawyer in and to get things settled while her mind is still in a reasonable condition. Dear, oh dear, I always seem to get involved in tricky matters. But I feel I must try and do something not only for the memory of David but after all for the sake of British history.

On 3 March 1973 Mountbatten flew to Malta.

John‡ gave a dinner party for me at Villa Portelli which was great fun as it included so many old friends. After dinner I had a long gossip with Mabel Strickland§ who is now seventy-four. She had evidently quite forgiven me for having befriended Dom Mintoff¶ in the old days, because there was a time when she wouldn't speak either to Edwina or me. Now I appear to be her best friend again. She still runs her own newspaper but there is a strike on and she is bringing out an emaciated edition with volunteers.

---

* Private Secretary since 1972. Later Lord Charteris of Amisfield.
† The agent at Broadlands from 1960.
‡ Rear Admiral John Templeton-Cotill, Flag Officer, Malta.
§ Grand Old Lady of Maltese politics and proprietor of the *Times of Malta*.
¶ Prime Minister of Malta and strong opponent of British rule.

SUNDAY, 4 MARCH. MALTA   John drove me in his mini to the country home of the Prime Minister at Delimara called l'Gharix. We arrived as Dom and Moyra Mintoff were returning with the 'boys' from a swim in the very cold sea just below the Villa. He greeted me with remarkable warmth and friendliness and I was then taken into the house.

The whole scene here baffles description. They had six of the 'boys' with them who all spoke very halting English. They appeared to be young working-class men who cooked and served the meals out of friendship. However, although everybody usually sits at one table, as a gesture to me he put all his 'boys' at another table quite a long way away in an alcove. I noticed that one of the 'boys' put his cap on to have lunch, and they all appeared the oddest collection but obviously gathering round Mintoff as the gang gathered round The Godfather in the book.

The Prime Minister said he would wait on me himself so that there would be no interruption from the 'boys', and we had a rather delicious local Maltese meal and the four of us had a fascinating long conversation; in fact we went on talking until after 1600.

After having congratulated him on his great success in getting more money out of the British and out of NATO than I had ever expected, I told him that I thought he had carried brinkmanship rather too far. I told him after he had got rid of 7000 British personnel and families and their pets, and even the Services polo ponies, that when the Commando Carrier *Bulwark* finally left the harbour with almost the last lot of Service personnel on board, leaving only the Admiral and 22 Service personnel in the island, he had reached the limit.

It had been generally felt that if the Admiral had embarked in the *Bulwark* with the other 22 none of the British Forces would have ever come back to Malta whatever Mintoff had offered. As it was I said he had really gambled very heavily on the goodwill which had existed for him, and I advised him to go steady and not try any more brinkmanship. He took all this quite well but explained at some length that if he hadn't done this he would not have got the money, which may well be true!

At 2000 I drove to the great formal dinner at San Anton Palace. It was very well done but curiously enough for such a formal occasion, with candelabra, silver and servants, the dress was a day lounge suit and not a dinner jacket. This was mainly because the Labour Ministers and one in particular, Frederick Sant, had always refused to wear dinner jackets. He used to be a militant Trade Union leader, but tonight he appeared in a dinner jacket with his pretty wife dressed up to the nines in my honour while the rest of us were wearing day suits on his account.

I must admit they have made a fine arrangement of all the Grand Masters' portraits in the dining room, but when I complained to the Governor-General* of the removal of our Kings and Queens he regretfully said he was acting under orders which he deeply regretted. He had, however, kept the Queen's own State portrait and had hung it in his study; he took me along to see it in the place of honour. I asked him whether he had told the Prime Minister yet and he said, 'No, and I hope you won't either'!

TUESDAY, 12 JUNE. LONDON   After dinner† I had a long and useful talk with the Prime Minister, Ted Heath, who particularly wanted me to help him out at luncheon with Indira Gandhi when she comes for half a day on 25 June. I pointed out that she had already asked me to see her at 11 a.m. at Claridges, and I had released him from coming to the luncheon on board the *Belfast* provided he came down afterwards to make his speech and cast off the yacht *Sea Star* on the round-the-world tour with the former students of the United World Colleges. As I was in the Chair and had issued the invitation, I didn't see how I could stay away to have lunch with him. However, he was most insistent and I said I would think it over and let him know, but would probably only be able to look in for drinks.

I also talked to him about the possibility of making the Chief of the Defence Staff a Life Peer about every three years, just to have some Service representation in the Upper House as the old Service Peers were dying off. He said he would think about it.

I also had a long talk with General Gowon chiefly about St Donat's. He promised to help and said I could talk to his High Commissioner who could go down to St Donat's and report to him.

THURSDAY, 14 JUNE. PARIS   At 1700 I went to have 'tea' (which consisted of a cold ginger beer as it was so hot) with Wallis at 4 Route du Champ d'Entraînement. For three quarters of an hour I talked about every sort of thing under the sun, and then I took the bull by the horns and told her I had heard from Grace Dudley that she had decided to make various generous bequests to charities in the name of the 'Duke of

---

* Sir Anthony Mamo.
† At Buckingham Palace. A banquet for General Gowon, President of Nigeria.

Windsor', and that I thought this was splendid. She seemed gratified. Then I suggested that it was rather a pity that this should be a 'once only' gesture which would be reported in the papers and would never be referred to again.

I suggested that she should form a Trust – put all the money into the Trust, invest it and then use the interest to give the benefactions. I suggested it should be under French law a *Fondation* and that she should choose the trustees herself. I suggested that Charles should be the Chairman, as he was the next Prince of Wales after David, and perhaps Rear Admiral Philip de Gaulle, the son of the great General, might be a French trustee.* She seemed to like the idea and asked me to write to her about it.

FRIDAY, 15 JUNE. WINDSOR   I am staying in ground-floor rooms of the Augusta Tower and the rest of the party only consists of Lilibet, Philip and Anne, which is very pleasant.

Lilibet was out but Philip came in at the same time as I arrived and I had a pleasant gossip with him before dinner. We dined on the Battlements to the accompaniment of the most tremendous noise of the aircraft approaching Heathrow. Every two minutes we had to stop talking for thirty seconds because one couldn't hear oneself speak. I find this even more trying than ever now I am getting rather deaf, though the others very often tried to talk on through the noise I could never follow them.

After dinner we watched television and went to bed early.

> *On 11 July 1973 in Stockholm Mountbatten resumed his campaign to persuade his brother-in-law, the King of Sweden, to abdicate or at least take a back seat.*

After dinner on the verandah when the coffee was cleared away everybody left Gustaf and me alone to talk. Gustaf immediately tackled me about the last letter I had written to him and we got into an unfortunate and rather cantankerous discussion. I suggested we should stop it and I asked him if he would let me go and talk to Stig Ericson† the

---

* An unsurprising suggestion, since Mountbatten had involved Philip de Gaulle in the affairs of the United World Colleges.
† Marshal of the Realm, a position roughly comparable with that of Lord Chamberlain.

following day to clear things up before we continued the discussion. He entirely agreed and then we turned on to happier subjects.

It takes a bit of courage poking my nose into Swedish affairs, but I don't think there is anybody else who really has as much influence with him, or, perhaps I should say, is prepared to talk so candidly to him. He always takes it very well, I must say.

I found Gustaf very cheerful but getting terribly deaf. He apparently has lost the sight of his left eye completely and is beginning to lose the sight of his right eye and is rather depressed about this.

I decided to pay this visit at short notice on receiving word from Gustaf he would not be able to pay his annual visit to Broadlands this year. I suddenly had a premonition that if I did not come over quickly I might never see him again. Although he looks well he is terribly frail and I fear may not last the year out. After all he was ninety last year.

THURSDAY, 12 JULY. STOCKHOLM   It was a lovely day today. We all breakfasted at 0900. After this Gustaf volunteered to accompany me down to Stig Ericson's house, but this was the last thing I wanted as I wanted to consult him quite alone. So I suggested that instead he should show me round the gardens and see what new additions he had made.

This went very well and we spent a happy hour going round the really beautiful gardens for which Sofiero has become so famous. I believe they are the finest gardens in Sweden, and they are certainly the biggest and best rhododendron gardens anywhere in the country. Gustaf is very proud of all that he has achieved and quite rightly so.

Finally at 1045 I was able to break away and go down and have an hour's heart-to-heart talk with Stig Ericson about the future of the Monarchy, the future of Carl Gustaf etc. He was extremely helpful and sensible and we together decided on a new line of approach to Gustaf.

Stig Ericson and Baron Palmstierma, the Private Secretary, were at lunch. After lunch when coffee had been served, Stig and I had a heart-to-heart with Gustaf which lasted quite a long time and really went surprisingly well. This time he was not so much on the defensive and far more willing to listen and discuss the situation. I undertook to write a letter summing up all my remarks to Stig which he could show to Gustaf afterwards.

At my suggestion Gustaf prepared Crêpes Suzette for dinner as usual. It was really great fun.

SATURDAY, 14 JULY   I had breakfast at 0650 in my room and Gustaf came in to keep me company and say goodbye. We embraced each other emotionally, almost tearfully. What a sweet and wonderful person he is.

SUNDAY, 23 SEPTEMBER. WOLFSGARTEN*   Golo Mann, son of the famous philosopher and writer, Thomas Mann, arrived at tea time to spend the night. He is the most famous professor of history in Germany and a charming and most intelligent man. He had been invited by the Swedish Ambassador to give the address at the memorial service for Gustaf† in Bonn and wanted to ask me questions about him. His questions were very penetrating and interesting.

MONDAY, 24 SEPTEMBER   Peg and I set out to go to Stockholm for Gustaf's funeral. The new King, Carl XVI Gustaf, was at the Palace to meet me and I at once realized that something had happened to him to alter his whole appearance and composure. He took me round to introduce me to some of the principal guests and then I insisted on going to change. He said he would wait dinner but I begged him not to. After all, they were supposed to be sitting down at dinner a quarter of an hour ago and I begged him to go in, but he said, 'No', he couldn't go in without me.

Philip was very friendly but slightly cynical, saying it was quite clear who seemed to be running Sweden; all the Crowned Heads of Europe had had to wait until I changed into dinner jacket.

Later that night:

Tino and Juanito led me round and when we came to Carl Gustaf's own bedroom they knocked at the door; there was a hurried scrabbling and when we opened the door there was Carl Gustaf busy turning over some enlarged coloured photographs of a beautiful girl.

I gathered afterwards this was Silvia Sommerlath, a twenty-five-year-old German girl with an Argentine mother whom he had met at the Olympic Games. She comes from a good and wealthy family and is

---

* Home of Princess Margaret of Hesse and the Rhine and last of the former palaces of Hesse still in possession of the family.
† King Gustaf had died on 15 September 1973.

apparently highly educated and talks five languages, and now that the restrictions which he suffered from as a Crown Prince, that he had to marry Royalty, are removed on becoming King perhaps he will marry her.* I certainly hope he marries somebody soon, because it is an appalling burden for him to bear alone.

I understand on all hands Carl Gustaf has done magnificently since his grandfather died; that the speech he made on his induction as King could not have been better, and that his whole bearing has impressed everybody including the Socialist Government. He has managed to solve the deadlock between the two Parties, and already has a following of the young people who previously were calling for a Republic but have now become Carl Gustaf fans. It is all very exciting if this young man has suddenly developed to the point at which he can make the Monarchy alive and able to continue.

TUESDAY, 25 SEPTEMBER. STOCKHOLM

At the airport on the return journey:

I put my head into the other lounge and there found my old friend U Maung Chit, the Burmese Ambassador to England and Sweden. I had had a long talk with Kenneth Kaunda, the President of Zambia, about the United World Colleges in the Palace. I have now heard that whereas he had asked if he could bring 28 members in his suite he arrived with no less than 78. I can only suppose he took the whole of the Opposition with him to make sure there wouldn't be a military coup in his absence, as has happened both in Ghana and Uganda.

On 29 September 1973 Mountbatten flew to Canada for a weekend of varying activities including an important television appearance for use in an Armistice Day programme.

At 0915 the producer arrived, a young Englishman, who insisted on asking all the wrong questions, but we finally agreed what questions I would answer and I told him if he asked any others I wouldn't answer them.

* He did, in 1976.

I then said goodbye to my host and hostess and drove off to Legion House where I met about a dozen members of the Royal Canadian Legion Council and officials.

They said they would look into what help they could give from RCL funds to the United World Colleges. Curiously enough, when it came to providing scholarships they said they wouldn't mind providing 'Mountbatten' scholarships but not 'Pearson' scholarships, because the Legion was so terribly upset at his having removed the old Union Jack and given them a new Canadian flag, which they didn't want.

At 1100 we drove to the Château Laurier Hotel. Here the television people had already set up their camera and recording apparatus. The High Commissioner had arrived to supervise the recording.

It went very well until the young interviewer deliberately put in a question which I had cut out. 'Would you say it was at the Battle of Vimy Ridge, April 1917, that Canada found her manhood and from then on started to become an independent nation?' I replied, 'You agreed not to ask political questions and specifically agreed to exclude this particular question. Before I give you any answer I would like to know what your reasons are for breaking your arrangements?'

He went very red and said that he would drop the question, and then we went on to the next question and the rest of the interview passed off very pleasantly.

Why do inexperienced television people always try and trap their victims into answering questions they had previously said they were not prepared to answer?

After various activities:

It took us half an hour to drive to the Park Plaza Hotel where I changed and had a bath and rested on a bed with a patent vibrator fitting. This shakes you all over and makes you feel very good. I congratulated the hotel manager on having it and he promptly presented me with one which I will have fitted to my bed at Broadlands.

The dinner was being given as part of the Reunion of the Dieppe Veterans and Prisoners-of-War Association. This is a fairly new association and when they asked me to come and address them about the Raid I could not resist accepting, because I have long wanted to tell the actual men who took part what a magnificent show they put up and how essential Dieppe was.

I don't think John Barratt had taken me seriously when I said that I was blamed widely in Canada for having murdered all the Canadians at Dieppe. He sat next to a French Canadian Officer and his wife, who on hearing he was my secretary told him that I had been responsible for the disaster – I had deliberately withdrawn the air support which was needed, and I had arranged the frontal assault which was impossible, and finally I had insisted on going on with the Raid after the date and target had been leaked to the Germans. John Barratt had much difficulty in keeping his temper but just advised him to listen to my speech and hear what the truth was.

When I started to speak I had great difficulty in being heard. I had to do two or three test counts, the loud speakers had to be adjusted, more seats had to be moved, but finally after the first five minutes of ineffective talking I gradually got going, and certainly the last twenty minutes of my half hour speech were heard by nearly everybody, and obviously they took it all in because at the very end when I finished with, 'The Duke of Wellington said "the Battle of Waterloo was won on the playing fields of Eton"; I say "the Battle of Normandy was won on the beaches of Dieppe"', I got a standing ovation much to my surprise. So obviously the object of my speaking to the Reunion had been achieved.

We then all moved into the Ward Room of the *York* where all the different Reserve Officers and their wives and friends had gathered.

I had hardly got into the room when a slinky, sexy, rather attractive young lady with dark eyes and dark hair came up to me and said, 'Lord Mountbatten, this is the thrill of my life, I have always been in love with you.'

She then took my hand and held on to it until I managed with my left hand to pull my right hand out of hers, whereupon she put her arms round my neck. With the assistance of Mark McCormick* and Joe Mylne† we got her arms off; she then started feeling me and fondling me all over and I got very embarrassed and I asked Mark and Joe to take over from me.

They advanced between her and me whereupon she struck Mark a very vicious blow in the kidneys and kicked Joe very hard on the shin. Finally, the Captain of the *York* had to come up with two men and lift her bodily out of the room. It is rather gratifying at the age of seventy-three!

---

* Mountbatten's ADC from the Life Guards.
† Canadian Naval Adviser.

FRIDAY, 9 NOVEMBER. BROADLANDS Soon after the twins* were born Patricia asked Charles if he would be their god-father, as she had been his god-mother and he had just been confirmed. I told her I thought it was a bit much having the Prince of Wales to be god-father of two children simultaneously, but she said that this had been balanced by having very ordinary god-mothers, Miss Sacha Phillips and Miss Amanda Lonsdale. By an extraordinary fluke both these girls are now married to Marquesses, and in the ordinary course of events Sacha will become the Duchess of Abercorn and Amanda the Duchess of Devonshire. I took great pleasure in pointing out to Patricia that the god-mothers were hardly the ordinary run of the mill for the twins.

I had invited Sir Robert Mark, the Commissioner of the Metropolitan Police, to come down for dinner as Charles very much wanted to meet him after having heard his fascinating Dimbleby Lecture on TV.†

It was a fascinating dinner party because of Bob Mark's discussion about the police and the administration of justice. He left at about 2230, and after he went we all agreed that it had been the most interesting dinner conversation any of us could remember for a long while. What a great man Bob is.

On 12 November 1973 Mountbatten went to London for the marriage two days later of his great-niece Princess Anne.

Lilibet had asked me to give a dinner party for unattached nephews, nieces and other relations who had not any other dinner party to go to before the big party at Buckingham Palace. So I arranged to have the big private room at the Royal Automobile Club of which I am luckily still President after 32 years.

I had arranged to have a coloured TV set put into an adjacent ante-room which was reserved for our pre-dinner drinks, and we sat round and watched poor Anne and Mark Phillips struggling with the *Panorama* interviewers. I was amazed that they had consented to be put through this ordeal, and even more amazed to hear that they had asked for it because they wanted to clear up their image. In fact I think they did very well, all things considered, and certainly Anne's character came through clearly and to her advantage.

---

* Nicholas and Timothy Knatchbull.
† A lecture which caused a furore because of its denunciation of dishonest lawyers.

Then we all had dinner and afterwards we set off in a convoy of four cars to drive to Buckingham Palace. The trip would normally take three or four minutes from Pall Mall, but the moment we got into the Mall we got into an absolute jam of cars going towards the Palace. I managed to get hold of a policeman and drawing his attention to the red crown on my car got him to hold back the oncoming traffic and let us go down against it. However, when we got to the Victoria Memorial the traffic joining from the right was so heavy we could not turn against it and we had to turn to the left to go round the Memorial. Then we found all four of our cars were locked solid in a jam so that we could neither advance nor reverse.

After about ten minutes John did a recce and came back to say that the jam extended right round the Memorial up to the gates of Buckingham Palace, and was getting worse every moment. I then persuaded him to take my place driving the Jaguar and got out and walked with some difficulty across to the Northern Gate into the Buckingham Palace forecourt. Here I found two policemen, and with some difficulty persuaded one of them to accompany me.

With his help we managed to get the cars that had got jammed behind us to move just sufficiently to let us back out on to the pavement; then our four cars got on to the pavement and led by the policeman and myself drove right round the traffic jam, and on reaching the approach to the Gate the policeman managed to push back the on-coming traffic sufficiently to let us through. So we all got to the Garden Entrance after a delay of only twenty minutes.

Most others were not so lucky. Nearly everybody spent three quarters of an hour in the jam.

The cause appears to have been that instead of allowing people to come early as they do for Garden Parties and giving them a single approach route, all guests were told to arrive between 2200 and 2210, and as there were 1700 guests all approaching from any direction they got themselves locked in and the police weren't ready for it.

The scrum inside the Palace was nearly as great. This was because they had had to keep the rooms to be used for the Wedding Breakfast locked up, and there wasn't the usual amount of space for the guests. However, it was all great fun and very gay. The women looked lovely in tiaras and jewels and all the men had decorations, except the Phillips' contingent who practically all came in hunting coats.

It was quite a job finding Philip and Lilibet and finally Anne and Mark to say 'Good-evening', but we all saw a great number of people we hadn't seen for a long time which was great fun. I danced with both daughters, both grand-daughters, Lilibet, and Grace of Monaco; but it was difficult to find partners in that scrum.

The atmosphere was tremendously gay and exciting, and it was one of the best parties I have ever been to.

WEDNESDAY, 14 NOVEMBER. LONDON   This was the wedding day of my god-daughter Anne with Mark Phillips. The weather was kind and the sun was shining, and the radio and TV were already dealing with the crowds and the excitement.

Lilibet looked absolutely radiant and Philip looked magnificent leading the bride in, though I noticed that he had obviously lost one of his stars on the way (indeed this proved true for he told me afterwards that the Thistle star fell off owing to the wretched fastenings which he and I now have).

Anne looked more beautiful than I have ever seen her in a tight-fitting white dress with a very slim waist, and the bridegroom wore the newly designed full dress uniform of the Queen's Dragoon Guards. As this Regiment had been amalgamated with the Queen's Bays they had no amalgamated uniform before, so it had to be specially designed but it looked very smart.

After we had kissed the bride and congratulated the bridegroom, photographs were taken. I kept discreetly away but Lilibet found me and said that I was expected in the group, and indeed a place had been marked on the key for me so I went in. I found that the platform to contain the family was much too small, and we all crowded one on top of the other in rather a ridiculous way; I doubt if all our faces will be visible in the group.

Then the bride and bridegroom and their respective parents went off to wave to the crowd from the balcony. I heard afterwards that it was the biggest crowd seen there since Armistice Day. It was a sea of faces as far as the eye could reach up the Mall, up Constitution Hill and down Buckingham Palace Road. All very exciting. What a contrast to President Nixon's image at the present moment with himself risking impeachment and his Vice-President having pleaded guilty to avoid going to prison.*

Meanwhile we all signed the special Visitor's Book and some of us

---

* The Watergate scandal was then very much in the news.

were invited to sign the Marriage Register. I was invited to sign the Register on the front as I had done so for the wedding of Philip and Lilibet, and the others signed on the back.

I looked back and saw their Marriage Certificate and noted that Lilibet had her surname down as 'Windsor'. I looked anxiously to see if they had given Anne a surname and was gratified to find it was filled in as 'Mountbatten-Windsor'.

There has been a curious dispute about whether the Royal Family can use surnames or not. They always have done up till now, but since the Order in Council, which changed the name of the descendants of Lilibet and Philip to 'Mountbatten-Windsor', stated that this only applied to those who were not Royal Highnesses and therefore had a surname, the implication was that there was no surname now that Royal Highnesses could use.

The great thing about this is that the ambiguity about the position of Charles, Andrew and Edward is now cleared up, for since Anne has been officially recognized as 'Mountbatten-Windsor' in the Marriage Certificate, so will the three boys.

The Wedding Breakfast was a very jolly affair at lots of little tables. I was at Charles's table and Grace of Monaco sat between him and me. He said Anne had placed her there out of love for us both!

Philip began his speech to toast the Bride and Bridegroom with the words, 'Unaccustomed as I am to public speaking'. This brought such a roar of laughter that he couldn't go on. He then said, 'I will start again. Unaccustomed as I am to public speaking at Breakfast.' Mark made a very modest and nice little reply in such a low voice that not everybody heard what he said.

When it came to the Bride cutting the cake with her husband's sword, the latter had got jammed in the scabbard and great difficulty was experienced in pulling it out.

There was a party for Charles's 25th Birthday at Buckingham Palace tonight. I heard the origin of this when Charles was speaking on the telephone to his mother and saying that he would like to have a birthday party that night, and she apparently said it would be rather difficult to arrange because the servants would have been busy all day but he was insistent that he must have a party for his birthday, and she finally gave way.

He then turned to me and said, 'I don't mind about a party for my own birthday but I don't want Mummy to be left alone and unhappy when Anne's gone.' What a sweet and thoughtful person Charles is.

In the event it was a great success. Patricia and John drove me there and there were about forty members of the family sitting at little tables – all very gay. I sat next to Elizabeth (the Queen Mum), Tino proposed thanks to Lilibet and Philip for the party and proposed Charles's health. Philip made a speech in which he thanked 'His Majesty for having come all the way from Chobham'. This raised a good laugh as of course Tino has now bought himself a house there since he has been deposed.

I have a feeling he will eventually get back; he told me he had a most successful two-hour conversation with Governor Connally* which I had arranged for him after meeting Connally at Julian Amery's† after lunch. Tino attributes most of his troubles to the Americans having idiotically backed the Fascist Coup by the Colonels for purely military reasons, without realizing that they were risking the future of democracy in Greece, for if Fascist dictatorship goes on too long there is the grave risk of Communism taking its place when they are overthrown.

That weekend the King of Greece was among the guests at Broadlands. On 17 November:

Eddie Kent drove Anne Marie and Tino back to London after tea. It has been exciting having Tino here during this weekend because every two or three hours he has been rung up from Athens or spoken with the former Greek Prime Minister, Karamanlis, in Paris, about the situation which has developed since the students rioted and made a demonstration against the Government. Apparently people have been out in the streets and there has been fighting and rioting all over Athens. They have had to declare Martial Law and suspend the elections; in fact everything is going exactly as Tino has prophesied for some time and as he foretold to Governor Connally quite recently, though of course nothing much can happen the first time this occurs because they can easily put down riots with tanks and soldiers, but they can't go on like this and if there is more dissatisfaction and rioting and demonstrations against the Government Papadopoulos‡ may have to go.

What a splendid thing it would be for Greece to have a really honourable, decent, intelligent young man as Head of State.

* John B. Connally, a former Governor of Texas and Secretary of the Treasury, had in 1973 joined the White House as a special adviser to the President.
† Minister of State at the Foreign and Commonwealth Office.
‡ As well as being President, George Papadopoulos was also Prime Minister, Minister of Planning and Government Policy, Minister of Defence and Minister of Foreign Affairs.

1974

In January 1974 Mountbatten visited China and
after a brief stay in Peking continued on the 28th to
Shanghai.

We were met by the only three members of the British community left,
and when you think of the thousands who lived in the International
Settlement in the days before the war, it was very sad to see how they
had dwindled. They were the manager of the Chartered Bank, the
manager of the Hong Kong and Shanghai Bank, and one of them was
married to a former Wren. I asked them how they managed to get
permission to stay on. They pointed out it was not a question of getting
permission to stay on, it was entirely a question of getting permission to
go, and the Banks were ordered by the Chinese Government to retain
British managers!

An extraordinarily boring but frightfully earnest and enthusiastic
young Chinese and lady assistant had been sent to meet us on behalf of
the local Foreign Affairs staff in Shanghai. He announced that he had
arranged a complete programme; we were to drive first of all to see their
handicraft experimental centre, etc. I told him as forcibly but as politely
as I could that we did not want to see the handicraft centre, which we
could see in any part of China, what we particularly wanted this time
was to see Shanghai which we were all interested to see.

With great reluctance he gave way, so we drove down to the
International Settlement consisting of a lot of extremely fine houses and
buildings on the famous Bund which is the embankment and quay
running along the Wham Po river.

David [Hicks] then suggested that we should go and see the Peace
Hotel. This had been built by the Sassoon family about forty years ago
as the Cathay Hotel. When we went there we found it was extremely
well kept up in every way, except of course there were boring propaganda slogans up everywhere about how wonderfully the People's
Republic was doing and urging the workers of the world to unite.

Nevertheless, in their upstairs restaurant I noticed that every table was laid up with European cutlery and glasses, and they were expecting a full house for dinner and dancing there tonight on the sprung floor.

WEDNESDAY, 30 JANUARY. CANTON   We dined together at the hotel without our Chinese friends at 1900 and had an early night. Patricia passed me a note to say that the delicious soup we had for dinner was snake soup but that she didn't care for the cold lining of sheep's stomach which we had for lunch.

When we arrived in Canton, John's back was extremely painful from his old troubles originating with his wound during the war.

Patricia arranged to go with him to No. 1 People's Hospital where a Chinese doctor treated him with acupuncture along his shoulder. The treatment was painful but the result was excellent and it relieved the pain almost completely during the night.

THURSDAY, 31 JANUARY   In Peking I had seen the entrance to one of the new Underground Stations and asked Madame Wang if we could visit it. She explained that the whole of the Underground was out of action because it was undergoing repairs! Further enquiry indicated that these consisted of building deep shelters against bombs. I enquired about these shelters, and it turned out they had not only living accommodation for the whole population but there were proper hospitals and schools built 60 to 100 ft underground.

Madame Wang seemed rather more indiscreet than the English-speaking Chinese and admitted that underground shelters had been built in every city and large population areas throughout China, and that this had been going on ever since the 'Russian Confrontation'. This was because the Chinese fear a pre-emptive nuclear attack by the Russians, before they have their own retaliatory weapons ready. They are determined to try and survive this attack and then come out and carry on. Indeed, the people have gladly agreed to give up all holidays except the three days at New Year and two single holidays on other days, but they do have one rest day a week.

They appear to make no bones about the fact that they are relying on their comrades among the Labour leaders of the West to break down the capitalist system. In the English language *Peking Review* of 8 January 1971 there is a very significant and sinister headline, 'WORLD

Classiebawn. Fishing with the family and being filmed for the 'Life and Times' television series.

London, 19 December 1968. The Queen arrives at the Imperial War Museum for a preview of the series.

HMY *Britannia*, 16 May 1969. A royal inspection of the Fleet.

Washington, 5 November 1970. At the White House for President Nixon's dinner.

IN GREAT DISORDER – SITUATION EXCELLENT', and from their point of course it is.

They are actually friendly with the British people, particularly now because of the Russians. In fact I heard a story of a dinner given to a Visiting Mission, at which the No. 4 man in the hierarchy in China ended his speech by saying something like this:

> Now I want to say a word about our relations with Russia. This is not usually mentioned but it's time it was. At the liberation in 1949 we regarded Russia as a Father figure. They were going to tell us about Communism; they were going to give us help; they were going to set us on the right lines. They let us have a lot of technicians and technical aid. Bit by bit we drifted rather further apart and regarded ourselves as cousins. When we refused to toe their line they started withdrawing their technicians and doing us so much harm we regarded them as very distant cousins.
>
> But it was not until Confrontation, when they moved 50 Divisions up on our borders and started attacking us, that our relationship changed. Now I can tell you candidly that we regard the Russians as *Yi De Kuan Renfen*.

The interpreter blanched and came to a stop, but was obviously instructed by the Chinese Minister to get on and translate it. So he took his courage in both hands and said, 'Very sorry to have to say that Minister regards the Russians as a great big lump of shit.'

Sensation and consternation! But it shows what the Chinese now feel about the Russians. In fact, they think that the Americans are going to join with the Russians as they realize that a pre-emptive strike made during the next three or four years might practically finish the Chinese off, but after that they will have enough nuclear retaliatory weapons to make it not worth the Russians' while.

I checked that shelters were being built even as far south as Canton where I got Shen to ask in broken Cantonese from the driver of our car what their shelters were like, and he told us with pride that they had fine schools and hospitals in their deep shelters already.

Armed Forces were to be seen everywhere. The army are dressed in a sort of light yellow-green uniform; the navy in light blue; and the air force wear army jackets and navy trousers. They have no badge or rank whatever, and there is no way of telling the difference between a Colonel and the men in his battalion. When I asked how they got on, I was told everybody of course knows who the Colonel is, but they couldn't explain what happened when a messenger came from outside to see him urgently except that all the private soldiers would point out where the Colonel was.

Mountbatten joined the royal family aboard Britannia *at Auckland and on 14 February was off Aneityum Island in the New Hebrides.*

The whole Royal party went ashore in the marvellous new Landing Craft the Yacht has acquired. She is known as a 'Sea Truck' and is 24 feet long with a 10-foot beam. She has a ramp which can be lowered and is very convenient indeed for landing dry-shod across a beach.

At first we went close to a village settlement on the main island where the school children had been collected and sang 'God Save The Queen' twice. I pointed out that they were wrong to sing 'Long to reign over us' because here we have the condominium with France and they would therefore theoretically only be entitled to sing 'Half to reign over us'.

FRIDAY, 15 FEBRUARY. *Britannia* The *Britannia* anchored in Vita Bay in the island of Efate. A joint Guard of Honour of twenty men of the British and French Divisions of the New Hebrides Constabulary were drawn up. Inspector Kalsakau of the British Division was in overall command and gave his orders in English, which the French Commander repeated in French as their rifle drill was quite different.

One has to admit that the French, with their little red Kepis, their baggy white trousers and spats and their French rifle drill, were noticeably smarter than the British contingent, who did a rather indifferent imitation of British Army drill.

The native Chief then came forward, and delivered a short speech of welcome on behalf of the people of the New Hebrides in the Efatese language. The Queen's Equerry was then conducted along a path of mats to receive gifts of food and colossal big black pigs with wonderful tusks. He touched the food and the tethering ropes and then came back. The Queen's 'Spokesman' then stepped forward, in the shape of Martin Charteris, who made a speech first in English, then he repeated the speech in French (having rehearsed his accent with me beforehand) and finally he made the speech in Pidgin English. He was a little nervous when he started but he warmed to his task and very soon had outdone Peter Sellers with his wonderful native accent.

After this, important natives came forward to give gifts. Lilibet got a six-foot slit wooden gong which was really magnificent and when carried away was set up like an Easter Island God in the ground.

Philip was given the tusks of the pig which he 'ceremonially killed' on his last visit, but which in fact was only slaughtered just before our arrival. Anne received a carved mask, and Mark and I each got a spear and a club.

The Family then did a walkabout round the whole of the assembled multitude on the outer edge of the British Paddock, which was rather trying because one never knew whether the person one addressed could speak English, French, or only Pidgin; it was all most friendly and very exciting. I was astonished how well Mark competed considering he can't speak any French.

Here I want to record an amusing incident. The Keeper of the Cabins congratulated me on my initiative in rearranging the tables to seat more people in a more commodious and comfortable way. I foolishly said to Philip I was glad my suggestion had been a success, when he, of course, showed great surprise as he thought it had been his idea.

What an extraordinary thing it is about VIPs. As we get older we always seem to think that new ideas are our own ideas. I naturally thought that I was the originator of the idea but Philip also thought he was, so I said, 'Well you're senior to me in this ship so you can take the credit', and left it at that.

At 1935 we re-embarked in the Royal Barge. After dinner I insisted on doing another rehearsal of the Household Haka for the Ship's Company concert. The du Boulays* had kindly brought a lot of native grass skirts for us which we tried on, and by this time Philip, Lilibet and Anne took a real interest and started advising us how the Haka should be danced and chanted. It was really all very useful and encouraging. I was asked to provide the words of the Haka which I learnt in 1920, and I have been training six of the staff ever since to chant it for the Ship's Company concert.

SATURDAY, 16 FEBRUARY We had an early family breakfast on the verandah and at 0830 the *Britannia* anchored in Bay Homo in Pentecost Island.

The natives of Pentecost have for countless generations performed a

---

* Roger Houssemayne du Boulay, British Resident Commissioner.

head down jump usually referred to as 'Land Diving'. It is more of a native celebration than a ritual ceremony and the natives are not keen on doing it for tourists. They usually choose a site deep in the interior of their island which is difficult to get to, but made a great exception in favour of the Queen by building a jump tower so near the beach at a place they had never been to before and at a time of year they don't normally jump.

They were offered a chance of keeping the jump tower up, and special tourist excursions being sent over by boat for the next day or two if they repeated the jumps, but they declined. In return the British Resident Commissioner undertook to provide them with a complete ox to be roasted whole for their feast that night.

Why they do this jump is hard to imagine; it is terribly exciting and obviously very dangerous. The native name is *Gol* which apparently means 'Fun'. It is usually performed after the first Yam harvest, a traditional time for celebrating and merry-making. The French very naturally call it *Sol de Gaul*, but it has nothing to do with the General nor did he see it on his visit to the New Hebrides.

The circumcision of youths, a very important customary ritual, is usually carried out shortly after the jump has been performed. The wood employed in the construction of the Gol tower is used for cooking the food for the feast that follows.

The structure in this case was built round a fairly thin tree, but to a height of 80 feet above the ground. The ground slopes away below it like a ski jump. There are at least a dozen 'diving boards' sticking out from different parts of the tower on either side, rising up to the top one which is over 80 feet from the ground. Strong lengths of lianas are attached, two to each diving board or jumping platform, carefully measured so that they just reach the ground when stretched.

The diver climbs up and attaches the end of each liana to each of his ankles. He stands on the jump platform while the crowds start chanting louder than ever in a frenzy of enthusiasm and excitement which communicates itself to everybody. And then unbelievably the man dives off the platform beginning with a motion as though he was going to dive into water and indeed his head comes down quite early. But instead of keeping his feet and arms together for a smooth entry into the water he splays them out so as to make as much air resistance as possible.

He lands with an incredible 'whump' on the fairly soft ground and we all thought the first man had been killed as he hit the ground with his face, one of the lianas having been broken from his ankle. However, after some help he got up and walked away, waving to us and smiling.

Jump after jump followed for five or six more turns and I did my best to get photographs with my little Instamatic camera. The third jump looked as though it had ended in disaster, as both lianas broke and the man entered the ground with his head disappearing from sight and his shoulders catching up against the earth. He was pulled out with his nostrils and mouth stuffed full of earth and was unable to breathe and was unconscious. They gathered round and started cleaning him, then they carried him away and our doctor offered to go but they said they had their own doctors. Philip sent one of the jumpers to enquire and he came back saying that the man was all right and would be only a week or two in hospital.*

The next jumper by contrast gave a perfect demonstration. Both lianas held; he hit the ground with his head and chest and then jumped up to his feet and waved to us.

All this was thrilling, made the more so by the chanting and excitement of the crowd. I don't think I have ever seen anything quite so dangerous in my life, or in a way quite so exciting. None of the high-up officials had actually seen the jumping before and were thrilled to be there with us.

Then we all walked down again to the boat, re-embarked and at 1030 the *Britannia* sailed.

There was considerable talk on the verandah deck about the Land Diving we had just witnessed. I said I thought it was the most exciting display I had ever seen. Philip said he thought that the display of high diving at Acapulco, which we had both seen at separate times, where a man dives from a great height and has to jump far enough out to miss some rocks and land in a pool as the waves come in, was even more remarkable. I agreed that that was just about as exciting.

However, Lilibet really hated the horror of seeing the man whose lianas broke and who pitched with his head right into the earth. After that she was terrified somebody would kill themselves outright. Fortunately, as I've written, the next man did a perfect jump and waved his hands to show how well he was.

---

* He died a few days later, one of the very few recorded jumping deaths.

SUNDAY, 17 FEBRUARY   At 1530 there was a rehearsal on the fo'c'sle of the whole of the first turn for the Ship's concert, which included practically everybody in the Royal Party.

At 2030 I got Ross* to make up my face as a Maori Chief having drawn out the design on a bit of paper for him. I wore a fine purple grass skirt which had been provided at Vila, and the little garland of purple ginger flowers I had been given at Pentecost round my neck. On my head I wore one of the extravagant spiked head-dresses from the dancers at Santo, and I carried the wooden club I had been given in Vila.

I had taught six members of the Household to dance and chant the Haka based on the words I learnt in the *Renown* in 1920 for the Haka Party which was run by the Prince of Wales. Incredible as it may seem, when Lilibet looked up in an encyclopaedia of New Zealand the words of this Haka she found that I had been almost word perfect in my reproduction after fifty-four years!

We all went for'ard just before 2100 to the fo'c'sle and the surprise turn of the evening was revealed. The first turn was to be the arrival of the Queen at Pongnastia. Finally we had the Haka party with myself and six other members of the staff.

The star of the show was Martin [Charteris] who, as Prime Minister of Pongnastia, read an address of Welcome in Pidgin, but the real surprise was when Lilibet and Philip turned up. Instead of being shown to their seats, they were shown straight on to the stage where they took part in a mock 'Official Arrival' and did it beautifully. It caused a sensation, as may be imagined, but I knew about it and had indeed noted that Lilibet was sickening for taking part in the concert because she had attended every one of my rehearsals giving advice and help.

The whole turn was a great success and I felt rejuvenated and thoroughly enjoyed myself.

How times and people have changed in my life-time. It is just not possible to imagine Queen Victoria, even Queen Mary, taking part in the Ship's Company concert on board the *Victoria and Albert*!

TUESDAY, 19 FEBRUARY   I arrived at breakfast time in the verandah to find Philip in a great state because his little pet Hermit Crab, Hermon, had really disappeared this time. He had picked up a beautiful spiral shell on the beach at the picnic party on the 14th February at Aneityum

---

* Ross Hallan, Mountbatten's valet.

Island not realizing the shell was inhabited. It was only some time later when he took the shell out that he discovered it was walking about and saw it had a Hermit Crab inside it. He then felt rather guilty and tried to look after it by getting a soup plate, putting in sea water and little pebbles.

It would climb out whenever it could, and every morning so far it has disappeared but usually has been found again in the Verandah. This morning, however, it required a full-scale search and was eventually tracked down outside my cabin at the far end of our deck. So he told Bennett to take it ashore and release Hermon on the beach at Government House, Honiara.

MONDAY, 25 FEBRUARY. PORT MORESBY We all went back to Government House and had a most amusing evening gossiping. I have always enjoyed collecting inverted proverbs, such as the story about the Pelota players who came to London and were put in an hotel with a revolving door. They got very excited about this and all tried to get out together and got stuck, and this proved, 'You should not put all your Basques in one Egsit.' Or the case of the Eskimo who during the Queen's Visit found his caique had got frozen, and as the skins can be damaged if left frozen too long he put it in his igloo to warm it by the fire. He left it there too long and the skins were charred. This proved, 'You can't have your caique and heat it.' Philip and Lilibet between them produced the best of all which apparently occurred when Margaret was visiting Tanganyika, and they visited one of the great Chiefs in his village and he insisted on bringing out the Chief's Chair which had not been used since his grandfather's time. When it was brought out it was found to be so weak and wobbly that it fell to bits. This proved that, 'People who live in grass houses should not stow thrones.'

TUESDAY, 26 FEBRUARY We left at 1000 in a car procession for the Hubert Murray Stadium which was packed with a dense excited crowd. The Seventh Day Adventists' Adult Choir sang a hymn called '*Fowl Bilong Papa*'. I made enquiries what this meant and nobody was quite certain, but some of the Papuans thought that 'Fowl' meant 'Bird' and the Bird referred to the Holy Ghost, and it evidently belonged to God the Father who was called 'Papa'. So this was evidently a song about the Holy Ghost in Pidgin English.

Then followed other dancers and school choirs singing, and it ended with the very fine large brass band of the Royal Papua New Guinea Constabulary playing 'I vow to thee my Country' which was sung by the choirs. Philip looked across and said 'Your hymn'. The whole show was ended by the playing of the Preobrajensky March. Philip looked across and Lilibet said to me, 'I had no idea your tune had got so far round the world!'

I should add that when the Chief Minister addressed the beginning of his speech he said, 'Your Majesty, Your Royal Highness' and then ended with 'Your Royal Highness Lord Mountbatten'. Philip looked across at me and said, 'He means, Serene Highness.'*

Lilibet gave a big official dinner party of fifty-four in the evening. After-dinner displays took place on the verandah deck. They began with eight quick short acts explaining the background to the dance we were to see. Act I introduced the house called Darimo which was used as a place to kill people. Act II showed two missionaries in their small sailing craft arriving. They were invited ashore by the people but refused to go ashore until the following day when they went to the Darimo. Here there was a fearful scene showing them being attacked and killed. The Captain and crew of their boat then sailed away, wailing and bemoaning the death of the white men. All this occurred in April 1910 in my life-time. The astonishing thing was that the whole play was performed showing how Chalmers and Tomkins were killed, and then a complete dance celebrating the events was staged.

I sat next to the coal black Bishop's wife from the Solomon Islands and she agreed it was a very odd play to put on in the circumstances.

During the drive from the airport I started to talk to the Chief Minister, Michael Somare, a thirty-eight-year-old brilliant Papuan with a good record as a journalist, about the Independence that was shortly coming to Papua New Guinea. I had been told by the High Commissioner, and by the Constitutional Adviser, that he had set his heart on having an accurate and comprehensive constitution drawn up before the transfer of power. I pointed out that I thought this would be absolutely disastrous, for either they would have to hasten the drawing up of the constitution so that it was full of loopholes and regrettable clauses, or else they would have to delay the transfer of power which in itself was probably not what he wanted.

---

* A mild jibe at the fact that Mountbatten's branch of the royal family of Hesse, stemming as it did from a morganatic marriage, was Serene rather than Royal.

I drew his attention to the fact that in India I persuaded the leaders to accept the transfer of power on the old constitution, and it was years before the new constitution was finally drawn up in time for the proclamation of the Republic. I advised him to think along the same lines. This seemed quite a new idea to him, and I promised to send him out a copy of *The Great Divide** so that his people could study what we did. I think I made an impression on him, and I repeated the advice in the presence of Dr Guise† later on and he also seemed to agree. At all events they expressed gratitude.

THURSDAY, 28 FEBRUARY   The High Commissioner invited me to dinner at Government House. I went up there and found that the American Deputy Secretary of State, Kenneth Rush, and his wife, and the US Ambassador to Australia and its Dependencies, Marshall Green, and his wife, were present at the dinner.

I had fascinating conversations with them all. Rush insisted on leaning across the back of his hostess to talk the whole way through dinner, but she told me she was fascinated and didn't mind. He was particularly interesting about President Nixon as he was a rabid supporter.

What astonished me was that he claimed that the action taken by Nixon's staff, such as bugging in Watergate, was perfectly normal in American politics and had been done by both sides over many years. He was sure the President was not aware of what they were doing. He now said that the American media had a personal vendetta against him because he always treated them rather badly and they were determined to get rid of him. In other words, the situation was not as clear as we thought in Europe.

He did, however, agree our system was much better, having a separate Head of State from an elected Chief Executive, and if they had this system in the US there would not be such great difficulties now.

TUESDAY, 5 MARCH. SINGAPORE   At 1500 accompanied by Robert Blackburn I paid my call on the Prime Minister, Lee Kuan Yew.

At my request Harry Lee had got a representative from his Ministry

---

* H. V. Hodson's seminal work on the transfer of power in India.
† Dr John Guise, the Home Minister.

of Education to be present, a charming man called Chan Kai Yao. The interview with Lee was as amusing as ever, and he more than accepted ideas for the reorganization of the UWC and gave certain views about how the SIS* should be treated which were of the greatest value.

I offered to send him a written note of the discussion but he said that would only mean he would have to answer me; he trusted me completely to give the written note to the Ministry of Education to get on with it; very friendly and very useful.

While discussing who the new Ministers of the Labour Government in the UK were going to be, I suggested that Jim Callaghan might become Chancellor of the Exchequer. Harry Lee replied, 'If he does I shall sell my pounds!'

WEDNESDAY, 6 MARCH   We drove to the City Hall which we reached according to the programme time at 1615. Here Run Me Shaw and his various officials were waiting to show me the great Surrender Tableau which the Prime Minister had asked me to help with, and which I have been doing through Run Me Shaw. In fact I found the original uniform I wore for the Surrender and gave it complete to the Tableau.

The Prime Minister had asked me through his Chairman, Run Me Shaw, to open the Tableau officially as it was just going to be ready at the beginning of March. I readily agreed. Then I got a telegram from Alec Douglas-Home, our Foreign Secretary, asking that I would decline the invitation on the grounds that it would be a pure Singaporean event. This seemed utter nonsense to me, but I gave in and this pre-visit took its place. The whole of the City Hall was crammed full of television cameras, photographers and reporters, the only thing missing was the actual audience for an official Opening. However, it complied with Alec's wishes.

Outside they had a sadly interesting display of the Fall of Singapore and the Surrender of the British. Inside the City Hall was devoted entirely to the Surrender of the Japanese.

As I entered the Hall I had a most uncanny feeling and I suddenly was transported back twenty-nine years to the scene of the Surrender. It was the same room, the same furniture and the same people were seated at the main table. I recognized them all and suddenly I looked

---

* Singapore International School, latest addition to the United World Colleges.

with a shock to find that there was I among them. It really was a most eerie feeling. Several people thought I had been in some sort of trance.

Then they ran some very interesting but rather bad old newsreels of the actual Surrender, which included my own voice speaking the Order of the Day and reading over the Terms of Surrender. After that I went round the display of photographs in the City Hall, and I found quite a number of small mistakes and one or two rather big mistakes in the captions, and I pointed these out.

The wax effigies are really surprisingly good. Everybody is recognizable without having to look at their names which are written below their chairs and so one can see them as one goes round.

What touched me very much was they found a special bit of film showing Edwina standing among the prisoners-of-war, whom she had released, on the main landing outside the Hall. She had agreed that it would be improper for her to take an official part in this purely military ceremony inside the Hall.

Memory is evidently very short because a perfectly intelligent lady whom I had met at dinner and was talking about the new Tableau asked me whether I was at the Surrender!

On 7 March Mountbatten visited the Singapore International School.

I was taken on a tour of the new Kitching Block which had been built since my last visit here two years ago, at a cost of 900,000 Singapore dollars (about £165,000). It is the most modern type of teaching block in the world and is right up to date, being based on the new integrated teaching system. I was fascinated to see this going on on the main floor in a vast room where there were no less than four separate classes in four different corners doing different things, but all in the open together with the teachers moving about and complete freedom of movement and discussion.

There were also separate classrooms, and in one of these a pitch-black Ghanaian was giving a fascinating talk on the history of Coloured Folk Music, giving excerpts on a tape recorder in between to demonstrate what he meant.

In another classroom I found a modern history lesson going on and the class was being taught the history of post-war Indonesia from the time of the Japanese Surrender. Needless to say I was asked questions by the class and by the teacher as well, and ended up by giving a quarter of an hour lecture myself on that period.

At 1245 I was taken to the Sixth Form House Dining Room which is between the two dormitory blocks. Here all the members of the Upper Sixth were sitting at tables, and at one of them I was invited to sit. Between every course the students got up, took my plate away and a new lot arrived with food for me and sat down at their place. I was thus able to have discussions with many. They came from every part of the world and all appeared to be imbued with the United World College concept.

In my talk I reviewed the progress which has been made in the United World College since I last talked two years before, and then tried to get questions. They were terribly shy so I went on talking and then tried questions again. Finally I went round and practically bullied one of the girls into asking a question. From that moment the flood gates opened and there were hands up all over the place from people who wanted to ask questions. The questions were all intelligent and friendly, and co-operative, and soon we had a general discussion going which I felt was of great value.

MONDAY, 18 MARCH. DJAKARTA At 1155 we drove by car the two hundred yards to the Istana Merdeka where we were received in the Credentials Hall by the President and his wife and conducted to the Saloon where we sat on sofas and armchairs, Madam Soeharto sitting between Philip and me. She asked me, 'Have you ever been here before?' Philip jumped in, 'Has he been here before! Don't you realize this is Lord Mountbatten who was Supreme Commander in charge of your country after the war?' She replied, 'Where did you live?' Before I could answer Philip jumped in again, 'I am pretty sure he would have pinched your Palace.' She took all this in very good part.

At 1300 we left again, this time to drive to the Istana Negara which more or less corresponds to St James's Palace. The entire Diplomatic Corps was present.

I was particularly interested to meet the Indian Ambassador, Mahboob Ahmad, as he had been a regular officer of the Indian Army going through the Military College and then being commissioned in 1940. He was captured by the Japanese, I believe in Singapore, and then joined the Indian National Army under Subhas Chandra Bose in 1943.

I asked him why he went back on his oath and went over to the enemy. He explained that this was entirely for ideological reasons as he thought that the best chance of obtaining the liberation of India from British Rule would be with the Japanese. He admitted his mistake and regretted now what he had done when in fact the British were intending to give India its freedom anyway.

I told him that while I saw his reasons I could not accept that the average sepoys who joined the INA did so for any other reason than to get out of the Japanese prison camps, leaving the great majority of soldiers who were loyal to their oath to receive horrible treatment at the hands of the Japanese, and from the INA themselves. I told him that the whole of the INA Division fighting alongside the Japanese against us in Burma had been valued at the equivalent of one regular Indian Battalion by my Intelligence people.

I also told him that I had advised Nehru not to overlook the service of genuine intelligent members of the Indian National Army later on, and no doubt he got into the Foreign Service through this advice. He quite agreed that this was probably so and was extremely friendly. A rather curious and interesting experience for me. Anybody who reads *The Great Divide* will see the extreme difficulties which the Indian National Army and their Courts Martial caused me when I became Viceroy.

WEDNESDAY, 20 MARCH. DJOKJAKARTA In the afternoon we drove out to Borobudur to see the famous Buddhist Temple. I drove with the Foreign Secretary, Malik, in car No. 2. We had a fascinating conversation.

Malik told me that he had been a great personal friend and supporter of Soekarno, who became the first President on declaring Independence. Soekarno had been a great personality to begin with but had grown more and more away from realities and ended up by having megalomania.

He greatly regretted his idiotic decision to have a military confrontation with the new united Malaysia which the British were setting up. Malik could never really make out why he was so keen to do this, and sometimes wondered whether in fact he had ideas of attacking and taking over Sabah, Brunei and Sarawak and putting them in to Kalimantan, as the large Southern part of Borneo which belongs to Indonesia is called.

However, he never actually did so, and I told Malik as Chief of the

Defence Staff I did everything in my power to prevent the Forces we had facing confrontation from actually attacking the Indonesians or opening fire except in self-defence. He said he was sure that wise counsel on both sides had prevented a disastrous war.

THURSDAY, 21 MARCH   Philip appeared in the breakfast room and told me of his terrible experience during the night. Anne rang him up from Buckingham Palace about 0500 local time to say that she and Mark had been held up in the Mall by an armed madman. He had shot her detective three times; he had shot the driver twice; he had shot another policeman who came from Marlborough House once; he had shot a man who came to help once. He also fired several other shots, one of which narrowly missed her.

It appears that he was trying to kidnap her and when he got the door of the car open started to pull her out, then Mark got hold of her waist and started pulling her in, so she was the subject of a tug-of-war. She kept on telling him to go away. He said he wanted £2 million and an amnesty from the Queen. He ended up by pleading with her to come with him. By this time other police had arrived; the man ran away and was caught.

I remarked what a very plucky girl Anne was, and Philip said, 'Yes! they tried it on the wrong girl, didn't they!' Then Lilibet came to breakfast. She had already heard the story from Philip and was of course rather worried but took it all extremely well. Philip added the remark, 'If the man had succeeded in abducting Anne she would have given him a hell of a time while in captivity!'

Philip was worried that this would immediately start a tremendous increase in security; armoured glass and armoured sides to the cars, surrounded by motor-cycle cops with police cars in front and behind and life wouldn't be worth living.

However, both Philip and Lilibet were very robust about it and made a great point that their own security should not be increased in Indonesia.

We arrived at 1410 at Djakarta Airport. This was the evening of the return State Banquet given by the Queen to the President of Indonesia. It should, of course, have taken place on board the *Britannia* as in every other case over the years. Surprisingly the Indonesians argued and argued against this.

First they said that the ladies might feel sick on board the ship! When they discovered she would be absolutely still and quiet they then said that there was a risk of sabotage to the whole party while they were on board the *Britannia*. When it was pointed out that this was the one place where one could be quite certain to prevent sabotage, they said it was a long dangerous drive to Tanjong Priok through very unhealthy suburbs of the town and it would be difficult to provide adequate security for the Queen. Finally they said that there were so many important Indonesian dignitaries to be fitted in there wouldn't be room for them in the Royal Yacht.

Bill Heseltine,* who was doing the negotiation, huffed them by pointing out that they could seat more people on board the *Britannia* than they could in the British Embassy, and at that the Military Secretary to the President finally admitted, 'Quite honestly we don't want the President travelling down at night in that area at this moment.' So we had to give up the State Banquet in the *Britannia*; the poor Master of the Household had to move up all the stewards, pages, footmen, cutlery, plates and everything else to the Embassy, and had a devil of a job fitting in just fifty at small tables.

However, it was a great success. I sat opposite Lilibet at the main table and Philip sat in the position of honour at the second table.

SATURDAY, 23 MARCH. BROADLANDS   So this is the end of the 1974 Spring Tour Diary. It has been two months crowded with excitement and interest. The visits of Lilibet and Philip appear to make an increasingly big impact with every trip, and the Royal Yacht is a really priceless asset for these visits.

Naturally I enjoyed living on board one of HM Ships and the days at sea particularly, but what moved me most of all is the increasing kindness of both Lilibet and Philip who treat me more and more as a really intimate member of their immediate family.

---

* Assistant Private Secretary and former Press Secretary to the Queen. Now Private Secretary.

On 4 October 1974 Mountbatten attended a meeting of former members of the Military Committee at SHAPE, military headquarters of NATO.

The Supreme Allied Commander Europe, General Goodpaster, USA, met us at the entrance. They had an Armed Guard from the twelve nations working in the Headquarters and a group photograph was taken.

We were then led into the main briefing room where Goodpaster gave us a welcoming address which was followed by a briefing by the relevant divisions of his staff. After this there was a discussion. Goodpaster opened this by saying he wanted to have constructive criticism, as never before had SHAPE had such a distinguished gathering of people who really knew about NATO and he thought I would be the right person to start.

I stood up and delivered a pretty heavy broadside. I congratulated the briefers on giving a really brilliant, concise and lucid report on the present situation of NATO and its plans. I had attended the first briefing ever held by the first SACEUR, General Eisenhower, at a hall hired in Paris in 1950. I had attended almost every briefing meeting and SHAPEX that had been held after that up to 1965.

Although this building was new, the atmosphere was very nostalgic of the old building and particularly the briefing, which I found was as good as ever, but what staggered me was that there was absolutely nothing new in it except technical improvements in weapons.

I found it hard to believe that in the nine years that had elapsed since I had left the Military Committee no new concepts whatever had been embraced. I reiterated my yesterday's remarks that the Arabs with their oil blackmail were not only breaking us financially and buying up the actual territory of the most important parts of NATO countries, but that President Ford's warning that this could not be tolerated hadn't even been reflected, anyway in the NATO briefing. If this was on account of the Middle East area not falling into SHAPE's field of responsibility, then why had this not been changed?

The Russian Naval threat had been colossally enlarged, but as it was mostly taking place in the Indian Ocean and in the South Atlantic, all of which were outside NATO's areas, presumably NATO felt no responsibility. If NATO (with SHAPE and SACLANT) were to continue to be a live going concern, they had to alter their boundaries and strategical areas of thought.

I was followed by others, mostly British, who supported my views, and it was clear after we broke up that my speech had caused a great deal of excitement and a lot of enthusiasm.

What has gone wrong with NATO leadership in the last nine years? It was a depressing experience coming here.

TUESDAY, 12 NOVEMBER. PARIS   At 1630 I went and had tea with Wallis Windsor at her lovely house in the Bois. As we had last parted on slightly distant terms because she obviously wasn't going to take my advice about what to do in her Will, I was amazed at the warmth of her reception. She complained that I hadn't been to see her recently, and I told her that the last time I came to Paris she had been in New York. She then wanted my views on whether she should continue to live in the house for the six months of the year she wasn't in New York, or whether she should give up the house and take a permanent suite at the Plaza Athéné Hotel in Paris.

I told her that she must have two budgets prepared, one, what her expenses would be keeping the house, and the other what her expenses would be living in an hotel in Paris for half the year.

She then said she would like to keep her best pictures and best bits of furniture in the suite in the Plaza Athéné. Did I think the hotel would accept them? I said they would jump at the chance, particularly if she allowed the hotel to rent the suite the six months she wasn't there to carefully selected clients, who would pay more because it was the Duchess of Windsor's suite with her own pictures and furniture.

The rest she said she would sell, and added that she had sold 'The Mill'* very well and found she had rather more money than she had expected. I reminded her I had always prophesied she would have a lot of money.

She then said she had always wanted to arrange in her Will for some money to become a sort of Duke of Windsor's Fund to keep his memory green. I said to her, 'What a wonderful idea', without a smile and without hinting that this was the idea I had put up to her which her lawyer had turned down. Anyway, I promised to write and give her advice on what to do in due course provided she could compete with Madame Blum her French solicitor.

So we are in business again, thanks largely, I think, to the fact that I

---

* The Windsors' country house in the valley of the Chevreuse, some forty-five miles from Paris.

didn't mention anything about the Will, or money, or anything else to her during the hour and a half I spent with her except in reply to her questions.

I am now going to discuss this with Lilibet, Charles and Martin Charteris, as I have already suggested to her that the way to keep David's name green would be in Wales, and the best thing would be through the United World Colleges of which I am the International President now, and Charles, I hope, will succeed me. In any case she said she wanted us both to be associated with the Duke of Windsor's Fund, and hinted that she had already asked me to be an Executor of her Will though she has never mentioned it before.

She begged me to come and see her again and said she wants to come over and see David's grave next summer.

THURSDAY, 21 NOVEMBER. LONDON   I had breakfast at 0700 and then at 0720 my Royal Marines ADC, Alistair Donald, arrived. After a lot of discussions it had been finally decided that I should represent the Queen at the State Funeral of the late President of Ireland, Erskine Childers, and although other Heads of States were expected to wear uniform it was agreed that I should wear plain clothes in case the IRA were to make a set at the funeral arrangements, as it was known that they were building up for some sort of demonstration today or tomorrow.

The Prime Minister sent one of his cars to collect me at 0730 and Alistair and I drove down to Northolt. Here the remainder of the party gradually collected; it consisted of the Prime Minister, Harold Wilson, with his Personal Physician, and two of his Secretaries. The Leader of the Opposition, Ted Heath, was also there. I had technically had to invite them to accompany me in the Andover of the Queen's Flight as it had been turned over to me as her representative.

The Prime Minister tried to make me go into the aircraft first, but I pointed out as we were still on English soil and he was the Prime Minister he should go in first, but I said I would naturally have to get out before him when we got to Ireland. We flew from rainy weather to fine clear weather and arrived at Dublin Airport at 1005.

I got out first by myself and was greeted by the Taoiseach (the Prime Minister), Mr Liam Cosgrave. I had never met him before but I have corresponded with him. He welcomed me not only as the Queen's representative but said what particular pleasure it had given all the Irish people that Her Majesty should have chosen me, since of course it was known I had property in Ireland and was in fact an Irish taxpayer.

Elaborate security precautions had been taken and the streets were well lined by police, and we drove fairly fast to St Patrick's Cathedral. Four special armchairs had been placed in the front row nearest the altar in the south transept. I occupied the first of these four and in due course they were filled by Trix* of the Netherlands, Johnnie of Luxembourg, and Baudouin of Belgium. The two Sovereigns had brought their Prime Ministers with them, and Trix the Deputy Prime Minister of the Netherlands.

The Service was a good simple Protestant funeral service,† very well conducted and only lasting about forty-five minutes. Then the coffin was carried out, followed by all of us in procession. Security was good everywhere, but round Harold Wilson's car behind mine it was almost ludicrous. There were eight plain-clothes men walking, four each side of the car; four policemen, two each side walking, and four policemen on motor-cycles so that if they had tried to shoot him they would have had to shoot through a hedge of human beings.

At luncheon Cosgrave said how much the Queen was respected; how he had heard from her former trainer, Cecil Boyd Rochfort, of the fantastic knowledge and genuine interest of Her Majesty in horse racing, and that all the Irish people loved somebody who really understood about horses and the more they knew about her knowledge the greater would be the feeling of affection towards her. I promised to convey all this to the Queen when I got back.

After all these remarks about the Queen's knowledge of horses I pointed out that the really remarkable thing was that she was a very able, competent and experienced Head of State. Cosgrave said that he realized this but he assumed that she only had to agree with the constitutional advice of Ministers and sign what was put before her.

I then asked him if I might bring Harold Wilson into the conversation. I told Harold that Cosgrave wanted to know what sort of Head of State the Queen was.

Harold Wilson said with sincere enthusiasm that she was really a wonderful Head of State. She had been one for 23 years; she had dealt with six Prime Ministers; she knew more about statecraft and politics

---

* Crown Princess and later Queen Beatrix.
† Erskine Childers was a Protestant, though his father had been executed by the British.

than any of the Prime Ministers she had had to deal with recently. He himself valued his audience on Tuesdays enormously. He had to do a lot of homework to be sure of giving her a good picture and answering all her questions: and he found it was an immense help to him to be able to unburden himself to somebody outside the Cabinet and then get their views and advice, without having to ask that sort of advice from the Cabinet itself. Cosgrave was obviously surprised but expressed great gratification.

Our Andover should have taken off at 1600, but in fact we taxied out at 1635 only to be recalled because Harold Wilson's overcoat had been left in the VIP lounge. So finally we took off at 1640 but luckily we had a strong tail wind and caught up so much that we arrived back at Northolt at 1805.

During this time I had a personal conversation with Harold Wilson. He talked to me first of all about Tino and expressed his personal affection and confidence in him and hoped very much that he would be returned as King. He had given him sound advice on what to do. In particular he suggested that he should not try and get British support; he should not give a press conference or have an interview on TV with Robin Day, all of which he had in his mind to do. He said he ought to make the best possible television film of himself and the Queen having an interview, talking Greek to a Greek interviewer, and send that over with the request that it should be shown. He thought the least thing that Karamanlis could do was to give facilities for supporters of the Royal cause to do some propaganda on behalf of the King they hadn't seen for seven years.

I then spoke to him about the situation in our own country. I told him I had been to the Eleven Club* to dinner and that there had been a general discussion on the state of the country, and that everybody said they were looking for a national personality 'in the wings' to come out and lead the country in its crisis. They seemed to think of somebody like Winston Churchill ready to come forward when called. I had pointed out to them that Winston Churchill was a Member of Parliament, in fact had already had a seat in the Cabinet as First Lord of the Admiralty, and it was easy for him to take over when a National Government was formed. I pointed out that there was no such person in the wings now except Harold Wilson himself, and somewhat to my astonishment they then came round to thinking that he would in fact be an acceptable

* Even the most clubbable of Britons seem unable to identify this body.

leader for the country if he formed a real National Government. This appeared to surprise Harold Wilson too.

I told him that they were all worried that he was trying to do a sort of balancing act keeping the left and right wings of the Labour party together, whereas what he ought to be doing was keeping together all the people of good faith who wanted to see the Monarchy and Democracy survive and to prevent the Communists from getting control through the Trade Unions.

Harold Wilson said that he was very strongly anti-Communist and had no intention of letting them gain power, but it must be left to him to decide when, where, and how to deal with these things. He pointed out that Denis Healey's budget had been designed to strengthen free enterprise and, by taking away the subsidies to nationalized industries, to show exactly the true economic situation of these industries. He thought that this would do a lot.

I said that this was a good beginning but not enough. Anyhow the conversation was very interesting and I felt rather encouraged.

Harold Wilson reiterated to me how strongly he felt about the help the Queen was to him, and he hoped he wasn't boring her by going on talking so much about all the problems in the country. I gave him a direct assurance that she was not bored and he asked me to confirm this, and if by any chance she was, to let him know. I will certainly do this and I am sure I am right.

As soon as we landed at Northolt, Alistair Donald and I were driven in one of the Prime Minister's cars at full speed to 2 Kinnerton Street which we reached in very good time at 1840.

I had already changed into a dinner jacket in the aeroplane to save time, much to Harold Wilson's surprise.

At 1915 the Prime Minister's car which had waited for me drove me to Buckingham Palace.

I met Anne and Mark and drove with them to the ABC Studio for the great Royal World Première of *Murder on the Orient Express*, John's new film.* We three were taken separately round the Officials and the Stars, and then Anne, as President of the Society of Film and Television Arts, and I as her predecessor, greeted Lilibet and Philip who arrived quarter of an hour after us.

The film was the greatest possible success and everybody was really thrilled; nobody more than me. What a great Producer John is.

---

* i.e., produced by Lord Brabourne.

After dinner Philip and Lilibet went back to Buckingham Palace, but all the rest of us, except Mark who had to go back to Sandhurst direct, drove to Claridges for the big EMI party for the Première. I sat between the remarkable author, Agatha Christie (Lady Mallowan), and Mrs Lumet, the Director's wife, who is the very attractive daughter of Lena Horne, the famous coloured singer.

I had a fascinating discussion about our early correspondence nearly fifty years ago with Agatha Christie, when I suggested the entirely novel switch in the plot which she used for her most famous book *The Murder of Roger Ackroyd*, which she admitted caused a great sensation.

1975

On 19 February 1975 Mountbatten, with the Prince
of Wales and the Duke and Duchess of Gloucester,
left London to attend the Coronation of King
Birendra of Nepal.

I was amused to find it was actually the same old Comet that had been
assigned to me when I was Chief of the Defence Staff. In the Royal
Compartment Richard and Birgitte sat at one table, and Charles and I at
the other table.

We had dinner on board and Charles told me with pride that he had
selected all the menus and had carefully arranged to have caviare after
we left Teheran. I said to him, 'I bet they've already bought it in
London.' He wouldn't believe me so I challenged him to ask the steward
who said, 'Yes, of course they got it in London'!

We landed at Teheran at 2215 local time. We were met by the Shah's
youngest brother and were driven straight to the Palace Guest House
where Charles, Richard, Birgitte and I are very comfortably installed by
ourselves while all the rest of our party are in an adjacent guest house.
We were asked if we wanted any refreshments before going to bed, so I
suggested we should have caviare and a large helping of caviare was
provided for us which was delicious.

THURSDAY, 20 FEBRUARY. TEHERAN   At 0940 Charles and I had
breakfast with another large helping of caviare each.

After lunch we drove back in the same large procession to the airport
and took off at 1435 local time. The Shah had given us a lot of caviare
which was served for tea. The clocks were put on two hours and we
landed at 2025 at Palam Airport, Delhi.

We were conducted to a new VIP Ceremonial Lounge where the press
had all gathered and an entirely unprogrammed press conference was
forced on poor Charles as the press gathered round filming, flashing
photograph bulbs and asking questions continuously with micro-

phones. Charles, I thought, did very well in coping with them. They were all very enthusiastic.

FRIDAY, 21 FEBRUARY. DELHI   We came down to receive the Prime Minister who was coming to call. Indira Gandhi is certainly ageing a bit under the strain, but she was relaxed and extremely friendly, and Charles took the opportunity of apologizing for the shortness of his first stay and asking whether it would be convenient for him to come again about the 24th October. Indira seemed very pleased at the idea and said that she would look forward to arranging the visit. Then she conducted us out into the Moghul Gardens to meet her luncheon guests on the lawn.

Just before 1500 my old friend Kewal Singh* came to see me. We discussed Charles's next visit to India about which he was absolutely delighted. And we then discussed the tragic story of the hidden treasure of gold in Jaipur. It appears that the Inland Revenue Department became suspicious of what might be hidden at Jaipur and entirely on their own went down and carried out a raid. Something like 150 Revenue officers went down, and they took everything apart and found no less than 7 krores worth of gold bricks worth nearly £4m sterling.

This has caused a sensation on the local television and radio, and now in the press, and I was very worried as to what would happen to the Jaipur family. However, Kewal was not too pessimistic about it and thought that they might be able to handle the case if they had any worthwhile explanation. He promised to do all he could to help them from his position as he was particularly fond of Ayesha.

We dashed off to the British High Commissioner's Residence at 2 King George's Avenue where a large party had been assembled, not just the British community but all people who had been connected with us, and a great many of my old friends.

Among them I was absolutely delighted to spot Ayesha who came looking exquisitely beautiful in a blue sari. I took her aside and gave her a kiss and said, 'What have you all been up to?' She was evidently in great distress so I told her to tell me all. She said her problem was – where did her loyalty lie in this matter and how could she best protect the memory of her dear Jai? I replied that that depended upon who had hidden the gold. She replied that she had known nothing about it, nor

___
* Indian Ambassador in Washington.

had her step-son, Bubbles, who had succeeded Jai and was now the head of the family, and in fact in the place of the Maharaja. But Ayesha seemed to think it was her duty to try and pretend that she was responsible so that Jai's memory would not be impugned.

I think I was able to set her mind at rest by saying that if Jai had not told her or his son about the gold this could only be because he did not wish to involve them in case it was discovered. It had now been discovered and if she or Bubbles took the blame this would defeat Jai's intention in having kept his secret from them. I was quite certain the right thing to do was to tell the truth and say that they knew nothing about it, because this is what Jai would have wanted.

She then gave me a kiss and said that this had taken a load off her mind but she was still very worried, and rightly so, as to what was going to happen. How idiotic could Jai be as to store nearly £4m worth of gold bricks without telling his family? I am afraid it is going to cause quite a lot of trouble for the family, even though they may ultimately convince the authorities that they were entirely innocent themselves.

At dinner, I sat between the Prime Minister and the wife of the Minister of Energy, K. C. Pant, whose father was with me as one of the politicians in the old days.

Indu was really very friendly throughout dinner and we had a profitable and long discussion, and I talked to her again about the United World Colleges; and we reminisced about the old days in a very friendly way. She is much more relaxed than she used to be, though I think she must be having a hell of a time.

MONDAY, 24 FEBRUARY. KATMANDU   This was the great Coronation day which we had come for. The crowd of VIPs who formed the audience were very colourful indeed; all except the Nepalese who invariably wear exactly the same costume – white jodhpurs, a white shirt, a grey ordinary civilian jacket which leaves the shirt hanging down outside, black shoes, and either a white sweater or a white shirt with a tie. This goes from the King down to the lowest officials and it is very confusing.

I had an excellent seat in the block immediately opposite the heads of delegations themselves. On one side of me I had the Vice-President of the Nepalese Planning Commission, and on the other side the place-card showed the delegate from North Korea. Luckily, he never turned up so I had room to put my cap, my gloves and the little Instamatic camera I had brought in my tail coat pocket, rather shame-facedly as I didn't think I would dare use it during the ceremony.

How wrong I was. Almost everybody had cameras, some had big 16 mm cameras, and one or two had the nerve to bring boxes with spare cameras and lenses with them and put them at their feet. It didn't matter how resplendently the particular people were dressed, they took photographs quite unabashed, got up from their seats, walked down to the religious platform to take close-ups and generally it was a rather unfortunate exhibition of bad manners all round. Nor can I entirely absolve the daughter of Sir John Kerr, the Governor-General of Australia, who was in my row, and frequently went down into the arena to take photos.

One of the most entertaining aspects of the Ceremony was that a large number of young waiters in bright scarlet jackets came round offering cigars, cigarettes, matches, drinks, biscuits and finally snacks.

A further stir occurred when the Crown was carried in in procession, again past my stand. It is not a Crown in the ordinary sense of the word; it is merely a very superior form of Nepalese General's hat such as they all used to wear when we went there in 1946. At that time there were at least twenty-eight of them, and the King's was only slightly more glorious. However, the only one now worn is by the King himself which is called the Crown. It is heavily encrusted in jewels and pearls, fits tightly over the head rather like an ordinary cap, and with a most magnificent Bird of Paradise plume at least three feet long.

Now everything was poised for the moment of the crowning. The Chief Priests held the Crown up where everybody could see it, and we waited breathlessly. Nothing happened. I asked my neighbour what was wrong and he said that the Head Astrologer was there with his wrist-watch and he alone would proclaim the auspicious moment when the Crown must be put on. Just to show his complete authority he kept everybody waiting for five and a half minutes before finally nodding his head, and down went the Crown with loud applause all round. My arms had been aching from holding up my camera but I just managed to last out and snapped it the moment the Crown was put on; I hope the photograph comes out.

As soon as Their Majesties had taken their place on the one single wide throne, the door of the Palace through which the Crown Prince had gone opened and out he came dressed in military uniform, looking too sweet for words. He went boldly by himself, his legs rather knock-kneed but very steady, climbed up the steps in front of his father and was the first to pay homage and presumably swear an oath. He then came and stood at one side of the throne, while all the nobility, members of parliament and officials of Nepal came by for homage. The soldiers saluted and bowed, the other officials gave the usual sort of oriental movement of the hands and bowed, but the little Crown Prince replied to each of them with the same gesture that they had given to him. In a way he really rather stole the show.

We got back to our hotel at about 1730 and rested, before getting into white tie and decorations. Charles and I wore knee breeches and the Garter. There was a hold up when Daborn* was unable to find my second pair of stockings which he had put away only half an hour before thinking I would only want one pair. However, at the last moment he produced them and all was well, and we arrived in perfectly good time at the Royal Palace for the State Banquet to be given by the King.

Fate seems to have put me continuously in contact with the Crown Prince and Crown Princess of Japan, who always come up to Charles for whom they appear to have a special affection. I couldn't avoid having a long talk with the Crown Prince Akihito who talked with some distress about the war, saying how young he was at the time, he couldn't remember anything about it. We talked a bit about Burma and from his conversation it was quite evident he had no idea I had had anything to do with that war. Anyway, this saved me some embarrassment, and I concentrated on my visit with the last Prince of Wales in 1922 when we had first met his father, the Emperor.

TUESDAY, 25 FEBRUARY   At 1200 I joined up with Charles and we went to the new Foreign Ministry Banqueting Hall where a lunch was being given by the Prime Minister. I continued to meet interesting people at this party and asked someone if they could tell me who was the man who looked like Yul Brynner playing General de Gaulle, and was told he was the Vice-Chairman of the Presidium of the USSR. So I went up and introduced myself through his interpreter and said I would very much like to have a chance of talking to him about Russian participation in the United World Colleges. To my astonishment the interpreter translated my words into German and the man replied in German for him to translate to me. At this I broke in and said in German, 'Why do

---

* George Daborn, Mountbatten's valet.

you speak German and not Russian?' to which he replied, 'Because I am the Vice-Chairman of the State Council of the German Democratic Republic.' I said that I was afraid I had made a mistake, I was looking for his Russian counterpart, could he point him out? He did so and offered to come over and introduce me. This was very useful because I then got introduced by one big Communist to another.

Turabai Kulatov was very friendly and we started gossiping about Russia and the war, the fact that we had been allies, the fact that I had been Supreme Commander in South-East Asia and had killed a lot of Japanese, and had met Stalin and discussed our future plans and so forth. Then he asked me if I had ever been to Russia, to which I replied I had been as a child and spoke of my connection with Uncle Nicky and Aunt Alix, to which he replied that he was only ten years old when all that happened and there was nobody alive now with any responsibility, and he hoped that I would not feel this a bar to paying a visit to Russia. I said I appreciated that new generations had grown up and I would gladly consider an invitation to visit Russia.

On 22 April 1975 Mountbatten was in New York.

It was really most inconvenient having to be called at 0640 but I had agreed to go on to the 'Today' television programme to publicize Dick Hough's book about my parents. It is being published this week in New York by Duttons under the stupid title of *The Mountbattens*. I say it is stupid because it had been used, without authority, by Alden Hatch some ten years ago; it should at least have been called *The First Mountbattens* if they didn't want to call it *Louis and Victoria*.*

I found Tony Snowdon there being interviewed before me about his photographic exhibition. When he came out he said to me, 'When you go in say to them, "The Great Grandfather of the chap who has just left you worked for my Grandfather in Germany." '† I did so, which rather shook the two interviewers.

They were a very famous couple, the beautiful girl was called Barbara Walters, and the fairly clued-up man was called Jim Hart. However, Barbara Walters chose to take charge of the whole thing and although it was agreed beforehand in some detail that I would mainly be asked

---

* Which was its title in England.
† Mountbatten got it slightly wrong. It was Lord Snowdon's great-great-uncle, the German architect Alfred Messel, who had worked for the Grand Duke of Hesse.

about the book, they never mentioned it but she went straight in and said something like this: 'It must have been terrible for you when you were driven out of Office by anti-Jewish demonstrations.'

I asked her which war she was talking about and she admitted she didn't know. I said was she talking about my father or me, and she admitted she didn't know. I said, 'Well, I can tell you it was the First World War, long before Jewish demonstrations which wouldn't have affected me anyhow; it was my father who was driven out by anti-German agitation when I was fourteen years old, so we had better start again.'

However, she wasn't deterred and she asked me most idiotic questions – 'What was it like to be an Earl? What do Dukes, Marquesses and Earls do for a living? What did I think of the Monarchy? Wasn't it out of date?' This gave me the chance to put in a good plug for the Monarchy, pointing out that far from being out of date it was obviously a much more satisfactory system than the American Presidency in view of what had just happened about Watergate. When they asked, 'Wasn't it very expensive?' I said, 'The Queen costs far less than your President costs you, even the British Embassy in Washington costs three times as much as the Queen gets.'

Then after twelve minutes there was a thirty-second commercial break, and I leant across and said, 'Suppose you two ask me some questions to do with the book?' They looked very shame-faced and apologized and I then said, 'Well, just let me talk, we've only another two or three minutes and I want to get the plug in.' This I did and I hope retrieved the position. But what really inane questions and what stupid interviewers!

FRIDAY, 25 APRIL. LONDON   At 1700 I drove myself to the Foreign Office where I had a meeting with Sir Tom Brimelow (the Head of the Foreign Office), Sir John Killick (one of our former Ambassadors to Russia), and two of the Foreign Office staff to discuss my visit to Moscow. It has been arranged for me to go as Head of the British Delegation to the 30th Anniversary Celebrations of VE Day in Moscow. The briefing lasted a full hour and was most interesting and valuable.

MONDAY, 5 MAY   I went to a big dinner given for me by Sir John and Aliki Russell. They had invited the Russian Ambassador, Lunkov, and his wife and altogether there must have been fifty guests. It was at 80 Chester Square, their private house which had recently been done up regardless of expense. There were about eight courses including complete poussins in a burning dish.

After dinner the main topic of conversation was my impending visit to Russia. I complained a bit that whereas the American delegate, Averell Harriman, would obviously be arriving in one of the Presidential planes, and the French representative, General Pierre Billotte, in a French Service aircraft, that my party was being sent by commercial flight, and in an Aeroflot Russian aircraft at that, which I thought was rather a comedown for our prestige. The Foreign Office made it clear that the Government couldn't afford to send us in an RAF aircraft, upon which Sir Kenneth Keith, the head of Rolls-Royce, said, 'Well, I will arrange for a special private aircraft, a Hawker Siddeley 125 with Rolls-Royce engines, to fly you and your delegation direct to the principal airport in Moscow, refuelling at Warsaw.' Sir John Killick, from the Foreign Office, thought this a splendid idea, and the Russian Ambassador, Lunkov, also agreed with it. So all was settled and I was delighted, and I promised to go in uniform ready for the investiture for the medal on arrival and for making my broadcast on Moscow radio. I therefore thought it was a party well worthwhile to have attended.

TUESDAY, 6 MAY   In the evening I got a telephone message from the Foreign Office to say that the Russian Ministry of Aviation had been unable to clear my private flight to Moscow, as they required a minimum of 48 hours' notice by statute regulations to process such a flight. I then got on to Sir John Killick and protested violently, but he said that with the two hours' change in time all offices would be closed in Moscow and it would be impossible to reach anybody. I had proposed telephoning to Kosygin myself, thinking the Prime Minister would be able to clear the flight. However, there was no way of getting in touch with him so with great reluctance I reverted to the plan to go by Aeroflot.

WEDNESDAY, 7 MAY   I complained a bit to Lunkov about the extraordinary lack of flexibility of the Russian bureaucratic machine that they couldn't clear a flight in under 48 hours. He assured me that this was inevitable and regretted the bureaucracy, but that there was no question of lack of courtesy to me, it was just one of those things one had to put up with in Russia. To make matters worse the Aeroflot flight arrived over an hour late from Moscow, and instead of leaving at 1510 we did not leave until in fact 1630.

There was a large welcoming committee headed by Mr Georgadze, Secretary of the Supreme Soviet, and of course our Ambassador, Sir Terence Garvey. I was informed, much to my horror, that all three Allied Delegations were being offered special VIP villas on the Lenin Heights, Americans, French and British, and I was asked if I would go to this villa. I asked the Ambassador whether he would be prepared to stick to the arrangement that I should stay at the Embassy, to which he replied he would be delighted if I could fix it.

Georgadze renewed the offer of the villa and hoped very much that I would accept the Soviet hospitality. I replied very cautiously to the effect that I had been given a private Hawker Siddeley 125 with Rolls-Royce engines to fly in, but admitted that I had only been able to give 40 hours' notice and the regulations required 48 hours. I therefore realized that my request couldn't be granted.

I applied the same rules to my residence. I said I had accepted the Ambassador's invitation to stay at the Embassy and required 48 hours' notice to change that. I had only been given about half an hour's notice, and this wasn't any more possible to me than the aircraft had been possible to them, and I therefore hoped he would agree that I should stay at the Embassy. I must say he was gracious enough to laugh and to say that I could do whatever I liked, so I stuck to the Embassy.

THURSDAY, 8 MAY. MOSCOW   I asked to go to see my old home in the Kremlin which was in the Nicholas Palace in 1901 when Uncle Serge* was the Governor of Moscow. Incidentally, I stayed there again in 1908 because his widow, my Aunt Ella, stayed on there after Uncle Serge was assassinated. I led them to what I remembered as Ivan Square, the Russian name being Ivanskaya Ploshchad. I took a look at the giant bell, Tsar Kolokol, which I remembered distinctly had fallen when it was being erected in the Belfry of the St Ivan Chapel, and a large bit had got chipped out which acted as a doorway so that it could be used as a small chapel.

---

* The Grand Duke Serge, who had married Elisabeth, second daughter of Ludwig IV of Hesse.

A bit further along was the biggest calibre gun ever made, Tsar Pushka, of 30″ calibre. To my surprise it had been moved at least forty or fifty yards nearer to the bell, as it was no longer opposite the corner of the Nicholas Palace. It transpired later that this was moved when they built the new Hall of Congress.

Exactly opposite this, as I expected, there was the old Nicholas Palace and I was able to point out that my nursery had occupied the first four windows on the second floor just next to the part where the columns ended.

We moved round the corner to the Government building where the Prime Minister has his office. I arrived punctually at 1030 in Kosygin's office where I was received by his interpreter, whom I remembered as being with him when we both shared the Viceregal Suite in Delhi at the time of Shastri's funeral. I must say that Kosygin received me with open arms, a great smile and a very warm welcome.

I had a most useful talk about the United World Colleges, which went really very well, and he promised he would talk to the Minister of Education and give him his support.

Finally, I handed him the David Hicks Company literature and asked him if he would give it to his son-in-law, as he had come over to the opening of the Aeroflot offices in London which David had designed. I said that I hoped his firm would be allowed to tender for the decoration of the nine new hotels which I understood were being constructed, and he promised to pass this on to his son-in-law. So I hope this will help.

At 1120 we arrived at the Naval Headquarters where Admiral Kharlamov received me and took me up to the Chief of the Naval Staff, Admiral Sergeyeef. He gave me a great welcome and was very cheery; we talked a lot about our respective Navies.

In glancing up at a shelf in his office I saw a model of the POLARIS submarine which I recognized immediately as one I had given to the Russian Naval Attaché. I drew his attention to this and told him I had sent it to his predecessor, the Chief of the Naval Staff, in 1958 through the Russian Naval Attaché, as I understood they were keen to know what a POLARIS submarine looked like inside. He also again expressed his great gratitude for this, and the trust I had shown in them by sending it over long before there were any plans available. I suggested he should put a little plaque up indicating that I had given it and he said he would. In fact I am thinking I am going to have a little plaque made and send it to him, as it is historically interesting.

The real truth of the story is really quite interesting. Round about

Bovington, 16 December 1972. Mountbatten masquerading as a soldier.

Vancouver, March 1972. At a press conference, wearing the United World Colleges' tie which he designed himself.

1958 I was visiting the American Chief of Naval Operations, Admiral Burke, and found he had on his desk quite a good little model of the POLARIS submarine, the side of which could be opened to see all the details of the lay-out. He was very angry and said that it had just been sent to him by a friend who had bought it in the open market at Schwarz's toy shop in New York. He complained bitterly that after all the trouble to keep all the plans absolutely Top Secret, the details had leaked to a toy maker who had the nerve to put a model on sale where everybody could buy it. I asked him if I could have the model, and he said certainly and gave it to me.

When I came back I put it up on my mantelpiece in the First Sea Lord's office. A week later, by chance, the Russian Naval Attaché called, saw the model and asked whether it was that of the POLARIS submarine. I replied it was; would he like to see the inside? He could hardly believe his ears when I offered this, and then I opened the side and he saw the full Top Secret details of the POLARIS submarine lay-out revealed. I asked him if he was interested, and he said he was absolutely thrilled at my showing so much confidence in him to show him this Top Secret model. I asked if he would like to keep it. Again he could hardly believe his ears, but I said it was on condition that he gave it to the Russian Chief of the Naval Staff with my compliments. This he did. Little did the Russian CNS realize that it had been bought in a toy shop, and it still is an object of the greatest interest in the present CNS's office.

FRIDAY, 9 MAY We had a short rest in the Embassy, and then at 1440 drove off to the Palace of Congress where an enormous reception of several thousand people was held on the top floor. Podgorny made the speech which was translated. This, I suppose, was appropriate as he really is the Head of State* and the senior of the Trinity of Podgorny, Brezhnev and Kosygin.

Incidentally Jack noticed Kosygin speak to Brezhnev and then they pointed towards me and nodded their heads violently. Gromyko, the Foreign Secretary, was sent for, and he came over from the top table and spoke to me in a friendly way and said that Brezhnev would like to meet me, so he took me over to him; we shook hands and had quite a long talk. The Minister of Defence, the famous Marshal Grechko, tried to come up and join our party but couldn't break through Brezhnev and

---

* Chairman of the Presidium of the Supreme Soviet.

Gromyko. Then Kosygin brought Podgorny over to speak to me and once more Grechko tried to join the party but couldn't break through them, so he finally gave up. This was a pity because I would like to have had a talk with Grechko.

SATURDAY, 10 MAY. LENINGRAD Peterhof Park only opens officially on 15 May when they expect to have over 200,000 people in one day, which must be quite horrifying. However, the Grand Palace itself was open and there was a certain number of people coming to see it.

We walked up along the famous row of fountains, which I remembered so well, but because the Park wasn't officially open most of the fountains were only turned on at half strength.

I asked if I could be shown the two Joke Fountains, which caused great surprise because nobody had ever asked before to be shown them. However, they found them with the help of a local guide, one I remembered was made like a tree with holes in the branches so that when you sat on the seats round the tree you were squirted with water and everybody roared with laughter. The other one was a big parasol with a circular seat under it. When you sat down it started off raining furiously all round the outside and you couldn't get away without going through the rain. It's funny how, after something like 67 years, my memory was so clear on these two Joke Fountains.

Then we went in to the Grand Palace to see the restored rooms. At this point I must admit I didn't realize the Germans had been so close to Leningrad that they had actually occupied both Peterhof and Tsarskoe Selo, and out of sheer vindictive vandalism had blown up as much as they could of these beautiful Palaces on their departure.

MONDAY, 12 MAY. LONDON Averell Harriman told several people that the Russian authorities had approached him on more than one occasion to try and find out how they should address me. They wished to call me 'Your Royal Highness' but Averell said that this was wrong, I was an Earl but I hadn't got a Royal title. They expressed great disappointment as they wished to honour a member of the late Imperial Family.

It was an interesting visit from every point of view, both historically and politically, and I was overpowered by the emotion of going back to a country I had known fairly well as a child, where so many of my closest family had lived in such tremendous splendour and then been murdered in this ghastly way. I felt it all the way through, and I was quite exhausted when I came back.

The only thing to be said is that the Russians appear now to have rather changed their attitude to the Imperial Family, and certainly their special attention to me, I am sure, came more from my relationship with Uncle Nicky and Aunt Alix than because I had been a Supreme Allied Commander during the war.

WEDNESDAY, 18 JUNE. BROADLANDS Yesterday Dodo* drove Nan Pandit down for the night. Nan had come over at my invitation to deliver the Nehru Memorial Lecture about her brother and was now going to spend a night at Broadlands. Pammy also came down separately to look after them. We had a very pleasant afternoon and evening gossiping. The reason I say it was pleasant – it was nice having Nan there but the gossip was sad.

First of all we talked about the fact that her niece, Indu Gandhi, had been found guilty of incorrect election practices by a very brave judge in the UP, which means that she loses her seat and is banned from public office for six years unless she can get the decision reversed in the Supreme Court.

She has not, of course, been corrupt in the ordinary sense of the word, but she certainly has got a great deal too big for her boots and is being very tough and difficult with everybody. Though she may get the decision reversed by an Appeal to the Supreme Court, this in itself will be regarded with great suspicion because, when the original Supreme Court rejected her action in getting the President to de-recognize the Princes she then managed to get rid of the Chief Justice and get in her own choice above the heads of three others more qualified. So people think she may have got the new Supreme Court in her pocket, but I hope not as it would be a bad thing for India. It remains to be seen what will happen.

We then talked about our dear friend Ayesha Jaipur who had been in trouble ever since they discovered gold bricks in her new Jaipur home when I was in India in February. I had a very long letter from Ayesha saying that her passport has been taken away and that they are using metal detectors searching everywhere for further treasure.

* Dowager Lady Brabourne.

SUNDAY, 29 JUNE When I was CDS Nelson Rockefeller and later Henry Kissinger both came to consult me about the strategic situation of the world. I was rather flattered at the time and told them that if ever they wanted to come and spend the night at Broadlands they would be welcome.

Now this invitation has borne fruit, but at the last moment Henry Kissinger had to go off on one of his urgent meetings in other parts of the world.

This light-hearted invitation to come and spend the night with his* new wife and her daughters turned into quite a military operation. As long ago as the 21st June, while I was still in France, three Secret Service security men arrived, and as Norton was then staying in the house he received them and they explained to him the precautions which would be needed for a visit by the Vice-President, which rather staggered him. In due course a further eight Secret Service men arrived on the 23rd, and were seen by Jack Barratt, and at their request he took them over the entire house, right across the roof, down along every floor, looking into every cupboard, and finally down to the basement looking into every room.

After that they said they wished to have a proper reconnaissance of the grounds and two helicopters spent two days searching the estate, presumably for the Mafia, or whoever was plotting to assassinate the Vice-President.

They said that they would have to station a very big helicopter in a hidden part of the ground near the house to lift out the Vice-President in case of an emergency. I subsequently sent them a message not to be stupid, because if it came to an emergency I and my gamekeepers with guns would clear a way through so that the cars could get out of the estate. They evidently felt rather foolish, and the helicopter, having been in position, was flown away together with the crew of five whom we would have had to put up in the basement of the house.

Meanwhile, when I got back I sent a message to say that we would not put up anybody else in the house, so they then took over the White Horse Inn where no less than 24 agents were billeted. About 12 of them seemed to be permanently on duty all round the house and it was very much like a Hollywood extravaganza film of Presidential life.

The Vice-President finally arrived by a Presidential jet at Eastleigh; Jack Barratt had offered to send a car to collect him but was told that it

---

* i.e., Rockefeller's, Vice-President of the United States.

would have to be a bullet-proof car and they had the only one available, so the Secret Service fetched him.

MONDAY, 30 JUNE The Vice-President had asked for a special interview with me to discuss the world situation and particularly the significance of the build-up of the Russian Navy. So we arranged to have an hour's talk after 0900 breakfast.

He had his Naval Aide with him and the three of us went very thoroughly into the significance of this colossal build-up of the Russian Navy and the general lines which should be taken by the Western World about it.

What a very nice and intelligent man he is. Indeed the whole family are delightful, and the daughters very pretty.

> *On 8 July 1975 Mountbatten was in Edinburgh for the visit of the Swedish King, Carl Gustaf. After a luncheon at Holyrood Palace:*

I heard the Prime Minister was going to have to leave immediately to settle a confrontation with the Trade Unions which might entail a constitutional crisis, and so I waited for him.

As Harold Wilson came out of his audience with the Queen he saw me and greeted me warmly. I then asked him if he would allow me to speak my mind to him, and he said 'Certainly'. So I pointed out that the situation in the country was such that all true patriots of any political persuasion would rally round him if he went out 'on his charger with a drawn sword and determined to do battle' against all those who were trying to bring the Government down by unrealistic wage claims or other attitudes.

I gave him a long pep talk, at the end of which he put his hand on my shoulder and said, 'Well, Dickie, you must say I always do take your advice, don't I?'

I replied, 'Yes, but I have a nasty feeling that you are going to try and make another compromise settlement for the sake of political party peace instead of really leading the country as Winston did in the War.' He said if he could not settle the problem within 48 hours he would certainly bear my advice in mind. However, I fear he will try further political manoeuvring to get a settlement which will avoid his having to lead the country with all patriots behind him as I suggested.

WEDNESDAY, 9 JULY. EDINBURGH All except Carl Gustaf and the Swedish and attached British Suites were at dinner, a total of some twenty. I sat between Lilibet and Elizabeth. After dinner we went to the drawing room where Margaret sat down at the piano and started to play. Soon we all gathered round the piano and were singing lustily.

This was still in progress when Carl Gustaf and his party returned from having attended a dinner and reception at Parliament House given by Her Majesty's Government. I encouraged him to come right up to the piano and join in the singing. Charles scored a great hit by singing, or rather chanting, to the tune of a Psalm words from the Official printed instructions for the State Visit. The section he chose referred to that afternoon's activities and was as follows:

> His Majesty will arrive at the British Petroleum Tank Farm at Dalmeny where Sir Eric Drake will present Mr G. G. Porter, the Resident Engineer. The motor-cycle escort group will proceed independently to the Control Room. The King of Sweden, and those in attendance, will drive to the top of the reconstituted shale tip from which the landscaping of the Tank Farm project can be seen. Thereafter the party will proceed by motor-car to the Control Room which will be inspected. The King of Sweden will, outside the Control Room, take leave of Sir Eric Drake and Mr F. M. Cook, and with the Suites in attendance accompanied by the motor-cyclist escort group will leave for the Palace of Holyrood House.

Charles, accompanied by Margaret, did a good job. It was hilarious, and amused Carl Gustaf a lot.

After this Carl Gustaf showed surprising initiative by collecting the whole of his Swedish Staff round him, headed by the Foreign Minister, and conducted them while they sang three amusing Swedish songs. Altogether a very pleasant and hilarious ending to the formalities of the State Visit.

SUNDAY, 27 JULY. BROADLANDS I had a long gossip with Juan* about the situation in Spain. He explained to me why he had made that

---

* Don Juan, Count of Barcelona.

very odd public speech which had so embarrassed his son, Juanito.* He said if only Franco had not taken back the power after his illness all would have been well. But now he was an old senile man holding on to power and it was going to be very difficult for his son to take over under the aegis of an ailing dictator. He thought it was much better that he should make an announcement showing that he was perfectly ready to rally the Democratic parties away from the Dictatorship, which he would not have had to do if Franco hadn't messed things up.

Ron Allison, the Queen's Press Secretary, rang up to say that there was intense press interest in Prince Charles's new girl friend (Liz).† I therefore suggested that when we got to Windsor Great Park the girls would change round, and Liz then got into my car with Norton, and Penny‡ got into Charles's car.

This worked surprisingly well from the point of view of confusing the press but unfortunately it had the effect of making them more interested than ever, and a great deal of idiotic captions were put under the photographs that were printed. One of the press people managed to get hold of Norton and asked him who Charles's new girl friend was, and he replied that she was his girl friend and not Charles's.

The international polo match was between England and South America. England led with two quick goals but was defeated by ten goals to six after a really splendid match.

The winners were given champagne in the Royal Stand, and then Lilibet had to leave. I stayed on with Norton and Penny until half time, and Elizabeth stayed on with Charles for the whole match, as Lilibet had said she could stay at Windsor for that night.

When we got back to Broadlands shortly before dinner, Daborn said that the press had been constantly on the telephone trying to find out the name of the new girl. He had managed to evade the issue. However, telephone calls continued to come in and the last one started just before midnight, but I answered the phone without speaking and left it connected up and I heard the man on the next telephone in their office saying to the person he was talking to, 'It is very important that we should locate the Brab Borns; they appear to have left their house in the

---

* Now King Juan Carlos of Spain. Don Juan had reasserted his own claim to the throne and said that Franco's plans for the succession would not lead to the essential democratic change.
† The press had had a short but merry field-day when they thought they had detected an incipient romance between the Prince of Wales and Princess Elizabeth of Yugoslavia, whose name had previously been linked with that of Richard Burton.
‡ Penelope Eastwood, now Lady Romsey.

South of France and must be on the road, and they ought to know what is going on in London about their son, Norton, and this girl.'

THURSDAY, 31 JULY. LONDON At 1845 Norton brought Penny round for a drink, and I gave them a quick dinner at the Royal Thames and then we drove to the New Theatre in Drury Lane to see *Kwa Zulu*; a very unusual production consisting entirely of Africans of Zulu and neighbouring tribes doing a sort of dance-and-song spectacle with a story running through it.

On coming out, while Norton went to fetch the car, I was walking alone with Penny when a photographer came up to snap us. This is real fame now, being snapped because I am walking with Norton's girl friend!

MONDAY, 18 AUGUST. CLASSIEBAWN Patricia told me that Amanda had made a mess up of her arrangements to have friends to stay; she had first asked a girl friend who couldn't come; then she had asked a boy friend who said he would let her know if he could come; then another boy rang up and said he could come, and as the first one hadn't answered she accepted him, and now both boys wanted to come together. Although it made a bit of a crowd in the Castle, I said I didn't mind and so she went to the station and collected a boy called Hughie.

His hair was longer than Peter's but did not actually cover his eyes, and he seemed somewhat bashful. I tried to talk to him but he couldn't understand what I was saying; he replied to me in an American accent which I found difficult, so between us we were not able to communicate very successfully.

The next day Amanda and Hughie went to the station to fetch her next boy friend, Donald. He had a vast untidy mop of hair and as he kept his head well forward most of the time I hardly ever saw his face at all. I discovered he was intensely shy and rather shattered by his arrival at a place he had not expected, and that he took refuge in hiding his face behind his hair most of the time.

Soon after he had gone out riding with Amanda and Hughie the telephone rang and a very Scottish voice asked if that was the house of 'Mr Knatchbull'. I replied that I supposed it was. He then asked whether his brother, Donald, had arrived and I said he had. I was intrigued by this and got Patricia to make enquiries.

316

From these it transpired that Amanda had told neither of her friends
that her father was called 'Lord Brabourne' and not Mr Knatchbull;
that the place they were going to stay at was a Castle and not a house;
that it was owned by her grandfather who, horror of horrors, was that
terrifying character Lord Mountbatten.

She freely confessed that she didn't think either of the boys would
have accepted the invitation if they had known what they were in for.
However, she seemed quite happy with them and looked after them
very well, and they were no bother to me, though I must say I was
somewhat put off by the messiness of the vast tangle of hair which
Donald had.

> *On 4 September 1975 Mountbatten was in Gothen-*
> *burg to unveil a plaque to the memory of Admiral*
> *Sir James Saumarez, British Commander-in-Chief*
> *in the Baltic from 1803 to 1812 during which time*
> *he had rendered great service to Sweden. After the*
> *ceremony:*

We drove back to the hotel where I had the chance of a good long gossip
with Carl Gustaf. I pinned him down on the question of his marriage,
and to my astonishment he not only listened but took part in the
conversation and agreed with all that I was saying.

Bertil had begged me to have a talk with him when I saw him
yesterday but warned me that I would run up against a stone wall. This
was not the case at all and he was most forthcoming. I told him that
everybody I had met, including Ministers, had said how well he was
doing, but that the one thing now lacking was a Queen of Sweden.
Everybody wanted him to marry and I felt he would be much happier
with a partner by his side. This he agreed with. I then said that my
attempts to find a bride for him in England, such as Jane Wellesley and
Leonora Grosvenor, had failed* and what was he going to do now.

I urged him to consider marrying his girl friend, Silvia Sommerlath; I
understood that she could speak several languages very well, including
Swedish. To this he replied she could speak a number of languages very
fluently but her Swedish was not very good yet, in fact he spoke English

---

* Neither the Crown Prince nor Lady Jane Wellesley had shown any conspicuous
enthusiasm for Mountbatten's project, while Lady Leonora had unsportingly become
engaged to Lord Lichfield before her royal romance had even had a chance to burgeon.

to her. He admitted, however, that she certainly could learn it quickly if she put her mind to it.

Her father is South German and her mother is Brazilian, and she apparently has very good manners and goes down well with everybody. All this he admitted. Then I said I thought it was a great mistake that he should invariably be reported in the newspapers as spending his holidays with her. I pointed out that if this went on the idea would come about soon that she was his mistress, and it would be difficult then for the mistress to become the Queen. He saw this.

I then asked him what he was going to do, to which he replied that he was fully taken up with his time-table and programme and wouldn't be able to do anything about it in the near future. I pointed out that the sooner he did it the better, because he could then alter his programme to allow for having a fiancée.

Finally, I put a proposed time-table to him that he should definitely make up his mind by the end of 1975, and that he should not see Silvia again until he was prepared to propose to her, or to tell her that he wouldn't marry her.

Even this he took quite well and said he would give it careful thought. I promised to put it to him in writing when I got back as I do want him to do something about it. He is doing so very well as King; if only he could get a good Queen now, he would really be firmly on the throne and the Swedish monarchy would be re-established.

Mountbatten was in the United States on 15 October 1975, having promised to visit Princeton University that day.

After breakfast in the New York apartment, Jack thought he had better ring up Warren Elmer in case there had been any sort of mix up as he still hadn't received the printed programme, although I had been requested by Frank Taplin to arrive just before 1200 for the lunch.*

To Jack's horror, but hardly to his astonishment, Warren said, 'Lord Louis should have left in the car by now to get here in time for the press conference.' It then transpired he had invited the press to meet me at 1100 and had put it in the programme, but as he had never sent me the programme and never told anybody, of course we didn't know anything about it.

---

* Frank Taplin was the Chairman of the United States UWC Commission; Warren Elmer the senior salaried executive, styled the President.

Walter* did arrive at 1020 and drove me as fast as he could to Princeton, and we arrived at the Woodrow Wilson Memorial Building at 1145. Frank and Warren and Ian Gourlay† were there to meet me and to dash me into the press conference. Frank was very good and began the conference by saying that it was entirely his personal fault that I had not been told of the conference. However, they were in an understandably hostile mood and a very difficult conference resulted.

A man from the *Philadelphia Enquirer* started off by asking me questions about the present state of India and various other extraneous matters. I tried to get out of this by saying that as we only had quarter of an hour left out of the hour's conference I hoped he would confine his questions to the thing I had come for, the UWC. To this he replied rather tartly that they had been waiting 45 minutes for me, and if I had arrived at the time they had been told I would then have had time to answer his questions. I explained that even then on principle I would not have answered questions on the state of India, and we left it on a rather bitter note, though I was able to improve matters, luckily, after lunch when he came up and was friendly.

Several other people asked me quite intelligent questions, particularly the local radio who were very friendly.

Then a very clued-up young journalist from Jamaica really started putting me through it. He said he was surprised that a man like me should have consented to be associated with the United World Colleges considering they hadn't even got as their main object the abolition of colonialism throughout the world.

I tried to explain to him what the objects of the United World Colleges were, and that there was nothing in writing about political aims. He returned to the charge; I then finally turned on him and said, 'How dare you criticize me about not being pro anti-colonialism?' I asked him who he thought had started abolishing colonialism and breaking up the British Empire and turning it into a Commonwealth. I said not only had I done this in Burma and in India, but I had even been consulted about Jamaica and had said that although I thought it was rather bad luck on Jamaica giving them their independence as early as all that, if they wanted to go bankrupt they should have their freedom to go bankrupt. I asked him how near they had got to their goal.

To my surprise he took this awfully well and laughed and said, 'You

---

* Chauffeur to Carola Rothschild, Mountbatten's old friend and hostess.
† General Sir Ian Gourlay, Director General of the UWC.

are quite right, we are very nearly bankrupt', and we ended good friends.

Then I was taken along to the luncheon which consisted of some four hundred of the most important people in the University, and in the world of education in that part of America, and their wives. I was called upon to make a speech and made one entirely on the educational aspects, and ended up with a very breathcatching statement. In effect I said that all these American Authorities on Education, and particularly those of Princeton, were now going to hear what the United World Education was like and how the International Baccalaureate worked. I said that this was a new revolution in Education which apparently had not hit Princeton before; how lucky they were to have the chance of hearing what Education should be like in the future, and realize how very far behind the times they were at Princeton. This brought a roar of friendly laughter and loud applause.

The conference itself was in two parts, one dealing with the International Baccalaureate and the other dealing with the principle of the United World Colleges.

They had excellent panels for each subject and the discussion afterwards was extremely illuminating. As I listened to it I realized that the words I'd used were being amply fulfilled and the Authorities of Princeton were being considerably shaken.

FRIDAY, 17 OCTOBER We landed at Heathrow at 0950. We shared the Alcock and Brown VIP Lounge with a large Saudi Arabian Delegation. I noticed a very pleasant young man and I suggested to the official in the VIP room that I would like to meet him. He said, 'That's funny, His Highness has just been asking if he could meet you.' So we met and he said he had been to Sandhurst and Cranwell and immediately asked me to visit him in Saudi Arabia. I said I would be delighted to come if I could do so on my return from Singapore, probably about the beginning of March. He was Prince Bander bin Sultan bin Abdul Aziz, son of the Saudi Arabian Defence Minister.

I was told by one of the airport officials that a Saudi Arabian Prince had bought a Rolls-Royce for his three months' stay in England, and on departure the chauffeur had asked him, 'What shall I do with the car?' And the Prince said to him, 'You can keep it.'

WEDNESDAY, 22 OCTOBER. LONDON   I was lucky to have quarter of an hour's talk with the Prime Minister and mentioned my invitation to Saudi Arabia and wondered whether I ought to accept. He said, 'I order you to accept. Nothing could be more important than that you should visit Saudi Arabia at this time. I will tell the Crown Prince when he sees me this afternoon.' Apparently Harold Wilson is relying on the Saudi Arabians to help him out of some of our financial troubles. No wonder he wanted me to go out there.

Patricia had come up from Newhouse arriving at Charing Cross at 1820. We walked together up to St Martin in the Fields, and were taken to the vestry where we were both met by Frank Harcourt Munnings, the enthusiastic Director of 'War on Want'.

He had arranged to have an annual Edwina Mountbatten lecture; the first one had been held a year ago and given by the Prime Minister which none of us could go to because we weren't given enough warning. This year Patricia and I represented the family.

The speaker was that famous little freedom fighter, Archbishop Dom Helder Camara of Brazil. He is a tiny man but with an outgoing personality and charm and had made a great name for himself, so much so that he had been called, unofficially, 'The Ambassador of the Third World'. I had been asked to present him with the Victor Gollancz Humanity Award and had to make a speech to a crowded church.

Then the Archbishop gave his lecture, which had fortunately been printed in English and distributed to a few of us but not to the whole congregation. He read the speech in the most delightful English which was almost un-understandable. However, the gestures with his hands and his whole movement were so emotional that it made a great impact on the congregation.

Then came the tricky business of his answering questions. How he could have understood the questions I don't know. What is certain is that nobody could have understood all the answers, though they were received with great enthusiasm.

1976

<hr>

*Mountbatten duly visited Saudi Arabia arriving at
Riyadh on 9 February 1976.*

At 1020 Bander conducted us to the old Palace of the late King Faisal
who had been assassinated by a nephew a few months ago. He had been
succeeded by a brother who had gone off with the Minister of Defence
on a hunting expedition for a month. Bander tried to persuade me to
change my programme so as to come at a time when they would be in
the capital, but I pointed out that as long as the Prime Minister and the
Minister of Education were present, as far as I was concerned they were
the people I was trying to do business with. Although of course I was
sorry to miss the honour of being seen by my real host, the King, I was
sure His Majesty would understand.

Bander took it in good part and went ahead with the programme, but
when later on my old friend the Sheik of Bahrain got his son to ring up
Bander to ask us to extend our programme by a day to go and visit him
again at Bahrain, which I knew well from the days when it was our main
Naval Base in the Persian Gulf, Bander replied, 'Lord Mountbatten
would not change his programme to meet our King; you can hardly
expect him to change his programme to meet your Sheik!'

It appears that the real power in Saudi Arabia now is the King's
younger brother, Crown Prince Fahd bin Abdul Aziz;* and the next
most powerful his younger brother the Minister of Defence, who is, in
fact, the father of our host, Prince Bander. Thus Bander is a nephew of
the reigning King and the grandson of the great King Ibn Saud.

The audience took place at 1100 and was fairly romantic. There were
a lot of people in a very large room with armchairs placed round the
walls – otherwise devoid of furniture. The Prime Minister, who was
sitting in a central chair, got up to greet me and then we were placed on
chairs round him.

The Prime Minister had at one time been Minister of Education and

* The First Deputy Prime Minister.

was not only extremely knowledgeable but very friendly and sympathetic to my approach. I took up the agreed line that we wanted to involve Saudi Arabia in the United World College movement both for the sake of our Colleges and for the sake of Saudi Arabia's image in the world.

They were particularly interested in getting American or English University degrees. In America they could have an easy entry into any university and in four years they got a degree. In England they required at least one year's English tuition, two years to get the necessary 'A' levels, and then three years to get the degree, making six years.

I now offered them a short cut. If they liked to come to any one of the three existing United World Colleges, we would accept them at a pinch for one year and at the same time as working up their English we would help them to pass the International Baccalaureate to get in to a university in England, and then in three years they could get a degree making four years, the same as the Americans.

This attracted the Prime Minister very much. However, I pointed out that ideally they should do two years at a United World College so as to get the full benefit of the International Baccalaureate, and in five years they would get an education and a degree worth a great deal more than the four years in America. This appeared to appeal to His Royal Highness. It certainly went over very big with the Minister of Education and his Deputy, whom we called on immediately afterwards, and they promised to look into it.

I do not want to be over optimistic, for I realize what the Middle East is like and their politeness may mean only that they are going to look into it and take a very long time making up their mind. I hope we can keep the pressure up.

On 11 February Mountbatten continued to Bombay.

The Governor, Nawab Ali Yavar Jung, came to call on me at 2025 for a brief talk as we are old friends.

The Governor was very keen that I should ring up the Prime Minister as an act of friendship on passing through India. I agreed and he tried to get through and found that Indira was actually in Goa at the time, carrying out some function, and was not available on the telephone. This was quite a relief to me as I wasn't sure what I should say to her. However, I sent her a message through the Governor to say that the single act she could take which would help the friends of India most in England would be if she removed the censorship and allowed the English correspondents to come back unhindered to India. The Governor absolutely agreed that this was the right thing to do, and said he would be very glad to pass on the message.

Dear Ayesha called me up from Jaipur as she had received my letter saying we were passing through Bombay. She had just been to Bombay for medical treatment and I was sad to have missed her. She sounded in rather good form and we had a nice but rather careful gossip. I gave her love from all the family and she sent love to everybody. It is clearly a devastating experience being in prison for so long but she felt all the more excited to be liberated. I only hope she doesn't have to go back to prison again as she has only been released on parole.

TUESDAY, 17 FEBRUARY. SINGAPORE   At 1445 I went for my interview with the Prime Minister. I must say I am very fond of Harry Lee and he was in particularly good form. We had a thoroughly enjoyable sparring match. When I couldn't find a date that would suit him for the Conference, I then challenged him with, 'You don't want to come and speak at it, do you?' He confessed this and explained that as the next year was an Election Year, and as he had been so busy and never accepted invitations to give prizes or do any Openings at his own schools, he would lose a lot of votes from the Singapore Education people and the parents if it was known he went and paid this tribute to what, after all, is a foreign school even though it were international.

I replied I did not wish him to lose any votes and therefore would let him off on condition that he allowed me to get his Minister of Education to make the speech. He promised not to dissuade him, but said I would have to persuade him myself as he also had to be elected.

I then gave him a long pep talk on what we had done to improve the image of the UWC in Singapore since I had last been with him, and this he accepted quite well. I told him that I hoped the President would give a reception for our delegates, to which he replied I could ask him. I said I had already done so and he had accepted. This took Harry Lee aback a bit but he countered by saying, 'Well, he is a sick man, the Americans put the wrong medicine into him and knocked him out for five days.' To which I replied, 'I suspect he'll survive all right but if he doesn't his successor will have to take on his commitments.'

After that we talked in general about the world situation. He is a most refreshing person to talk to and great fun.

Mountbatten flew on to Australia and embarked on the long railway journey from Perth to Sydney. On 20 February:

At about 1430 we entered the famous Nullarbor Plain, so called because there are literally no trees whatsoever. It is like the dried-out bottom of the ocean, pretty flat with a sort of rough scrub blue-green stiff grass, and little tufts that rise to about 12 or 18 inches, and every now and then some sort of bushes in little groups of a dozen which rise to about 2 or 3 feet.

Keith Smith* offered to let me go on the footplate and drive the train, so he had the train pulled up on the Nullarbor Plain after we had walked right forward through the corridors to save time.

There were two drivers who were very friendly and one of them gave up his seat, but I let the other one carry on driving so as not to cause complications. I had seen the line stretching both ahead and astern 56 years ago, and I had brought a copy of my 1920 Diary with me.

Across Nullarbor Plain the train runs 300 miles without a turn or dip, the longest perfectly straight railway track in the world. I cannot improve on the description I wrote 56 years ago in my Diary.

> There is a weird fascination about this great plain which, to look at, reminds one of the sea, the horizon being distinct and unbroken all round. The sky was blue and almost cloudless. Looking ahead one can see the shimmering rails running straight on until they appear to join and melt away in the distance, a second set of rails being occasionally visible in the air when a mirage occurred.

While on the footplate we saw a certain amount of life. At least half a dozen rabbits and hares scampered away from the railway line as we approached; and one big kangaroo on the embankment raced off with enormous hops.

A fox slunk away on the other side, and finally the star turn was a great eagle sitting on one of the telegraph posts; it took off slowly as we passed, and its wing span must have been about 8 foot as it flew very slowly along the train and then wheeled away.

This is my fourth very long train trip; my first one being on our honeymoon in October 1922 when Edwina and I went from Florida to California on the Atchison, Topeka and Santa Fe rail road in a private

* Chairman of the Australian National Railway Commission.

car. Then I also went by the famous Orient Express from Paris to Constantinople in January 1923, and having had the Trans-Australian experience already that was three, and this makes my fourth.

I must say a long train journey has a very peculiar fascination of its own. One gets to know the other people as one gets out and walks up and down the platform or goes through the saloons, and one gets used to one's own little cabin after three or four days as though it really were home.

Jack asked Keith Smith what would be an appropriate tip to give the drivers, to which he replied that no tip which we could offer would be of any interest because they were both paid the astonishing salary of $20,000 a year for their broken life in crossing Australia so continuously. This works out at £13,000, over £250 a week. So we decided to give them each a specially designed David Hicks tie which they liked very much.

THURSDAY, 26 FEBRUARY. SYDNEY   We got back to the Admiralty House steps at 1200 and I went up to Kiribilli House and freshened up a bit. Then Jack and I walked over to Admiralty House, only a hundred yards away, at 1230 and were met on the doorstep by the Governor-General, Sir John Kerr, and Lady Kerr, and their staff.

Their Excellencies took me into their private room for quarter of an hour's extremely interesting discussion about the general situation, and I congratulated him once more on the decisions he had taken and told him that wherever I had been in Australia everybody had admired his courage and thought he had done the right thing; indeed, the Chief Justice told me it was the only possible constitutional step that he could have taken.* I told him that it seemed lucky that Gough Whitlam now appeared to have become involved in a $500,000 gift by the Iraqis to the Australian Labour Party, and he said it was indeed a very fortunate development from his point of view.

I finally got away at 1300, rather late for luncheon, and we drove straight on out to the house of Sir John and Lady Pagan.† I met Marjorie Pagan and their daughter briefly, when it was explained to me the luncheon was to be an all-male affair and quite small – only nine people.

---

* The Governor-General had recently caused considerable controversy when he dismissed the Prime Minister, Gough Whitlam, and called a general election.
† Brigadier Sir John Pagan was a man of many roles, which had included that of Agent-General for New South Wales in London.

The conversation was stimulating and brilliant, and they gave me the complete low-down on the whole of the Australian constitutional crisis. I had not appreciated before that Sir John Kerr was not only a political appointment by Gough Whitlam, but that he had been made to realize by the Prime Minister that if he failed to fall in with the Prime Minister's wishes he would have him dismissed by the Queen. Constitutionally, however, the Governor-General could dismiss the Prime Minister but only so long as he was still in office. Therefore Kerr had to choose a time at which this was a feasible proposition, and he chose to do it just before he went off for the Armistice Day Commemorative ceremonies on the 11th November so the Prime Minister could not get hold of him or take any steps to prevent his dismissal by trying himself to get the Queen to dismiss the Governor-General.

This largely accounted for Whitlam's fury and the fact that he made those terrible remarks on TV: 'God Save the Queen because no one can save her Governor-General. Kerr by name and Cur by nature', which we heard on TV in the UK.

Everybody round the room agreed that the next Governor-General they all wanted was Charles, appropriately married but even unmarried, as soon as Kerr's time was up.

I then raised the point that had Charles been placed in the same constitutional crisis he could hardly have acted in the same way. And this they were inclined to agree with and said the matter wanted further consideration, but they still thought the solution for Australia was to have Charles as Governor-General, at least during a period when no constitutional crisis could be foreseen.

WEDNESDAY, 10 MARCH. LONDON   At 1740 I joined Anne and we drove together to the new Headquarters of the British Academy for Film and Television Arts (BAFTA). If there is one man really responsible for having brought the film and television sides together in one organization it is John. He formed a unified Society for Film and Television Arts originally with Philip as Chairman; then after some years I took over from Philip; and then after some years I managed to get Anne to take over from me.

Lilibet and Philip very kindly gave the £60,000 that they received as royalties on *The Royal Family* film to BAFTA in order to create a wonderful new international film and television centre at 195 Piccadilly. Here again John was instrumental in raising most of the money, finding the premises, and getting the property reconstructed with the most up-to-date form of equipment imaginable.*

On arrival Anne and I were greeted by the various officials and found John and Patricia at the entrance to the Centre. A few minutes later Lilibet and Philip arrived to perform the Opening Ceremony, which they did in the marvellous new theatre for which most of us have sponsored the seats and which she then christened the 'Princess Anne Theatre'.

Anne made a witty speech in which she referred to her 'Parental and Avuncular predecessors'. John had got Charles to do a most amusing recording for the occasion which was shown on half a dozen television receivers. They gave an exhibition of the actual capacity of the equipment starting with a 10 by 10 foot screen which gradually opened until it was something like 25 by 50 feet.

After that we were taken round the various other places such as a smaller theatre and separate individual projection rooms.

Then there was a party for all the guests, who were all distinguished, beginning with the Prime Minister himself. But perhaps the most exciting of all was my dear old friend Charlie Chaplin, who received in person the trophy which goes with an Honorary Fellow of BAFTA. Poor old Charlie really is a chronic invalid. He was in a bath-chair; he could hardly speak; he just smiled; and Philip came over apparently on the television recording saying to Lilibet, 'He can't see either.' He could see a bit but not in the glaring lights.

THURSDAY, 11 MARCH At 1400 I went to Thames Television Studios where I recorded an interview about the United World Colleges with Eamonn Andrews which went well. He surprised me by his ending and I surprised myself by hearing what I replied. He said, 'You have been retired since 1965 from active duty and yet everybody tells me you are as busy as ever. How long are you going to go on working like this?' I replied, 'Anybody who has worked hard all their lives must never stop but go on working if they want to live. So I intend to go on working; I intend to die before I stop.'

SUNDAY, 21 MARCH. BROADLANDS I worked hard clearing up my papers and dealing with left-over correspondence. At 1700 Jack came for a last-minute check of all my papers, and I asked him to make

---

* Lord Brabourne maintains that this account exaggerates the importance of his contribution.

arrangements to have me represented by Ronnie Brockman at Monty's funeral since his son had sent a message saying he was likely to die in the near future, and of course I won't be able to get back.* After all, Monty didn't come back for Winston's funeral when he was on holiday in South Africa, and I shall be doing official business for at least another week.

However, I was fond of the old boy and we have been friends since 1941 and I was indeed sorry to hear that he was dying. He was the last great General of World War II and a very fine battle winner. I am afraid he was no good in office, and was definitely a failure as CIGS, and I was glad when I was able to persuade Attlee to recall Bill Slim to the Active List as a Field Marshal to take over from Monty.†

> *Mountbatten's 'official business' took him to Canada. On 23 March 1976 he was in Ottawa staying with the Governor-General, Monsieur Léger.*

At 1210 I was asked to have a formal interview with His Excellency in his study in the nature of a call. Then at 1230 he took me into the drawing room where a party had been assembled for Patricia's Investiture. I had originally been asked to bring a morning coat to wear, but I thought it inappropriate and was allowed to wear uniform instead. There were many others there in uniform.

Patricia had been awarded the Canadian Decoration (CD) as Colonel-in-Chief of Princess Patricia's Canadian Light Infantry. She rang up the Queen when she heard she was being offered it to ask if she might accept, to which she received the reply, 'Why not? I have got the same decoration myself.' Being told it was hardly the same thing and she wondered whether there would be any trouble if she did accept it, she received the reply, 'If anybody gives you any trouble I will do my best to speak on your behalf.' So Patricia had now agreed to accept the decoration and there was a formal investiture.

After lunch I had agreed to give a television interview about the new book *Bodyguard of Lies* which has just been published, which gives a most distorted picture of what happened at Dieppe.‡ So once more I

---

* Lord Montgomery duly died on 24 March 1976.
† A somewhat picturesque assessment of Mountbatten's role in this appointment.
‡ This ingenious book, by Anthony Cave Brown, *inter alia* argued that Dieppe was planned by Churchill as a means of proving to the Americans that any immediate invasion of Europe would fail.

had the chance of telling my story on Dieppe on television, and I hope this time people will begin to understand it.

SUNDAY, 28 MARCH. WINNIPEG   At 0945 I drove with Patricia to Kapyong Barracks. An Interdenominational Church Service was held in commemoration of the Battle of Kapyong. All the important Patricias were present – Patricia, Colonel Jim Stone, Lieutenant Colonel Bob Stuart and I sat on special chairs. During the Service Patricia was asked to unveil a new memorial window to her Regiment.

The sermon, though it could hardly be called that, was preached by the Chaplain General to the Canadian Forces who had been the Chaplain attached to the 2nd Battalion of the PPCLI* during the actual battle. He spoke very much from the heart in a very effective way.

He mentioned how much encouragement he got from going round the various United Nations Operational positions which were occupied by Canadian troops. On one occasion he went to an outpost where a little mess had been built with some flower beds arranged round it, and on the path up to it was a little tombstone which he thought might be for some pet dog. On the way back he stopped to look at it; there was just one word on the tombstone: 'Sex'.

He then proceeded to speak of Patricia in a manner I have rarely heard a living person praised in church; the inspiration she was to the Regiment, and how thrilled the Patricias were to have a 'Lady Patricia' once more as their Colonel-in-Chief. When it came to the turn of the Roman Catholic Padre, he prayed that, 'Our Colonel-in-Chief may be guided in her duties by God's almighty hand.'

At the end of the Service the Colours were marched out and the other 50 men followed and formed a Guard of Honour once more to Present Arms to Patricia when she left.

Then we all walked over to the Officers' Mess where a sherry party was held to bid farewell to the Colonel-in-Chief. At this party I was able to have a really good word with the Minister of Defence, Richardson. Although he had been nearly three years in the job this is the first time he has actually attended a ceremonial parade, and he told me he couldn't get over how impressive the Trooping the Colour was. He said nice things about Patricia and what it meant to the Regiment having her as

* Princess Patricia's Canadian Light Infantry.

Colonel-in-Chief; and I said nice things about the Regiment and what a thrill it was for Patricia.

I then took the opportunity of trying to do some propaganda for the Services as a whole, and above all for restoring the right coloured uniforms and ranks for the Navy, the Army and the Air Force while still keeping their administration unified. Finally, I put in a very strong word that senior officers should be allowed to have volunteers from their own units to come in service hours and look after the house and food.

A farewell luncheon party was given at Government House for 34 people. This time Patricia had to make a speech. The Lieutenant Governor started off telling, in rather a pompous voice, the great thrill and pleasure it had been to have Lady Patricia and her distinguished father, Lord Montgomery, present. I chipped in with 'I am not dead yet' before the general laughter which inevitably followed this remark. From then, of course, the speech couldn't go on being serious, and both speeches were light-hearted and pleasant, though Patricia's did end on a very sentimental note which moved everybody very much.

WEDNESDAY, 21 APRIL. WINDSOR   There was a birthday lunch of 16 which did not include Anne as she and Mark had had to leave the dance soon after midnight to go off to a cross-country riding competition. In the middle of lunch Lilibet was called to the telephone and came back with the shocking news that Mark had just rung up to say that Anne had had a terrible accident. Her mare, Candlewick, had turned away from a jump and tried to jump an impossible obstruction to one side which she hit with her legs, and turned a somersault throwing Anne 15 feet on to the hard ground where she immediately passed out. The horse landed only a few inches from her, then rolled on her. If it had landed directly on her I think it would have killed her. As it was she was still unconscious with a black eye and badly bruised, and was now in the local hospital.

SATURDAY, 24 APRIL. LONDON   In the morning I went to see Anne at the King Edward VII Hospital for Officers where she had been moved from the local hospital in the West Country after her accident.

She was in the same room I had occupied and I found her surprisingly cheerful. She told me it was the first time she had been able to keep her eyes open while having a visitor. So far she has only had her parents and Charles and, of course, her husband, Mark.

I have been working hard to ensure that Sir Charles Strong* should give her treatment as soon as she was ready for it, and she told me she had now decided to start it on Monday morning having moved back to her own home at Sandhurst on Sunday evening. She expressed great regret at having had to cancel her coming to the Burma Reunion and sent a very good message to be read to the assembled company.

John drove me to St Paul's Cathedral for the Slim Service of Thanksgiving, after the unveiling of the Memorial Tablet put up to him in the Crypt by the Burma Star Association.

I had arranged to represent Philip, who was a Burma Star Holder and hadn't been asked in time, and so the Canon in Residence met me at the West Entrance. The Cathedral was pretty full with over 2000 Burma Star Holders in the congregation.

The Canon was not very clued up; he asked me who I was representing and when I said Prince Philip he didn't seem to understand, so I had to say the Duke of Edinburgh. He then said, 'In that case you had better sit in this chair', pointing to the special chair put in front of the rest of the congregation. I told him I was going down to the Crypt first, which surprised him, so he took me down to the Crypt where Bill's family and close friends were gathered waiting for the Canon in Residence to dedicate the Tablet and for Aileen to unveil it.

As he led me up into the body of the Cathedral again he said, 'I knew you had an interest in India but I didn't realize you had a connection with Burma!' It is very good to have one's ego deflated like this from time to time.

SUNDAY, 25 APRIL. BROADLANDS   In the evening we had an extraordinary film called *Rancho de Luxe* which was an X certificate. I had the Fowler family there and was worried for Angela was only sixteen. I had every reason to be worried as there was the most pornographic shot I have ever seen of two people having ridden off into the woods, stripped and then copulating naked together with appropriate noises. Why do all ordinarily decent films have to be ruined by this sort of display of sex? I suppose I am old-fashioned but I do think that sort of thing one wants to keep private and not see it exposed in public.

---

* A physiotherapist in whom Mountbatten had total confidence, whether the patient was a princess or a polo pony.

TUESDAY, 27 APRIL. LONDON   I woke up in agony and could hardly get out of bed because I had clearly displaced my sacro-iliac joint during my sleep. This was an old injury which I originally did in a severe polo collision, and every season or two it used to go out but Strong always manipulated it and got it back. He has even taught me how to get it back myself and help others, though it is much more difficult.

I was in such pain that I decided to get hold of Sir Charles Strong only to find that he had gone over to treat Anne. I could hardly complain as this had been at my own suggestion.

So I rang up Oak Grove Lodge at Sandhurst and spoke to Mark. He said that Charles Strong was due in quarter of an hour and I asked him if he would ring me up at once if Anne and he would agree to my being manipulated at their house. They agreed. Charles Strong rang up and I fixed up an appointment with him for 1015.

I got up with great difficulty and was helped to dress and helped downstairs, and then was driven to Sandhurst.

We had some coffee, then Anne came down to see me. She has made a remarkable recovery already due entirely to Strong's treatment. In fact I was now an old cripple and she was a bright young bouncing girl.

I then crawled down and got into a special car and was driven up to the hospital. Here Colonel Young* took us to a private ward in which there was a bed with a wooden board on it for manipulation. He then offered to retire. I suggested he should remain and see the miracle which was about to be performed.

Strong put me on the board, felt all round and then said, 'Right, here we go.' He then manipulated me to the right – there was a loud report; then he manipulated me to the left – there was another loud report; then he said, 'All right, you can get up now.' I got up and found myself standing erect virtually without pain.

Colonel Young was really impressed, but what impressed him most was that I was ashen grey and looked really ill and old when I got on the board, and a minute later the colour was coming back into my face and I looked young and healthy. What a miracle man dear old Charles is; it is a tragedy that Lady Strong has died but lucky for us that he is going to move back into practice above his old flat in Portland Place.

FRIDAY, 30 APRIL. WINDSOR   At 1730 the new Prime Minister, Jim Callaghan, arrived for an audience and to spend the night at Windsor

---

* Commandant of the Military Hospital at Sandhurst.

with Mrs Callaghan. The Court in residence attended the dinner which was very gay, and after dinner, Philip, the PM and I had a three-cornered conversation which so pleased Callaghan that he consulted me afterwards about what he could do to get into personal contact with the Chiefs of Staff. I suggested that he should ask the four of them to dinner and just get to know them a bit without any agenda. He said he would have to ask the Secretary of State, Roy Mason, and I said that would be all right as long as Roy Mason realized that he must not interfere with free discussion with the Chiefs, as had regularly happened with Harold Wilson, Harold Macmillan, and, of course, Winston Churchill.

He liked the idea very much, and then asked whether I thought I could come, and I said that was out of the question – I couldn't do back-seat driving. He then wondered whether he could ask Philip, and I said I thought he probably could provided that Roy Mason and the Chiefs of Staff agreed he should only come on a social, informal basis and I offered to clear it with Philip and with Lilibet. I did this afterwards and they liked the idea so it is now up to the PM to see what he does about it.

SATURDAY, I MAY   There was a luncheon with members of the Court present at 1300; and at 1415 I drove with Lilibet and Philip in their car, followed by the Court Officials in another car, to Wembley. We did the trip, in spite of record crowds for the Cup Final, in 35 minutes.

I was very keen to go to the Cup Final this year because for the first time in history our own local home team, the Saints of Southampton, were in the final against that formidable team, Manchester United. The betting odds were 6 to 1 in favour of Manchester United, but on the way up I kept on saying I was undaunted in my backing of Southampton and reminded Philip how often when one is playing with a low-handicap team against a high-handicap team in an open tournament, the low-handicap team could surprise the high-handicap team who then got rattled and the low-handicap team won.

The world now knows that that is exactly what happened; within the last 7 or 8 minutes of the game Southampton shot the one and only goal. The whole place went mad but the Royal Box sat rather glumly there, so I stood up by myself and cheered and waved and shouted. I gathered later that this did not pass unnoticed by the Southampton supporters!

I have been to several Cup Finals, particularly with Edwina who loved them, but never before have I enjoyed one so much because previously I had no personal feeling about which team won. This time I madly wanted Southampton to win, and it was frightfully exciting. It was a nice clean game too, with hardly any violence afterwards such as has recently been disgracing these big soccer matches.

As Philip was dining out as Colonel-in-Chief of the Royal Irish Hussars, Lilibet and I dined alone. She let me choose the menu and of course I chose caviare again which Tino had brought back from Iran. This is my third consecutive night with this most delicious Beluga caviare. However, what was real fun was having the whole evening by myself with Lilibet gossiping until Philip came back from his Regimental dinner.

MONDAY, 3 MAY. LONDON   At 1130 I drove to St Paul's Cathedral to attend the Memorial Service for Field Marshal Lord Montgomery. I walked up the steps with a lot of camera clicking and then was met by a young officer who said, 'I am going to conduct you to your seat.' I asked where I was sitting and he said, 'Right up in front.' The Field Marshal's family were all sitting in the front pew to the right, and the front pew to the left was for the VIPs. I was given seat No. 1; next to me was Edward Short representing the Prime Minister; then Roy Mason, the Secretary of State for Defence, and somewhat down the line to people like Ted Heath, etc.

It was a large congregation with many important people to pay tribute to this marvellous old man. Monty was such a remarkable man with whom I became good friends. He is the last of the great wartime Generals left, I believe, on either side. As far as the Chief of Staff and Supreme Commanders go, I have for some while been the last because I was appointed so very young. Rather an odd feeling now.

On my way out his son, the new Viscount Montgomery, stopped to speak to me for a moment to thank me for my letter explaining why I couldn't attend the funeral and to thank me for coming. I reminded him that I had been to see him at Winchester when he was at school there at the request of his father after the Sicily landings.

I must say I am really horrified that Lord Chalfont should have written a book with such very unkind remarks about poor old Monty just at the time of his illness and death.* The British seem to love denigrating the great men of the War.

* * *

* *Montgomery of Alamein*, a somewhat tendentious biography.

Nan Pandit's daughter, Rita, who is married to Autar Dar, the Indian Ambassador in Sweden, is over on a short visit to London and had asked to see me, so I gave her and Patricia lunch at the Royal Thames Yacht Club. She gave us a horrifying account of the Police State in India and said they were surrounded in their Stockholm Embassy by what they called 'Intelligence Officers', which were obviously like the German Gestapo or some sort of Russian Commissars of the KGB as they reported on their every movement and on everything they said to the Swedes.

WEDNESDAY, 5 MAY. PORTLAND   The *Bronington* had just got alongside when we arrived. I was piped on board and received by the Captain, my great-nephew Charles.

We sailed at once and passed the German large modern Frigate *Hessen*. This was such a coincidence that I suggested Charles should send her a signal in German which translated was as follows:

'My Uncle Grand Admiral Mountbatten, nephew of the last Grand Duke of Hesse, greets *Hessen*.'
    The reply came back in English: 'Thank you very much.'

As we passed the breakwater a second mine sweeper of the same class, the *Bildeston*, joined up. Her Captain was three months junior to Charles so the latter was the senior officer of the two ships in company and enjoying it very much.

I must record that I was really impressed at the way he handles the situation on the bridge. He is quite clearly the Captain and in very definite command. Yet he lets his officers put up their suggestions and will listen to them and then make his decision. I found that he really ran the bridge quietly and efficiently.

After we had cleared the breakwater he carried out Officer Watch manoeuvres with the *Bildeston*. Then we made a *rendez-vous* with his first ship, the Guided Missile Destroyer *Norfolk*. They got a jack stay across and transferred an officer from the *Norfolk* to *Bronington* and back. I had volunteered to go over if they really wanted me but on the whole Charles thought it was better not.

Charles had arranged for me to go down to the Chief and Petty Officers' Mess for some coffee during the morning. It was great fun talking to his 7 Chiefs and 5 Petty Officers who were full of enthusiasm, and obviously had a very high regard for Charles.

I was amused to see that while doing the jack-stay transfer he hoisted as his RAS (Replenishment at Sea) flag his own Royal Standard. I asked him why he did this and he said that ships all flew any fancy flag they liked while the transfer was going on. I told him that it was very lucky that the *Norfolk* hadn't fired a 21-gun Salute when he broke out his Standard, but he said there was not the remotest chance of that happening.

Charles looks very magnificent with his beard, of which he is proud, but he caught it in the wire cage over one of the naval telephone transmitters and found it quite painful!

After lunch the First Lieutenant showed me round the ship. He was an Upper Yard Man (that's to say a promotion from the Lower Deck) and was really excellent. He showed me everything, and then finally I discussed the ship. I asked him what the ship's company felt at having the Prince of Wales as their Captain. He replied that they were tickled pink and absolutely loved it. They bask in the reflected glory of the publicity and their tails are right up. I asked what the discipline and defaulters were like. He said they had had no defaulters at all, except for the odd leave-breaker which Charles dealt with pretty strictly.

I then asked what he felt about serving the Prince of Wales as his First Lieutenant, and he said he couldn't have liked it more; he was a delightful Captain to work with, and the *Bronington* was a very happy and efficient ship. It is clear to me that this is true.

SUNDAY, 16 MAY. BROADLANDS   I worked on my RAC speech. In the evening we had a film *All the President's Men*, the incredible story of how two *Washington Post* reporters, Bob Woodward and Carl Bernstein, unravelled the corruption of President Nixon and his gang and pushed the case through to the point which finally caused the President to resign to avoid impeachment. It is a sad story because I really quite liked Nixon; he was always very friendly to me and very sensible about India and helped me with the UWC, but he turned out to be a real crook and what he did was quite unforgivable. And on top of that the Vice-President he had chosen, Spiro Agnew, had to resign to avoid corruption charges as well. And he presumably nominated Gerald Ford to be his Vice-President on condition he pardoned him after his resignation. Nixon's top men are also likely to end up in jail.

MONDAY, 17 MAY. LONDON   I went to Claridges, where a large Supper Ball was given by EMI to celebrate their Première.* I sat between Diana Wellington and Marianna Monckton. Diana said how much they had appreciated my being kind to their daughter, Jane Wellesley, after the papers had been hounding her because Charles had been seen a lot with her.

She was very bitter about the way the press had treated not only Jane but Valerian† and herself about the whole affair. If they had committed some ghastly crime the newspapers could not have persecuted them more. She said the media could kill Charles's chance of having a happy marriage because what young girl could possibly put up with this appalling persecution. Any girl who would accept a proposal in the face of such prospects would surely not be the right one for Charles to marry in any case. So what was he going to do? She thought he was absolutely charming and it certainly wasn't his fault. She wished him luck in finding the right wife, but unless he could in fact meet her quite secretly, without the media knowing about it, she thought the chances of a marriage coming off with the right person would be really rather slim.

SATURDAY, 22 MAY   The *Kelly* Reunion Association is an extraordinary organization. It was started by the Lower Deck as long ago as 1951. They used to have annual dinners; then recently I suggested they should have them every even year. This was the 25th dinner that they have had. The old ship herself went down in the Battle of Crete 35 years ago tomorrow.

When Charles came in 1974 we had a record number of survivors attending, a total of 43. Since then 6 have died and miraculously 6 more whose names were known have agreed to join the Association, bringing it back to the original strength, and we had 43 again tonight. In fact there are 68 including 8 living overseas, 7 of whom I have seen in the last few years. That means there were 17 in the United Kingdom who could not come to the Reunion, partly through ill health, partly long distances to travel; in any case it is very expensive for them to come with their families and put up for the night. So it was another wonderful occasion.

Sub-Lieutenant Edward Ashmore of the *Jupiter*, one of my Flotilla in whom I used to go out while the *Kelly* was being repaired, came; he is

* Of *Aces High*.
† The Duke of Wellington.

now the First Sea Lord. Then a Midshipman from the *Valiant* who met the survivors when we landed also came; he is now an Admiral of the Fleet and is in fact Philip. The speech proposing [the health of] the Captain himself is usually made by the First Lieutenant, Rear Admiral 'Egg' Burnett, but he had this time asked the Signal Officer, Dusty Dunsterville, to make it and a very good one it was.

Then I had to make my usual 'cabaret' reply in which I succeeded in pulling Philip's leg a bit. After that I was asked to present a Bell to the TS *Kelly* Sea Cadets' Unit at Hebburn, and my godson, Jeremy Bradford, was allowed to present old Admiral Sir Joe Kelly's miniature rum tub, which he had acquired somehow. After that Rocky Wilkins presented Ship's badges to Edward Ashmore and Philip as a result of which they made very nice thank-you speeches, Philip being in great form and pulling my leg in return.

Then we had the 'absent friends' toast, and altogether we ran about 10 minutes later than we expected.

TUESDAY, 25 MAY We drove on to the Palladium for the Shirley MacLaine Show. The first half has a comic and then a singer; the second half is Shirley on the stage by herself supported part of the time by five dancers and a band. She was on stage for an hour and thirty-five minutes and put up the most marvellous show imaginable, which brought the house down.

Afterwards we all drove off to Annabel's. Shirley joined us there, twenty minutes later, and was the life and soul of the party, and we had a very gay evening. I asked her if the story was true that when a large official lunch was given for Philip in Hollywood she sat next to him. On his asking her, 'What have you done to my old Uncle?' she is said to have replied, 'If you stay here long enough I will show you!' She blushed and admitted it.

SUNDAY, 13 JUNE. WINDSOR Lilibet gave an official luncheon for the President of Israel and Madame Akatzir. I sat next to her. When the dessert plates were put round with finger bowls on them, Madame Akatzir started to put the raspberries on the doyley alongside the finger bowl. I suggested tactfully she would find it easier if she put the finger bowl and doyley on the table. She thanked me and said, 'This is really stupid of me as one of my favourite stories concerns a visiting Israeli team being given a formal dinner with finger bowls on the dessert plates. The Captain stood up and asked the Chairman's permission to propose a special toast in Yiddish and said, "You ignorant fools, you don't drink from the finger bowls, you wash your hands in them. Now pick up your glasses and drink a toast."'

I persuaded Lord Rothschild and Sir Marcus Sieff to accept membership of the Friends of the United World Colleges. As we all split up after lunch Lilibet came up to me and said, 'You won't forget your programme, will you? At 1700 you are going to see Anthony Avon, and at 1800 you are going to Andrew Yates's cocktail party; and dinner is here at 2015.' She really knew my programme better than I did myself, and it was very sweet and thoughtful of her to remind me.

I lost my way going to the Provost's Lodge at Eton College and only arrived at 1715. Clarissa Avon and Lady Caccia were in the garden waiting for me and took me up to see Anthony in his bed upstairs. He looked very ill and rather sad. He told me that on top of all his other troubles he had finally got cancer of the prostate which wasn't discovered in time so it had spread up to his lungs. However, there is a wonderful new drug which can cure cancer or, at all events, arrest it, and he had taken it with great success. However, it had had a lot of unfortunate side effects from which he was now suffering and he would not be able to go to the Investiture tomorrow but would come to the luncheon and the Installation Service. He had particularly asked to see me to complain about a statement in an article in the *Sunday Times* Magazine in which the author, a man called Lacey,* had made a statement implying that people close to the Queen knew how much she disapproved of the combined operation against the Egyptians† but there was no constitutional means of her stopping it.

He then showed me a letter from Lacey saying he had got this information from two very intimate friends of the Royal Family who were in a position to know. He assumed one might have been Philip but I pointed out that he had been in the Antarctic at the time; and the other might be me. I didn't attempt to deny it; I said that I had been asked to see this man to help him and had answered all his questions. It was the author himself who had put the question, and I thought I had answered

---

* Robert Lacey, whose *Majesty*, for which this article was a trailer, was the runaway success of Jubilee year.
† In 1956, after Nasser's nationalization of the Suez Canal.

China, 27 January 1974. On the Great Wall with his daughter Patricia.

HMY *Britannia*, 17 February 1974. Dressed as a Maori chief for the ship's concert.

Pentecost Island, 16 February 1974. Land diving.

it tactfully not to produce the particular statement that had appeared. I was sorry about this.

Anthony then told me that if, in fact, this statement was repeated in the book which he understood Lacey was writing, he would have to take official action on this, and he hoped therefore that it would not appear in the book.*

MONDAY, 14 JUNE   I went back to my room and picked up Pammy and we went to the Throne Room where I found that I was left in the position of Senior Knight and had an armchair next to Philip. The other Knight invested was Harold Wilson, our late Prime Minister. Both Investitures went off very smoothly.

I do think that Lilibet had been wise to get Harold Wilson to become a Knight of the Garter because to have a Labour Prime Minister, like her father had Attlee, is an excellent idea to keep a balance between parties and classes.

After the Garter luncheon

I finished off my correspondence and then worked out the postage which was £1.61. I found the Queen's Page, Bennett, going in to Lilibet's room. I followed him in and asked him if he would kindly arrange to have the letters posted and gave him a £5 note. Bennett said it would take him at least five minutes to go to the Post Office to get change, whereupon Lilibet offered to produce the change. She unlocked one of her Red Cabinet Boxes and took out an envelope full of money. I said I only wanted £3 – I didn't want the odd pennies – so she gave me £3 and turned to Bennett and said, 'Bennett, don't forget you owe me £3.'†

On 17 June Mountbatten flew to Stockholm for the wedding of his great-nephew King Carl Gustaf.

The party consisted of about 40 members of the bridegroom's and bride's families; a sort of get-together. I met Silvia, the bride, briefly, and thought she looked very attractive and nice. I was asked to sit next

---

* It did not.
† The mathematics of this transaction are, to say the least, obscure.

to the bride's mother, Frau Sommerlath, as she could only speak German and Portuguese and there weren't many people who could compete with her.

People could choose their own seats and Silvia came up a few moments later and asked if she might sit next to me. I was, of course, flattered that she should have chosen an old man as her dinner partner but I must admit that by the end of our dinner I had fallen for her and thought her charming in every way.

This opinion was fully confirmed by Carl Gustaf's sisters who all went out of their way to say that their new sister-in-law was going to be a most successful Queen and a wonderful wife for Carl Gustaf.

FRIDAY, 18 JUNE. STOCKHOLM   There were about 450 guests to a dinner party of which the more important sat in the famous Hall of the Sovereigns. I was at the top table. By this time Baudouin and Fabiola of the Belgians had turned up, as well as Richard and Birgitte of Gloucester. I took the opportunity of having a good conversation with the Prime Minister, Olof Palme, about the United World Colleges and he promised his support.

I also had the chance of a good gossip with Kekkonen, the President of Finland, and Scheel, the President of Germany, and a brief word with Eldjarn, the President of Iceland. Apparently the Presidents of many other countries such as France and Jugoslavia had asked if they could come, but they were told that only the two Scandinavian Presidents and the President of West Germany, as the bride came from that country, could come.

Poor Juanito and Sophie of Spain were turned down by the Socialist Swedish Government, which is unkind for they are doing their best to liberalize in Spain now.

After dinner we all moved to the Ball Room. I noticed a whole lot of beautiful girls and some nice-looking young men who appeared after the supper for the ball, and gathered these were all Carl Gustaf's old flames come for a farewell party.

The ball was opened in the most formal manner by Carl Gustaf and Silvia dancing a waltz by themselves while everybody looked on and clapped. I helped to get other people on to the floor because we couldn't leave them doing a cabaret turn by themselves for the rest of the evening. Then everybody danced. I danced quite a lot, mainly with Carl Gustaf's sisters. I was determined to be a Cinderella and left soon after midnight, but many of the others stayed on till 0230 I am told.

Silvia appeared for the first time wearing the Ladies' Order of the Seraphim. It was explained to me that Carl Gustaf had to give it to her before the Wedding while she was still of German nationality. The new Government regulations about Honours say that the King can award Honours to foreigners but the Government alone can award Honours to Swedish subjects. This would mean that the moment that Silvia was married and had become a Swede, the King could no longer give her the Seraphim, and although the Government might Carl Gustaf naturally preferred to give it himself while he still had the power to do so.

SATURDAY, 19 JUNE

After the wedding ceremony a dinner was given for relatives who had not yet left. The newly married King and Queen somewhat unexpectedly attended.

They arrived looking sweet. She was very trim in her cream going-away dress and hat holding a bouquet of flowers, and he in a gay light blue country suit. There was much applause and loud cheers when they arrived full of smiles. We all went up and greeted them and then sat down for dinner.

The food was absolutely delicious, as might have been expected since Bertil is a Cordon Bleu Chef himself. The conversation was very gay and there was unrestrained laughter everywhere. We all got up together and went into the next room, and then the bride and bridegroom tried to slip away unnoticed but two of his sisters rushed up and shut the door and put a chair against it, then they put me into the chair and gave me the key. Meanwhile Daisy and her sister, Anne Marie,* stood guard, so the bride and bridegroom were held. Silvia said, 'What do I do to have the key?' I replied, 'Give me a kiss.' So she came up and embraced me warmly and took the key.

By this time the rest of the party had gathered round with a supply of rice, and as the door opened and they tried to escape they were smothered with rice. In fact Tino actually emptied a tin of rice over Carl Gustaf's head.

* Queens of Denmark and Greece respectively.

They left greatly dishevelled, covered with rice, but in high good spirits, and I don't suppose there has ever been a Royal departure on a honeymoon quite so extraordinary since my sister, Alice, hit her Uncle, Nicholas II, on the head with her slipper. It was a wonderful ending to a gloriously mixed day of high Royal Ceremonial and family leg-pulling, and later friendly demonstration by the crowds.

I blush to add an astonishing incident; after Silvia was given the door key by me and the family were standing round, Tino came up with Daisy and Anne Marie and said to Silvia, 'Let these two young Queens be a lesson to you. You will soon find that all young Queens invariably fall in love with Dickie.' Anne Marie added, 'Dickie likes you very much and approves of you; is it true he had never met you before?' Daisy added, 'He may not actually have taken any part in choosing you but in a few years time you will find that he was the person who chose you to be Queen of Sweden!' I suppose I deserve that crack – it certainly brought out a lot of laughter.

WEDNESDAY, 23 JUNE. LONDON   After supper I had a splendid opportunity to have a long conversation with the President.* He was very friendly and interested in the fact that his brother† had just been to see the United World College of South-East Asia. He made a great point that I should come and see him again when I came over to France on the next occasion, which I said would be towards the end of October.

He then surprised me by asking what I thought of the Resistance hero Rémy.‡ I said I thought he was a really splendid man who had done a wonderful job in the war in supplying us with information for various raids and the invasion at great personal risk, and has done a great deal since for ex-service-men. He asked me if I would write and put my views on paper as he was considering promoting him in the Order of the Legion of Honour, and whereas he himself was only seventeen years old when he was in the Resistance he wanted a contemporary to put up the case. I told him I would be delighted to do so as I admire Rémy and he is a very old friend.

---

* Valéry Giscard d'Estaing, President of France, who was paying a State Visit to Britain.
† Olivier Giscard d'Estaing, a staunch supporter of UWC.
‡ The *nom de guerre* of Lieutenant Colonel Gilbert Renault.

WEDNESDAY, 7 JULY   An Indian from South Africa called Lodhia, and his wife and son, came to try and persuade me to go to South Africa to lay a wreath on the great statue of Mahatma Gandhi at Johannesburg. I said nothing would give me greater pleasure if I found it possible to visit South Africa at all. I had already been asked three times by the Government to go there, and on each occasion had made the condition that they would give me complete freedom about how I answered questions that the press might ask me about apartheid. They have never agreed to this and I didn't see they were likely to agree to this in the future.

I said I had an outstanding invitation from the Royal Naval Association of South Africa to go as their guest – I could certainly do both events if ever the atmosphere improved sufficiently for me to visit the country. I pointed out I would very much like to do so as this was one of the few big countries in the world I had never been to, certainly in the Commonwealth.

THURSDAY, 8 JULY. BROADLANDS   I arrived rather late at Amport House, the RAF Chaplain's School, which they lend to the Navy from time to time. Here I was received by the Chaplain of the Fleet, O'Ferrall, and thirty-six Naval Chaplains who had been having a three-day conference, with some RAF Chaplains who normally run the place.

The Chaplain of the Fleet made an informal speech and then I was asked to speak. I decided I would make it a cabaret turn reminiscing about all the incidents that I remembered about Chaplains which were amusing, or from which something could be learnt, or which indeed were very much in their favour. I enlivened the talk with a few jokes and I must say they seemed to be extremely well received with loud applause, and afterwards many of the Chaplains came up and said they must try and remember those stories and they felt they had something to learn from them.

The Chaplain of the Fleet disappeared to another room for an interview with somebody, and it wasn't until I was going to go away and wanted to sign the book that I asked if they could find him. He came up full of apologies and then led me to the car and said goodbye.

I discovered from Alistair Donald on the way back, who is a great friend of the Chaplain of the Fleet, that he felt I had let the side down by not speaking in a sufficiently dignified and inspiring way about religion, and actually making jokes about sex at a Chaplain's dinner.

TUESDAY, 27 JULY. LONDON I drove to St James's Palace for the Annual General Meeting of the Association of Lord Lieutenants of Counties.

At 1100 Master (Duke of Beaufort) took the Chair. I was only asked to speak once, which was to express my opinion about the terminology of the appointments of Deputy Lieutenants saying, 'The Queen having not disapproved.' There appear to be some legal difficulties about this phrase and I said that I had already arranged with the Isle of Wight not to use such gratuitously ungracious language, and had found a perfectly good way round it by saying that I was appointing the Deputy Lieutenant in accordance with Regulations without specifying the Queen did not disapprove.

The meeting finished quite early but resumed at 1200 when Charles and a couple of dozen members of his Silver Jubilee Trust Appeal Committee came in. Charles made a really excellent address explaining what the Appeal was all about and enlisting our help. There were a lot of questions asked and he got his various Chairmen to give answers.

Charles dropped me back at Buckingham Palace. I lunched alone with Lilibet, Andrew and Edward.

They had all just arrived back from attending the Olympic Games in Montreal and the three of them gave me a fantastic account of Anne's courage in the Cross Country event. It appears there had been a cloud burst on the course and one jump had become so dangerous that the Judges had decided it was to be cut out of the course and not attempted. They sent runners on foot with special instructions stuck in a coloured cleft stick. Anne's runner was arrested by her Security Police, and stupidly they prevented him from getting anywhere near her in time to let her know to cut out this jump.

Anyhow she took the jump; her remarkable horse, Goodwill, cleared it and landed in three or four foot of sticky mud where the horse came down and threw Anne very hard over its head. She was knocked unconscious and lay there while some people managed to get the horse out without any damage. Anne then insisted on going on, although the doctor who was present made her wait for at least four minutes.

She got up, started off in the wrong direction but was told which way to go and with a gay wave of her whip set off and cleared a further seventeen very difficult jumps beautifully. She wasn't just a passenger, she was actually riding the horse very intelligently at each fence. On arrival she dismounted in a complete daze; it then transpired she was suffering from concussion and could not remember a single jump and didn't even know what had happened. Sheer determination, guts and courage carried her through; a really remarkable performance.

FRIDAY, 30 JULY. PORTSMOUTH   I had a long and interesting talk with the First Sea Lord who told me, with some embarrassment, that he had been approached by the Minister for the Navy, a new man called Duffy, to ask him to register a complaint to me about the inappropriate speech I had given to the Naval Chaplains at their course recently when he was present. He said that I had introduced sex and had not taken religion sufficiently seriously, and that he thought that my speech had been damaging to my reputation as he knew what a high reputation I had for making good speeches.

Edward Ashmore was rather apologetic about this but said he would like to be able to tell Duffy that he had seen me and mentioned it to me, and I told him that he could say that I was sorry if I had said anything that he didn't like, but he ought to know that after dinner most of the Chaplains gathered round me and thanked me for the speech which they said they had enjoyed enormously, and even last night, at the *Pembroke*, the Chaplain there came up and said what a splendid speech it was. So perhaps I didn't do as much harm as Duffy, and perhaps the Chaplain of the Fleet, thought.

FRIDAY, 27 AUGUST. CLASSIEBAWN   We have been seeing our Gardas in lots of about three at a time to give them a drink and say goodbye and thank you. A total of twenty have been guarding us including a man with a labrador that sniffs out explosives! I asked him how he knew when the dog had found an explosive. He replied that he barked. I said, 'What do you do then?' He replied, 'I run like hell.'

THURSDAY, 9 SEPTEMBER. BROADLANDS   Today was the publication date of the new book called *The File on the Tsar* produced by two BBC journalists.* From all accounts it is unsatisfactory. I have managed to get a copy which confirms my worst fears. They still seem to think Anna Anderson is really Anastasia which of course we in the family know is not the case, much as we would have wished it to be true.

---

* Anthony Summers and Tom Mangold. Certainly it was not unsatisfactory to the publishers, it sold massively.

TUESDAY, 28 SEPTEMBER   At 1930 Michael of Kent and his friend, Marie Christine Troubridge, came down. They apparently arrived at 1910 and thought they were too early so they went round Romsey Abbey.

We had dinner together and a very good discussion afterwards. She apparently runs a very successful interior decorating firm called 'Szapary Designs'. Her marriage to Tom Troubridge is being annulled by the Pope and she will probably take her maiden name, which includes the title of Szapary as she is a cousin of all the Szaparys we know, Yvonne the wife of Karl, and also my old friend Anty. What a very nice girl she is.

I took her all round the house; she was, of course, particularly interested being an interior decorator.

> *In October 1976 Mountbatten visited South-East Asia. On 4 October he was in Singapore for an International Council Meeting of the United World Colleges.*

As we were driving back up the Istana grounds we saw a man playing golf who waved violently, so I stopped and realized it was the Prime Minister; Pammy and I got out and he ran over towards us to greet us. I think Pammy was duly thrilled to meet the great Lee Kuan Yew who was as gay and active as ever though his hair was beginning to go slightly grey. I told him of the arrangement I had made with Ramphal;* he turned to Pammy and said, 'Your father is the greatest fixer in the world!'

After a while I said, 'Anyhow, this meeting can surely take the place of my call on you as you must be very busy and it was only a courtesy call on you tomorrow anyhow. I am sure you will be glad to be released from this as I know how busy you are.' He thanked me very much and said he hoped it was convenient to me, which of course it was because I would have had to leave the Council Meeting tomorrow for at least three quarters of an hour to go and do my call.

TUESDAY, 5 OCTOBER. SINGAPORE   We arrived at 0800 at the Equatorial Hotel where the Council Meeting was being held. First I

---

* Mountbatten had persuaded 'Sunny' Ramphal, the Secretary-General of the Commonwealth Secretariat, to fit a visit to the International College into his extremely crowded schedule.

went in to see the arrangements for the official Opening; then I went out and received the Corps Diplomatique as they arrived. I had had a bit of a set-to with the Russian Ambassaor at the Tripps' cocktail party.* I said I understood from his colleague in London, Lunkov, that he had passed on my invitation to him to attend the Opening and that he had accepted and I was looking forward to seeing him there. He staggered me by saying he had never received a written confirmation of the invitation and therefore had made other arrangements. I asked him what the other arrangements were, and he said he had to be somewhere else at 9 o'clock. I said, 'Well we are starting at 8.30 so you can come along from 8.30 to 8.45 just to the Opening speeches, then we will let you go.'

He appeared to be very unwilling. I said, 'I insist; you accepted my invitation once; if you will turn up as promised I will make sure that a message is passed to my friend, Mr Kosygin, to say how much I appreciated your coming.' He saw the point and said that he would come; in fact he turned up quite early and remained right through the Opening ceremony and to the coffee party afterwards.

The Council Meeting was opened by a speech from the First Minister of Education for Singapore. I replied with a fairly carefully thought-out speech explaining the general policy behind the United World Colleges for the benefit of the Ambassadors. All this was being recorded on television by a German company. During the coffee party for the Ambassadors the Dutch Ambassador said to Pammy, 'That was a brilliant performance of your father's. How old is he?' When Pammy told him I was seventy-six he said, 'Well he has a great future in front of him.'

I managed to let every delegate address the meeting at least once, and Frank Taplin made quite a sensation by announcing that the US Commission was the first one to have elected a former student, Bob Dickerson, to be their new Chairman, but it was the only good news he gave us. I managed the proceedings so that we finished 30 seconds before the announced time of 1800. It had been a hard slogging match virtually lasting ten hours, but I have no doubt it has been the most successful of the seven International Council Meetings at which I have taken the Chair.

---

* Sir Peter Tripp was the UK High Commissioner.

THURSDAY, 7 OCTOBER. KUALA LUMPUR   We went to have a look
at the principal shopping street which had been called after me after the
liberation of Malaya. I had been warned that they had changed its name
and found, in fact, that they had put up both names, the new one being
'Jalan Tun Perak' with '(Jalan Mountbatten)' underneath it. Several of
the shops still had 'Jalan Mountbatten' on their notice boards outside,
and I was told that practically nobody used the new name.

The change had been brought about by a hysterical nationalistic
declaration in the elections that they would abolish foreign names of
streets. Fair enough. But I was somewhat mortified in driving round to
find that there was a circus called 'Bulatan Edinburgh', and I thought it
was a bit much that my nephew should have taken my place as he had
not liberated Malaya, though of course he had married the Queen.

Pammy then discovered a 'Jalan Hicks'. It turned out not to be called
after my son-in-law, but a well-known headmaster, as was explained to
her by our host at luncheon who served under him at school.

The Sultan of Johore (who has now become a Royal Highness) had
sent four cars to collect our party of four. We arrived at his Palace on the
outskirts of Johore Bahru, forty minutes late, when it was beginning to
grow rather dark, at 1740. I was anxious for Pammy to see Bukit Serene
as it out-does almost any Indian Maharaja's idea of extravagant
tastelessness. Among valuable objects there is a lot of junk. Exotic caged
birds all round the Palace kept up a ceaseless chant so it was difficult to
hear oneself speak.

We sat down to a very formal tea party, but the Sultan, who is now
eighty-three and has been told he is going to die on the 8th May next
year, was quite cheerful.* Whenever any subject turned up he had an
archivist ready to produce the appropriate papers. For instance, he said
I looked very much better than when he last saw me, and I attributed
this to Barbara Cartland's health pills; he snapped his fingers and within
two minutes he had twelve Christmas Cards from Barbara on the table.

We talked about his garden, and Beverley Nichols came up; he
snapped his fingers and a long fascinating letter from Beverley Nichols
was produced which he insisted Pammy read aloud. And so it went
on.

Finally I gave him an inscribed copy of the sixth edition of my
Introduction to Polo for his library. He has certainly done more for

---

* He had reason to be cheerful. He outlived Mountbatten and died in May 1981 – and
not even on the 8th.

polo than anybody in the Far East; he still keeps 150 ponies and lets people play them free.

Afterwards we went round the house and were fascinated by the vulgarity and ostentatiousness of everything on display, and finally we penetrated to his private study where the centre piece was a large oil painting of a beautiful girl, all in white, astride a snow white horse, which was kneeling on the ground. He said it was a picture of the finest rider he had ever seen.

FRIDAY, 8 OCTOBER. MAURITIUS Our High Commissioner, Brind, came on board the aircraft to fetch us. We were greeted by quite a Reception Committee, headed of course by our host, Peter White.

By an astonishing coincidence the Prime Minister of India is paying an official visit during the exact three days we are going to be in Mauritius. She had arrived a couple of hours before us, and was due to depart three or four hours before us on Monday. The result was there were many flags out, and TV cameras were still there who took my arrival which would otherwise have gone unnoticed.

Brind and Peter White were somewhat concerned about how I should participate in the festivities. I said, 'Not at all, I am here on a private visit to rest.' They had an invitation for Pammy and me to go to the three State Banquets given by the Governor-General, the Prime Minister and Indira Gandhi herself. These I refused out of hand. But they both urged us to go to the inauguration of the Gandhi Institute the following morning to show friendship and willingness towards India and to be seen on TV by the people. With some reluctance we both finally agreed.

Peter White drove us out to his charming house, an old French house on to which he has built a delightful guest house with its own dining room, sitting room, bedrooms and entrance. Peter is a delightful Western Australian brought up in India, and now the most successful expatriate businessman in the island as he runs the big Lonrho branch here who employ 5600 people in their sugar fields and factories, and other activities such as a textile factory.

SATURDAY, 9 OCTOBER The Prime Minister said he wanted to come and call on me and would arrive at 0915 to take me on to the Gandhi Institute. In fact we had just finished breakfast and I was putting on a tie and jacket when he arrived at 0900. Then for forty minutes we sat together on the patio having a fascinating discussion. He is Sir Seewoosagur Ramgoolam and is the same age as me. We had made friends on my last visit and I had seen him once or twice in London, and he greeted me as a long-lost friend and asked what he could do to help the United World Colleges scheme which he heard I had come over to launch. He gave his blessing to what I was trying to do, and said he would leave it to his Minister of Education to fix up the details.

He explained to me, with the utmost regret, that the Opposition party had put forward a demand that the island should become a Republic and the Governor-General should become a President, which he had strongly opposed. But he had to agree not to make an election issue of this, which would have been bad, and so was going to accept it as he really was only following the footsteps of all the other similarly placed Commonwealth countries, and would of course be loyal to the Queen as Head of the Commonwealth.

Then he drove me off in his car, and Peter drove Pammy in the second car, and we arrived in about seven minutes at the new Gandhi Institute which had been built with money from India and for which Indira had laid the foundation stone six years ago.

The Prime Minister just had time to introduce me to the members of his Cabinet and the Committee of the Institute when Indira arrived with a large escort of motor-cycle police. The Prime Minister took Pammy and me along by hand so we were the second and third people to greet Indira on arrival. She was far more warm and friendly, though Pammy and I were a little bit chary at this as we are still not certain about the part she has played in the Emergency in India where so many of our friends were in jail.

Pammy's old friend, Jagat Mehta, who is now the Foreign Secretary of India, came to call. Apparently Pammy had been great friends with his wife, Rama, thirty years ago, and had got to know Jagat five years later and became great friends, so they embraced warmly. He was absolutely fascinating and really explained the circumstances of the Emergency in quite a new light. He was deeply distressed at the number of people who had been put in jail and the treatment they had received, but he said that he thought that India had been saved from Communism and complete chaos. In fact, people were now working punctually and hard and enthusiastically; the economy had made a startling recovery, and he hoped that soon everybody would be out of prison and allowed their freedom.

I told him that I had urged Indira to remove censorship at least for the media from England, otherwise the BBC and *Times* would not send back their correspondents.

I said I was delighted to hear that she had taken my advice, and he said she had been keen herself on doing it. He was sorry her programme for going round the island had run 2½ hours late and she couldn't see us tonight, but was keen to see us tomorrow.

SUNDAY, 10 OCTOBER We drove back at 1600 and I rested until 1830 when Pammy and I called on the Governor-General at Le Réduit. We had an interesting talk with him and then we went on to call on Indira Gandhi. She was unusually forthcoming and friendly. I suppose she realized how much the family disapproved of some of the things she was doing, but we kept off politics and all the people she had put in prison.

FRIDAY, 15 OCTOBER. LONDON I had a haircut at 0930, then at 1100 went to see my heart specialist, Lawson MacDonald. Lilibet had said she would be delighted for me to carry the Sword of State again if my doctor gave me a clean bill of health.

Lawson went at it very thoroughly and made me bring up an object weighing the same amount as the Sword of State with a strap to go round my neck to carry it. One of the very new portable electro-cardiogram instruments was attached to me and I walked about climbing over stools and standing still for ten minutes at a time for a total of half an hour, at the end of which he said that he thought I had passed with flying colours. I must say I felt very well right through and grand at the end of it all and delighted.

We drove back to Broadlands for a late lunch. Lawson rang up to say that there had been a very disturbing flicker on my ECG, and if I had half a dozen of them I should have felt giddy and would have swayed. He didn't think I would fall over or would do any harm but he thought it would worry the Queen, so I reluctantly had to write to Martin Charteris to say the doctor didn't advise me to do it. I am very disappointed.

THURSDAY, 21 OCTOBER We went for a drink at Admiralty House and Fred Mulley, the new Secretary of State for Defence, drew me aside to ask if he may send me a brief so that I could tell the President of France more about our Forces which he didn't seem to understand. I agreed.

Then I went over to Duffy, the Under-Secretary for the Navy, and said I was sorry to hear he disapproved of my speech to the Chaplains. He hotly denied this and when I told him that the First Sea Lord had told me so he said, 'He had no business to tell you at all.' In fact he implied it was a very good speech.

> *On 21 October 1976 Mountbatten visited France for various ceremonies, mainly connected with the wartime activities of the Resistance. He lunched near St-Germain-des-Prés.*

I sat opposite the Préfet* as in fact our host was only the Parliamentary representative as Deputy of the District. It was a large gathering and I sat next to the Princesse de Ligne, and also met her husband who is a cousin of the Belgian de Lignes whom we knew in Delhi when he was the Belgian Ambassador in 1947. When I asked whether the family were Belgian or French, as they seemed to have such big properties in both countries, the Préfet leant forward and said, 'The de Ligne family are much older than Belgium.' They made a great point that I should visit their home the next day and I said I would try.

I had great trouble in finding the loo afterwards because apparently you don't go to the loo when visiting other people's houses in France. Finally, I was taken right through the house to one of the best bedrooms which had a bathroom attached.

Vincent Howard,† who is married to a nice French girl, called Genevieve, told me a delightful story of the different points of view in France and England about the loo. When her French parents came over to England to stay with his parents for the wedding, old Mr Howard took his French guest up to the bathroom, saying, 'You must be tired after your long trip, let me show you to the bathroom.' The Frenchman, at a loss what to do, felt he was expected to have a bath, so thereupon he undressed, turned on the water and had a bath. When the English couple discovered he was having a bath they thought he was mad. However, when the French couple discussed the matter they thought the English must be mad to want them to take a bath on arrival.

---

* René La Combe, Préfet of Maine et Loire.
† The British Naval Attaché in Paris.

THURSDAY, 26 OCTOBER. PARIS   We arrived 10 minutes early at the Naval Attaché's flat, 244 Rue de Rivoli, at 1620. Here we washed and brushed up, and Rémy managed to produce the Croix de Guerre ribbon to wear with my Legion of Honour button-hole for my visit to the President.

We drove round to see the President at the Elysée at 1700.

I was with the President until 1740 and he was extremely friendly. He first asked how the Queen was, and had she sent any messages to him, to which I replied that she had asked me to enquire how her labrador was getting on. The President said he had expected this, rang the bell and the dog immediately appeared and wagged its tail and came up and rubbed himself against me. A very friendly dog.

Fred Mulley had asked me whether I could do some propaganda about the strength of our Armed Forces with the President. I managed to bring this in fairly easily by referring to the honour I was about to receive the next day by being elected to the Académie de Marine, and asking if I could make certain statements the acknowledgment of which by him would in fact have the effect of pushing home the points Fred wanted me to make.

THURSDAY, 18 NOVEMBER. LONDON   I had a useful conversation with the new Saudi Arabian Ambassador and also with the Foreign Secretary, Crosland, and Michael Palliser, the Head of the Foreign and Commonwealth Office, about John making the Agatha Christie film *Death on the Nile*. I told them that Norton had said that the Location Manager for the new James Bond film, who had been out there for three weeks, had reported that the chaos, corruption and incompetence were indescribable and he couldn't understand how it took the Israelis six days to defeat them. He went on to say that had he been given £10,000 a week he wouldn't go out himself and take on the job again – they were lucky to be able to get away by night having had to deal with the extremists to get any sort of co-operation.

I asked whether HMG would advise John to proceed with the film in Egypt or try to do it elsewhere. They both said they thought it important he should try and do it in Egypt, and he should work through the Ambassador and try and get Sadat, the President, to give real support on the top level. I promised to tell John this, and I will write a letter to the Ambassador which I hope may prove useful.

WEDNESDAY, 24 NOVEMBER   Much to my mortification I discovered, after having turned down carrying the Sword of State because I couldn't get an 'all clear' from Dr Lawson MacDonald, they put in Field Marshal Sir John Harding who must be about eighty; certainly older than me.* He very nearly tripped up twice when his spurs caught the back of his robe. I complained about this afterwards to Lilibet; she thought a blunder had been made in asking such an old man to carry the Sword of State. I warned her I might insist on carrying it if I got an 'all clear' next year.

WEDNESDAY, 15 DECEMBER   I had to leave at 2055 to get to the BBC Theatre at Shepherd's Bush. I had undertaken to give the Sports' Personality of the Year Award and they wanted me to come early before the programme started to see the lay-out of the stage and what I should do.

I had a buffet supper with the Heads of the BBC in a special box overlooking the stage with TV monitors. This was very useful because I was able to learn the names of a dozen odd people I had to refer to in my speech, and see what they actually looked like and what they did.

I found it was a difficult occasion and rather nerve-racking. I felt I had to break the ice first with a genuine personal funny story; so I told the story of a polo match in March 1922 in Hong Kong when my number 3 hit the ball up to me playing number 1 and hit a bull's eye (if you can describe the back-side of a horse like that) and I rode through the goal post, pulled up and the ball dropped out.†

Then I managed to remember the names of all the different people I had been asked to refer to. Finally, I made a rather stirring appeal that the Nation should try and think not of themselves but to work hard, as these sportsmen did in their sport, to raise the prestige of the country. If I had known that the Scene Shifters' Trade Union were going to prevent them from moving the scenery so that the drinks could be served comfortably to the 50 sports personalities who had come, I am afraid I would have stuck my neck out and said, 'And in half an hour's time we shall see what is wrong with the country when the Scene Shifters refuse to make facilities for entertaining these Sports Personalities who you

---

* Lord Harding was in fact already eighty. He had been a Baron since 1958; an unusual slip on Mountbatten's part, perhaps indicating his sense of outrage at Harding's designation for this honour.
† i.e., from between the horse's legs, where it had lodged.

have all seen.' The BBC kindly sent me down in a car to Broadlands which I reached long after midnight.

SATURDAY, 25 DECEMBER. BROADLANDS   Christmas Day, and at 0950 I drove with the entire Hicks family to Romsey Abbey for the Christmas Day Sung Eucharist Service. We arrived in good time and waited and waited for the Brabournes to arrive with Dodo. Dodo's watch had gone wrong and for the first time in her life instead of being quarter of an hour early she was five minutes late. So we started to walk into the Abbey just as the choir entered and had to wait for the choir to file into their seats. Then we walked by the whole congregation in a rather embarrassed way to the family pews which were occupied by fifteen of us, that is all except Nannie. Then the main tremendous Christmas Day procession started.

At 1110 we all drove to Edwina Mountbatten House to wish all the inmates and staff a very happy Christmas. We all gathered round poor Frank,* who is getting so deaf and blind he hardly knows who is there but keeps on saying how happy he is and how grateful he is. He came to us first in 1924 when Patricia was born, and our recently retired butler, Charles Smith, came to us in 1929 when Pammy was born. He hopes to go with his wife to the Edwina Mountbatten Home one of these days, but at present he is helping in the house over Christmas.

Then we had our usual Christmas lunch in the dining room with sixteen of us including Nannie, with crackers and general excitement.

SUNDAY, 26 DECEMBER   I should add that to save work in the house we have breakfast, lunch and tea in the shooting room – it is all a buffet help-yourself organization. We do, however, have dinner in the dining room with about ten of the older members of the family, which is a properly served meal and a great thrill for the younger generation.

I thought Lilibet's Christmas Day broadcast to the Commonwealth particularly good, and in fact TV went on for most of the day with large crowds in the Library to watch it.

MONDAY, 27 DECEMBER   In the evening we saw on television the famous film *Tora, Tora, Tora*, the story of the Japanese attack on Pearl Harbor.

---

* Frank Randall, for many years butler at Broadlands.

After that was over I gathered the family in the Wedgwood Room to tell them of my time in Pearl Harbor in October some seven weeks before the actual attack, as I of course knew all the main Americans in the story. We had to go to the Wedgwood Room as Norton curiously refused to give up seeing the television News by himself in the Library.

FRIDAY, 31 DECEMBER   And so ends the monumental Diary for the year 1976 showing a typical year in my post-retirement period.* Next year I will only keep a Diary of my actual tours, but my programme is already pretty full for the whole of 1977; I still seem to be doing too much but enjoying it and thriving on it.

It is wonderful to have such a delightful family and all ten of my grandchildren are absolutely enchanting. I am indeed a very lucky person, and don't feel too lonely at Broadlands as Jack Barratt is a great companion and I have at least two long talks with him every day mainly about business, and I also have two rides a week with Mary Lou† who is a most enchanting companion; very gay and very talkative, and great fun. And, of course, I see a lot of the family; and indeed in January I shall be going down to stay with Philip and Lilibet at Sandringham as usual, which is always great fun. So I can't complain, in spite of the economic difficulties which the country is facing, and indeed which all of us are facing.

---

* The diary for 1976 runs to some 180,000 words, as long as two substantial novels.
† Mary Lou Emery, principal groom at Broadlands and Mountbatten's most regular riding companion when no member of the family was staying.

1977

SUNDAY, 16 JANUARY. SANDRINGHAM I walked to church with the rest of the family. The usual large crowds were gathered. The Bishop preached a very sensible sermon.

Afterwards I went up to see Lilibet for a moment, and Kimberley disgraced me by cocking his leg on one of the spare pictures she had standing on the floor leaning against the bookcase. She said she didn't mind in the least and said that male dogs always did that in strange houses and had blotting paper and soda water ready to mop up the results.*

TUESDAY, 18 JANUARY. LONDON At 0825 Jack drove me to Heathrow. Here we were met by Barbara Cartland's friend, Sirdar Aly Azziz, who was to be my host for the day. †

Barbara was very anxious that I should accept his invitation to launch one of his ships as she had launched the last one, and as I have never launched a ship in my life I accepted. Normally it is ladies who launch ships; it has been left to the Far East and the Philippines, for whom the ship is being built, to have men doing the launching.

Having entirely redrafted my speech on the way up, I discovered from Aly Azziz that, far from being satisfied with the work they were doing, all that he could admit was that they now had reduced the delays by industrial strife from six months per ship to three months. But even this wouldn't be good enough for the next lot as his customers kept on saying, 'Can you guarantee it will be on time?' He said he had already warned the Management that unless they could give this guarantee he would not be able to place the orders for the next twelve ships at that yard, and he thought most people would stop sending orders. So within two or three years the yard would have to close down once more.

---

* This surprising observation presumably says more about Mountbatten's syntax than the prescience of male dogs visiting strange houses.
† In Glasgow.

I put all this in my speech and I gather it caused quite a sensation.

After the speeches when we mingled with the guests, I asked to be introduced to the Shop Stewards who were present, to find that none had been asked and none expected an invitation. I then told the Senior Manager that I wanted to meet the Shop Stewards, at least socially and have a drink with them, and have a quiet talk about the problem facing the next order.

He seemed extraordinarily reluctant to produce them but he spoke to his Industrial Relations Manager who thought it would be a good idea. It took some time to collect them and then he came in and said that they had expressed complete astonishment at being allowed in to the 'Golden Trough' with the VIPs, but as I had invited them they said they would come along.

Half a dozen of them did come. I shook hands with them, made friends with them, introduced them to some of the VIPs, and above all to Aly Azziz himself. Then we had a friendly talk in which I explained exactly the situation about whether they get the next order or not. They all said that this was the first time they had fully appreciated how serious the situation was and they had every intention of seeing they secured the order.

There was a photographer present and I then said to the Convener, 'Will you allow a photograph to be taken of you shaking hands with Aly Azziz in token of your promise that whatever happens industrial strife would not delay future orders?' To my surprise he said he would; all the other Shop Stewards murmured agreement so the photograph was taken, and Aly Azziz couldn't believe his luck.

What shocking bad man-management that they don't even have the representatives of the Shop Stewards at the celebrations for the launching. No wonder they have industrial troubles.

Mountbatten spent the afternoon visiting the Royal Navy's Faslane Base.

We had been going through two security fences, and now we came to a third one which was the most tight of all. It is the first time I saw armed guards in any Naval Establishment in peacetime. This was the Royal Marines guard on the actual nuclear POLARIS submarine lying alongside. She was in fact the *Renown* with the starboard crew on board.

Jack and I were taken all over the submarine which is as big as a *Phoebe* Class Cruiser. It is the first British POLARIS submarine I had visited, although I had been to an American one. The centre section which contained sixteen missile tubes is as impressive as ever, each tube about six foot in diameter in two rows of eight going through three decks. The crew were all at instant readiness stations for firing a missile from alongside to back up the submarine out on patrol. They were waiting to go off on their two months' submerged patrol.

TUESDAY, 8 MARCH. LONDON   Robert Blackburn was waiting for us and we went through a careful briefing before my meeting at 1500 with the Minister of Education, Mrs Shirley Williams, in her room at the House of Commons.

I took an instant liking to her and I think I started well by shaking her considerably. I said I had read in the newspapers that she had been considering abolishing the curriculum for the GCE and the SLC* and was looking for a common core curriculum. I described to her what I thought she was looking for and she said I had got it exactly right.

I then pointed out to her that the International Baccalaureate was based on the same curriculum, and that she could save two or three years of work through committees and probably £200,000 spent on investigation if she adopted the International Baccalaureate as the National Baccalaureate for the United Kingdom. This evidently startled her but after a while she said she thought there was something in the idea and set up a working party with our International Baccalaureate people. After that she accepted willingly to be the host in London at a conference of the International Baccalaureate, but couldn't do it in 1977 – she couldn't do it before early 1978. I accepted in principle as I thought we could have a small official meeting in Geneva to arrange matters before the end of 1977.

SATURDAY, 26 MARCH   We boarded the Concorde at 1315 and were airborne by 1335. I must say it really was rather exciting travelling supersonic for the first time. There was a big Mach indicator showing our speed relative to the sound barrier. Within a quarter of an hour after take-off we worked up to Mach 0.94 and five minutes later we went through the sound barrier without any appreciable indication. By 1407

---

* General Certificate of Education and School Leaving Certificate.

we were doing Mach 1.50; then as we passed over the English Channel at 1419 we got to Mach 1.90 reaching Mach 2.00 at 1435.

They then served a good lunch, after which they passed round the Entry Cards for the United States, and before we knew it we had arrived having taken 3 hours and 25 minutes to cross the Atlantic instead of the usual seven hours. The clock had been put back six hours, so we arrived over the Dulles International Airport at Washington at 1100 local time whilst GMT was still only 0900.

It was a very remarkable trip. There were 96 passengers on board which I think is a full complement. The Captain invited me to come up to the flight deck which is a mass of instruments, and he told me that once they have gone through the sound barrier the aeroplane is always flown entirely automatically with a few manual adjustments only. The aeroplane is narrow and long and there are only four seats in each row with a gangway down the middle. They are rather close together but I can't complain that they were uncomfortable. It certainly was a most exciting experience to arrive 2½ hours ahead of our departure by local time.

SUNDAY, 27 MARCH. WASHINGTON   I got back in good time for luncheon at 1300 to which the Ramsbothams* had invited Rick and his new wife, Mrs Rickover. We were told he never spent more than an hour, or perhaps an hour and a quarter over luncheon, but this time, to his new wife's astonishment, he stayed until 1630 gossiping about old times and trying to get some of the misunderstandings cleared up. He was particularly good talking to Jack Barratt. I am determined to try and get him a long overdue honorary KBE which he certainly deserves (but says he does not want) for all he did to give us the first complete SKIPJACK Propulsion Unit for our nuclear submarine *Dreadnought*.

At 1700 Senator Mike Mansfield, the former President of the Senate, called on me, having accepted Carola Rothschild's invitation to become Chairman of the US Commission for the United World Colleges. Jack and I spent an hour and a quarter briefing him fully about the United World Colleges project, and I think he is going to be very useful.

I told him I had nearly got Senator Bill Fulbright to join after he was given an honorary KBE during my last visit to Washington, but his wife

---

* Sir Peter Ramsbotham was British Ambassador in Washington.

had intervened and said he had too much to do and stopped him. Mike Mansfield said he had much less to do now, was much fitter, and if I liked he would approach him again. I said I would send him a letter to pass on to Fulbright and hoped he would get him to join, as we need high-level support to put the US Commission on its feet again.

FRIDAY, 8 APRIL. BROADLANDS   I am busy reading *Edward VIII*, the biography of the Duke of Windsor by Frances Donaldson. I helped her a bit over the book and I find it absolutely fascinating and fair.

TUESDAY, 19 APRIL. LONDON   This turned out to be the most astonishing day of my life.

John had offered to pick me up at 1750 to drive me to Thames Television Studios for Pammy's birthday party. He offered Jack a lift if he wanted to see programmes 7 and 8 of my television series, which were being run by arrangement at the Thames Studios before the birthday dinner.

I had with me a large bouquet of flowers for Pammy's birthday and a gift-wrapped parcel for her. As we neared our destination John told me that Howard Thomas, the Chairman, was arranging some publicity about a new book he had just written and there might be a photographer there, so it would be better to leave the flowers and present in the car until the birthday dinner at 2015 as we only had the projection room for two hours from 1815.

On arrival punctually at 1815 Howard Thomas met me himself at the door and took me over to where the family were gathered, looking unusually tidy and cleaned up, waiting to go to the projection room. I greeted them all and wished Pammy a happy birthday and then said, 'Let's go.'

I turned round and saw a man step out from behind a pillar and advance on our party with a big red book in his hand. I said to Howard, 'Is this your new book?' but before he could answer the man in question had arrived and held up the book in front of me and said in a loud voice, 'Earl Mountbatten of Burma, this is YOUR life.'

I couldn't quite make out what he meant at first and then with an appalling shock I realized it might be Eamonn Andrews, who catches people unawares to put them on the programme 'This is Your Life'. I had never seen it on TV but I knew about it and I was absolutely shattered.

I felt stunned. I stammered out, 'What do you mean?' and then when realization dawned on me I said, 'Well, I'll be b . . .' but I checked myself in time as I knew we had the grandchildren present.

I was led off in a daze to a corner of the foyer where a make-up girl powdered my face and then I was led straight into a large studio with an audience of 300. To my utter amazement I recognized most of them. First of all I saw all the surviving officers and ship's company men of the *Kelly*. Then I saw a lot of men I knew from the Burma Star Association and from the Far East Prisoners of War Association, also shipmates and friends. I then realized I was in for a much more serious time than I had at first supposed.

We sat down in the left-hand row of sixteen seats. This included Jack Barratt but there were two empty seats.

Eamonn Andrews started off, 'Lord Mountbatten this is your daughter Pamela's birthday. As you know she has three children, Edwina, Ashley and India.' He then turned to India and said, 'Why are you called India?' This nine-year-old child stood up and in her penetrating voice said, 'Because my grandpapa was the last Viceroy of India!'

Now I realized the situation was indeed more serious than I realized, for the family had not only double-crossed me by getting me there under false pretences but they had obviously been rehearsing what they were going to say. But my shocks were by no means over.

After introducing the Brabourne boys he said, 'Your two eldest granddaughters, however, aren't here.' To which I replied, as far as I can remember, 'No, Joanna is in Australia 10,000 miles away and I left Amanda three days ago in Nassau to go off and visit a boy friend in Boston, so you can't get her either.' Then the door opened and both girls walked in and this time I really very nearly fainted with surprise, but it soon turned to pleasure.

After a while, when I realized what I was in for I remembered the old saying, 'When rape becomes inevitable, relax and enjoy yourself.' I did just that and for the next hour and twenty minutes an assortment of old friends, some almost forgotten, turned up to give their reminiscences about me. Several of them were inaccurate and I had to correct them, but it was great fun and by the end of the evening I had completely recovered myself and had enjoyed it all.

After the recording was over there was a big party for everybody, with a large birthday cake for Pammy and drinks for all my friends in the audience. It was certainly a day I shall never forget and I only hope that the result doesn't turn out too badly when it is networked on ITV on the 27th April. Unfortunately I won't be able to see it as I shall be in Monaco, but I will ask Daborn to make a recording on my cassette recorder.

WEDNESDAY, 20 APRIL   I attended the Presentation of Colours by Lilibet to the 1st Battalion of the Scots Guards in the Buckingham Palace Gardens. Afterwards I had drinks with the staff and at 1300 I had lunch with Lilibet, Philip and Edward.

I told her about my surprise last night and she said she had only heard of it three days ago when Charles consulted her as to whether he should take part in the programme or not.

I told her that I knew from John he had told Philip about it months ago and had presumed Philip would tell her. To this Philip had the nerve to reply, 'John told me not to tell anybody, so of course I didn't tell her.' However, she said she would watch the programme herself, but again said she wished she had had more warning.

After lunch we had a delightful tête-à-tête and I gave her a wrist watch with a dial that changes colour according to mood for her birthday tomorrow.

THURSDAY, 21 APRIL   I arrived at Millbank Tower for the NEC meeting at 1450 in time for a brief word with Eddie Kent, for this was an historic meeting for me. It was the last time I took the Chair at the meeting of the National Electronics Council which I founded twelve years ago and of which I had been the Chairman ever since.*

Over the last five or six years I have been training Eddie to take my place as Chairman and he has been my deputy, getting better and better all the time. This time the meeting passed an amendment to our constitution creating the office of President. I was elected to this office which is really an honorary position as the Chairman will continue to run the Council.

Eddie was elected to take my place as Chairman and after the first two items I vacated the Chair in his favour, but remained on to see how it all went. Eddie had not wanted me to do this as apparently he thought my

---

* A body set up, in Mountbatten's words, 'to make sure Britain did not neglect the key to the future – electronics'.

presence would be rather embarrassing, but I insisted and saw how well he did it and I think he was finally happy I had stayed.

TUESDAY, 7 JUNE   This was the day of the Jubilee Thanksgiving Service in St Paul's. I got up early at Broadlands and was driven to London 0730–0900. Here I changed into Naval Full Dress with the Collar of the Garter and the Broad Ribbon of the Bath and the Grand Master's Badge of the Star of India as well as the Order of Merit.

A farmer whom I had met in the Isle of Wight kept a pair of carriage horses and produced them to draw our carriage, and he was dressed as one of the Royal Coachmen.

Outside the forecourt* were drawn up the Service Guards of Honour, Royal Navy, King's Company of the Grenadiers and the Royal Air Force with a large Royal Marines Band to play the National Anthem.

This reminded me of a story my mother told me of the Golden Jubilee of 1887 when there had been no State Ceremonial for so long that few appeared to remember what the routine was.

She saw the King's Company of the Grenadiers mounting a full Royal Guard of Honour in the Inner Quadrangle on the right of the line. She knew this was wrong and waited to see what would happen when the Royal Navy arrived. The Naval Guard came five minutes later, halted in the middle of the Quadrangle and the Officer in command went over to the Grenadier Officer and pointed with his sword that they should move down to the left and make room for the Navy. The Grenadiers finally realized they might be the right of the line of the Army, but in fact the Navy was the Senior Service so they had to move down. This time they were in their right order.

I found myself sitting next to Alice Athlone† who, at the age of ninety-four, had taken part in practically all Jubilees from Queen Victoria's Diamond Jubilee onwards. What a remarkable person she is, she is getting very bent but is very alert and bright. Then came the entrance of the Queen's procession which was done with full ceremonial marvellously well. Lilibet and Philip were placed on two thrones by themselves out in front, where everybody could see them and so could TV.

I asked her afterwards why she had looked rather cross and worried

* Of Buckingham Palace.
† Only daughter of the Duke of Albany and Queen Victoria's last surviving grandchild.

at one time and she laughed and said, 'I was just thinking how awful it would be if Amin (the horrible dictator of Uganda) were to gate-crash the party and arrive after all.' I asked her what she had proposed to do and she said that she had decided she would use the City's Pearl Sword which the Lord Mayor had placed in front of her to hit him hard over the head with.

At the end of this Service the procession left in the reverse order and then Lilibet and Philip did a 'walkabout' in between the Cathedral and the Guildhall where they were due for luncheon. She said afterwards she asked a group of particularly enthusiastic young people where they came from. She was gratified and surprised when they said, 'The London School of Economics'.

In the meanwhile those of us who were selected to go to the luncheon drove in a carriage procession, I driving with Margaret. The only people invited by the Lord Mayor were the Queen and her immediate family, husband, children, sister and mother. The Banquet was superb. I sat between Margaret and the Prime Minister's wife, Mrs Callaghan. The Lord Mayor made a witty and appropriate speech as a former Naval Officer, and the Queen's own speech was just what was wanted.

For the return we all got into carriages, Lilibet and Philip this time going in a State Landau and not the State Coach. We drove back through the streets packed as densely as they were in the morning so people must have been standing there ever since. The enthusiasm was even greater if that were possible and when we finally arrived at Buckingham Palace a heavy shower came down as the Queen stepped out of her open Landau into the Palace.

I then stayed back discreetly to let the family go on, but was sent for by Lilibet no less than three times saying she wanted me to come up and go out on the balcony. When I arrived she asked me what had been delaying me, and said that she wanted me to be there when the family went out together, so I was pulled out and stood behind her and I was glad that this had happened because I would never have believed the sight of the crowds if I hadn't been out on the balcony and seen for myself.

The whole of the flower beds round the Victoria Memorial were packed solid with people and they were jammed in Birdcage Walk and Constitution Hill and Buckingham Palace Road. But far more staggering was the Mall which was full from end to end right down to Admiralty Arch through into Trafalgar Square with a tight mass of wildly enthusiastic people.

I was told there were 1200 geraniums planted especially for the occasion and the crowd walked all over them and only damaged 12.

WEDNESDAY, 8 JUNE   I drove up again from Broadlands in time for the State Banquet and Reception for the Commonwealth Heads of State and Prime Ministers. The dress was dinner jackets with decorations but there was a misunderstanding on my card and the result was I was almost the only person to have no decorations at all at the party. This at least compensated for having worn more than my share yesterday.

I sat at the Queen Mother's table with the new Prime Minister of India, Morarji Desai, and the wife of the Prime Minister of Samoa,* who told me her husband had been absolutely thrilled at reading *Freedom at Midnight.*†

Afterwards I went round meeting the Prime Ministers and other representatives of countries in which I was trying to get something done for the United World Colleges. I must have had at least a dozen separate interviews which all appeared to go off rather well.

THURSDAY, 9 JUNE   I got back to Buckingham Palace at 2000 and at 2025 left with the Beauforts for Shell Mex House on the 24th floor. Here we met the rest of the Royal Family except Lilibet and Philip who were afloat for the River Pageant. The Chairman gave a small dinner party in his own room for the Queen Mother and the new American Ambassador‡ and Mrs Brewster, who sat next to me.

The others were entertained in different rooms, and when Lilibet and Philip got back we all gathered together and went out on the roof to watch the firework display. It was a rather misty night with a low cloud ceiling, the effect was absolutely staggering.

As Philip said, I have never been at the top of a firework display before because in fact the highest rockets were bursting level with where we were standing, or else they went through into the cloud cover and came out again in the most remarkable way. They had loud speakers which played appropriate music such as Handel's Fire Music and Water Music, etc., edited to fit in with the programme. It was certainly the

---

* Tupuola Efi.
† An ebullient account of the transfer of power in India by the American Larry Collins and the Frenchman Dominique Lapierre.
‡ Kingman Brewster, lawyer and academic.

finest firework display I can ever remember seeing in my life and there were people up and down the Thames everywhere.

Dodo and a friend went to the House of Lords to see the display from the terrace but although John and I managed to get her in there was such a crowd that they couldn't get anywhere near the buffet to have supper, and she remarked that for the first time in her life she saw Peers of the Realm sitting down cross-legged on the floor eating sandwiches. 'Not hereditary Peers, of course,' she added.

After the display was over we met all the VIPs who had been up there at a drinks party, and then went down to drive back in a carriage procession through surprisingly large crowds who had waited up to see us although it must have been nearly midnight.

I was in the carriage procession and it was all very thrilling. When we got back to Buckingham Palace the crowds gathered round, and, although one couldn't see them all, those that were within the range of any lights appeared to be as dense and enthusiastic as ever. In fact cries of 'We want the Queen' meant that Lilibet had to go out three times. When it was all over Edward said to the assembled company, 'Result of tonight's performance, the Royal Family three, Opposition nil.'

WEDNESDAY, 29 JUNE. BROADLANDS I was driven to Southsea Castle to have a look at the *Mary Rose* Museum with all the bits that had been recovered from this marvellous ship built in 1519 and sunk in 1545 in the Battle at Spithead. I am very keen that we should salvage the whole ship and bring it into a dry dock in Portsmouth and have been working to this end for quite a while with Philip and Charles.

On 10 July 1977 in Nairobi:

We went to the VIP lounge where we ran into the Prince of the Netherlands on his way out to stay with Kenneth Kaunda, the President of Zambia. I hadn't seen Bernilo since his troubles over the Lockheed bribery* and gave him an especially warm embrace which he warmly reciprocated.

After family talk he couldn't resist telling us that on his way to an airport in Italy recently he had actually sighted two 'flying saucers'. I

---

* Prince Bernhard was alleged to have accepted a bribe of over $1m from the American manufacturer, Lockheed, in exchange for supporting that company's efforts to secure military contracts in the Netherlands.

asked him if he had any witnesses and he said two policemen and his chauffeur, but alas there was no chance to photograph the UFOs. They discussed the incident afterwards between them and all three were agreed that two separate UFOs were seen not very far away which appeared to be carrying out some sort of aerobatics for fun. As Bernilo put it, it was almost as though they were trying to mate with each other. After three or four minutes they gave this up and then disappeared at high speed. He had never believed in 'flying saucers' at all and was simply staggered at what he saw.

I told him that my son-in-law, John, had seen a UFO crossing the Atlantic; the Senior Naval Officer of the South Atlantic had twice seen a UFO with all the men on duty on the bridge at the time. I told him that Sitta (Queen of Rumania) and her sister, Tim (Duchess of Aosta), had seen one together in the South of France so he was in good company. I told him to give Kenneth Kaunda my regards as I know him quite well.

1978

On 25 February 1978 Mountbatten was in Cairo for talks about the United World Colleges and sight-seeing with his grandchildren Norton and Joanna.

The Ambassador was supposed to be accompanying me all the morning but excused himself as Cyprus has asked the British if they will look after their diplomatic interests on the withdrawal of their own Ambassador from Cairo with his staff. President Sadat had decided to throw them out and more or less terminate diplomatic relations because he is so furious at what happened at the abortive attempt by the Egyptian Commandos to intervene in the hijacking incident at Larnaka.*

It had seemed that the Egyptians had behaved very foolishly about trying to intervene when the Cypriots announced that they had come to terms with the hijackers, who were about to release the hostages when the Egyptian Commandos attacked.

It now transpires that there was a good likelihood that the Cypriots would have turned the terrorists over to the Palestine Liberation Organization so that they would have escaped. Anyway, poor Sir Willie Morris was now having to wear two hats and the Cyprus hat is going to be a fairly uncomfortable one. He sent his Councillor to represent him and look after me.

MONDAY, 27 FEBRUARY. LUXOR   As we approached the Valley of the Queens we suddenly came across the two Colossi of Memnon, both of which represent Amenophis III seated in front of his funerary

---

* Two Palestinians shot an Egyptian newspaper editor in Nicosia, commandeered a plane and took hostages. Fearing the Cypriots would let them go, Egyptian commandos intervened and fifteen were killed in a set-to with the Cyprus National Guard.

Temple. The Temple has long since been destroyed and disappeared, but the two Colossi sit there magnificent in the middle of a field. They are some 60 feet high and I suppose if the Pharaoh had stood up he would have reached to a height of about 90 feet. His principal wife and mother stand each side rising no higher than his knee.

Norton took photographs of us standing alongside the Colossi to give an idea of their size. We re-embarked and drove on up to the Queens' Valley. We only entered one tomb here and paradoxically it was the tomb of a Prince. This was Amon Her Kopshef, one of the sons of Ramses III. The tomb has the most beautifully preserved colours and one of the attendants had a board covered in tin foil with which he reflected the sun's rays all round to light up the colours.

Norton was amused to see the remains of a specially lightweight stone which he had had constructed to be dropped, just missing the murder victim, in the Agatha Christie film *Death on the Nile*. The rest of us went into the courtyard and Norton climbed the pylon to take a photograph of us from the top.

Finally, we headed for the Valley of the Kings. We saw an ancient guide who had been present when Howard Carter had actually discovered the Tomb of Tutankhamen in November 1922.

We arrived at a rather interesting moment as the Chief Inspector of Antiquities from Cairo had arrived with some of his staff to take photographs and measurements of the inner sarcophagus in which the mummy of the King still lies, as they are afraid to move it in case it is damaged.

On our tour programme we should now have visited the Tomb of Ramses VI, but I was persuaded by the others to have some more refreshment. During this time I noticed that Joanna was missing and discovered she had been down with the rest of our party to this tomb while Norton and Jack had stayed with me to try and persuade me not to do another tomb. I felt rather double-crossed but she is a real enthusiast.

Then we re-embussed and drove down to the landing where we were taken across in a different ferry boat, and one very dear to Norton's heart as he had chartered it for the film company as their kitchen and restaurant, having flown out all the kitchen equipment from London.

I must say we have all been most impressed by Norton's tales of his experiences during his recent five months working on the film, as they come out quite modestly at different times. He showed us for instance in the Temple of Karnak where he had walked across a very narrow stone

HMY *Britannia*, 31 May 1975. Arriving at the Isle of Wight in Royal Marine uniform with Queen Elizabeth, the Queen Mother.

Leningrad, 10 May 1975. Sitting under one of the Joke Fountains in the Peterhof Park.

Pocentico Hills, 12 October 1975.
A visit to Nelson Rockefeller,
posing in front of a piece
of painted sculpture.

Cairo, 3 March 1978. Mountbatten's
granddaughter Joanna inspects
a model of the sun boat.

bridge between two of the 70-foot-high huge columns just to make sure it was safe for others to follow, and even then some hadn't got the courage to follow him.

When we got back on board the *Osiris*, two Egyptians fell on him and practically kissed him. It turned out that one was the leader of the second 'Mafia' who had appeared to be the most honest of the two. The leader of the chief Mafia openly threatened that if he didn't pay blackmail his body would be found floating face down in the Nile.

He also told us that the Chief of Police of Luxor had demanded £500 personal gift before he would supply the policemen. Norton went back to Cairo and saw the Government officials with whom he was well in, and the Chief of Police was told to provide all the police necessary and to guard Norton against the threats of the senior Mafia chief. It all went off so well that on Norton's birthday last October, the second Mafia chief had prepared a big birthday party for him as a surprise.

WEDNESDAY, 1 MARCH. ASWAN We went on upstream between the dramatic little rock islets which cause the cataract, and had a closer view of Elephantine Island. We landed and drove past the old Cataract Hotel which Norton had painted to smarten it up, as the old paint was peeling off. He also pointed out the site where he had had a gigantic head, about 60 feet high, built at the request of the Director. It cost £40,000 and at the end of it all they gave it to the authorities as a farewell present.

We discovered afterwards that the town had broken up this tremendous head and were using the steel and concrete for other purposes. Norton accepted it very gracefully and later still we discovered that all the scenes shot in front of the head, except one, had been left on the cutting room floor.

FRIDAY, 3 MARCH. CAIRO We were met at the Museum by the Director, Mrs Sania Abdel Aal. I told her I had been to the Cairo Museum in 1958 before the Tutankhamen treasures had been properly put on display, and said I had really come to see them as I had been round the rest of the Museum before. This made no difference to her plans and she took us round all the places she wanted to show us, which I must admit were interesting in themselves.

I was looking everywhere to see whether the stool, of which Edwina and I bought a reproduction in 1928, was there. Sure enough I found it prominently displayed. It was a little stool in ivory and dark wood, the seat was concave and thus comfortable to sit on. It had been one of the few authorized reproductions at that time, and was quite expensive, and I really must look for it when I get back to Broadlands.

Next we drove to Ghiza to look at the pyramids. I have seen these colossal pyramids over and over again and every time they impress me anew. I was delighted to see how deeply impressed Joanna was by them. However, we drove past the pyramids as we had an appointment at 1130 with the Director of the sun boat. On arrival we found all his staff were there wringing their hands and saying that the Director had left a few moments ago to attend his prayers, but would be back after lunch if we would like to come back then. As the time had been arranged with the sun boat authorities weeks ago, it was very odd. However, we filled in the time by going into the great pyramid of Cheops.

We left at 1515 and in half an hour we had driven to the great Sphinx. Norton was keen to show us the exact angle from which they took their filming of the Sphinx, but when we tried to go into the enclosure at the side a very officious old Arab refused to open the locked grille door to let us through. Our security officer showed his security pass but it made no difference.

Finally, John Manley, the Naval Attaché, who has been out here two years and talks a surprising amount of Arabic, went up and in a few short words said we were personal guests of Sadat and he had better open up quickly. This did the trick and we were allowed in. The first time I saw the Sphinx the sand covered its paws, but it has been excavated right down to its original base and I now saw that the tail itself embodies a series of steps for climbing up the Sphinx which is so huge.

Next we went on to the space between the pyramids of Cheops and Chephren where a structure that reminded me of the Vasa structure in Stockholm, but on a smaller scale, had been built. We entered and this time we were expected, but the dear old Professor had gone out and arrived a couple of minutes later. He was a tubby little fellow with a goatee beard and a twinkle in his eyes. He spoke no English so we had to talk through interpreters. Professor Martin* had told us he was the greatest Egyptologist reconstructor in the world. He had certainly done a staggering job.

Not very long ago somebody poking about discovered a large stone

---

* Leader of the British Archaeological Expedition.

slab about ten feet long and two feet wide. On digging round it they found it was in the form of a beam, the first of a row of them covering a deep trench. As they removed the stone beams they discovered the remains of something or other consisting of wood, ropes and netting material, which the old Director decided formed a boat. They took all the bits out. Then he decided that he would have to go round and see what he could discover about how boats were built thousands of years ago before he could reassemble this one.

He spent some two years gathering his necessary information and then got all the bits laid out and put them together. He had to put them together three times to get them right but the third time every part fitted, like a jigsaw puzzle. He explained to us it was really a funerary boat though it had been given the name of the sun boat and was now known as such.

The boat is very long and narrow. The keel is curved up very high at each end, its length is 150 feet. There is a large deck house in which the body of the King was placed when it was taken from the nearby delta up to the site of the pyramid.

From here the Naval Attaché guided us half a mile further along to the oddest sight we have seen in Egypt. It appears that the Japanese Government have got permission from the Egyptian Government to carry out a scientific experiment to see how the pyramids were built. The blocks used are only about two or three foot square and made of a fairly light material, but some are also made of stone. They are placing the blocks by ramps, the old method the ancient Egyptians are believed to have used, to see what they can learn from this. The extraordinary thing is that they have been given 90 days in which to complete the construction and 90 days to examine the results, and after 180 days they have to remove the whole little pyramid which I am told will cost over £1,000,000.

On the other hand I was told that a very sophisticated computer was asked to work out the best way of building the original pyramid of Cheops with practically no implements available, and it turned out that the computer advised them to build it in exactly the way the ancient Egyptians actually did.

SATURDAY, 4 MARCH   We had breakfast at 0830 in my bedroom as usual and at 0940 we drove to the Almaza Egyptian Air Force Base near the International Airport.

The Ambassador came with us on this trip and at 1015 we embarked in a really super VIP helicopter of British construction and flew in the utmost comfort, sound-proofed, to Ismalia Base where we landed two or three hundred yards from the Canal. We were met by two of the President's bodyguard in full dress on each side of the steps and a couple of ordinary soldiers in khaki. We were driven to what I am pretty sure was the old official Residence of the General Commanding the British Troops in Egypt, not the British Land Forces C.-in-C. of the Near East, who was senior to him.

We were met with the minimum of formality and shown into a pleasant simple large room where we all sat down, and within a couple of minutes the door opened and one man walked in by himself, and that turned out to be President Sadat himself. I introduced the party and he sat down and we had three quarters of an hour of the most interesting conversation. I really do admire him and I told him that in the UK everybody admired his courage, initiative and enterprise in trying to get the Israeli-Arab talks started again. He was obviously very pleased with this.

I did ask him what had happened about the Commando raid he sent into Larnaka in Cyprus. He said originally he had got permission to do the raid at Djibouti, but that the hijacked aeroplane had flown off just before they could get there so they followed it up to Larnaka, landed without any problem and were asked by the President Kyprianou to remain in the aircraft as he had the situation in hand.

By some means they were able to discover what negotiations were going on and when, after ninety minutes, the Commander of the Egyptian troops found that the Cypriots were proposing to give the two hijackers an air ticket and a safe conduct out of Cyprus he then stormed to the attack and both sides opened fire. Luckily the aeroplane was not set on fire and the hostages were in any case being released, but it did have the effect that the hijackers were then put under arrest. That was one of the conditions on which the Egyptian Commander insisted. So Sadat was very pleased about this.

I then initiated a full talk about the United World Colleges and the International Baccalaureate, and said that with his permission we were going to set up a National UWC Committee in Egypt. I explained the proposed composition and he liked the idea. I asked him if he would honour us by being the Patron of the Egyptian Committee, and he said he certainly would. I also brought a couple of books from Barbara Cartland to give to Mrs Sadat who she understood read her books.

However, the President said, 'No, no, I shall read them first, I am a great fan of Barbara Cartland myself.' He then suggested she might come out to Egypt and get some background information for writing one of her novels set in Egypt. I said I would pass on the invitation.

MONDAY, 15 MAY. LONDON   I had arranged with Charles to see the President of Zambia, Kenneth Kaunda, during his visit getting Government support for the United World Colleges in Zambia. It was agreed I should go as it would be rather tricky for Charles, so I sought an interview. The only day and time which were in any way convenient both to the President and myself were Monday morning, and the young lady High Commissioner invited me to come and have breakfast with the President. I accepted.

I was told breakfast was going to be at 0730 at the Hilton Hotel, but just before I went Jack Barratt received a warning that there would perhaps be a dozen or so other people at the breakfast but nevertheless I would have a good opportunity of talking to the President.

What actually happened was that Jack drove me round to the Hilton at 0725, I went up to the large restaurant at the top of the building on the 28th floor with its unrivalled view of London. Here I found a large gathering of other guests. Some thirty were already assembled and I was rather touched that the leaders of three political parties came forward on their own to seek me out and talk to me. They were Jeremy Thorpe (Liberal), Reggie Maudling (Conservative), and Lady Llewellyn Davies (Labour). There were all sorts of important people at the meeting, about twenty white and ten black.

I then discovered that the breakfast was really 7.30 for 8. I introduced myself to the High Commissioner, who appeared surprised to hear that I was 'Lord Mountbatten' though she admitted she had arranged for me to come and knew all about me. I found that she was quite enthusiastic for the United World College and was prepared to go down to St Donat's.

I said I hoped I'd have a chance of at least a quarter of an hour's personal talk with the President, and she said that this would be quite impossible because the plan was that he would sit at the head of the table with his Minister of Finance on his left and the British Government representative on his right, and thereafter people would go in order of precedence and there could be no separate conversations though he would address the meeting after the breakfast was over and answer questions.

I didn't argue with her but I stood on the two steps between the great breakfast room and the Reception Lounge so that when Kaunda arrived, attended by half a dozen of his acolytes, he couldn't easily get by me without speaking to me, so he paused a moment. I took his hand and said, 'Mr President, how nice to see you again, I haven't seen you really since you attended my brother-in-law's funeral in Sweden.' A broad smile broke on his face and he said, 'Ah, Lord Mountbatten, of course.' He then went on, 'But I have seen you at the Buckingham Palace parties since then.'

This was a good beginning. I then went ahead into the breakfast room and hunted round and found I was three places down on the right hand side, much too far to be able to talk to him. The first thing I did was to move the card of an Ambassador one down and took his place next to Lady Llewellyn Davies, and so was within shouting distance of the President.

I took an early opportunity to tell Kenneth Kaunda that I came representing the Prince of Wales, and at His Royal Highness's special request, and I brought greetings from him and explained that he was now President of the United World Colleges and I said I would like to talk about it. At this point Lady Llewellyn Davies said that as it was clear that I wished to talk business and as she had nothing whatever to say to him, she suggested we should change places. We did so rather dramatically and this, of course, improved the situation very much.

I then had twenty minutes' uninterrupted conversation with Kenneth Kaunda and found him really interested in the United World College concept. I gradually worked him up, gave him a brochure and an *aide mémoire* and told him exactly what I wanted him to do. He gave it some thought, then he said, 'All right, I'll do everything you say.' We then stood up and dramatically shook hands on it.

I then said, 'Will you now tell your Finance Minister and your High Commissioner?' He turned round and told the Finance Minister that Zambia would back the United World Colleges and he told his High Commissioner that the sooner she went down to St Donat's Castle and sent him a report on it the better. It was all quite dramatic and a complete change over the rather apathetic attitude of Zambia up to now.

At about 0900 the President addressed the entire assembly on his views of the present situation in Rhodesia, Southern Africa, but above all on the precarious financial situation in Zambia. It was a remarkable performance of a long talk without notes. After this he asked for questions and bit by bit they came in from all parties, from all sorts, all of which he dealt with deftly.

I think he rather upset people by saying that the present local agreement between Ian Smith and Bishop Muzorewa and the Reverend Sithole was bogus, and a trick which should not be accepted by anybody as it would only perpetuate the war which might well spread throughout Africa.

TUESDAY, 16 MAY   At 1545 Jack and I called on the Commissioner for Police at New Scotland Yard. We were taken up to Sir David McNee's room which I knew so well from having visited his predecessor, Bob Mark, there on several occasions.

We discussed the likelihood of my being kidnapped in view of a letter that Peg had written to me after seeing Moritz of Hesse when he had been released by the police and from his kidnappers.

She said that one of Moritz's captors had spent most of the ninety minutes before they were caught by the police, boasting about his complete study of Moritz's life and habits. He had mentioned in particular that he was interested in his uncle, Lord Mountbatten.* on this I wrote to David McNee to seek his advice.

McNee began by saying, 'If you want a permanent security officer attached to you, you can have him.'

However, when we went through the steps he had taken the situation appeared rather different. He had sent the Head of the Security Branch out to Schleswig-Holstein to make contact with the German Security Police there. This had revealed that the gang who had carried out the kidnapping of Moritz recently consisted of five young amateurs, two Swiss and, I think, two Italians and a German. They indignantly denied any connection with the Baader-Meinhoff gang or the Red Brigade. They said they had no political motivation and they were only out to make money by way of ransom. They were sorry that Moritz had got quite badly hurt with broken ribs and a pierced lung but he shouldn't have fought them. I might add that David McNee said that if ever I were

---

* Prince Moritz, who had been briefly held captive by a rather inefficient group of kidnappers, was in fact a distant cousin of Mountbatten's.

captured the stupidest thing to do would be to fight, particularly at my age.

The young man who spoke to Moritz most of the drive boasted of the careful study they had made of his whole life and habits. They had spent four or five months studying them and they had also got hold of a genealogical tree which showed how closely he was related to me. They had had to put off their attempted coup from Christmas time until April because Moritz's movements were different from what they had expected.

I should add that on the way one of the men was very talkative. The second remark he made was, 'We know all about your uncle, Lord Louis Mountbatten, we have been going into his case very carefully.' Peg had told me of this and I had reported it to Lilibet and the Commissioner of Police at Scotland Yard, Sir David McNee, who immediately sent out the Assistant Commissioner for Crime and one of the high-up people in the Security Service. The Germans, up to now, had never been really helpful but when they found it was a question of the Royal Family they became very co-operative. McNee told me that Scotland Yard was very grateful because this had been a break-through with the German police, who now fully understood the importance of co-operating.

To sum up, David McNee said he did not think I was in any more danger now than I had been before, but he also said he did not think the idea of kidnapping had really taken hold in England. He said that the man who tried to kidnap Anne was slightly deranged and acting on his own.

He pointed out that Moritz had admitted that he had not locked his doors nor had he switched on his burglar alarm.

I pointed out that at Broadlands my bedroom door was always locked with a shunt lock and the key kept nearby, so that anybody could obtain access by using the key and I then entered by the bathroom door and bolted it. I pointed out that if anybody did manage to break in they would have to break down one of my doors to get at me, and during this time I could easily press the alarm bell-push by my bed and set off the siren on the top of the house immediately. It would also ring a bell directly in the Butler's and Valet's bedrooms. McNee thought this was adequate security.

Jack pointed out that he thought I was in greater danger in London, although we had quite a good burglar alarm for 2 Kinnerton Street. I often drove myself back alone from places like Buckingham Palace, especially late at night when I could easily be grabbed on arrival before I entered the house and came under protection of the burglar alarm. He said he would warn the Gerald Row Police Station to keep a bit of a closer watch on 2 Kinnerton Street, particularly when I was in residence, and so we hope to see some Panda cars going by there more frequently.

On 30 June 1978 Mountbatten flew to Vienna for the wedding between Prince Michael of Kent and Mrs Marie Christine Troubridge.

At 2000 there was a great Gala dinner in the magnificent dining room of the private part of the Palais Schwarzenberg. I didn't actually count the number of guests, but there must have been between eighty and one hundred. The dress was white tie and decorations and the ladies wore tiaras. It was all very smart and reminiscent of pre-war Vienna.

I sat beween Olga of Yugoslavia (Marina's sister) and Marie Christine's mother, Countess Koczorowska. She had married again after she had divorced her von Reibnitz husband. She was fluent in many languages and spoke perfect English with a very slight Australian accent. She was great fun and very sensible.

Eddie asked me whether I would propose the health of the bride and bridegroom at a suitable moment, but I said I thought he should do so as he was head of Michael's branch of the family and had acted as 'best man' at the civil service.

He thought that the toast should be proposed in German which he couldn't do, so I finally agreed to do so. It was short but went well and the toast was drunk with great enthusiasm.

Then after we had sat down poor Peter Scott* had to stand up and say that he now had to make an announcement which was far from pleasant and which indeed was painful for him to have to make.

He then explained that that afternoon they had received written instructions from the Cardinal Archbishop of Vienna to say that the Mass to which the family were going to be invited had to be held in the small Scottish Chapel of the Benedictine Monastery. There was barely room for thirty people to attend which meant that only the most immediate relations could go.

---

* Sir Peter Scott, former British Ambassador in Oslo, had become Private Secretary to Prince Michael.

There were all the many other people who had received printed invitations to the Mass to be said in the big church who had to regard their invitation as cancelled, and there would be no part they could play in the religious service.

This announcement caused a good deal of consternation among the guests. Many people, both Catholics and Anglicans and Orthodox, were horrified and deeply distressed, but everybody, of course, accepted it.

Then Michael stood up and made an absolutely charming speech thanking everybody for coming out to support them at his wedding with Marie Christine and generally made an excellent impression.

Then we went out on to the verandah of the great ball room where the Vienna ballet company from the State Opera House had volunteered to give a special performance of eight dancers. They danced in the floodlit gardens of the Palace on the broad main walk, and though it had been well rolled down it must have been pretty painful dancing on the end of one's toes on gravel! It all went off very well.

Then an orchestra struck up in the ball room, a waltz, and Marie Christine and Michael opened the ball and danced three times round by themselves. Then I took Anne on to the floor and others followed us, and presently everybody was enjoying themselves hugely.

I had the next dance with Marie Christine and after that she introduced me to a very attractive cousin of hers. I noticed that Tiny, Olga and others started stealing away before midnight and I finally said I, like Cinderella, must go at the stroke of midnight, and succeeded in doing so.

I gather that the others stayed on a long while, some as late as 3 a.m.

Some of the most prestigious Hungarian families came to the dinner and ball, most of them I gather related to Marie Christine. Famous family names I noticed were Apponyi, Batthanyi, Esterhazy, Szchenyi and others.

SATURDAY, 1 JULY I had been pretty tired last night and Marie Christine had kindly said that she was sure that Michael would not expect me to attend the British communion service at the English church and would both be quite happy if I came on to the Mass at the Schottenkirche. I drove with Anne to the Benedictine monastery where quite a large and enthusiastic crowd was waiting to greet us with a lot of photographers.

We were barely thirty all told in the tiny chapel. The service was held in English by a charming priest who included parts of the marriage service and blessed the gold rings of the bridal couple and then prepared for the communion service. We had been led to understand that the Pope would have no objection to a communion service being held in the small church, as long as it wasn't in the big church.

The priest brought out the wine and the water in a chalice, blessed it and drank it and he blessed the wafer and ate it, he then cleaned out everything and washed his hands, dried his hands, and started again as usual, pouring out water and wine and blessing fresh bread. At this moment we all thought he was going over to offer it to Marie Christine, only to find that he consumed the host himself.

On the way out I could hardly contain myself. I went up to him and said, 'I thought it was a beautiful service, you did it in a most moving way, but why, oh why, did you consume the host yourself, why did you not offer the sacrament to the Princess?'

He said he was very glad I had asked that question as that enabled him to explain. He said that he had designed the service himself to be particularly satisfying, including part of the marriage service and the blessing of the rings and communion. Not long before the service he had received written instructions from the Cardinal Archbishop to say that on no account was the Princess to be allowed to take communion. He had therefore done the only thing he could do which was to consume the host himself. He was bitterly sorry about it but he had to do what he was told.

I don't think I have ever come across such unchristian behaviour by anybody, let alone the Pope and the Cardinal. I think it was really horrible and I was delighted to find, on return, that Charles had spoken out against the behaviour of the Catholic church at the Salvation Army Congress on the day of the wedding.

Anyway, we all drove off to the British Embassy, which is a really magnificent building with a fine garden dating way back to the days when the Austro-Hungarian Empire was large and powerful, now reduced to a population of only six million.

The Ambassador behaved in a very queer way. He said that he would, of course, meet Their Royal Highnesses at the airport and see them off, but he had received no instructions to help over the wedding. He apparently resisted the idea of giving any sort of party for the wedding, and, when asked whether he would permit Prince Michael to borrow the Embassy to give a party, demurred to such an extent that the organizer was unable to convince him until Peter Scott came in; being considerably senior in the Diplomatic Service to Morgan he persuaded him to allow the Embassy to be used for Michael's luncheon, and all the chairs, cutlery, table cloths, tables, etc., were provided by the Schwarzenberg Hotel. He did, however, allow the table at which the immediate family sat to be covered with their own table cloth and cutlery.

I noted that the Ambassador and his wife were not asked to sit at the Royal table which, considering it was his Embassy and he was the Queen's representative, was distinctly odd. However, I did my best not to get involved with all these extraordinary upsets.

1979

FRIDAY, 23 FEBRUARY. BROADLANDS   At 0815 Charles, Norton and I had breakfast in the Dining Room. Sharp at 1020 we left in a Buckingham Palace Rolls and drove at a comfortable speed to Portsmouth. We arrived without having had to increase or decrease speed, a few seconds after 1100, alongside the *Bulwark*. We had an argument as to who should go on board first, he or I. He argued that he was not entitled to be piped until he got four stripes and if we were to be piped I had better go first and take the pipe. I suggested that the solution would be for him to go first and for me to follow closely behind him so that nobody could distinguish who the piping was for. That worked very well.

We were then taken by the Captain to his cabin, as he had wisely left an eight minutes space between arrival and starting the programme in case we were slightly adrift.

On Charles's arrival on board his Standard was broken and Fort Blockhouse and ships in harbour fired a 21-gun salute.

At 1115 we both arrived in the hangar. It was a bright sunny day but cold outside, so it was very welcome for the ceremony to take place in the hangar. The entire ship's company was fallen in with a Royal Guard and a Royal Marines band. The proceedings were started by a fanfare by the trumpeters of the 4/7 Royal Dragoon Guards who are the affiliated Regiment to the *Bulwark*. Charles then inspected the Guard and the front ranks of the ship's company and came back to the dais.

The Captain read the commissioning order. We all took our caps off and the ten-minute recommissioning service was held. Charles then made a speech to the ship's company, a difficult thing to do as the First Lieutenant had left the entire ship's company standing to attention for the speech: an unfortunate oversight as, of course, it made it more difficult to get through to the men. However, Charles did successfully do so and even got them laughing at attention. He certainly made the right sort of speech though he had so little time to prepare it. The speech was followed by three enthusiastic cheers for Charles and then the senior official guests were escorted to the quarter deck.

We were able to get rid of sword and medals in the Captain's cabin and came back to the hangar where Charles cut the recommissioning cake, assisted by the ship's youngest rating, 'Junior Marine Engineering Mechanic Dwyer'. (What I would have called a 'stoker' in the old days.)

I asked him how old he was and he said he was sixteen years six months old. I pointed out that that was seven months older than I was when I went to sea in the First World War and we both laughed, particularly when I congratulated him on having gone to sea at the right age.

The same day the Prince of Wales received the Freedom of the City of Portsmouth.

Charles made a speech. Realizing that he had written most of his notes on his knees in the car going to Portsmouth, I was rather apprehensive about what the result would be. I needn't have worried, he always seems to be able to pull things out of the hat at the last moment. He made a very moving and excellent speech which was improved by the fact that it was quite obviously extemporaneous.

Now Charles went out into the Guildhall Square while we all lined his route. He then carried out a walkabout with great success. In one corner there was a group of young student demonstrators shouting, 'What a waste of money – What a waste of money – What a waste of money.' He went right up and faced them and however he did it I don't know, because they suddenly stopped demonstrating and kept quiet.

As a matter of fact the National Union of Public Employees had called a one-day strike, and in particular nothing was to be done to co-operate with the City authorities in preparing for Charles's Freedom.

However, as Charles had made these remarks criticizing the employers and by implication backing the strikers, the strikers in Portsmouth had a quick meeting and decided they would co-operate. The result was that the town hall square which had been filthy was miraculously tidied up. The crash barriers which were not going to be put out were put out so that the crowd could be controlled, the red carpets were laid out, the heating was turned on and the flowers were put on the stage and everything worked.

1979

SATURDAY, 31 MARCH. BROADLANDS

Preparations were in full swing for the opening of Broadlands to the public.

In the Library we are changing the pictures round. The First Viscount and Viscountess Palmerston will be put there from the South staircase. The picture over the mantelpiece of him riding away from the House of Commons in his old age as Prime Minister is the Third Lord Palmerston. His wife is being put above the bookcases. A nice pair of pictures of love in an old age, their first love affair, is shown in the Drawing Room by Sir Thomas Lawrence. I have moved the Second Lord Palmerston from the South staircase up over the other side of the bookcases next to the picture he originally bought from Joseph Wright of Derby, 'The Iron Forge', which has been for 200 years at Broadlands apart from the 17 exhibitions since the Second World War alone. I am going to put the sword table in there and I have got the three Russian Coronation books, Alexander II, Alexander III and Nicholas II to display in the room.

They are getting on well transforming the dairy into a place where the public will pay for their ticket and buy a guide book to go into the House. We have got two expensive portaloos, costing £7000 before installation. I wanted to put them in the car park, but Ken Robinson, the great expert who is advising us, said that that would be fatal, as people would go away having used the portaloos, without going in to see the House. He said it was essential they should pay their entrance fee to the House, before going to the portaloos. He also said it was essential they should enter by the front door, and the result is we have to knock a doorway in the semi-circular wall between the front door and the back door.

It is all very exciting and I hope it will work well, but I am glad to be away from it for three weeks.

That day Mountbatten left on what was to be his last visit to New York.

In the evening I drove down to the Radio City Music Hall. We had gone this time last year at the private entrance where we met Lawrence Rockefeller and were informed that the Music Hall was closing down because it couldn't afford to stay open.

We went up with the House Manager to see the last performance of my beloved Rockettes, the 36 best dancing girls in the world.

However, a miracle happened and they had been reprieved at the eleventh hour and were carrying on, although the House Manager said that they were going to close down for re-decorations this month and not open again until June.

They had the usual Easter show which was delightful and the Rockettes were as enchanting as ever.

THURSDAY, 5 APRIL. NEW YORK I thought of Mama today. This would have been her 116th birthday. It is incredible to think that she died twenty-nine years ago and my father fifty-eight years ago.

> *This was the last entry in Mountbatten's Tour Diary. Some five months later, on 27 August 1979, he was killed by an IRA bomb while on holiday at Classiebawn.*

INDEX

With the exception of the British royal family, crowned heads are listed under the name of their country.

A comma rather than a semi-colon between entries denotes that both entries are covered by the preceding heading. Lord Mountbatten is referred to throughout as M.

Index

Beaverbrook, Max Aitken, 1st Baron, 7, 16
Belcher, Ronald, 91
Belgium, M visits 1964, 103–5; and in 1971, 218–21
Belgium, Prince Albert of, 104
Belgium, King Baudouin of, 96, 103–5; at Eisenhower's funeral, 173, 175, 218–20, 295, 342
Belgium, Queen Fabiola of, 103, 220, 342
Belgium, King Leopold of, 50
Belgium, Princess Paula of, 104
Belize, 67
Bennett, Ernest, 187, 283, 341
Berlin, 38, 54
Berne, 190
Bernstein, Carl, 337
Bernstein, Leonard, 192
Betancourt, Rómulo, 73–4, 80
Bevan, Aneurin, 37
Bildeston, HMS, 336
Billotte, General Pierre, 306
Black, Eugene, 148
Blackburn, Robert, 219, 285, 361
Blandford, Marquess of, 69
Blum, Maître Suzanne, 259, 293
Bodyguard of Lies (book), 329
Bombay, 16, 81–2, 85, 323–4
Bonn, 62
Borneo, 13, 40, 50, 54–5, 121, 234–5, 289
Bose, Subhas Chandra, 288
Bottineau, Captain, 216
Boucher, Gene, 180
Bourguiba, President Habib, 174–5
Bousfield, Commander Robin, 142
Bowles, Chester, 88
Boyd-Rochfort, Sir Cecil, 295
Brabourne, Doreen, Lady, 258, 311, 357, 369
Brabourne, John Knatchbull, 7th Baron, 42, 60–1, 66; in Los Angeles, 115–16, 118, 142, 146–7, 179–80; on Pacific cruise 1971, 206–7, 211–12, 229, 241n, 249, 258, 271, 274; in China, 276; produces *Murder on the Orient Express*, 297–8, 317; and BAFTA headquarters, 327–8, 355; and 'This Is Your Life', 363–5, 369, 370
Brabourne, Patricia, Lady (later Countess Mountbatten of Burma), in Africa, 42, 45–8, 51; at Classiebawn, 60–1, 66, 82; in India and Burma, 87–9, 91; on 1965 world tour, 107–9, 112–15, 118, 121, 128; in Ethiopia, 133, 141–2; in Burma,

151–2; in India, 153–6; in Canada, 157–61, 179–80, 200; on Pacific cruise 1971, 206–7, 210, 212–14; in Burma, 229–30, 254–5, 258, 270, 274; in China, 276, 316, 321, 328; invested with Canadian Decoration, 329–31, 336, 357
Bradford, Jeremy, 339
Bradley, General of the Army, Omar, 205
Brasilia, 76–7
Brecknock, Marjorie, Countess of, 5, 9
Brewster, Kingman, 368
Brezhnev, Leonid, 309
Brimelow, Sir Thomas (later Baron), 305
Brind, Arthur Henry, 351
Brisbane, 55
Britannia, HMY, 135–6, 186–7; cruises in Pacific 1971, 206–16, 229; 1972 cruise, 233–44, 255–7; 1974 cruise, 278–91
British Academy for Film and Television Arts (BAFTA), 327–8
British Broadcasting Corporation (BBC), 86, 182, 200, 353, 356–7
British Commonwealth Ex-Services League (BCEL), 56, 145, 244
British Honduras, 67
Broadlands, 50, 79, 92, 94; farewell garden party at, 127–8, 142, 151, 176; M's seventieth birthday at, 196–7, 203, 221, 265, 270; King Constantine at, 274; Nan Pandit at, 311; Nelson Rockefeller at, 312–13; Don Juan at, 314–15, 332; Prince Michael of Kent at, 348, 353; Christmas at, 357–8, 366, 368; kidnap risk at, 380, 385; opened to public, 387
Brockman, Vice-Admiral Sir Ronald, 4, 51, 57, 82, 91; on 1965 world tour, 107, 120, 131, 137, 168, 329
Bronington, HMS, 336–7
Brooke, Rupert, 214
Brooks, General Sir Dallas, 56
Brown, George (later Lord George-Brown), 94, 137–8
Brunei, 235–8, 289
Brunei, Sir Omar, Sultan of, 235–7
Brussels, 103–5, 218–21
Buckingham Palace, 90, 204; marriage of Princess Anne, 270–4; and Jubilee, 366–9
Buenos Aires, 77–9
Buganda, Kabaka of, 47
Bulwark, HMS, 262, 385–6
Bunche, Ralph, 166
Bundi, Maharoa Raja of, 15

390

Index

Burgh, John (later Sir John), 137
Burke, Admiral Arleigh, 25, 166, 309
Burma, 14; M visits 1956, 17–18, 22;
    M visits 1964, 89, 98, 125; filming
    in, 144, 151–3; M visits 1972,
    229–32, 303
Burma Star Association, 332, 364
Burnett, Rear Admiral Philip, 339
Burnham, Forbes, 63
Burton, Richard, 192, 227
Bush, Admiral Sir John, 186
Busk, Sir Douglas, 72–4
Bustamante, Sir Alexander, 66–7
Buxton, Aubrey, 206

Caccia, Sir Harold (later Baron), 29, 70,
    104
Caernarvon Castle, 183–6
Cairo, Conference of Non-aligned States
    at, 100–1, 371–5
Cakobau, Colonel Ratu Edward, 58
Calgary, 157–9
Callaghan, James, 185, 286, 333–4,
    367
Camara, Archbishop Don Helder, 321
Campbell-Johnson, Alan, 143
Canada, M visits 1958, 24–5; M visits
    1959 for National Exhibition, 32–3;
    1965 visit, 123–4, 127; 1967 visit,
    157–61, 178, 247–8; M speaks on
    Dieppe in, 267–9, 329–30, 331
Canberra, 21–2, 56, 112–13
Canton, 276–7
Caracas, 72–4
Caradon, Hugh Foot, Baron, 124–5,
    166
Cardinale, Claudia, 118
Carreras, Sir James, 167, 191–6
Carrington, Peter, 6th Baron, 199, 201
Carson, Johnny, 166–7
Cartland, Barbara, 350, 359, 376–7
Cave Brown, Anthony, 329n
CENTO (Central Treaty Organization),
    40–1, 80–1
Ceylon, M visits 1956, 22–3, 90; filming
    in, 144–6
Chalfont, Arthur Gwynne-Jones, Baron,
    335
Chalk, Denis, 251–2
Chameleons, 11, 102, 122
Chan Kai Yao, 286
Chaplin, Charlie, 224, 328
Charteris, Sir Martin (later Baron), 251,
    261, 278, 294, 353
Chaudhuri, General Muchu, 83, 120–1
Chavan, Y. B., 81, 120, 139
Checkley, Irene, 55

Chiang Kai-shek, Generalissimo, 11,
    27n, 29
Childers, Erskine, 294–5
Chile, 75–6, 80
China, 53–4; and war with India, 81,
    83–4; M visits, 275–8
Christian, Elwyn, 213
Christie, Dame Agatha, 298, 355, 372
Christie, Sir Harold, 179
Churchill, Sir Winston, 11, 21, 57, 123,
    181, 182, 192, 204, 296, 313, 334
Clark, General Mark, 180–1
Clarke, Sir Arden, 100
Classiebawn Castle, 60–1, 172, 221,
    257–8, 316–17, 347; M murdered at,
    388
Cobham, Charles Lyttelton, 10th
    Viscount, 58
Collector, The (film), 117
Colombo, 22–3, 90, 144
Commonwealth Immigration Mission,
    107, 116–20, 122
Concorde, 361–2
Conduct Unbecoming (play), 188
Connally, John B., 274
Connaught, Arthur, Duke of, 158
Cooper, Simon, 137, 148
Corwin, Sherrill, 246
Cosgrave, Dr Liam, 294–6
Cousteau, Commander, 140–1
Coward, Noel, 166n, 199–200, 224
Crawford, Sir Frederick, 47
Crosland, Anthony, 168, 353
Crosland, Susan, 167–8
Cumming-Bruce, Sir Francis, 101–2, 122
Curle, Colonel, 7
Cyprus, M visits 1953, 1–3, 95, 97, 124;
    Immigration Mission in, 125–7,
    371, 376

Daborn, George, 303, 315, 365
Daily Express, the, 7–8, 16, 22, 60, 78,
    128, 188
Daily Mirror, the, 238
Dalton, Peter Gerald, 116
Dar, Rita, 336
Dartmouth, 256
Darvall, Air-Marshal Sir Lawrence, 169
Darwin, 55
Davidson, Professor Robert L., 180–1
Day, Robin, 296
Dean, Sir Patrick, 165
Death on the Nile (film), 355, 372–3
Delhi, 14–16, 82–6, 87–9; Immigration
    Mission in, 119–22; Shastri's funeral
    in, 138–40; filming in, 155–6,
    299–301, 354

Index

Index

Paley, William, 163
Palliser, Sir Michael, 354
Palm Springs, 246–7
Palme, Olof, 222–3, 342
Palmstierma, Baron, 265
Pandit, Shrimati Vijaya Lakshmi (Nan), 81, 88, 92, 119, 134, 156; at Broadlands, 311, 336
Pant, K. C., 301
Papodopolous, George, 274
Papua, New Guinea, 283–5
Paris, 71, 228–9; M visits Duchess of Windsor in, 259–61, 263–4, 293–4
Park, Air Chief Marshal Sir Keith, 58
Parr, Thomas, 179
Pearkes, George R., 24
Pearl Harbor, 116, 357–8
Pearson, Lester, 123
Peking, 275–6
Peking Review, the, 276–7
Penang, 240–1
Penn, Sir Eric, 250–1
Pentecost Island, 279–81
Perth, 325
Peru, 74–5, 80
Peters, Squadron Leader Dick, 70
Philadelphia Enquirer, the, 319
Phillips, Princess Anne, Mrs Mark, 97, 184–6, 196, 199–200, 203; on 1972 *Britannia* tour, 235–7, 254–6, 264; married, 270–4; on 1974 cruise, 279; attempted kidnap of, 290–1, 297; opens BAFTA headquarters, 327–8; riding accident to, 331–3; at Olympic Games, 346, 382
Phillips, Mark, 270–3; on 1974 cruise, 279, 290, 297–8, 331–3
Pickford, Mary, 117
Pincher, Chapman, 128
Pipilis, General I., 94–5
Pitcairn Island, 212–14
Plunket, Patrick, 7th Baron, 254
Podgorny, Nicolai, 309–10
POLARIS, 308, 360–1
Portal, Marshal of the Royal Air Force, Viscount, 173, 198
Port Moresby, 111–12, 283–5
Portsmouth, 347, 369, 385–7
Power, General, 34, 59n
Pramoj, Seni, 51, 109
Prasad, Dr Rajendra, 15
Previte, Keith, 64
Preston, Surgeon-Commander, 200
Price, G. C., 64
Princess Patricia's Canadian Light Infantry, 158–9, 329–31
Princeton University, 318–20

Puerto Rico, 192–4

Quemoy and Matsu, 27

Radford, Admiral Arthur, 166
Radhakrishnan, Sir Sarvepalli, 82–3, 91–4, 121–2, 138, 140, 155
Rajagopalachari, Chakravarti, 155–6
Ramgoolam, Sir Seewoosagur, 216–18, 351–2
Ramphal, Shridath 'Sunny', 348
Ramsay, Lady Patricia, 159
Ramsbotham, Sir Peter, 362
Ramsden, Caryl, 6–8
Rancho de Luxe (film), 332
Randall, Frank, 357
Rangoon, 17–18, 23; filming in, 151–3, 229–30
Ravensdale, Irene, Lady, 7
Rémy, Colonel (Gilbert Renault), 344, 354
Renown, HMS, 360–1
Rhodes, Michael, 151
Ribadu, Alhaji, 102
Richardson, James, 330
Rickover, Admiral Hyman, 28, 30–1, 33–4, 362
Rikhye, General, 166
Rio de Janeiro, 76
Riyadh, 322–3
Roberts, Rachel, 128
Robinson, Kenneth, 387
Rockefeller, Lawrence, 387
Rockefeller, Nelson, 312–13
Rockettes, The, 388
Rogers, Ginger, 246
Rogers, William, 204
Roosevelt, Franklin Delano, 11, 74, 204
Rostow, Walt, 165
Rothschild, Carola, 319n, 362
Rothschild, Victor, 3rd Baron, 340
Royal Life Saving Society, 25, 64, 148
Royal Naval Film Corporation, 26
Royal Overseas League, 64, 200
Rumbold, Sir Anthony, 150
Rush, Kenneth, 285
Rusk, Dean, 85, 92, 94
Russell, Aliki, Lady, 134, 225, 305–6
Russell, Sir John, 134, 225, 305–6
Russell, Rosalind, 246
Russia, Grand Duchess Olga of, 33
Ryde, 135–6

Sadat, Anwar, 355, 371, 374, 376–7
St Donat's College, 168–70, 182, 191, 205, 219, 222, 230, 245, 247, 263, 377–8